PENGUIN BOOKS

The Condé Nast Traveler

Book of Unforgettable Journeys: Volume II

THE CONDÉ NAST TRAVELER

Book of Unforgettable Journeys: Volume II

GREAT WRITERS ON GREAT PLACES

EDITED AND WITH AN INTRODUCTION
BY KLARA GLOWCZEWSKA

PENGUIN BOOKS

PENGUIN BOOKS
Published by the Penguin Group
Penguin Group (USA) Inc., 375 Hudson Street,
New York, New York 10014, U.S.A.
Penguin Group (Canada), 90 Eglinton Avenue East, Suite 700,
Toronto, Ontario, Canada M4P 2Y3 (a division of Pearson Penguin Canada Inc.)
Penguin Books Ltd, 80 Strand, London WC2R 0RL, England
Penguin Ireland, 25 St Stephen's Green, Dublin 2,
Ireland (a division of Penguin Books Ltd)
Penguin Group (Australia), 250 Camberwell Road, Camberwell,
Victoria 3124, Australia (a division of Pearson Australia Group Pty Ltd)
Penguin Books India Pvt Ltd, 11 Community Centre,
Panchsheel Park, New Delhi - 110 017, India
Penguin Group (NZ), 67 Apollo Drive, Rosedale, Auckland 0632,
New Zealand (a division of Pearson New Zealand Ltd)
Penguin Books (South Africa) (Pty) Ltd, 24 Sturdee Avenue,
Rosebank, Johannesburg 2196, South Africa

Penguin Books Ltd, Registered Offices:
80 Strand, London WC2R 0RL, England

First published in Penguin Books 2012

1 3 5 7 9 10 8 6 4 2

Copyright © Condé Nast Publications, 2012
All rights reserved

The essays in this book first appeared in issues of *Condé Nast Traveler.*

THE LIBRARY OF CONGRESS HAS CATALOGED THE FIRST VOLUME AS FOLLOWS:

The Condé Nast traveler book of unforgettable journeys : great writers on great places /
edited and with an introduction by Klara Glowczewska.
p. cm.
ISBN 978-0-14-311261-7 (volume I)
ISBN 978-0-14-312147-3 (volume II)
1. Travel—Literary collections.   I. Glowczewska, Klara.
PN6071.T7C66 2007
808.8'032—dc22   2007026230

Printed in the United States of America
Set in Adobe Garamond Pro • *Designed by Elke Sigal*

CONTENTS

INTRODUCTION

"It is easy enough to make fun of birders," writes E. L. Doctorow, one of the contributors to this second volume of *The Condé Nast Traveler Book of Unforgettable Journeys*. He is on a tour of India with a group of American enthusiasts of the earth's winged life and is struck by the wisdom in their curious passion. "Birders ask only to see something. Not to shoot it, not to touch it, feed it, cage it, mess with it in any way. To see something and give it a name. That's all. Birding celebrates non-possession. At this time in the history of a planet dammed, deforested, and drilled to its deepest dingles, isn't this a blessed thing? It is the practice of reverence. It is knowledge for its own sake. Here are these birders traveling halfway around the world to amaze themselves."

The best travelers—and the best writers on travel—belong to that same wandering tribe and share that same fundamental passion (if not necessarily its object). They are obsessive, wildly alert observers of what nature and man have wrought. Amazement is their Holy Grail, and they come upon it, as do all the contributors to this collection, in the most varied ways and places. In Berlin's impressively licentious nightlife (which, as Guy Martin concludes, "has something fundamentally im-balanced and headlong about it, something Slavic and not quite fully Western"); in the hallucinatory quality of the Arctic summer's endless sun (where, as Wade Davis reports, one can witness an annual convo-cation of wildlife "of such stunning magnitude and beauty that [it] shatter[s] all notions of a world of human scale"); or in the gastronomic oddities on display in a market in Cuenca, Ecuador (including something that appears to be the result, Calvin Trillin delightedly observes, "of crossing a large strawberry with an exceedingly small porcupine").

These and countless other aperçus in the pages that follow are travel writing's pots of gold, the reason some of the very best observers of our world—be they novelists, poets, playwrights, art critics, political reporters, screenwriters, essayists, or naturalists—journey forth and report back on what they see. The telling seems for them a goal in and of itself, and their generous compulsion to make note of the earth's myriad seductions akin to that of those birders thrilled with recording "the fleeting glimpse, a blurt of color, a call, the bend of a branch." Witness Amy Wilentz's rapture in Senegal: "The women are beautiful to look at, the men are elegant and sometimes jazzy, and there are corners where a painted wall, even though it's made of cement block, will stir you with its raging deep-maroon color, and a single palm tree and a single sheep in a village compound, up against the flat ocher of a quick-falling sandstorm sunset, will make you sigh with poetic ecstasy."

Most of us are not likely to buy a ticket anytime soon to the Swat Valley, in the wilds of Pakistan's North-West Frontier Province, but how eye-opening to read William Dalrymple's account of his travels through the magnificent and forbidding region that stopped Alexander the Great in his tracks during his conquest of the world. And no wonder it did. "Machismo is to the Frontier," Dalrymple writes, "what prayer is to the Vatican. It is a way of life, a raison d'être, an obsession, a hobby, a philosophy." The ultimate status symbol? "You can drive to work in a captured Russian T-72 tank." We are definitely not in Kansas anymore.

But how tempting to table-hop in Patrick Symmes's footsteps as he eats his way through Italy's Emilia-Romagna—the fecund plain that produced the food that *did* conquer the world, or at least the table (think prosciutto di Parma, Parmesan, porcini, and half of all pastas known to man). On his menu? A meal that ended with "a stunningly simple dish: *gnocco fritto*, or pillows of fried dough topped with a few intense drops of sixty-year-old balsamic vinegar . . . so thick that it had to be coaxed from the bottle."

Introduction

We live in a cabinet of endless curiosities and possibilities for enchantment, and since *Condé Nast Traveler*'s founding in 1987, the magazine has made it its mission to provide the key: travel intelligence and information that is both authoritative and inspiring. Authoritative because it is based on our unique motto, Truth in Travel, which stipulates that neither the magazine's writers nor its editors accept free or discounted travel—not from airlines, not from hotels and resorts, not from tour operators. It is a simple proposition but also a profoundly consequential and liberating one, since it allows us to report freely and fully—with no ulterior motive, hidden agenda, or allegiance—on what we see and experience. And inspiring because it is so often presented through the lively, evocative lens of some of the world's finest observers—our contributors.

The authority of *Conde Nast Traveler*'s advice is on display each month in its print and digital pages (and daily on its Web site). There you will find the best and the latest, the most reliable information possible on all the often nettlesome mechanics, the must-know how-to's of modern travel. The thirty stories collected in this volume, on the occasion of the magazine's twenty-fifth anniversary, speak eloquently to travel's whys—the reasons so many of us set forth on what Joan Juliet Buck calls, at the start of her tour of the wonders of Rome, "exhilarated wanderings."

Here's to exhilarated wanderings.

Klara Glowczewska
Editor in Chief, Condé Nast Traveler
New York City, 2012

THE CONDÉ NAST TRAVELER

Book of Unforgettable Journeys: Volume II

The Liberation of Sydney

by

ROBERT HUGHES

In the 1950s, when I was growing up in Sydney in a house above the harbor, one of whose blue lobes showed through the glossy foliage of a loquat tree in which red-arsed bulbuls flirted at the edge of our garden, two things seemed obvious to me.

The first was that the place would never change much.

The second, also wrong, was that foreigners would never make a point of coming in any numbers to see it: It was too far away from the rest of the world, just as the rest of the world (known from books, names in the atlas, skimpy press stories about the revolt in Hungary or the Suez crisis) was too far away from us.

You could grow up in Sydney in those days without seeing an American, except for sailors off the Pacific fleet. Sydney was full of Americans during the Second World War—"oversexed, overpaid, and over here"; girls wore ankle-strap shoes known as Yank-catchers. The town would fill up with them again in the Vietnam years. But in the fifties and early sixties, the Americans were so uncommon that one could pick them out easily: Once in a while, the Matson Line would decant a couple of hundred elderly tourists at Circular Quay, the ladies in billowing muumuus and their husbands in peculiar burgundy- or saffron-colored blazers. As soon as they were on the concrete, they would gaze around with mild ruminant alertness, looking for the kangaroos and platypuses they had heard so much about. Texas with cute living fossils: That was their idea of us.

As for the Japanese, the very idea of Japanese tourism would have struck any Sydneysider as ludicrous. The last Japanese visitors anyone remembered were the crews of three midget submarines that sneaked into the harbor in May 1942. Two midgets sank in deep water. The third fired its torpedoes at the U.S.S. *Chicago* but missed and sank a ferry, the *Kuttabul*, tied up for the night with thirty sailors sleeping the booze off on board. What happened to it after that remains a mystery. So much for Japanese tourism.

Not now. Apart from the fact that the Japanese, as any Sydney taxi driver will complain to you, "own half the bloody country anyhow," tourism (including Japanese) has turned into one of the chief Australian industries, and the vast majority of visitors come into the country through Sydney. Hotels have mushroomed, and Sydney has become, rather self-consciously, a visitors' city.

The provinciality that seemed to characterize Australian society, and could be plainly seen in Sydney twenty-five years ago, is all but gone. To a striking degree, the city's habits have softened. Its harsh, intolerant machismo—the bad-dream side of "mateship," which ran from the Anglophilic stuffiness of the Establishment clubs to the raucous all-male suburban pubs—has toned down. Sydney is no longer quite so keen on the Ocker (Pacific redneck) image of the Australian: beer gut, thongs, nasal foghorn voice, and a truculent certainty that, short of Paradise itself, Australia is the only ticket and that the rest of the world only displays its inferiority by not necessarily wanting to come here. ("Which the bastards all do, but they don't admit it.")

People worry about Ocker and would not want you to suppose that he lurks under their skin. The Australia he represents (or so people in Sydney will tell you, not without an apotropaic glance over the shoulder) is a thing of the past. However, it was preserved in "export culture" during the eighties—especially in the films that Australians made with an eye to the American market, like *"Crocodile" Dundee*—with the result that Americans still land in Sydney expecting, if not a welcoming of marsupials, then certainly the last refuge of unself-conscious masculinity.

And if they come in February, what do they get? Among other things, the gay Mardi Gras, which draws up to half a million people and once featured (right along with the leather-jacketed lesbians on their motorcycles and the blue elephant shambling along with a condom over its trunk and a sign announcing that elephants never forget to have safe sex) a truck bearing a longboat in which stood an aboriginal dancer attired as Captain Cook. "It is enough trouble being black, let alone gay," he told the press at the time. "That is why I am determined to put this float in the Mardi Gras."

A black, gay Captain Cook? Can this be the same city as the one in which, thirty years ago, the minions of "Bumper" Farrell—the corrupt and much-feared chief of the Sydney Vice Squad—used to decoy homosexuals in the public lavatory in Martin Place? Was it from here that Sir Eugene Goossens, head of the Sydney Symphony Orchestra, fled in disgrace when "rubber articles and masks" were found by customs officials rummaging in his bags?

The answer, broadly, is yes and no.

Fundamentalist religion, the motor of American moralizing in the eighties, never caught on in Australia. Hot-gospeling evangelists rarely crossed the Pacific from America; Oral Roberts tried once in the fifties but came up so empty that he is said to have proclaimed, on departure, that Sydneysiders were godless and irretrievably damned—old news to us. Sydney has a raucous lobby shoving plastic fetuses in the faces of scared teenagers outside clinics, just like America. But these clone movements have nothing like the political power they have in the United States and are unlikely to get it, because at this level, Australians—especially in Sydney—are more tolerant than Americans.

Nevertheless, the struggle between the Good and the Unredeemed runs quite deep in Sydney life: How could it not, in a city that began as a jail? Compared with America, this is still a surprisingly authoritarian society: laid-back and easy, the visitor thinks, but without a Bill of Rights or a popular constitution (ours was couched entirely in terms of British imperial interests and contains hardly one democratic clause).

In the fifties and early sixties, Sydneysiders could put up with every sort of constraint and still tell you that they were the freest people in the world because they could knock off and go surfing at lunchtime. A residue of this feeling still lingers, and it may help explain the talismanic importance Sydney attaches to its emblems of leisure and pleasure—the sun, the harborside life, the benign blue sky, the white squeaky-sand Pacific beaches covered with tanned and glistening bodies, the wine, the beer, the prawns.

In any case, one would have to be crazy *not* to revel in them. In my twenties, having overdosed on Cyril Connolly and his nostalgic vision of Mediterranean hedonism in *The Unquiet Grave*, I was longing to leave; when I did, it took me two years of living on the coast of Italy to admit that, apart from ruins, tombs, and frescoes, much of what I had wanted on the edge of that dying sea was what I had left behind in Sydney, and some of it not as good. "Can you imagine," an ecstatic English painter remarked to me a few years ago, as we were walking from his visitor's studio in the Art Gallery of New South Wales across the green expanse of the Domain, in the blowing salt air and the high crystalline light, "what Matisse would have made of this if he had seen it?"

What Sydney made of Matisse is another matter. It used to be the case that local art museums, wherever they were, tended to concentrate on local art, so that what one saw on their walls gave a strong impression of the culture in which they were rooted. For the last twenty-five years there has been an increasing degree of internationalization, so the same *menu touristique* of contemporary art tends to reappear all over museum walls in the West. This has never been quite so in Australia, partly because (when Picassos and Pollocks and Beuyses were relatively cheap) the museums did not want the work of European and American avant-gardes and so tended not to buy it, and partly because when taste changed in the seventies and eighties, the overseas art had become far too costly for their limited buying budgets. The same, in Sydney, was true of Old Masters. Thus, when you approach the tawny sandstone bulk of the Art Gallery of New South Wales, superbly sited on its bluff above Woolloomooloo Bay, you will see inscribed on its facade in bronze letters a kind of cultural mantra: the names of a whole string of artists—from Giotto to Andrea del Sarto, Michelangelo, Donatello, Rubens, and Rembrandt—who are not, in fact, represented in its collection. This queer expression of Edwardian cultural fantasy—whistle and they will come, so to speak—used to strike us as the height of deceptive advertising. The gallery has no significant works by French Impressionists, either, because the trustees were simply too provincial to want them.

But does the visitor really care if he finds no Rubenses at the end of the long flight to the Antipodes? Of course not. He will want to see Australian art, which is represented in profusion. The Art Gallery has a superb collection of Australian Impressionists—Tom Roberts, Arthur Streeton, Frederick McCubbin—the generation of the 1880s that gave vivid form to the particular light, color, and structure of the Australian coastal bush. It is also one of the three "collections of record" (the others being in Melbourne and Canberra) of modern Australian art, from 1940 through to our fin de siècle. For art of the colonial period, our first century, the visitor should cross the Domain and study, or at least skim, the collections of the State Library of New South Wales, which are unrivaled. For aboriginal art, a subject of ever-increasing fascination to visitors, the place to go is the Australian Museum.

And for gardeners, or strollers, the "green museum" of Sydney is the Royal Botanic Gardens, the city's finest Victorian artifact, surrounding the spot by the harbor where the first furrows for corn were dug and sown by convicts in 1788. A very good way to start the day, if you are an early riser and staying in one of the big inner-city hotels, is to take a taxi to the saltwater Boy Charlton pool, which opens at 6 A.M., swim a few laps, and come back on foot through the gardens.

"Take it easy, mate. Just do a few every day and it gets like walking. Easy as walking. Just like Jesus." Thus the twenty-year-old to the floundering fifty-year-old. It may not. Stay in the duffers' side lanes, where you can stop and hang on to the edge—the middle ones are reserved for the serious lap swimmers, who will churn over you like trucks on the Hume Highway. The walk back through the Botanic Gardens, acres of terraced green between the harbor and the city, whose wakening growl of traffic seems very far off, is a capsule introduction to Australian nature: thousands of species, exotic to you (and many of them to us), from tiny delicate cacti and ground covers up to the huge Moreton Bay figs with their ridged, elephant gray roots, in whose branches kookaburras laugh and colonies of white cockatoos sit squalling in the limpid early light.

A city changes greatly in twenty-five years. The physical changes are the ones that strike the returning expatriate first. But even more striking is how much Sydney's very language has altered. We have learned psychobabble, public relations cant, and New Age blather. One hears the transpacific words: *self-actualization, creativity.* Granted, the mincing euphemism that has rotted American public speech has not quite attained its full force here: In Australia the blind can still lead the blind, without obliging one to speak of the visually challenged adopting a hierarchical relationship to their peers. My Californian wife was once jolted to read SPASTIC BUS on the flank of a Sydney public health vehicle.

But the great Australian vernacular, with its sharp slang and improbable flights of metaphor, in whose pungency a rich national literature was rooted, is going, smothered by Australian TV. Sydneysiders still have their laconic habit of chopping off the ends of words and tacking on an *o* or an *ie*: "garbo" for garbage collector, "gerrie" for geriatric. But you no longer hear them complain that the weather is "wet enough to bog a duck," that they are "flat out like a lizard drinking" (very busy), or that, when luck is bad, "If it was raining palaces, I'd get hit by the shit-house door."

Only the accent is imperishable—high in the nose, drawling, flat, and brown. It is not, as so many Americans imagine, related to Cockney, and its origins remain an utter mystery. One knows only that it was in place, and being complained about by supercilious visitors as a "detestable snuffle," as early as the 1820s.

Sydneysiders are what everyone says—hospitable, friendly, and curious. They were egalitarian once, and still preen themselves on that reputation, but they no longer are. Under the surface of a fraternal style, the breezy exclamations of "G'dye, mate," and the ready approachability that visitors are apt to interpret as signs of an unworried society where divisions of class play no big part, the lessons of the 1980s bored in deep.

Not that Sydney isn't still a genuinely civil city. Its citizens keep to standards of public behavior that simply no longer exist in any American city of four million people. A visiting American journalist, Susanna Gaertner, wrote with amazement some months ago: "You sit on one of those benches under a splendid palm beneath a sky the colour of prewar Meissen and no one will bother you, beg, hassle, play a boom box, much less mug or rob you."

But in the eighties, just like New York or London, Sydney learned to be obsessed with indexes of status, wealth, and power. There was serious money around in the Sydney of the fifties and even the early sixties, but it tended not to flaunt itself. In the Sydney of the eighties, as in America, wealth not only came out of the closet, but it ripped the hinges off as it emerged. People still remember a party one of the newer plutocrats threw for his daughter's twenty-first birthday. Said to have cost upward of $350,000, it featured tranquilized lions and tigers by the swimming pool, an elephant dropping its huge turds on the tennis court, and a level of catering worthy of the climactic orgy scene in *Salammbô*; this was thought unusual, maybe even a bit extreme, but not entirely off-the-wall.

In the eighties, Sydneysiders got used to popping flashbulbs, limos, society shrinks, lifestyle magazines, and a national credit binge. Until the real estate market lapsed into a coma in 1990, houses in the posher parts of Sydney—Vaucluse, Bellevue Hill, even Paddington—cost more than their equivalents in New York or London. But funny money is no longer king. Alan Bond, the prototypical Australian plute of the eighties, went down the tubes along with many lesser fry; only the lawyers get rich, as former moguls devote themselves to suing one another like maddened scorpions in a sock. Businessmen look back on those lost days as on a vanished paradise, as well they might. On my last visit to Sydney, I went with a couple of such friends on a thirty-six-foot ketch for a Saturday sail down the harbor, through its incredible traffic jam of yachts. At day's end, we were beating east toward the harbor entrance, with the jagged profile of skyscrapers, once the graph of the speculative capital of downtown Sydney, silhouetted against the pearly westering light.

"Sad sight, isn't it?" one of them said to the other.

I squinted at the setting sun and could see nothing sad about it.

"Yeah. Look at it," said the other.

"Only one construction crane. Used to be dozens of them."

"Well, that's the way it's going to be. It's normal. It's going to be normal for years. No new building. Welcome to the real bloody world, eh?"

Australia is notably short of the icons by which countries make themselves known. It has one famous building, the Opera House, which is in Sydney. It has the Sydney Harbour Bridge. It has Sydney Harbour and Ayers Rock—one evoking community, the other remoteness. After that, when pressed to name their images of Australia, most Americans (at least the ones I have asked) are apt to go straight to the animal kingdom: the roo, the Qantas koala, the prawn on the barbie. One notes that Sydney has a majority, if not a monopoly, of these Identa-kit images. Elsewhere in Australia this is regarded as horribly unfair, but nothing, it seems, can be done about it. The harbor is the master image of Sydney's culture, both high and popular. None of the other Australian state capitals—Perth, Adelaide, Hobart, or Brisbane—has anything so identifiable; and Melbourne, as Sydney chauvinists insist, is stuck with the River Yarra, a stream so muddy that its bottom flows on its surface. The harbor is also the only thing that holds Sydney together visually. To one of the most cluttered cities in the world, it gives scale, measure, and—blessed relief—an inviolable plane of nature. It is the city's lungs and heart.

Which is just as well, since most Australians, and Sydneysiders in particular, have never given a zack (archaic slang for "sixpence," an obsolete coin of small value) for town planning or anything that smacked of visual control of the urban environment. Consequently, the parts of Sydney that look coherent today—Macquarie Street, for instance, with its remaining Georgian buildings, the Hyde Park Barracks for convicts, the Parliament House, the hospital, and the graceful town houses raised from local sandstone; or Paddington, once an area of cheap workers' terrace-housing built in Victorian times and now sedulously gentrified—are exceptions surviving amid the sprawl and high-rise eclecticism of the rest of the city. During the "naive" years of Sydney's prosperity, which lasted roughly as long as America's (a quarter of a century, from 1945 through 1970), the wrecker's ball had more say than any architect. Australia then loved a tabula rasa. If there was nothing to tear down except trees, then well and good.

But if there was actually something to tear down, then the Parthenon itself would not have been allowed to stand in the way of progress. "As beautiful as fifteen different colors of paint could make it," wrote an acerbic English lady, Louisa Anne Meredith, of a new pub she saw by the road in the Blue Mountains in 1840, comparing it to "a new toy, freshly unpacked." The spiritual heirs of that pubkeeper have been developing Sydney ever since, and have conferred on its downtown area an almost hallucinatory lack of scale and inconsistency of texture, with the looming cliffs of eighties-style "prestige" corporate buildings jammed into the small layout of what began as a straggle of Georgian mud huts.

One could compile quite a *sottisier* of Sydney's flashy blunders in urban design, every one of which has been promoted as a leap into the

future and as marking yet another tide of fashion that rippled across
the Pacific to cast its secondhand detritus on our shores in the eighties.
It is hard, under the circumstances, to name one's least favorite Sydney
building. Mine would probably be the Centrepoint Tower—a ridiculously overweening space needle webbed with guy cables and ruining
the once-agreeable scale of the midcity skyline with its rise.

But there is also some very serious new architecture in Sydney. Its
risen star, among the younger generation of architects—those who entered professional life in the 1960s—is Philip Cox. His main work in
the eighties was the development of an enormous site at Darling
Harbour in Sydney—an industrial wasteland—into exhibition and conference centers, an aquarium, a maritime museum, malls, and other amenities, buildings that carry their size with a subtly lyrical optimism full of
complex allusions to maritime structures in the spirit of the Opera House
downharbor.

And for the last ten years, with the mania for new signature
buildings on the wane, Sydney has done fine things for itself in preservation and conversion. Its star projects include the Queen Victoria
Building on George Street, an extravagant Romanesque palace converted, with great tact, into a shopping mall; the fine Victorian arcades
that run between blocks in the inner city; the onetime-slum dock district of Woolloomooloo; and, perhaps best of all, the whole Paddington
area, which has the most fetching concentration of ornamental cast-
iron work outside of New Orleans.

The natural place for the visitor to begin is Circular Quay, maritime
hub of the city. The ferries churn out and in, stopping in a backpedaling froth from their screws. Today, there are also Jetcats, closed shells
that scoot down the harbor at forty miles an hour. When you go, do
not take them. Get on one of the older boats and sit outside. The trip
down the harbor—past the unfolding headlands and islands to the immense sea gate of the Heads, beyond which lies eight thousand curving
miles of ocean to America—takes thirty minutes and is worth every
second of it, because the harbor is such a spectacle of nautical democracy.

Especially on weekends, its water swarms with thousands of craft—from kayaks and cockleshell sailing dinghies through catamarans and eighteen-footers under their bustling press of sail, up to the big ketches and the gin palaces of local plutes; a dazzle of bunting and white triangles leaning under the wind, every hull stuffed to the gunwales with sun-flushed Strines (local for "locals") waving their stubbies and tinnies. Only from the water can one truly appreciate the blue, branching arm of the Pacific that Captain Arthur Phillip, its discoverer, called "the finest harbor in the world, where a thousand sail of the line may ride with the most perfect security."

The ferries dock between the two chief emblems of Sydney: to the west, the great arch of the Harbour Bridge, roaring and resonating with traffic invisible from below, which vaults from the south to the north shore of the harbor in a single span and was our emblem of modernity before the Opera House—our second emblem—went up.

Jocosely known as the Coathanger or the Toast Rack, it is the largest rigid single-span bridge in the world, and when it opened in 1932 it was the largest construction project ever undertaken in Australia. Like Rockefeller Center in New York, its building went on through the depths of the Depression and became an immense symbol of social survival. All around, Sydney was static, decaying, hopeless: a city of unemployment lines and soup kitchens. But the bridge gave thousands of people work, and was known as the Iron Lung, because it kept people breathing. Whether by coincidence or by design, when seen from afar it is a solar emblem. Its mighty arch ribbed with vertical columns is an engineer's version of the badge on the Australian Army hat—the rising sun of Australia. Its four pylons—now reduced in scale by the sheer size of the office blocks around its south and north approaches, but in their time among the highest secular structures in Sydney—are Art Deco versions of Mayan sacrificial step pyramids, structures dedicated to the cult of the sun.

The New South Wales government paid for the bridge. Thirty years later, it began its second huge emblem, the Opera House. Australia—with reason—has been proud of its operatic tradition since the 1890s, when Nellie Melba, its national nightingale, the great soprano from Melbourne, climbed to the peak of fame at La Scala and Covent Garden; by the 1960s, when the construction of this immense prestige object began in earnest, Sydney had a major opera company, and Melba's emblematic role had been assumed by Joan Sutherland, or, as her Australian fans call her, Wonderlungs.

Opera meant prestige. It needed a home, and there was an international competition for its design. It was won by an unknown thirty-eight-year-old Danish architect, Jørn Utzon, whose name would acquire a painful, two-edged celebrity in Sydney. Australian public cultural projects are often slowed up by angry, reflexive criticism: Why aren't those millions going to health care or old-age pensions? With the Opera House this reached heights of asperity, because opera was undoubtedly an "elitist" art, and Australians, who dote on elitism in sport, have trouble with it in other fields and use the word as a stick to bash ambition with.

Utzon, a quiet beanpole of a man, had never been to Australia and had no idea what was waiting for him. He soon found out, landing at the center of a hellish political imbroglio between some politicians who wanted the building up right now and damn the cost, other politicians who wanted to slash the budget, and his own ideas of design.

His Opera House was a brilliant poetic conception, the kind of metaphoric leap toward nature that hardly existed in architecture thirty years ago: Its form suggested blown spinnakers, birds' wings, seashells, all that was appropriate to the great port. Its small, remote cousin was Eero Saarinen's TWA terminal at Idlewild (now JFK) Airport, but it is utterly unlike its stodgy corporate-state American counterparts of the sixties—Lincoln Center in New York and the Kennedy Center in Washington, D.C.

In retrospect it seems extraordinary that Sydney, whose architectural tastes tend to be conservative when not blatantly vulgar, should have taken a flier on it—but Australians *are* gamblers. No one really knew how to build it or (even after nine years of planning and seven years of construction) how to finish it.

Those complex membrane shells would be difficult even with to-day's computer modeling. Thirty years ago, with engineering not far out of the slide rule era, they were a nightmare. Nor did Utzon's own inexperience help. He resigned halfway through the job in 1966 and limped back home, dropping a postcard to a friend: Postmarked Yucatán, it read, "The ruins are wonderful so why worry? Sydney Opera House becomes a ruin one day." He never saw it completed.

Finished by a Sydney architect, Peter Hall, the Opera House was opened by the queen in 1973. It had taken nineteen years from the first esquisses and had cost $102 million, fourteen times its projected budget, most of which was paid for by the profits from a state lottery. Utzon was lionized by most Sydney writers, artists, and architects in the sixties, but in functional terms the building was, and remains, far from satisfactory. Some of Utzon's original aims were never fulfilled. It is only an opera house by the skin of its teeth. You cannot produce Wagner or large-scale Verdi in it, for instance, because the main theater became a concert hall.

Nevertheless, the $102 million turned out to be a spectacular investment. In the year the Opera House opened, Gough Whitlam's Labour government was in power, and Australians were beginning to feel the oats of cultural identity after long decades of dependence, first on England, and then, in the Vietnam years, on America. What were we? Transplanted Brits or second-rate Yanks? The main thrust of Whitlam's cultural politics was to assert that, yes, there was and should be a specifically Australian identity, that we could create a culture of our own across the board, from "popular" to "elite."

One omen of this was the Opera House; another, in 1973, was the award of the Nobel Prize for Literature to the novelist Patrick White. Thus the Opera House—the only building erected in the entire history of Australia that the rest of the world had ever been interested in—was seen, no matter whether it "worked" or not, as a totem, assuaging insecurities, something "for the ages." Through it, we could watch others watching us. And most Australians, who couldn't care less about reverberation times or scene changing and who had no intention of going inside the thing, continue incessantly to use its outside—its steps, the immense plinth on which it rises above the harbor—as a logo, a platform from which to view the harbor, or (half-consciously) as the biggest environmental, site-specific sculpture south of the equator. An inversion, yes; but you are in the Antipodes now.

If you look straight out from Circular Quay, past the Opera House, you see a third building on a little island: Fort Denison. It was built at the time of the Crimean War to repel the Russians, who never came. But if its military history is nil, the symbolic power of the rock under it is considerable. In the 1790s it was known as Pinchgut, and on it "desperate" convicts were hanged until the seabirds stripped their bones, and "refractory" convicts were marooned until the sun broiled them into submission.

What is now Circular Quay is, in fact, the place where European settlement in Australia began, on January 26, 1788, when Captain Arthur Phillip brought his eleven sea-battered vessels to anchor and his men began ferrying their freight of convicts ashore—in all, more than seven hundred souls, including children who had been born on the long voyage from Plymouth. This squadron, bearing to banishment in the unknown Antipodes what all right-thinking people in England regarded as the dregs of criminality, is known to Australians as the First Fleet. About 160,000 people would be exiled to Australia over the next eighty years, most of them arriving in Sydney—until transportation there was abolished, under popular protest, in 1840—and many others going to Van Diemen's Land (modern Tasmania), until "The System" shut down there in 1853.

At the time the first whites came floundering off the longboats, a little stream rippled down into the harbor here, through a gully of tree ferns. This was the embryo colony's freshwater supply, known as the Tank Stream. Because the naval and marine officers' tents were pitched east of it, and those of the convicts and guards to the west, a lasting social division was set up in Sydney: To this day, the rich live in the eastern suburbs beyond Kings Cross—Paddington, Edgecliff, Double Bay, Point Piper, Bellevue Hill, and so on, out to Vaucluse—and the not-rich west of the line.

Who were they, these most unwilling of pioneers, the first convicts who provided the reason for the new colony and the labor to build it? It used to be a cherished Australian myth that our Founding Fathers were innocent working-class rebels against a grindingly unfair political system. Also, that our Founding Mothers, the convict women, were prostitutes.

Neither is true.

There was not one political prisoner on the First Fleet. Nor were any women on it transported for prostitution, since whoring in George III's England was no more a criminal offense than it is in Sydney today.

Almost all of the 736 prisoners, like the many thousands more to come, were small-time offenders against the property laws. They had stolen ribbons from shops, cheese from pantries, cucumbers from gardens, horses from stables, razors and watch parts from their employers. Most were in their twenties, theft being a trade for the young— and the young and strong being needed to make new colonies. They had only one thing in common: They had been caught, swept up in the broad, inefficient net of the late-eighteenth-century system of English criminal justice and turned into the guinea pigs of a social experiment whose outcome nobody, from the crown to the courts, could predict: "Thieves, robbers and villains, they'll send 'em away / To become a new people at Botany Bay."

Today's "new people" are only marginally composed of convict stock—perhaps a quarter of a million people in Sydney (but, significantly, no one really knows how many) can claim direct descent from transported Irish or English convicts. What happened to New York in the 1890s happened to Sydney after 1945: Its social structure and cultural habits were transformed by a surge of government-sponsored immigration from Europe.

The "reffos"—or "New Australians," as they were politely known—are now old Australians, and the person next to you in the Bondi bus is much more likely to be the scion of a shopkeeper from Skopelos, a veggie farmer from Palermo, a Hungarian machinist, a Lebanese accountant, or a Vietnamese lawyer than the bearer of an English horse thief's genes. Although the bulk of immigration continues to be English and Irish, Sydney has a wide mix of minorities, one of the smallest being the aborigines—or Koories, as they call themselves—several thousand of whom live in Sydney, mostly congregated in the terraces of Redfern. None of these people—and especially not the aborigines, for whose race and culture the white invasion of Australia was a genocidal disaster—have any reason to want to commemorate convicts.

This does not, of course, mean that traits were not passed down the cultural line. Ever since its convict days, Sydney has remained a Barbary Coast, a seaborne Mahagonny of hustlers, swifties, thugs, and hoons and lairs (pimps and dandies), where astoundingly crooked deals were matter-of-factly hatched over the Tooheys lager (or, latterly, the Hunter Valley chardonnay), between raw wealth and the "pollies," our elected representatives; and where the police force has retained a reputation for graft and heaviness. But the combination of "native" amnesia and "migrant" indifference has meant that there is no monument to the convicts in Sydney, not even a wall with the 736 names on it.

The effort of amnesia, working its way out through the social pores, produced a mind-set that *always* preferred the new to the old and rarely enjoyed the Australian past for its own sake. Hence Sydney has only one exception to the national dearth of good monuments, and it commemorates not the "shame" of convictry but the blood sacrifice that was thought to have redeemed it. This is the Anzac War Memorial, which stands in Hyde Park in Sydney and is one of the most beautiful Art Deco ensembles in the world: another Mayan sun temple, whose red-granite steps lead up to a first floor with a wide circular well. You peer over the edge of the parapet, and there below, laid in crucifixion

The Liberation of Sydney

on a sword, is a naked bronze soldier, borne up by grieving caryatid figures of his mother, sister, wife, and child and seen against a burst of formalized bronze flames set in the marble floor. This coup de théâtre is the work of Rayner Hoff, whose death in 1937 at the age of forty-three deprived Australia of a potentially major artist. Here you sense, as nowhere else, the veritable cult of death that rose out of Australia's appalling losses in World War I, when its men were used as shock troops at Gallipoli and elsewhere and suffered the highest casualty rate of any army in the war—64.8 percent killed or wounded, as compared with 47.1 percent for the British and some 54 percent for the Germans. Traumatized by their losses, every town in the country put up its war memorial, but none with such a tragic pietà as this.

The place most redolent of convictry—and even here its whiff is faint—is on Dawes Point, the spit of land that runs out into the harbor from the west side of Circular Quay, from which the bridge makes its jump. It is known, from the sandstone ledges to which it clings, as The Rocks. From the early 1800s to the end of the century, The Rocks had a lurid reputation as the Clap Alley of the South Pacific. It was a hive of foul shanties and shebeens bearing such Dickensian names as The Sheer Hulk and The Black Dog. Here was sold colonial rum laced with tobacco juice and vitriol to give it a bite. (In the 1830s, four and a half gallons of distilled spirits were drunk for every man, woman, and child in Sydney. People wanted oblivion; few thought it was the Best Town in the World then.)

But among the mellow, sun-struck alleys that clamber up and down The Rocks, there are reminders of the convict past that cannot be effaced; they are carved in the very bone of the headland, and the most evocative of them—if you pause to look at the pick marks in its high walls and reflect on what they mean—is the Argyle Cut, hewn straight through the sandstone of Dawes Point to link the docks on its west side to Circular Quay. Many of the nineteenth-century houses of The Rocks—now containing bookshops, restaurants, and opal vendors, along with

17

boutiques selling souvenir T-shirts and (for the urban jackaroo) R. M. Williams rabbit-felt hats and Driza-bone bush raincoats—were built with stone mined from this slit of punishment.

A particularly good hotel, the Park Hyatt, follows the curve of the waterfront, and from its balconies you have one of the best takes on the harbor a visitor can get. In the early morning, a working replica of Captain Bligh's *Bounty* is docked beneath your window, with the Opera House right behind it; ferries with the names of the First Fleet convict ships—*Fishburn*, *Lady Penrhyn*, *Supply*—bustle in to dock in the opal light; and there is a tinny screeching of red rosellas arrowing through the gray girders of the bridge behind. The best place to have lunch at The Rocks is a Chinese restaurant called the Imperial Peking. Reserve ahead if you want a table by one of the windows overlooking the water. Sit and gobble your salt-and-pepper mud crab. Drink your Pooles Rock chardonnay (although beer is perhaps better with this un-equaled, quasi-ritual dish), and watch the sun spots move across the white shells of the Opera House. You will not be sorry.

The milder heir of The Rocks was the Cross. Kings Cross, on a ridge to the east, around the curve of Woolloomooloo Bay, began as a site for the big mansions of the 1840s and '50s but became Sydney's bo-hemia in the 1930s and acquired a louche reputation: The sleaze was there, the nightclubs and whores, with most of Sydney's once-minuscule subculture of druggies. Its little hole-in-the-wall restaurants and coffee shops, from The Arabian in the forties to Vadim's in the early sixties, were shunned by good suburbanites but were hospitable to writers, artists, and other misfits, who found subdivided rooms in its old man-sions and in the tall Victorian terraces along Victoria Street, their back windows looking on the panorama across Woolloomooloo to St. Mary's Cathedral. Woolloomooloo, down by the docks, was then the proletarian id of the Cross. Its streets were run by a formidable network of hoons and madams, the most famous of the latter being Tilly Devine, née Matilda Twiss (1900–1970), who ran two generations of girls with a strong ma-ternal hand and withstood no fewer than 204 charges of prostitution, assault, and malicious wounding.

The old Kings Cross came to a grinding close in the late seventies, with Vietnam and the drug epidemic. It ceased to be the locus of the "soft" bohemia that I gravitated toward, like hundreds of other vaguely arty kids, when I got out of school. Today, the Cross is dirtier, harsher, fifty times more dangerous, and riddled with crack. One is not tempted by the needle-tracked teenage whores along their specified strip in William Street, or by sex shops and strip shows, with their loudspeakers blasting over a pavement crunchy with broken bottles: "Point yer erection in our direction!"

"Eat like a pig, drink like a fish, smell like a rose." Glimpsed on the side of a deodorant delivery van in Bridge Street, this motto says something—to put it mildly—about the Sydney appetite.

We know about Australian wines by now. They are often much better than California wines, and always cheaper. But nothing is more surprising to the visitor than Sydney food. In the fifties most of it—except Chinese—was the gastronomic pits, a wilderness of steak Diane and watery ravioli relieved only by the frilly-shelled, delectable Hawkesbury oysters, which, being served raw, no culinary intervention could wreck—unless you used the ketchup they were served with.

By the early sixties, when I left for London, things were changing because of the European influx and (at home) the ecumenical influence of Elizabeth David. By the start of the eighties they had really begun to move, and today there must be a score of places in Sydney whose food is in every way as serious, inventive, and respectful of its ingredients as any restaurant's in New York City or California.

For though Sydney has no deep tradition of fine cookery, it has sublime ingredients—particularly in seafood, which is best viewed at the Pyrmont fish markets: among crustaceans, for instance, not only the spiny crayfish and the formidable two-pound mud crab but the Balmain Bug, the yabby, and six or seven kinds of raw prawn. So, too, with meats and vegetables, and even cheeses. And the temple of Australian cooking—a plain, airy restaurant in the middle of the national park where the Hawkesbury River enters the sea north of Sydney—is the Berowra Waters Inn, run by Gay Bilson, whom one would call the Alice Waters of Australia if such comparisons were worth making.

But the chief index of Sydney's popular pleasures are the beaches. Nowhere else in the world, except maybe Honolulu, is urban space so integrated with beach culture. You can't "read" Sydney without its beaches; the relationship of city life to beach life here is fundamental.

To Sydneysiders, the beach and the city are culturally adjacent, and only the thinnest membrane of use—the act of shucking one's shoes, slipping on a pair of thongs, and grabbing a towel—separates them. Going for a quick dip is not an event. It is something people do at lunchtime. Not until the sixties, when surfing really took hold among Australian kids and established its own elaborate subculture of tribal loyalty and daring, did Australians start looking for empty beaches, away from the flats and bungalows.

Those who want still water go to the public beaches around the harbor—little coves, each with its blond meniscus of sand covered with oiled bodies slowly turning mahogany under the fierce barbie of the southern sun: Camp Cove, Seven Shillings Beach, Lady Martins Beach, Parsley Bay, Watsons Bay on the south side; Shell Cove, Little Sirius Cove, Taylors Bay, Chowder Bay, Clontarf, Forty Baskets Beach, and Manly on the north. Many are topless now, some are gay, and no one cares.

The Pacific beaches are another story: They are where the big waves come in. The best known is Bondi, where ocean surf meets suburban scurf: rundown hotels and fish-'n'-chipperies all along the back, and in front a wide, baking curve of sand where Sydneysiders gather by the thousands to worship Helios. But they also go to Tamarama and Coogee and other beaches south, each of which has its particular character and wave pattern to challenge the surfboarders; and to the northern ones, of which the most popular are Palm Beach and Whale Beach.

And what about the sharks? The very thought of the gray nurse, the tiger, the thresher, the hammerhead, and so on up the scale of anxiety to *Carcharodon carcharias*, the great white itself, has always scared the bejesus out of visitors. The harbor beaches have sharkproof nets. But the sharks are there. Once, forty years ago, bobbing at anchor in a dinghy while hand-lining for red bream in the channel that goes around the tip of Point Piper, I became aware of a scraping and bumping that was out of sync with the slap of the little waves, as though the hull were against a log. Turning around, I saw the tip of a dirty-gray fin sticking up a good foot above the gunwale: an enormous elderly brute rubbing its skin on the hull like a cat on a post.

One must refrain from swimming in the open harbor. On the ocean beaches, of course, there are the lifeguards, Sydney's surf police and swimming wardens, who keep nit for sharks—from beach towers, and now by radio link to spotter planes—and practice their rescue routines in long, light mahogany skiffs rowed out, with insouciant skill, into the combers. No one has been eaten by a shark in years. You are in much more danger from the undertows and rips, and of course from the increased UV levels in the sun's rays: This is where the Big Hole in the ozone layer makes itself felt.

The shark bulks large in Australian iconography because it is the continent's only large animal that is in any way dangerous to human life. The nearest thing to the spectacle of a public hanging in Sydney is the weighing station at Watsons Bay, where the big game boats tow in their catches and where crowds of people converge, silently licking their ice creams, to watch the giant malefactors dangling—eight-hundred-pounders or more, blood streaming from their gill slits and gaff wounds but still alive enough to take a tooth-crunching swipe at a post as they are hauled clear of the water.

At such moments, one gets a flash of the sheer otherness of Australian nature, an otherness that is generally benign but still shows itself through chinks in Sydney's urbanity. It has always mocked, and sometimes defeated, attempts to impose an English or European mask on the place. I went to lunch a couple of years ago with some art collectors who lived in an exquisitely restored Victorian manse on a western arm of the harbor. Sun, chardonnay, ice buckets, prawns—served in a shady garden where boronias and creepers cascaded over the rocks, between whitewashed walls. A lot of trouble had been taken over that garden since the hostess and her husband had come back from the Aegean. "Sometimes," I heard her say from a nearby chair, through my postprandial drowse, "it makes me feel as though I'm in Greece." At that moment, a shadow passed and I looked up: Flying foxes, fruit bats three feet across, were passing low overhead, their black, leathery wings cranking archaically in the sun.

"Oh yes, Greece," her husband agreed.

"Of course, Greece," I muttered, watching the pterodactyls sail out of sight in the dazzle above the yachts.

1993

Peeling Away the Masks of Vienna

by

STEPHEN SCHIFF

The outdoor café at Vienna's Sacher hotel has its charms—not much sunlight, maybe, but the sound is hard to beat. Across the street looms the State Opera House, one of the three finest in the world (along with the Paris Opera and Milan's La Scala), a gaudy pile so huge and proximate that its faux-Renaissance bric-a-brac seems to be glowering down into your soup. The strange thing, though, is this: Every few minutes or so, the café's swank aplomb is shattered by muffled choruses, musical chants, euphonious bellows. When the opera's doing *Boris Godunov,* everybody within a five-block radius knows it.

And *knows* it. "Mussorgsky," murmurs my Viennese companion, a young woman whose American contemporaries generally believe that opera was invented several centuries ago by The Who. "You know, we live in paradise here." So it seems, at least for the moment. Our forks are raised over Sacher tortes with *Schlagobers*—whipped cream to you—and the Viennese coffee, dense and bitter and fresh, bears its own sweet *Schlagobers* mound. "There is no crime in Vienna," she continues. "No poverty. No slums. No war. We were once the capital of an empire of more than fifty million; now we are the capital of this little place with wine and mountains, Austria. We are shrinking. In 1910 Vienna had two million people, and now only one and a half million. So you see, there is enough here for everybody—more than enough."

"It seems very pleasant," I say.

"It is," she replies. "After Budapest, we have the second-highest suicide rate in Europe."

Has she just delivered a *Schmäh*? Vienna has given the world Mahler and Schubert, Freud and Wittgenstein, Klimt and Kokoschka, Musil and Schnitzler, Stroheim and Billy Wilder. But perhaps its greatest gift to the world is the *Schmäh*—without which all those illustrious figures might never have seen things in the way that made them so illustrious. *Schmäh* is what the Viennese call their peculiar brand of mordant, ironic humor. The writer Paul Hoffman defines it as "blarney, Viennese style," but that doesn't quite get at the knowingness and sarcasm, the deadpan charm and, in some cases, the darkness that constitute it. A *Schmäh* is dual, binary. There's the cheery outer face of the joke—the *Schlagobers*—and the dark, dense, bitter, ambivalent quality beneath it. Listen to the way the airiness of Schubert at once masks and accents the melancholy behind it. Look at the way Klimt's gilded meticulousness somehow brings out his lust for the macabre, the sensual, and the chaotic. Freud posits an unconscious mind below the conscious one, hidden yet always manifesting itself. He could have been describing every Viennese when he wrote, quoting Goethe, "Where he makes a jest, a problem lies concealed."

I had been told that Vienna was a "three-day city." And three days is what the guidebooks usually allot for a solid itinerary. Don't believe it. In three days you'll get the whipped cream, all right, but to understand the *Schmäh*, you have to see not just the grand museums but the eccentric ones, not just the towering church in the center of town but the jewel-like one on the grounds of an insane asylum, not just the opulent historicist buildings of the Ringstrasse but the wild, forestlike cemeteries where lovers romp among the tombs.

I spent the first few days walking the streets of the Old Town, drinking in its dichotomies and contradictions. This district, which is Vienna's first and innermost (there are twenty-three in all), has blocks reserved for pedestrians only, and its buildings range from the medieval to the just born. As you stroll, statues of fierce naked maidens glare down at you, fantasias of Art Nouveau gold leaf swirl above, august palaces give way to chic clothes shops, art galleries, even a diverting clock museum. The appeal of Vienna's inner city arises from a legion of intrusions and oppositions, all of them now coexisting in a harmony not unlike that of a cemetery, in which tombstones of every period reside comfortably side by side—a harmony of the dead.

Right in the middle, in a beguiling stone-paved street called the Graben, there are two remarkable, and remarkably gruesome, objects. The most visible is a gnarled Baroque column some sixty feet high: a meringue-like tower of clouds and angels and, yes, corpses that strain and dance upward until it seems they were shot from some subterranean cannon and then frozen to stone on their way to heaven. This is the *Pestsäule*, the Plague Pillar, erected by Emperor Leopold I, who had prayed for an end to an outbreak of the plague in the late seventeenth century and had vowed that he would reward God's mercy by building a column. He did; it's at once an imposing and strangely grisly sight. Nearby, a more diminutive monument: a low white wall on which hang grim black-and-white photographs depicting Vienna at the end of World War II—bombed out and devastated, the trashed, paranoid Vienna of Carol Reed's film *The Third Man*. As you look around at the cheery restored shops, at the handsome Baroque Church of St. Peter around the corner, at the teenagers strumming and crooning beneath the contorted Plague Pillar itself, it's as though the ironic dualities of the *Schmäh* had invaded every block and building of this city, imposing a kind of higher order—an order that belongs not to man but to nature and the gods.

How is it that Vienna's mood manages to be at once so sanguinary and so sanguine? Somehow the city's fondness for the morbid and the bizarre never seems at odds with its sunny stability. Rather, all Vienna works the way its graveyards and its Graben work. The order here is rich, organic, and complex. Death takes its place alongside life, the old alongside the new, the eccentric alongside the conventional, the mad alongside the sane.

Even the city's geography is orderly in an organic, inspiriting way. Vienna is a series of concentric circles, or, more accurately, half circles, rippling outward from its center in the inner town (where Vienna began as the ancient Roman camp of Vindobona) to the Vienna Woods themselves, which are the ultimate foothills and fingerlings of the Alps. At the nucleus, the first district, you find this vigorous hodgepodge of old and new, sublimity and grotesquerie, urbanity and coziness. Around it, in a protective and officious circle, there is the Ringstrasse, a collection of public and private buildings, all planned nearly simultaneously (in the mid nineteenth century) on an enormous scale. The buildings are charmless but imposing, and they were all designed as though they were theatrical sets, with an eye to the illustrious past: fake Renaissance for the university, fake early Baroque for the Burgtheater (the Baroque being the period when commoners joined with the gentry in flocking to the theater), fake Gothic for the Votive Church and the Town Hall (since the medieval commune represented the source of Viennese government), fake Greek for the democratic institution of Parliament. At once expansive and forbidding, the Ringstrasse hems in the vibrant inner town and formalizes it. It was built where the fortress walls of Vienna once stood, and even today it acts as a sort of wall, inside which the city carries on with the appropriate metropolitan bustle, and outside which Vienna can sprawl and relax and indulge itself. Small wonder that the next ring beyond the Ringstrasse, the Gürtel, is best known as the circle where streetwalkers ply their trade—streetwalkers who, by the way, are carefully regulated and legally bound to submit to periodic physicals.

Beyond the Gürtel, Vienna fans out into neighborhoods, pleasant, almost bucolic districts that retain the character of their past lives as quaint Austrian villages. There are workers' regions (including the beautiful and still-functioning Karl Marx-Hof housing project, built during the utopian twenties, when the city was often referred to as Red Vienna) and posh residential areas. Good mansion viewing can be had in the nineteenth district, where you can and should visit the Geymüller-Schlössel. Although its clock collection is its greatest draw, the Geymüller-Schlössel is one of Vienna's most delicious repositories of Biedermeier furniture, the ingenious and beautiful stuff made to amuse the upper middle class during the early nineteenth century, when Metternich's secret police became terrifying enough to drive the populace indoors. There the haute bourgeoisie played with cabinets that look like ballet sets, full of secret drawers that revealed themselves at the punch of a button; with sleek oblong boxes that magically transform themselves into multitiered sewing tables; with frightful fake-flower arrangements that turn out, on closer inspection, to be made of hundreds of dead butterflies.

Now we are almost at the city's outskirts, and here something wonderful happens. On the edges of Vienna are two final rings that form a kind of passageway to the untamed natural world beyond. Let me begin from the outside in, from the Vienna Woods themselves, which have been carefully preserved in all their density and wildness. Virtually no one has been allowed to build or develop here for over a century. Hiking paths abound; the roads are stone-paved and unadorned. The woods remain the lungs of Vienna (few Middle European cities are so pollution free), a source not just of physical but of spiritual inspiration. As the superb Viennese journalist Traudl Lessing says, "Every Viennese autobiography begins with the hike in the summer woods, with the rucksack and the parents who know every tree by its unpronounceable Latin name. The Vienna Woods begin at the terminus of the streetcar—we have very lucky surroundings."

Between the woods and the outskirts of the city itself there is a kind of transitional ring allowing wilderness to segue into civilization: a belt of vineyards. These, in turn, give way to yet another transitional circle: the hilly districts of Grinzing, Sievering, Nussdorf, Neustift am Walde, Salmannsdorf, Stammersdorf, Streberdorf, Heiligenstadt, and several others whose winding narrow roads abound in *Heurigen* (little restaurant-like places devoted to the sampling and celebration of young white spring wine).

If the vineyards themselves are where man tames nature, the *Heurigen* allow nature to tame man. (Avoid Grinzing, by the way, unless your taste in drinking companions runs to streams of haggard tourists fresh off the bus.) And when the proprietor—who is also the winemaker—leaves a cluster of fir twigs hanging outside his door, that means the new wine (the *Heuriger*) is ready to be drunk in his garden. In many *Heurigen* you will be served bread or crackers slathered with Liptauer, an orange-colored cheese spread full of paprika, capers, cucumbers, anchovies, onions, and mustard. You will also invariably be served a packet of obscene and enormous chocolate wafer cookies manufactured by a firm called Oskar Pischinger. These cookies are considered de rigueur, although they make as foul a companion to the generally tart, dry wine as anything you can imagine.

But then the *Heurigen* are not about fine dining. They are about communion: communion between the life of the city and the life of the woods—communion, in fact, between life and death themselves, since there are often *Schrammelmusik* bands (violin, accordion or zither, guitar) that serenade the customers with endless ghoulish songs about the fine art of passing away. (One well-known favorite, by Roland Neuwirth, simply lists Viennese euphemisms for dying: He made an exit, he studied the potatoes from underneath, he put on wooden pajamas, and so on.) Mostly, though, the communion is between strangers. "People go from table to table," says Traudl Lessing, "and then they see somebody else they know and go to yet another table. We all know each other in Vienna—it's a small town. If you come to one of the *Heurigen* regularly, you will get a postcard from the owner saying, 'We have the bush out.' And then you go, and everybody you know is there."

Not that you have to know your neighbors in order to commune properly. "In this city of Freud," says Peter Weiser, the sly and saturnine gentleman who ran the Mozart bicentennial festivities in Vienna, "there are fewer psychiatrists per capita than in any other major Western city. And that's for two reasons—the *Heurigen* and the coffeehouses. At these places you talk about your problems for hours with complete strangers. You never intend to see them again, so you say anything." Connoisseurs prefer quiet *Heurigen*, where you bring along your own "picnic" and the mood can turn deliciously melancholy and introspective. On a good night, no one needs any *Schrammel* musicians to remind him that, like Vienna with its woods, our little life is rounded with a sleep.

Food, music, death—these are the Viennese obsessions, and it often seems as though the first two are so much whipped cream sweetening the third. Among the tourist attractions the Viennese hold most dear is the Kaisergruft, the vault in which the fantastically elaborate and macabre tombs of the Habsburgs are kept. And not far from that is Zum Schwarzen Kameel, a gleaming lunch restaurant where you can eat the tantalizing open-faced sandwiches that are a Viennese specialty and listen to Peter Weiser explain that the most devout wish of every Viennese is to have a *schöne Leiche*—which means a lovely funeral, or, more literally, "a beautiful corpse." To a typical Viennese, his funeral is the central event of his, um, life.

"Funerals are the most important thing we do," says Weiser. "So funeral dress and behavior is very strict. You don't wear makeup, no sunglasses, and everything black. Black suit—not navy blue—white shirt, black tie, black socks, black shoes. Even the poor have to have a funeral outfit. I remember once I had a black trench coat and it got soiled and my wife panicked. She said, 'You need to get a new one, quick. What if there's a funeral?' Not 'What if it rains?' but 'What if there's a funeral?' We tend to be rather morbid here in Vienna."

Rather. Where else would you find a place like the Elektropathologisches Museum, which concerns itself with those who have "made an exit" by dint of lightning and other electrocutions? What other city has not one but two museums devoted to wax replicas of the human body and its parts—the Josephinum, in which the wax bodies are generally "healthy" (student army surgeons used them before the dissection of actual cadavers became customary), and the ominous Narrenturm, a scary cylindrical tower built in 1784 to house mental patients and now used to display icky wax re-creations of various diseases.

If this isn't thrill enough, Vienna has the only museum in any European capital devoted entirely to funerals, the Bestattungsmuseum, at Goldeggasse 19. You get in by appointment only, and an affable Viennese gentleman named Heinz Riedel, who runs the place, shows you around with a subtle smile on his face, exuding *Schmäh* in waves. The funeral museum is not just about the pomp that goes into *les pompes funèbres*. It's about the peculiar refinements that only a populace that thinks about death *all the time* could have hatched. Here, for instance, is an innovation promoted briefly by the beloved eighteenth-century Emperor Joseph II as a cost-saving measure. It's a coffin fitted with a removable bottom: You suspend the thing over the open grave, slide the bottom out, drop the corpse, and then carry away the coffin for reuse. A swell idea, and it was only because of an unprecedented outburst of public dismay that the emperor withdrew it six months after its introduction in 1784. Nearby, an elaborate toy: You wind a key and a miniature funeral procession marches by, diorama-style, while a hidden music box produces tinkly Diabelli and your average (but rich) nineteenth-century child presumably undergoes paroxysms of delight. A glass case across the way exhibits various elaborately painted skulls from Salzburg—painted because burial space there was scarce and disinterred bones were thought unsightly without a little decoration.

And, most bizarre of all, there are two examples of the provisions Vienna's wealthier classes made to relieve a peculiar nineteenth-century fixation: the fear of being buried alive. Here on the wall is a device patented in 1828 and meant for use during the forty-eight hours or so in which the putatively deceased lies aboveground awaiting burial. A string is looped around the corpse's wrist. It extends underground to the office of the cemetery caretaker, where it is attached to a horrifically loud bell. Should the corpse suddenly prove not to be one, he or she has only to tug on the string, whereupon the bell clangs and the caretaker comes running. In a glass case not far from this contraption is a deceptively simpler one, an ordinary-looking stiletto. For a fee of one hundred crowns, the doomed but well-to-do patient was guaranteed that after he had apparently breathed his last, a duly authorized medical doctor would arrive, take said stiletto in his well-schooled hands, and plunge it into the client's heart. When it comes to death, the Viennese don't mess around.

Nor do they find their own morbidity in the least awkward or embarrassing. When I first meet Peter Weiser, he wants nothing more than to show me Vienna's cemeteries. There are miles and miles of them. First he drives me to the attractively unkempt St. Marxer Cemetery, where Mozart is said to be buried—not precisely where his gravestone is, to be sure, but certainly, Weiser says, within a hundred square meters of it. Viennese graveyards are unusually absorbing because many of the tombstones are graced not just with names and dates but also with the dear departed's occupation. "Beautiful, isn't it?" says Weiser as he whisks me off to the more carefully groomed Zentralfriedhof—the Central Cemetery. "People sometimes go hunting in the cemeteries, you know—although the city has now banned hunting on Saturdays." He purses his lips regretfully, preparing his next *Schmäh.* "Of course, the cemeteries are also favorite places for mating." Of course. And, evidently, for Japanese tourists. They crowd around the graves of Beethoven, Brahms, Gluck, the Strausses, and Schubert, all conveniently (and rather undemocratically) arrayed in the *Gräbergruppe* (literally "group grave"). A little way on, you can find the mutually antagonistic architects and designers Adolf Loos and Josef Hoffman, the playwrights Arthur Schnitzler and Johann Nestroy, the filmmaker G. W. Pabst, and, beneath a tombstone that looks like a wobbly Jell-O cube, the great serialist composer Arnold Schönberg.

But the place to ask the Viennese about their death obsession is not the cemetery. Instead, you repair to the spot where every truly serious matter is discussed—the coffeehouse, to which many great Viennese and countless obscure ones have gone since the seventeenth century to sip a *Melange* (cappuccino to you) and read a newspaper, have a chat, or write, sketch, or compose the works that would change the course of history. Freud liked the Café Landtmann, Mahler the Café Imperial, while the habitués of the Café Central, now a picturesque tourist trap, included Leon Trotsky, Alfred Adler, Robert Musil, and occasionally Lenin himself. The terrific little place I'm sitting in now, The Bräunerhof, with its vaguely Jugendstil look, was launched in 1911 as a hangout for auctiongoers and is known now for its fabulously rude waiters and its thick, almost chewy coffee. "Inside the coffeehouse," says my young companion and guide, Elke Pittersberger, "everyone's equal—rich, poor, young, and old. It's not only a meeting place but a place to work, and sometimes you just watch people—you watch people and make up stories about them. We all have time here, and taking your time is very important. You don't see people running after trams in Vienna. They just say, 'If I miss it, I take the next one.'"

Elke can't quite explain the Viennese infatuation with death, but she thinks it has something to do with a certain native moroseness. "We love to complain here," she says, "and we hate change. If things are the same, we feel secure. Vienna is a kind of cocoon, and it's impossible to break free. You should see it in the winter. The city is full of old people—the percentage of old to young here is very high—and you see these old, bitter women everywhere, complaining, complaining about the weather, complaining about the foreigners, et cetera. Long ago they held their wartime households together, cooking the potato soup, but now they're not even useful. And the influence of these old people is very strong."

I think she has something there—not so much about the winter and the old soupmakers but about being useful. Glorious though it is, Vienna has clearly outlived its former usefulness—hence this sense of finitude and duality, of the brevity of life and even of empire.

"There's too much past for a small country like ours," says Traudl Lessing. "By marriage, we had the Netherlands and Burgundy all the way up to Savoy, and large parts of Poland and northern Italy. It's a real burden, all that history—the nostalgia is breaking our backs. What are we doing in this little mousetrap? We've never had it so good, really, and yet the comparisons remain."

Coffeehouses may offer consolation, but life in the mousetrap can take its toll. One proof of that—the ultimate *Schmäh*—lies on the edge of town, in the fin de siècle architect Otto Wagner's most captivating work: a church on the grounds of an insane asylum. As you drive through the gates of the Steinhof hospital, its denizens may eye you curiously. Up a winding road at the top of the hill is Wagner's Steinhof church (1904–1907), sleekly functional yet suffused with genuine spirituality, with a dome that's at once Byzantine and peculiarly modern, with magnificent stained-glass windows by the great Jugendstil designer Kolo Moser, and with an interior that feels at once devout and ineffably light. There are features designed expressly for the needs of the mentally ill: The pews have rounded corners so that falling bodies won't be hurt, for instance, and the floor tilts for easy cleaning. Yet none of the pragmatic touches detract from the work's sublimity. Here, at the Steinhof, is the ultimate example of the Viennese ability to accommodate the dark with the light, the graceful with the grotesque. For surely this humane and spacious building, erected to allow the worship of God by madmen, is one of the two or three most beautiful churches built in this century.

The Viennese, of course, treat their boggling cultural past the way New Yorkers treat skyscrapers—they studiously take no notice of it at all. To the inhabitants of Vienna, facing the past can only emphasize the tininess of the present. No wonder they'd prefer a glass of *Heuriger* or an evening spent gorging on pork at the *Beisel* (the local version of a bistro); no wonder their young disappear nightly into the so-called Bermuda Triangle of clubs and bars, or into well-appointed by-the-hour hotels like the Orient, where the room rate includes a lissome Slovakian blond. For the natives, only the pleasures of the present can ease the opprobrium of the past.

Which may be why we who come from afar don't always understand the Viennese. To us, the city's past and its present are inseparable enchantments. How can those who live here not revel in it? But the delight we take can only remind them of what they've lost; it can even make them grouchy. "We accept the fact that tourism and travelers are important," says Oscar Bronner, the editor in chief of Vienna's newspaper *Der Standard*. "But we aren't really interested in foreigners. The Viennese would prefer it if the tourists would just send the money and stay home." He gazes at me impassively for a moment. Still I'm not convinced. I can't help thinking of all the welcoming Viennese I've met, all the merriment I've gleaned through their deadpans, all the *Heuriger* and coffee and lively conversation I've enjoyed at their behest.

Besides, I know a good *Schmäh* when I hear one.

1993

An Island of Old Europe

by

LUC SANTE

For years I suffered from a condition that might be termed "fear of Belgium." This sounds comical to you, probably, but I am among those who have in their bedside drawer that maroon passport—EUROPEAN COMMUNITY, it says at the top these days—displaying a crowned shield with lion rampant and crossed scepters and motto scroll disproportionately long so that it can say "Union Makes Strength" in two languages, one of which I can't read. Like many holders of this passport, I am aware that my ancestors lived in the territory now called Belgium all the way back through the centuries when it was Dutch, Austrian, Spanish, French, Burgundian, and so on, and possibly as far back as when it was originally Belgica and conquered by Julius Caesar. On the other hand, I haven't lived there myself since childhood, have never voted or paid taxes there or fulfilled my military duty.

At some point it became clear to me that I needed to knuckle under and confront the place as an adult. On my last visit, I had been twenty years old and having a wild summer in Paris—ostensibly studying, but just barely—so I protested and dragged my feet when my mother ordered me to go visit various aged relatives. It was a good thing I did go, as it turned out, because all of them had died by the time I made it there again.

The lapse was a staggering eighteen years. Some of that time I was restricted by artistic poverty to places I could get to by bus, but later on I visited other countries, many of them in Europe, some of them actually adjacent to Belgium. My fear of my native land was a complex brew, but among its ingredients was surely the notion that the place could not possibly live up to my memories, that either it had changed beyond reckoning or I had changed so much that I'd be incapable of appreciating it—or, for that matter, that my memories were so inflated by distance as to bear little relation even to the original reality. And then, too, I was in some way returning to the powerlessness of childhood itself, or so it felt. This was quite a lot of baggage to be packing.

My jitters abated a little as I looked out the airplane window at the reality of Belgium: patches of woods where the trees are planted in ruler-straight rows, and tiny villages composed of two lines of row houses facing each other narrowly across a road, each house backed by its vegetable garden and the whole surrounded by fields. One would hardly imagine, from these ordered landscapes, that trilingual Belgium is riven by extraordinarily bitter cultural differences and that it was the battlefield of a hundred wars waged from beyond its borders. It has a reputation for conservatism, perhaps complacency, perhaps repression. The caricature would portray it as a flat, gray place with great museums and rich cream sauces, a country that should occupy no more than two days of any package tour.

There's truth in that picture, but the Belgium it depicts is largely the northern region of Flanders. As it happens. I'm from the south—Wallonia—which is neither flat nor particularly well endowed with museums (and the rich cream sauces have thinned out considerably) and, furthermore, is completely passed over by those package tours. It would, in fact, be difficult to package, but what it lacks in immediately identifiable landmarks and easily digested characteristics, it compensates for in density of atmosphere. It seems to partake of the old Europe, the one that existed before everything got, first, Americanized, then globalized.

The gateway to both Belgiums is Brussels, set almost at the country's midpoint and possessed of its principal airport. On my family's first trip to the United States, our flight had been grounded by a storm and the airline put us up at the gloriously Art Nouveau Hôtel Métropole. The hotel, I was pleased to see, is still there, still glorious, but the center of town has moved away from it. Now it borders a section of the old city that has been allowed to go to seed. In Brussels, that can only mean it will soon be demolished, or at the least flanked by glass towers. This is the flavor of Brussels, where, beginning in the 1950s, whole neighborhoods were razed and rebuilt and bona fide architectural masterpieces, such as Victor Horta's Maison du Peuple (1896–1899), casually destroyed.

The resulting grid of nondescript high-rises and jarringly omnipresent multilane highways is, of course, suitable for the city's function as headquarters for a variety of international agencies, the latest being the EC. What remains of old Brussels mostly exists in patches within the web of highways: the dizzyingly overdecorated houses of the Grand-Place; the tight cluster of old streets still bearing the names of their ancient trade designations (Cheese, Herb, Butter; Butchers, Brewers, Dyers, Spur Makers) that are now principally given over to restaurants and souvenir shops; the district around the Royal Palace (seldom actually inhabited by the royal family, who prefer the garden setting of Laeken Palace, on the northern fringe of the city) with its symmetrical parks and rows of embassies.

And then there is the Marolles, the old proletarian district, which I discovered on this trip by accident. I had strolled by the Royal Palace and then along the formal and dignified Rue de la Régence, which abuts the Palais de Justice, a monstrous domed juggernaut perched on its cliff as if ready at any moment to spring down on the cowering populace below. I went around this frightening structure and turned right onto a narrow street partly composed of steps, which plunged hundreds of feet down into the Marolles. My walk might as well have diagrammed the class structure. The neighborhood is, as it has always been, both picturesque and poor. The old Marollien culture is passing, as is its language (an improbable fifty-fifty mix of French and Flemish, spiced with Spanish expressions that go back to the seventeenth century, when Madrid was the ruler), but they are steadily being replaced by the language and culture of more recent arrivals, mostly from North Africa. On the Rue Haute, cafés with an inflexible population of veteran drinkers sit peacefully next to halal butchers, and at number 132 stands the house of Pieter Brueghel the Elder, marked with a plaque: FROM THE PEOPLE TO ITS PAINTER. A little farther down the slope is the Place du Jeu de Balle, where, every morning, the flea market is held.

I quickly became an aficionado of Belgian flea markets, which can be divided into two rough categories: *marchés aux puces*, which trade in junk; and *brocantes*, which feature a better class of junk up to and including antiques, although the upper bracket of these is purveyed at *marchés d'antiquités*, which are something else again. But flea markets, in all their randomness, come close to possessing the unconscious mind of a nation: They are true museums of its recent cultural history, its follies and cults and ambition and dread. At their best, flea markets seem to have the artist's gift for seizing vast questions and unnameable areas of ambiguity and defining them with perfectly apposite detail. George Orwell once wrote that you can best tell what most people feel and think by sampling the contents of a small newsagent's shop. Flea markets extend this divining capacity into the past. The things people saved because they thought they would one day be valuable, for example, are often worth less than the ephemera they unloaded right away. The Jeu de Balle market, from Monday through Saturday, serves up trash of interest mostly to advanced students. It is here that you will find your inexplicable machine parts, your broken shoes, your defective appliances, your boxes of miscellaneous papers. On Sundays its interest broadens.

Almost the first thing I saw was an elaborate stand covered with stationery supplies. How odd, I thought, that a *brocanteur* should be offering merely the contents of a paper-goods shop. And then I realized my error. The goods in question—which were in mint condition— seemed common enough to me because I had used them when I attended school in Belgium: nib pens, inkwells, blotter paper, wooden pencil boxes, thin paper-covered notebooks, hard erasers. Kids were examining them as if they were potsherds from the Merovingian era. I began to doubt my own memories until a beefy guy about my age, overcome with emotion, held up a notebook and cried, "When I was a boy, I had notebooks exactly like this!" "We all did, pal," came the reply.

Everywhere I looked as I walked around the square, I saw objects I once knew, even things my parents still own: the very same reproduction of *St. Martin Dividing His Cloak*, by Van Dyck, in the exact same frame! Celluloid trays, covered with a mosaic of cigar bands and then shellacked! Hadn't seen those in years. I'd nearly forgotten the kitsch Africana, the albums of the pictures included as premiums with chocolate bars (slipped between the foil and paper wrappers), the hammered brass (a national fixation), the aestheticized dirty pictures, the pious cards given out at funerals (boxes of these). This may all have been memory lane stuff for me, but it also had the makings of a crash course on the Belgian national psyche.

Later, as my wife and I sat drinking dark beers under the extraordinarily deep awning of the Taverne Falstaff, opposite the Bourse, another element in this course presented itself. A woman in her fifties sat with a younger woman, who might have been her daughter, and the latter's putative boyfriend, all chatting in Dutch. When the waiter came, the three ordered in French. Brussels is officially a bilingual city, and for various intricate political reasons there are no published statistics of who speaks what within it, but the French-language dominance is believed to run as high as seventy percent. (On another occasion I was sitting in a café when an elderly Flemish man came in. He spoke no French, and nobody else spoke Dutch, personnel or customers, so consequently his order could not be taken.) The French language was formerly the tongue of the ruling class, and held sway over the entire country. More recently, however, the rising commercial strength of Flanders and the declining industrial power of French-speaking Wallonia, in the south, have combined to increase the prestige of Dutch ("Flemish" is a dialect of Dutch, but use of the main language has become standard). Linguistic nationalists have even succeeded in passing laws aimed at dividing the country into strict language zones. Because a southeastern sliver of the country is German-speaking, the government has gone so far as to have many cabinet positions represented by three ministers: Flemish, Walloon, and Germanic or Bruxellois.

According to the great Belgian historian Henri Pirenne, the Flemish-Walloon division dates to the first half of the fifth century, when Roman legions controlling Belgica were called back to Rome and in their wake a Germanic tribe, the Salians, invaded Flanders. The Walloons in turn are descended from remnants of the original Celtic Belgians and elements of other Germanic tribes. The line of demarcation follows the frontier of Salian settlements but otherwise had no obvious markers, no topographical features of any sort, and yet it has remained fixed and absolute to the present. How these two distinct populations became a nation is a complex question—they were linked many times over the centuries before the foundation of modern Belgium in 1830, when it broke away from the Netherlands at least partly over the question of religion, Belgium being predominantly Catholic. The Flemish are fair-haired and on the tall side, industrious and precise, pious and conservative. The Walloons tend to be dark and shorter, have a reputation for a "Mediterranean" indolence and disorder, mostly vote Socialist, and harbor notable anticlerical elements.

Or so it is said, at least. But the two sides have a great deal in common, from popular culture to the basic cuisine, and from architectural styles to the styles of vegetable gardens. During a long wait in the arrivals room of the Zaventem airport, I set myself the test of trying to guess which among the parties present were Flemish and which were Walloon. I would pick out a cluster—three women who looked like my aunts, say, or a complicated family grouping with members of various complexions. Then I would sidle by to hear them talk. I guessed wrong fifty percent of the time. My "aunts" spoke Dutch; a rail-thin blond guy spoke French with a thick Walloon accent.

These days, the most obvious distinguishing feature between the two halves of the country has to do with signs of prosperity. Basically, Flanders is rich, Wallonia is hurting. Flemish Antwerp glistens with health, as does Bruges, a century and a half ago called a dead city and now serving up its artistic and architectural treasures as if on a bed of velvet; even the motley, stubborn city of Ghent exudes a certain glow of satisfaction. Compared to these, the Walloon flagship city, Liège, is a woebegone place with wobbly self-esteem. Its main square, Place St-Lambert, has been an excavation site for more than twenty years—a metro project that got tangled up in political and archaeological considerations—and its riverfront, once lined with ancient houses, became obscured in the 1950s and '60s by phalanxes of clumsily functional apartment complexes. Yet this was where I came to stay for three whole months, to stroll its streets, sit in its cafés, shop in its markets, and generally soak up the Walloon character it expresses. My aim was to write a book that would somehow enable me to come to terms with my Belgian past, and while its shape remains hazy in my mind, the city's appeal in that time became somewhat clearer.

Liège's ancient heart emerges in the Sunday morning market called La Batte (the Walloon word for "quay"), which sometimes stretches more than a mile—depending on the weather—down the riverbank. The market has convened for untold centuries, an omnium-gatherum of goods that range from vegetables to puppies, live turkeys to children's shoes, handguns to fake bonsai. Customers come from the Netherlands and Germany (neither is very far away, admittedly), and so all three currencies and languages are in constant use. The roiling crowds, the squawking fowl, the yammering pitchmen, the odors of frying, all seem to have been transferred in a straight line from the fairs of the Middle Ages. There is nothing quaint about this market, and no concession to "good taste"; for every display of sumptuous produce, there is one of polyester stretch pants. The Friday morning flea market on the other side of the river, in the old working-class district called Out-remeuse (where Georges Simenon grew up), is also the real thing, where vendors could almost be vying with each other for some extreme defi-nition of randomness: rare children's toys alongside false teeth, spare tires, and boxes of American license plates.

I found more of Liège's past on its outskirts. Beyond the ruined Place St-Lambert and the immense Palace of the Prince-Bishops that faces onto it is a street called Hors-Château. Low archways lead back between the houses to labyrinthine alleys of tiny dwellings, formerly reserved for the servants of the rulers. It is easy to get lost among these paths, which eventually issue into the woods that cover the side of a hill. Atop the hill is the Citadel, which dominates the city, and today its walls enclose the hospital. You can still find places in Belgium where urban streets end in farmland, without any suburban mediation, but far less often than I recalled from my childhood.

A Belgian city is, above all, a place deeply conflicted over the role of the automobile. In the early sixties, the country was still feeling the aftereffects of the war and there were relatively few cars to be seen. Car fever has since arrived with a vengeance, and along with it the begin-nings of a warehouse-outlet, strip mall culture. The streets were not meant for cars—many are actually too narrow for even one car to pass—and parking is a nightmare, with multistory garages doing the equivalent of draining the river with a spoon. Often, as I walked the streets of Liège, I would see an overlay, as if in sepia, of buff-and-red trolley cars jerking along beside the rush hour traffic, sparks shooting from their overhead cable connections, while streams of workers bi-cycled home from the factories at dusk.

Fortunately Liège, like every other Belgian city, has at its heart a pedestrian zone, both to curtail traffic and to encourage the country's historic love of strolling. As a consequence, the art of the window display is still taken very seriously, with some of its most beautiful and refined examples issuing from places of business that seem unlikely to tempt the purchasing instincts of the passerby—rope stores, for example, or casket dealerships.

Food and drink, also best found while strolling, are taken so seriously by Belgians that various tiers of accommodation have been established, to avoid any confusion regarding the precise degree of hospitality required. A restaurant involves tablecloths, aperitifs, wine, and at least three courses. You do not enter a restaurant with the intention of having a sandwich. That you can purchase at an outdoor stand, or through the sidewalk window of a snack bar. If you do not wish to consume it while perambulating, you can go to a café. If, however, you want to sit in a café and eat fried potatoes, you will more than likely be out of luck.

Fried potatoes (let's not call them French fries—even the French will concede that they're a Belgian invention) are best if they're obtained from a *frituur* (Dutch) or a *friture* or a *friterie* (old and new French styles, reflecting Belgian insecurities about the correctness of their language). These, traditionally, are trailers, although more often now they're small stores, usually without tables. In the past, the potatoes always came in newspaper cones, but now the polystyrene boat prevails. Generally they are eaten with mayonnaise, although here as well innovation has reared its head and proposed a dozen or so alternatives, including something called "Américaine," which tastes as if conjured up from a recipe for barbecue sauce transmitted in code. I betray no chauvinism whatsoever in asserting that Belgian fries are the greatest in the world. Purists will claim that they have declined, and cite as proof the fact that the potatoes are now fried in vegetable oil whereas animal fat was once the rule, but that is an academic question. Fries are a meal in themselves, usually lunch, although they can be consumed with a variety of sausage products or with *boulettes*, baseball-size spheres containing an approximate two-to-one ratio of bread to meat.

Cafés are not, by and large, associated with food, although a few of the fancier ones will have a restaurant wing. The café is a place to sit, since that is an important component of the strolling ritual, and, of course, to drink. Belgian cafés sell anywhere from six to three hundred of the country's beer varieties, of which there are said to be nearly five hundred. (In 1900 there were 3,223 breweries in Belgium, nearly one per village; today the number has fallen to exactly 100.) These range from the basic lagers like Stella Artois or Jupiler to the sweet-and-sour top-fermented *gueuzes* from the Senne Valley outside Brussels (where ambient enzymes that exist nowhere else in the world assist in fermentation), and from the dark, robust abbey beers like Leffe or Maredsous or Chimay, which frequently come in different alcohol-percentage grades (generally no more than twelve percent), to the "white" wheat beers like Hoegaarden. Many cities and resort towns will purvey a local brew available nowhere else. In addition, cafés may also feature pinball machines, inexplicable pinball machines (where the object of the game is something akin to bingo), radios blaring pop music (jukeboxes are rare), arcane dice games, billiard tables, cats and dogs, extended families, old soaks, courting couples, and, occasionally, extraordinary modernist furnishings that no one has noticed since they were installed in the 1930s.

I was so happily ensconced in the pedestrian comforts of Liège that it was some time before I thought to venture beyond the city limits, past even the concentric rings of surrounding small towns. There I rediscovered the beauty and seeming remoteness of the Walloon countryside.

Countryside in Belgium comes in many flavors: the polders of northwest Flanders, the rich plains just below them, the fertile Kempen in the northeast. South of the Meuse, the land begins to rise and the high plateaus of the Condroz and the Hesbaye give way to the rippling Ardennes, small mountains comparable to the Berkshires. Nothing in Belgium is terribly elevated—the highest point, the Signal de Botrange, is a mere 694 meters up, less than 2,300 feet—but in the hilly regions, there is constant change as the road flows with the landscape, and you can never be sure what the view will be around the next curve.

Although farms have been consolidating in Belgium over the past thirty years, just as they have in the rest of the Western world, resulting in ever larger and more streamlined operations, you wouldn't necessarily know this from, say, the Pays de Herve, the pastureland east of Liège famous for its potent cheeses and its cider. As we drove around this pocket of land nestled against both the Dutch and the German borders, we kept seeing what appeared to be little hills inhabited by one cow apiece. Here, as in many other rural areas, there remain numerous fortified farms—walled compounds made of stone, some of them very old, which appear at once redoubtable and homey, especially if the windows have lace curtains in them, which show very well against the stone. As our car was stopped by drovers bringing a herd across the road and through the gate of one of these establishments, I felt as if I were getting a glimpse of the deep past.

The best way to see southern Belgium's countryside is by car, starting out on one of the "green," or scenic, routes, then letting serendipity take over. The roads grow increasingly narrow until you find yourself on lanes cutting through fields that would appear to be intended only for farm vehicles. Every so often, however, a village appears. Many are hamlets of six houses and a church, untouched for centuries and seemingly abandoned, their residents either out in the fields or in the kitchen.

As we traveled, I kept lists of my favorites: Maffe and Somal, Vêves and Gendron, Herhet and Thynes, Beffe and Soy, Bra and Trou de Bra. Some are so tiny that they appear only on the most detailed maps, some are more substantial and were built in steps down a slope, some are clusters of houses clinging to the skirts of a church, some are so undisturbed that dogs sleep in the middle of the road. My mother's side of the family issues entirely from three specks on the map—Fraiture, Odeigne, and Malempré—that have just lately seen more business because they happen to sit near some decent ski slopes, but modernization has thus far consisted of little more than the construction of the odd chalet. Fraiture in particular has retained a certain classic status by virtue of its position at the end of a road—barring unforeseen developments, there will never be any through traffic there, so the chickens can range pretty much undisturbed.

Elsewhere in the Ardennes are more traditional attractions. I had indistinct but tantalizing memories of the original Spa, twenty-eight miles southeast of Liège, known as a mineral spring since antiquity and mentioned by Pliny the Elder. It reached its peak as a resort around the turn of the century, when Queen Marie-Henriette, who couldn't abide her husband, Leopold II, established a separate and permanent residence there. Not surprising, then, that what I found was a faded and melancholy place, though spotless and still grand. The Parc de Sept-Heures, for instance, is a covered promenade strewn with cast-iron pillars that speaks of the exercise habits of a vanished race; now it is a surrealist object, its only practical use being as a runway for skateboarders, who are specifically prohibited.

We drove farther west without a plan, passing through farmland interrupted by valleys, and got to Dinant. This place also evokes bygone forms of holidaymaking, but it has remained more viable and is less poetic as a result. It is a cool-seeming place between cliffs on the lower Meuse, with a citadel on the cliffs above, accessible by cable car, and with the ice blue onion dome of its *collégiale* filling the eye just below. There is not a whole lot to do in Dinant, but Belgians by the busloads, by the hundreds, fill up the town's cafés and exclaim over its grotesque souvenirs, which are the very same ones sold across the street from the Manneken-Pis (the famous pissing-urchin fountain) in Brussels. We observed the same phenomenon farther south in the hills, in Durbuy and La Roche-en-Ardenne, two more charming old resorts from a time when the vacation regime consisted largely of quiet walks and visits to slightly rusticated cafés. Nowadays, both are choked with crowds of people drifting uncertainly through the streets, elbowing each other to get into the watering holes, staring at window displays of smoked sausages as if they'd never seen such a thing. This behavior, which pretty much vanishes in the off-season, has much to do with the country's small scale: Old resort towns are simply not expandable, and nearly everyone is exhausted from the ordeal of finding a parking space.

For my part, I found the greatest enjoyment in visiting the towns not outlined in any color on the giveaway maps. Charleroi, for example, is noted for its flame-belching smokestacks and barely rates a mention in the guidebooks for its glass and photography museums. While not conventionally picturesque, Charleroi has benefited from its enviable reputation by being allowed to keep its tough urban look without deleterious improvements. The best time to visit is probably after dark, when the mystery of its streets is at its height. Charleroi's central commercial district is marked by a relatively narrow range of styles, from Victorian industrial to a sort of thirties brutalist moderne. There is a tall, curving arcade, disproportionately narrow, that spits one out into a movie set of sooty churches and blaring neon. A restaurant called L'Hippopotame is advertised in enormous red letters; you imagine the food arriving on conveyor belts. An inexplicable colonnade runs unanchored for what looks like a mile, too thin to contain rooms, too wide to be merely ceremonial. People are selling blood sausages from a cart. There seems to be bottle-breaking in the Chinese restaurant. Over all stand the open flames from the glassworks. The entire establishment seems to have escaped from some dark prewar movie by Marcel Carné or Marcel L'Herbier.

Perhaps I'm drawn to this because my hometown, Verviers, possesses some of the same flavor. A textile center for more than five hundred years but now considerably deindustrialized, Verviers sits in the precipitous valley of the Vesdre River. As a result, many of its streets are stairs, and numerous are its surrealist ready-mades, such as the Tyrolean-looking three-story building, oddly made of wood in a country of brick and stone houses, that turns out to be a false front built to conceal a boulder that sits about five feet behind its front door. Verviers is full of romantic sinister sights: a destroyed cemetery, an enormous mansion built into the rocks with a highway running directly above its roof, a private bridge club with large round windows through which can be seen the furnishings, which are chinoiserie. No tourists ever come to Verviers, and in truth there's not a lot to do, except maybe visit the Wool Museum, or have a drink at the Aux Pays-Bas, which looks as if it were designed by a renegade member of de Stijl and is frequented exclusively by pensioners. It's probably just as well that Verviers isn't overrun with tourists—they'd just force the municipal authorities to maintain the ghostly riverside park, which at present turns into wilderness almost right away.

This is what I hoped Belgium would be like after all those years: simultaneously gritty and not quite of this earth. I had an uncanny sensation, as if I'd invented the town, but, of course, it had invented me. As I walked around, every successive example of eccentricity, stubbornness, unmarketability, and obsolescence filled me with pride. For the first time ever, maybe, I felt a kind of patriotism. I remembered the ironic tag line of an old Richard Pryor routine: "My people!" I said, shaking my head.

1994

A Miracle in the Caribbean

by

MARTHA GELLHORN

 The airport terminal at Belize City is very encouraging. It is an overgrown shack. Passengers off the once-daily flight from Miami queue in the sun, slowed down, chatting with strangers. After each passport has been examined as if passports were newfangled inventions, you enter a square wooden room where the baggage has been dumped in the middle of the floor. A free-for-all follows. The taxi is a large old American car with fins. A handsome river runs to the right; the road is dirt and potholes. My heart rose like a lark; this is how it used to be, before the Caribbean was homogenized by tourism.

There is a quick impression of the town, small wood houses on stilts draped in greenery, and you are deposited at the Fort George Hotel and whisked by a lift to a high floor and a spacious room, stylishly European, complete with marble and tile bath and the sea below your window. Unexpected and unique luxury. I needed local advice, as I knew nothing about Belize except that it has a reef, which is why I was there.

Not just a reef, for heaven's sake, but 174 miles of same, the second longest in the world, after the Great Barrier Reef of Australia. Besides the spectacular reef, there are three atolls, islands encircled by their own reefs, with their own calm lagoons (exactly what I want for Christmas), and some four hundred other islands, called cays, mostly mushroom specks but a few are large, frequented by tourists. I was thrilled by this very special unknown geography—unknown because I had not heard of it—and eager to start on my winter plan of snorkeling, reading, writing, and baking in the sun. Though luggage is the curse of travel, it could not be escaped for such a project: a typewriter and rich supply of stationery; a book bag, weight half a ton; a portable chemist's shop, because of a disastrous snorkeling trip in the Pacific without a chemist's shop; a single caseful of the flimsy rags suitable to cover nakedness in a very hot country.

Alight with hope, I set off in an open boat laden almost to the gunwales with backpacking Americans and my luggage. I didn't mind being soaked to the skin by spray, nor the prospect of sinking with all hands, but I minded Cay Caulker, recommended as picturesque and nontouristy. In my opinion a rural slum, just bearable if one is sloshed to paralysis on inexpensive Belize rum. Wild with impatience, but hope intact, I got the first available boat for Ambergris Cay, touted as the up-market resort. The sky immediately turned gunmetal gray and an unseasonal norther roared over the island. Weather is now unseasonal everywhere, as we know, but this was hell. After the cold slicing rain, the wind blew hard and steadily day and night, like a cosmic fingernail on a blackboard. Tourists, not natives, wandered barefoot around the tacky village, where the residents, expatriate and Belizean alike, were fully occupied in overcharging them: minimum value for maximum money. Tourism, even this minor, modest tourism, corrupts.

I wondered why no one braved the wind, admittedly disagreeable and chill, to swim. What is an island for? When I tried it I saw the reason; the seabed is slimy with turtle grass and so shallow you cannot swim your way out of it. To snorkel, you could take a half-hour boat ride to the reef, twice a day, and paddle in the choppy waves among other bodies. Boats are all right for divers, who carry all that clobber, and of course for fishermen, but for a snorkeler this was a profoundly lousy setup. Cold, depressed to the point of panic, maddened by the wind, I stood it for five days, then rose in the dark, packed my crippling bags, and caught the first jitney plane back to square one, the Fort George Hotel. I never saw the famous reef, and I thought I had done it at last, traveled myself into a no-exit dead end.

Belize City is a fine little town, seedy and colorful, and I approve of it warmly, but not for a whole winter. It does not look or feel like anywhere else; best of all, it does not seem to belong to the last decade of this century. There are pretty clapboard houses with gingerbread trimming around the eaves and wide verandas, such colonial remnants as the courthouse and the old iron market, and pleasing oddities, such as an upstairs Hindu temple with three pink domes, like plaster powder puffs, above an airline office. Untainted by tourism, Belizeans are lovely, and because of their variety the place has a curiously cosmopolitan air. To me, it comes under the generic heading of Somerset Maugham. Ambling or loafing or shopping are Creoles, mestizos, Mayan Indians, perhaps some black Garifuna, Hindus, Chinese, as well as a few Americans and Europeans. Mennonites, a strangely pallid white, are not seen in this city of sin.

On Saturdays, market day, the town is jumping, and a man, carpenter by trade, stands in front of the Bank of Belize, the center of town, with a loudspeaker rigged on his bike, and preaches to the population from early morning until late afternoon. Passing in a taxi, I caught an interesting tidbit: ". . . sexual intercourse, he don't know if he de fadder. Mebbe stranger . . ." The taxi driver said, "He's good. If everyone was up-front like him, it would be better here." A well-dressed café au lait salesman in the hardware store said, "He's disturbing the peace. He shouts about religion, politics, even business, about which he knows nothing."

The carpenter has been bellowing away for six years, and nobody dreams of stopping him. The point, the deeply important point, is that nobody in Belize, with or without loudspeakers, is afraid to say anything he likes; simply, nobody is afraid. Belize is in Central America, where you breathe fear in the air. Tucked between Yucatán and Guatemala, this little country, fractionally larger than Wales, has been spared the horrors that have afflicted the region from the Spanish conquest up to this minute. Ongoing horrors. I look at Belize as Belizeans do not, thinking of murderous El Salvador, the regular manhunts for Indians and intellectuals in Guatemala, the miserable poverty and unsafety of Honduras; thinking of dictators, lawless armies, death squads, torture.

Belize is a miracle in this part of the world because it was a crown colony and the crown, without much bother, served as hands-off protection. Colonialism did its best here, leaving behind the habit of elections; Belize is a genuine, not a rhetorical, democracy. And British colonialism failed to do its worst—the nasty racism I used to detect in other colonies. Belize is as multiracial (and as multireligious) as you can get, and it is serenely color-blind and serenely tolerant. These splendidly mixed, independent people are loyal subjects of the queen, because Belize is a member of the Commonwealth with a lady governor general. They don't know how lucky they are, past and present; they are also safe from the evil meddling of Washington in Central America.

Added to the problem of what to do with the winter was the ridiculous problem of what to wear. Belize is not tropical, as I had assumed; it is subtropical, with the mean low temperature ranging from fifty to eighty degrees Fahrenheit. Flimsy rags were a bad joke; a bit of thermal underwear would not have come amiss. A far-flung friend of a London friend rescued me by finding an agreeable house to rent, some thirty miles west of the city, on the bank of the Belize River. Mainland Belize had not occurred to me as an option. I have never lived beside a river and have never lived anywhere as I did here for five weeks; I was entranced, not moving more than fifty yards from the house, content to watch the same view of the river. It is wide and smooth, changing color in the changing light of the day. Tall, feathery, close-growing trees on both banks reflect in its mirror surface. Except for jacaranda, royal palm, and mango, all the trees were strange to me. There was no wind.

I thought the beautiful frieze, undisturbed by the silent flow of the river, was perhaps the secret of this magic, but I cannot explain it.

The house was next to the main road west, one of four main roads in Belize—packed dirt, potholes like lakes (unseasonal rain), first-class bumps and furrows. I could see the only bridge that crosses the river, an old, iron railway type with plank floorboards. Scant traffic rumbled over it like outgoing artillery. Otherwise, the silence was broken by remarkable birdsong from invisible birds; once I saw gray cranes at the river's edge. And howler monkeys, a real novelty. Asleep on branches, they are two-foot-long packages of gleaming black fur. Awake, they sound like apprentice gorillas, their grunts and shrieks echoing over the forest. They awake at any odd time, but at night they seemed to besiege the house—very exciting. Giant orange iguanas, another novelty, also sun on trees; they look like baby dinosaurs and leap like flying squirrels. The house had all mod cons, and I felt that I was living alone in the depths of a romantic jungle wilderness.

The rule says that you cannot get something for nothing, and I accepted the three types of biting fly, which persecuted me outdoors, as payment for bliss. They are fast, silent, sting just as efficiently through clothing, and make mosquitoes seem like piffling amateurs. One day I stood under a huge old mango with orchids growing on its trunk and shouted, "STOP, STOP," to the insect world, so the situation must have been pretty bad. Later, after I tore myself away from the river to explore the country, I realized that the productivity of these flies was largely a *spécialité de ma maison*, due to long grass and a standing pond at the back of the property. When I moaned about the killer flies, people looked at me with polite amazement. There is plenty of wildlife in Belize, including jaguars and crocodiles, but insects are no serious hazard.

It is not possible to explore much of Belize, because seventy-five percent of the country is uninhabited. And of course roadless. It is not very inhabited anywhere: under 200,000 residents in all, cays and mainland. Many more people than that live in Cardiff. I cannot exaggerate the pure physical pleasure of underpopulation and a sense of empty space. Sometimes, dotty characters ask me about the changes I have noticed in my long life, as if I could remember, but I do notice always and with gloom the suffocating increase in bodies. Half a century ago, I thought this ghastliness of packed humanity was peculiar to China; three decades later, I fled India because I could not endure the crowds. Much of the world I knew and loved is lost, ruined because there are too many of us and we move everywhere. For my taste, Belize is ideal.

Places to stay outside Belize City are few and far between and small. Those I saw were distinctive and delightful and attached to rivers. Nearest to me was the Belize River Lodge, where you eat superb food (not all that usual) in a room that feels like the inside of a sailing ship's hull: varnished natural mahogany walls, floor, and ceiling. I think this is a secret society for fishermen, one whispering the good news to an-other, with the proviso: Keep the women out. Two blissful brothers from Boston were the only guests; at most there could be twelve fishing fanatics. They can fish in fresh or salt water from dawn to dusk and talk about it at night in that captivating room.

Cayo District, in the high western part of the country, is the most handsome landscape. On the way, we visited the Gurkhas, happy as sandboys with their posting to Belize. A British brigade rotates every six months, presumably to practice jungle warfare, no doubt much more fun than NATO exercises. It is noteworthy that there are no civilian-versus-soldiery brawls in Belize City when the British troops have Saturday night leave.

Chaa Creek Cottages spreads over a hilltop above its river ravine, facing a tapestry of rain forest. It was the largest and most elegant of the inns and can house thirty-six guests in its pretty thatch-roofed cot-tages. The maids are Mayan Indians from a nearby village. The good humor and helpfulness of working people in Belize may be due to decent living wages, unheard of in the rest of Central America.

From Chaa Creek, a semblance of road leads up into the Mountain

Pine Ridge Reserve. The pines do not look like the sad, dull things that the forestry commission plants in cabbage rows. The needles grow in fluffy bunches, and light pours through. The Rio On leaps in cascades between huge slabs and boulders of gray granite, falling into wide, deep pools; and there is no one around. Instant visions of naked Gauguin-style swimming.

The cabins of El Indio Perdido, owned by a Frenchwoman, lie on meadowland among enormous trees ("The iguana like the wild fig, the toucans like the rowan"). You reach the place by pulling a flat-bottom boat across the Mopan River, hand over hand on a cable. Since not everyone wants to sit and moon at rivers, you can fish, swim, kayak, canoe, rubber-raft in them. You can ride through the forests. If you are knowledgeable, you can bird-watch, and if you are a botanist, you will be in heaven. There are 250 kinds of orchids alone and four thousand types of flowering shrubs. The extra treat is archaeology, because Belize abounds in Mayan ruins.

At Chaa Creek I refused the chance of a bone-breaking twelve-hour day to visit Caracol, a Mayan city said to be larger than the famous ruins of Tikal in Guatemala. Caracol was discovered by accident in the jungle a few years ago. Instead, I opted for sociology in San Ignacio, the district capital—seven thousand souls and little wooden houses painted green, yellow, or nothing. The Sacred Heart school there teaches twelve hundred kids from infants to age sixteen. The education system in Belize is simple and odd; schools are given to the charge of the two main religions, Catholic and Anglican, though no child is obliged to adopt either faith. English is the official language; Spanish, the home speech of about one-third of the citizens, is taught as a second language. Kids end up bilingual. The Maya and the Garifuna also speak their tribal tongues, the Creoles speak an indecipherable patois based on English, and the Mennonites, who have their own schools, speak their own German.

Statistically, Belize is ninety-three percent literate, and I believe it. The classes in the Sacred Heart school are large, forty to forty-five children, and without discipline problems. I bet they come out with their three R's solid as rock, unlike too many of our children, who are functional illiterates. I keep trying to understand why Belizeans are so different from all others in Central America and feel that their self-assured literacy may be a partial explanation. And perhaps two hundred years of peace has something to do with it. In El Salvador, poor people have been illiterate forever and are hounded to death as subversives when they try to teach themselves to read from the Bible.

In the north, I was more interested in the ride than in its purpose, to visit the Mayan ruins at Lamanai. Two Mayan brothers own a classy speedboat; we whizzed up the New River, slowing only so as not to capsize Maya fishing in the river. Their boats, called dories, are carved by a Mayan specialist from tree trunks; they have pointed bows, flat sterns and bottoms and paddles, and look like children's toys. Seeing a man alone in a tiny dory, fishing in the shade of mangroves, I thought for the first time in my life that fishing would be fun. They do not use rods, and as we slowed, the older Mayan brother called out and the fisherman pulled up his catch, a heavy bunch of golden fish.

Leonardo, the Mayan caretaker who has worked at Lamanai since 1974, led the way through the jungle. My brief previous experiences of jungle were wet muck underfoot, leeches, and claustrophobia. This jungle was dazzling, innumerable intricate leaf patterns splashed with sun. Then the trail widened to reveal a half-cleared, time-blackened stone pyramid. Leonardo said the pyramid was nearly seventy feet high and had been started around A.D. 100. I was transfixed by a portrait head on the side of the pyramid, a slab of stucco carved with the face of a god, a priest, a king; the turban headdress might mean a priest. I can only guess its size, but think it was twenty feet square. The ears were placed open and flat beside the cheeks; the face was powerful and stern, but not cruel. The features resembled those of Antonio, the older Mayan boatman. The head dates from A.D. 500, said Leonardo.

He and the younger brother, Erminio, spoke with knowledge and pride; it is no mean thing to descend from such an ancient line. The site covers one and three-quarter square miles and has 718 structures scattered in the surrounding jungle. All I know about the Maya fits into a few hearsay sentences. They flourished for a thousand years, from Yucatán down through Central America. Archaeologists believe there were between 400,000 and one million Maya in Belize alone. They were sophisticated and peaceful and monumental builders, though they had not discovered the use of iron. Sometime between A.D. 900 and 1000 their successful civilization mysteriously leaked away, long before the Spaniards came to bring Christ and death. That hurried tour around Belize opened up to me vast vistas of my ignorance.

The quickest way south is by six-seater plane. You land on a grass field at Big Creek, where the outgoing passengers are waiting under a tree. You walk across the grass to the Toucan Inn, a charming little caravansary for travelers on the long bad road from Yucatán to Guatemala, and a merry drinking hole for the local banana growers. Mr. Burgess, a stout, elderly, very black Creole, took me sightseeing in his truck. At Haul Cabbage Creek there is a Mayan village—Spanish-speaking birdlike little women, all married at fourteen, all giggly and happy with hordes of children. Five miles away on the coast is Hopkins, a Garifuna English-speaking village—poor board and tin-roofed shacks, the only solid building being the school. The Garifuna are matte black, with sharp, strong Indian features and a reserved, ungiggly manner. "They come from St. Vincent," said Mr. Burgess as if they had arrived last week, not in the nineteenth century. The Garifuna descend from a distant intermarriage between African slaves and Carib Indians. In the eighteenth century the British booted them out of St. Vincent as troublemakers and left them stranded on an island off the Honduran coast. How they made their way to Belize and how they have kept their physical and cultural identity for two centuries, I do not know. I am full of not knowing.

By truck and boat I moved on to Placencia. We stopped for gasoline at a place that could hardly be reckoned a village, though there were seven churches. Belizeans are ardent churchgoers, but religion must be more sociable than cramping, because about half the children are illegitimate, which does not mean abandoned or denigrated. Perhaps a proper wedding party costs too much. I stayed in an outstandingly well furnished cottage at Rum Point Inn, and at last the Caribbean looked and behaved as it ought to. The long sand beach shelves quickly into deep blue water and you can snorkel from the reefs on nearby cays, so I know where to go next time.

A young American in the shortest possible frayed shorts was questioning the American Rum Point owners about the effects of tourism on the population and the environment, his thesis for the University of California at Berkeley. We agreed that tourism is a destroyer and that Belize is far too good for it. None of the inn owners I had met— English, French, American, Belizean, Irish—want to expand, though between them they could take care of less than a hundred perceptive guests. They are Belizean patriots; they love the country as it is. How much better if oil is found in viable quantities in the north, and tourists go somewhere else.

It is astonishing at my age to stumble on a new country. I feel astonished.

1991

Heaven and Earth

by

JAMES TRUMAN

 Arriving in Bhutan for the first time can give a person a bad case of the Shangri-las. The dirty monsoon heat of New Delhi quickly becomes a stifled memory, a brief stopover in Kathmandu the staging post for the heart-stopping flight east across the Himalayas. Everest, enveloped by clouds this afternoon, cedes to a hundred-mile chain of monumental, lethal snow cones with the legendary names of Gauri Shankar, Lhotse, Kanchenjunga, and, to the east, Jannu, known to its visitors as the Peak of Terror (and successfully climbed for the first time only this year). Then the plane begins its descent, and the darkly wooded crests and ridges of the Himalayan foothills mark our crossing into Bhutan. The approach to the Paro airport is notoriously dicey; only a handful of pilots are certified to attempt it. A series of hard banks and looping figure eights puts us alongside a cliff face, and suddenly we're a wing's length from Bhutan's most famous site, the monastery of Taktshang Goemba, held in miraculous suspension halfway up the rock wall. One final bank and we just clear the chimney of a house beneath us, then bounce to the ground, roaring to a halt a few yards shy of the runway's end.

Out in the cool afternoon air, we're still somewhere between earth and sky. Billowing mists cascade down the hillsides toward the valley floor, while funnels of smoke spiral up to meet them—the sacred offerings of alder wood and juniper that burn constantly, scenting the air. The impression is magical, the invitation compelling. Here, it seems, is a place to rest one's head in the clouds.

The drive into the town of Paro takes us along a narrow country road lined with willow trees; beyond lie meadows and rice fields and clusters of farmhouses in the traditional Bhutanese style, handsome and baronial with their white-plastered walls and timbered beams. Pedestrians thread the roadway, all of them in some manner of national dress. And in one form or another, everyone does wear a dress. We pass farmers sporting the *gho*—the male costume of a patterned smock worn with knee-high socks—and monks on afternoon recess in the traditional Tibetan Buddhist robes of saffron and burgundy. Packs of schoolgirls seem to be competing for who can wear the most colorful *kira*, the kimono-like dress that for women fulfills every duty, from farmwork to fashion statement. We see a group of girls being hauled into the back of a police truck. Have they gone too far? Not at all. With so few crimes to solve, the police fill their days with other things, such as ferrying children to and from school.

Meanwhile, through an open window I detect a pungent, dimly familiar smell and glance out at what looks like a giant marijuana bush. My hunch is correct. Marijuana grows wild, and voluminously, throughout the country. But, miraculously, there is no drug trade in Bhutan—nor, from what I can discover, even a single pothead. Only the pig farmers harvest the accidental crop, to fatten their animals. They've discovered that it gives pigs an insatiable appetite.

Paro itself is a broad main street of shops and tiny bars, with a town square that doubles as a parking lot. Most of the merchants sell exactly the same things at exactly the same prices. The Wal-Mart philosophy has yet to arrive in Bhutan. Shopping here is based not on bargains or convenience but on long-standing relationships between families and shopkeepers. There is no agony of loyalty: You shop according to friendship.

We stop on the other side of town, at our first hotel. Tourism in Bhutan is so recent—it began only in 1974, after the coronation of the present king, Jigme Singye Wangchuck—that there is no consensus about how visitors should be architecturally acclimated. Our hotel, the Kyichu Resort, is built in a fanciful Alpine Modern style; our rooms, though perfectly clean and comfortable, are wedges in a concrete octagon.

Our traveling party numbers four: my friend Sebastian Beckwith, an epicurean tea merchant and old Bhutan hand; Sonam, our driver, who has recently left the monastic life to become a soldier ("less hard," he explains); and Karma Lotey, our tour organizer and guide. There are generally two kinds of trips available to visitors: the trekking tour and the cultural tour. I'd opted for the latter, with a few days of trekking thrown in. Over dinner at a tiny restaurant in Paro, the Sonam Trophel, where we are the only customers, Karma goes over the itinerary. I was warned about Bhutanese food before leaving New York; Ruth Reichl, the editor of *Gourmet*, assured me that it was well known to be the world's worst cuisine. In fact, she was investigating a story that the king was negotiating with some chefs in Bangkok to invent a few national dishes less off-putting to visitors. Our dinner, which will turn out to be the best of the trip, is an appetizing multicourse affair of fried beef dumplings, chicken soup, a vegetable casserole, deep-fried chicken, and the popular *ema datse*, hot peppers stewed with cubes of cheese. Pungent and sour, it is an acquired taste, and there are many opportunities to acquire it: It is the national custom to eat it for breakfast, lunch, and dinner.

During Karma's briefing, it becomes clear that being a travel guide in Bhutan is no ordinary task. The usual particulars of history—of great leaders and commemorated dates and authenticated happenings—are in short supply, either lost or unrecorded. And what is known doesn't make for light reading. Buddhism's arrival in Bhutan in the eighth century unleashed a thousand years of bloody conflict between rival schools and sects, interrupted only by pitched battles with warmongering lamas invading from Tibet. In the seventeenth century, a layer of civil government was added to the theocracy, plunging the country into nearly two hundred years of civil war. The appearance of the British in India led to another hundred years of skirmishes, squabbles, and uneasy truces. So while Bhutan's survival as the world's last Buddhist kingdom has an aura of grace to it, the visitor has to give up the idea that it's because the people are New Age peaceniks.

Perhaps unsurprisingly, the Bhutanese prefer to relate their history through folklore and legends. In this version, the country's founding story occurs in the middle of the eighth century, when a reincarnate Buddha, Guru Rinpoche, unified both Bhutan and Tibet under Buddhism, first subduing the local animistic deities and then, in an enlightened example of missionary work, installing them as protectors of the new religion. Thus was born the fascinating interplay of historic and prehistoric traditions that still defines this country's (and Tibet's) religious practices. In one of Guru Rinpoche's most celebrated feats, he rode a winged tigress over the mountains of central Bhutan to alight on a cliff ledge outside Paro. This is the site of Taktshang Goemba, the monastery we saw from the plane the day before. It seems like a promising place to begin, so the next day we set off for the long hike up.

Today is a public holiday, "The day of Rain," marking the end of the monsoon season. Though the sky is a hard, brilliant blue, Karma assures me that it will rain before nightfall. As we apply ourselves to the upward trek, groups of schoolgirls wearing the traditional full-length *kira* come barreling past us, shyly amused by the lead-footed foreigners. The heavy traffic, Karma explains, is the result of the country's being in a special period of mourning, occasioned by the recent death of the Royal Grandmother, the wife of the present king's grandfather. In a few weeks, her body will be carried in procession across the country for cremation; until then, according to Buddhist belief, prayers and pilgrimages will still have a beneficial effect on determining her next earthly incarnation.

Ascending through pine forests, we emerge in a clearing to find a teahouse and a group of German hikers, our first sighting of fellow tourists. The trek to Taktshang Goemba is the obligatory first-day warm-up for hiking tours, acclimating visitors to both the rugged climbs and the airless nine-thousand-foot elevation. After this, they'll be off the map for ten or fourteen days, in the highlands where (many Bhutanese believe) yeti still prowl. Together, we grit our teeth and sip cups of butter tea, the national beverage made of meat stock and yak butter. (It tastes much as you would expect.)

A short climb puts us on a lookout shelf directly across from the monastery, which is closed to foreigners. But the miracle is fully apparent from across the gorge. Guru Rinpoche's arrival by flying tigress may sound like a story, but the human feat of building a monastery into the face of a sheer cliff couldn't have happened without it. So the story resonates with a kind of fulfilled truth. And since open-fire cooking and continuously burning butter lamps ensure that monasteries are vulnerable to regular devastation (this one last burned down in 1998), the toil of reconstruction marries story and fact in perpetuity, keeping both alive.

We turn around and make a leisurely descent, stopping to chat with a middle-aged man who is sweeping the path with a homemade twig brush.

I am intrigued that someone would spend his holiday engaged in this particularly useless task. He explains to us that he is accumulating merit. With both their present lifetime and many thousand forthcoming reincarnations to worry about, the Bhutanese devote themselves to accumulating merit—and thereby erasing bad karma—with the ardor of pilgrims. While I'm mulling this over, another man joins our party, jabbering in an excited approximation of English. He is returning from the monastery and is joyously, wholeheartedly, astoundingly drunk. I notice that Karma and Sonam treat both men—the do-gooder and the good-for-nothing—with equal graciousness and respect. There's a practical aspect to this: In a small country of large, related families, ripples of conflict make big waves. But one also begins to see that a Buddhist culture holds pride and shame, piety and earthliness, as something other than polar opposites. Just as we reach the end of our trek, the perfect blue sky clouds over, and to Karma's unsurprised satisfaction, it begins to pour.

From its mountainous border with Tibet to the north. Bhutan slowly descends south and east in a series of forested ridges and lush valleys. All travel is a labor-intensive procession of heaving ascents and plunging, twisting downhills. The public buses making the cross-country trek earned the nickname of Vomit Comets from the first generation of visitors, and as the name has stuck, so have tourists taken to the more commodious means of minibuses and SUVs. Our small group climbs into a black Toyota for the two-hour hop to Thimphu. A tiny village until the 1960s, when the present king's father decreed it the new capital, Thimphu is now an almost-bustling town of fifty thousand, with a raggedy commercial main street of government offices, traditional shops, and new minimalls. A kind of Beverly Hills is taking shape in the slopes above it—an enclave of guarded driveways and smart, Western-style apartment buildings. But the core of the town is its *dzong*, the magnificently medieval fortress that, reflecting Bhutan's power-sharing arrangements, houses the separate offices of the king, top government ministers, and the Central Monk Body, the Bhutanese Vatican. Surrounding it, rather incongruously, is Bhutan's only golf course.

My hope in Thimphu is to meet some of the royal family, who enjoy the nation-defining popularity once shared by the British Windsors. This seems especially notable since the king has four wives, all of them sisters, and has had children with each (a fact the Bhutanese don't find nearly as fascinating as foreigners do). But the situation has been complicated by the Royal Grandmother's death, and negotiations for our visit seem to have stalled.

And then, after lunch, we receive a summons: We will be allowed to pay our respects to the Royal Grandmother. We pile into the SUV and take off past the *dzong* and the foreign ministry and head out of town. Soldiers line the road as we turn into a private driveway that leads past the royal palace and uphill to a clearing where two brightly colored marquee tents flutter in the gathering wind and rain. We're led toward them and sit on benches surrounded by obediently silent schoolchildren. An attendant offers us tea or coffee; when I decline, she looks quietly furious and tells me I must have a cup. A few moments later, an older woman wearing Western makeup—the first I've seen—approaches, proffering a newly opened pack of Benson & Hedges. Not wanting to make the same mistake twice, I take one, and we sit together smoking, watching the misty squalls roll down the hillside toward us, bemused spectators at some washed-out Felliniesque pageant. From the nervous chatter around us, I slowly deduce that I am actually sharing a smoke with royalty—this is the king's aunt.

Invisible ice has been broken, for we are quickly led back to the SUV and escorted up the hill to a modest bungalow that once served as the Royal Grandmother's meditation retreat and is now the scene of her lying in state. Billowing clouds of incense and the gravelly sound of Buddhist chanting fire the air with a voluptuous solemnity. A dozen or so monks, some of them mere children, are wearily intoning the sutras of death and rebirth; they've been here for weeks, barely sleeping, and they will remain for several weeks more until the funeral procession heads east. In Buddhist culture—and one where, until recently, the life expectancy was in the low forties—death is held as an opportunity as much as an ending, the necessary bridge between lifetimes. For the Bhutanese, the Royal Grandmother also served as a bridge between generations, and their mourning is freighted with history. Her husband was the second king in the royal lineage that, beginning in 1907, brought an end to the centuries of civil war, skirmishes with Tibet, and struggles with the British colonizers to the south. A delightful fiction-alized memoir of this period, *The Hero with a Thousand Eyes*, tells the story of the second king's court: With its unfathomable intrigues, capricious punishments, and outrageous entitlements, it could be the story of any feudal, medieval kingdom. Except this one occurred in the era of Roosevelt and Churchill. Indeed, it wasn't until the ascension of the third king in 1952 that serfdom was formally abolished in Bhutan.

The handsome woman who greets us, dressed in a dark *kira* of mourning, is introduced as Ashi Dechen, the daughter of the third king and the sister of the current king. She leads us into an airy sitting room furnished in an Anglo-Indian style, and over the droning and cymbal-clattering sounds of the monks outside, we share tea and marble cake. Hearing my English accent, she reminisces about her and her brother's schooling in southern England. I struggle to picture the dislocation of a Himalayan prince and princess leaving the closed kingdom of Bhutan for 1970s Britain, with its tabloid press and Socialist politics and abrasive pop culture. But our conversation stays within royal protocol, with an occasional detour to discuss meditation practices and religious beliefs. At one point, I mention our difficulty in getting permission to enter some of the more sequestered monasteries. She nods her head sympathetically. From that moment on, as if by magical decree, every door in Bhutan opens to us.

The following morning we leave Thimphu for the next valley east, climbing higher this time through mists and pine forests on roads still wrecked from the monsoon rains. Bears, tigers, wolves, and antelope live freely in an environment that the government fiercely protects, for reasons of superstition as well as ecology. As we drive through the clouds to the pass at the ridge's peak, a *chorten*, or shrine, divides the road. Surrounding it, as far as the eye can see, tall masts of prayer flags bow and flutter in the cold misty air, a sight that manages to be both godforsaken and godly at the same time. In a country that still assigns deities to most actions and places, who would not anchor his or her prayers to the top of the world?

From the peak we cruise down through hairpin bends to the lush valley of Punakha. Sonam, whom I've come to regard as a reincarnated New York cabbie, honks and jousts with oncoming trucks decorated like carnival floats and roars past the wheezing, overstuffed public buses. A burst of sunshine suddenly colors the rice fields in yellow and viridian, and I see that we are now in a subtropical zone where orange trees and banana plants supplement the ubiquitous apple orchards, the backbone of a lively export trade to India. On the roofs of the white farmhouses, bright red peppers are drying in the autumn sun. Punakha was once the capital of Bhutan; in a eureka (or Brasília) moment in the 1960s, the king decided that rather than try to modernize it, he would start again, in Thimphu.

The Punakha Dzong, once the national headquarters, guards one end of the valley, at the confluence of the Pho (Father) and Mo (Mother) rivers. The dramatic location was foretold by Guru Rinpoche, and construction was begun in 1637. How much of the original remains is, like most Bhutanese history, a matter of conjecture. A fire in 1986, followed by a huge flood in 1994, destroyed half of this *dzong*, including the main hall, and its replacement has just been completed. We walk around it, admiring the lavish wall paintings of deities and demons (which, in Buddhist belief, are closely related if not identical). It's a strange feeling: I wonder if we would hold such reverence for a rebuilt Ponte Vecchio or a repainted Sistine Chapel. The issue of authenticity— and artistic preservation—is a recent one in Bhutan. Historically, paintings have been touched up or painted over as they've faded: The action brings merit and, besides, artistic styles have stayed within a continuum of tradition. (It's also worth remembering that a quintessential form of Buddhist art, the mandala, is a celebration of impermanence.) But with the country's opening to Western eyes, its older treasures have become more valued. And protected: At a similar moment in Nepal's history, its cultural heritage was being scavenged and sold off. So while more visitors are being admitted to Bhutan, the doorways to its greatest art are quietly starting to close.

Our visit to the *dzong* is a few weeks short of the resident monks' return here for the winter season. A small caretaker staff is in place, along with a herd of dirty-faced initiates who are playing a game that involves throwing rotten fruit at one another. Upstairs in the sleeping quarters, we meet one of the monks. He shows us his dormitory, a tiny room with no beds that usually sleeps four and also serves as a workshop for making drums. His mouth is stained a deep red from chewing betel nuts, a mild, naturally occurring stimulant that rural Bhutanese seem to munch on from morning till night (at first glance, everyone looks like they just went a round with Mike Tyson). He is a lifer, one among the tens of thousands supported by the government. Back in Thimphu, I will get to meet reincarnated lamas—the kind that get us foreigners hot for spiritual fireworks—but it strikes me that the everyday reality of Bhutan's Buddhist state lies here, in a gentle, toothless old monk whose family once found him a reprieve from rural poverty in the local monastery and whose exclusively religious education ensures that he'll never leave. Later, we watch the ragamuffin boys in their evening class being drilled in a chanted prayer. But for differences in language and doctrine, I imagine we could be in any Catholic monastery during the Middle Ages. It comes as a mild relief to walk outside and see the townspeople congregating for Bhutan's other popular religion, the game of soccer. Even the king likes to play: He dares the opposition by keeping goal.

The next day we haul ourselves up and over to the neighboring valley of Bumthang, Guru Rinpoche's first destination in Bhutan and now the revered site of numerous sacred temples and monuments. Preparations are under way for the arrival of the funeral cortege in two weeks, and road crews are out in force. Nevertheless, the main street, a muddy tract bordered by shops and guesthouses, has an untamed Wild West aspect to it; the Bhutanese seem to share with us a romantic inclination for rougher times. In the surrounding hills are the caves where Guru Rinpoche once lived and meditated, and it is to these that the Bhutanese repair for contemplation. Retreats are a crucial part of Bhutanese life—an enforced shift from doing to being. But as life speeds up, the doing naturally predominates. And so, testing the Buddhist belief in human interconnectedness, many Bhutanese no longer make their own retreats; they sponsor monks to do it for them.

At the beginning of our two-day trek the following morning, we climb through wildflower meadows and pine forests to a small temple built into a rock face. The lone resident monk is instructing a visitor in some detail of ritual, and we're invited to attend. As they chant and pray, incense smoke trails through the open screen windows behind us, tracing a passage between the hard blue sky and the hushed forests below. It's easy to fall into a picture of a life in retreat up here; but it's easier to leave, to keep moving. On our way out, we pass the cabin of a man who stayed, now several months into a year's solitude. From inside we hear a low moaning, a sound that haunts me for days; I have no idea if I've eavesdropped on a conversation with the divine or the later stages of a nervous breakdown. Afterward, I ask a senior monk who's completed the obligatory three-year retreat what I'm to make of this. He shrugs and suggests that the difference between the two is not as significant as I might think.

Our hike takes us deep into the valley, through alpine meadows and terraced rice paddies. At journey's end, we set up camp beside a large, traditional Bhutanese farmhouse, the home of the local village's chief, a rustic swashbuckler whom everyone addresses in English as Uncle. We're invited into his house for tea, and it's a shock to see that even the more prosperous Bhutanese live without furniture. A whole family will sleep in one room, which is often the kitchen, on floor mats; another large room will hold the family shrine; the rest of the space is used mostly for agricultural storage. Over tea, it becomes apparent that there is a family drama involving Uncle's daughter, a ravishing young woman of twenty-four. Her husband of two years is in America studying, leaving behind a son he's never seen. His most recent letter announced that he was staying on for two more years and couldn't raise the money to make a visit home. What makes the situation especially delicate is that the faithless husband is Karma's younger brother. As Uncle and Karma go at it in Dzongkha, the most common of Bhutan's multitude of languages, I gather enough meaning to work up a typical Western response: outrage against the transgressor, pity for the victim. Yet neither of the parties seems to share my reaction. Later, Karma explains that this is just a cordial negotiation about child support. As in all disputes, it is understood that karmic destiny ultimately plays the cards; individuals do the best they can within a clearly rigged game.

That night after dinner, Uncle commandeers the young women from the village to entertain us around the fire with traditional songs and dances. I had begun the evening by sampling some of the wild marijuana. Uncle, meanwhile, had worked his way through several tumblers of *arra*, the local moonshine. Together we make an appreciative audience, and the girls perform with gusto, singing in high, keening voices reminiscent of Chinese folk melodies. During one particularly heart-wrenching tune, I ask Karma what the girls are singing about. "This is a very beautiful song about impermanence," he explains. I ask if Bhutanese schoolgirls are much concerned with impermanence. "Almost certainly not," he replies, howling with delight.

The meeting of spirituality and earthliness may be Bhutan's most delicious mystery. Driving across the country, the first thing you notice is the religious apparatus: the shrines and temples and prayer flags. The second is the multitude of houses adorned with colorful drawings of penises—small, medium, and large, but mostly extra large. While these do duty as atavistic symbols of fertility, they also underscore the casualness with which the Bhutanese approach sex. The courting rituals of the young would, in the States, probably qualify as date rape. (The popular teenage practice of night hunting involves boys breaking into their crush's home and pouncing while the family sleeps.) Nevertheless, women hold equal status in marriage, inherit most of the family property, and, as far as I can tell, have no inhibitions about expressing themselves. One day, feeling queasy from the pepper-heavy diet, we go to a country market to look for bananas. The market women find this inexpressibly hilarious. They make numerous suggestions to Karma about where the foreign men should look for their bananas. One says that we'd be better off buying her cabbage. We leave the market empty-handed and red-faced.

The patron saint of Bhutanese mischief is a seventeenth-century lama called Drukpa Kunley, also known as the Divine Madman. Kunley is so popular in Bhutan that the national newspaper publishes an ongoing comic strip devoted to his legend. In the holy-fool tradition, he wandered the land doing battle with demons, carousing freely, and insulting all religious dogma. His crazy-adept verses and sexual antics—exposure to his Flaming Thunderbolt was said to bestow enlightenment—were recently published in English, and they're irresistible reading. One typical segment has him interrupting the devout prayers of prostrating monks with his own litany, which ends:

> *I bow to philanthropists with self-seeking motives;*
> *I bow to traders who exchange wisdom for wealth;*
> *I bow to renunciates who gather wealth secretly;*
> *I bow to prattlers who never listen;*
> *I bow to tramps who reject a home;*
> *I bow to the bums of insatiate whores.*

Kunley's status as a saint holds true to an aspect of Tibetan, or Tantric, Buddhism that embraces sexuality as a gateway to enlightenment. But he may also embody the animistic beliefs that Buddhism overlays. The painted penises are an unashamed petition to the fertility god, and not just for the Bhutanese. In recent years women from all over the world have been coming to Bhutan in hopes of receiving Kunley's fertility assistance.

We make our own pilgrimage to his monastery, Chimi Lhakhang, on our drive back through the Punakha Valley. A brisk half-hour walk through rice fields and up a grassy hill brings us to the white-walled compound that, to my astonishment, also houses a school for young monks. We find the resident lama inside the main temple attending to an altar laden with offering bowls of *arra*. I ask him about the school and how one goes about teaching holy foolishness. He counters that Kunley's actions were the spontaneous expressions of an enlightened being and cannot be understood or tolerated in an initiate. (In other words, don't try this at home.) Before he can elucidate, our attention is drawn to two young couples who have just arrived carrying newborn infants. Both were apparently conceived after visits to the Kunley shrine, and the parents are now asking the lama to name them. With an unimaginable nonchalance, he strolls over to the altar and retrieves a longbow, a horn-shaped flask, and a large bamboo phallus, and while touching each baby on the side of the head with the latter, announces their names. As we say our good-byes and leave, I realize that I've just witnessed two children being baptized with a dildo.

Traveling through Bhutan, hoping to make sense of its multiple personalities, one is reminded of Charles de Gaulle and his exasperated comment about the impossibility of governing a country with 246 different kinds of cheese. The situation in Bhutan somehow seems worse: nineteen different languages, two competing schools of Buddhism (with growing Hinduism in the south), hundreds of national and regional deities, many with numerous manifestations and conflicting meanings, climate zones ranging from mountain glaciers to tropical valleys to sunbaked plains, and only one main road. The ringmaster of this unruly enterprise begins to assume the aspect of a hero, for visitors as well as for the Bhutanese. His photograph is everywhere, in temples and shops and street-corner bars. The king is now in his thirty-second year on the throne (he landed there at age sixteen), and to him has fallen the epic, camel-through-the-eye-of-a-needle task of bringing Bhutan into the modern world without destroying it. Around him lie only cautionary tales: Tibet, insular and isolationist, occupied by China since 1951; tiny undefended Sikkim, annexed by India in 1975; and laissez-faire Nepal, overdeveloped and overrun by tourists, plundered of its national treasures.

The king's solutions include a push toward economic self-reliance, a preserved—some would say enforced—national identity, and a reduction of his own powers. In 1998, in a largely unpopular move, he handed the daily administration over to a national assembly, which he also invested with the power to vote him out of office in an annual referendum. This isn't quite a democracy—the king chooses the candidates who stand for election to the assembly. But this is supposedly an interim measure before he unveils the fruits of his present labor, which is nothing less than the writing of Bhutan's first constitution.

Adulation of the king is widespread and contagious. It is the national climate. I start to picture him as a kind of Kennedy-Jefferson-Emerson hybrid—a charismatic, God-chosen genius dreaming a new nation into being, equal parts visionary, emperor, and monk. While the four queens live up in the Beverly Hills section of Thimphu, the king lives alone in a modest log cabin that he built himself, and is said to spend his private time in quiet contemplation. The cabin's entrance, at the foot of a hill just outside town, is manned by guards, but petitioners still sometimes congregate in the mornings and the king will hear their grievances. Sadly, he rarely meets foreign journalists. However, Sebastian has used his connections to gain an audience with the king's confidant, the home minister Lyonpo Jigme Thinley, and one bright morning we head down to the capital *dzong* for our appointment. Compared with the regional *dzong*s we've visited, this one feels brisk and businesslike. The Central Monk Body occupies one end, the king's offices take up a corner tower, and the top government ministers are housed in the rest. From the middle of the inner courtyard, rising with the mad, voluptuous geometry of a beached galleon, the *utse*, a three-story structure of private chapels, holds the center.

We are ushered into a well-appointed second-floor reception room to meet the *lyonpo* (minister), an elegant middle-aged man of weathered face and martial bearing. My immediate interest was to question him about Gross National Happiness, a core Bhutanese philosophy on which he had spoken widely. Introduced as an idea by the king in the late eighties, Gross National Happiness can first strike cynical Western ears as a dodge—something dreamed up by an international ad agency to cover the bald spots in a threadbare economy. But listening to the *lyonpo*, I begin to understand GNH—which is essentially the quantifying of progress in measurements both spiritual and material—as the ingenious melding of Buddhist mindfulness with everyday pragmatism. "Our first question about any new program is to ask how it will contribute to Gross National Happiness," he explains, before rattling off the four supporting structures of GNH. The first, to create equal education and health care throughout the country, is already succeeding. Life expectancy has risen from a dismal forty-eight years to more than sixty-three in just fifteen years, and the literacy rate from seventeen percent to forty-eight percent. The second is rigorously enforced green policies that keep twenty-six percent of Bhutan as protected forestland and an agreement with India to build hydroelectric plants in the country's narrow, teeming gorges that promises clean energy and economic deliverance. The third is the forthcoming national constitution, the final step to a multiparty democracy. And the fourth leg in GNH is the promotion and preservation of traditional Bhutanese culture.

It's around the last one that things get a little sticky. Fifteen years ago, the Bhutanese government began expelling tens of thousands of Nepalese immigrants after a census showed that they were becoming a majority of the population. At the same time, the wearing of the *gho* and the *kira*, the traditional Bhutanese dress, became mandatory in schools and public offices. On our travels, we see a lot of Bhutanese, especially the young, walking about in Western-style clothes without censure. We also see many Nepalese men, women, and children, but we see them exclusively on the sides of the roads, living in tarpaulin shantytowns, working on road gangs. Their underclass status is unmissable.

The closer one looks, the easier it becomes to see a government presence in many aspects of daily life. At the new video game parlors in Thimphu, inspectors drop by to check that no one is playing games with violent content. Cable TV recently arrived—but only the channels approved by the government. At the end of our journey east, in the beautiful wildlife preserve of the Phobjikha Valley, we spend an evening with the local populace, watching a variety show put on by the district high school. In the first sketch, a group of children ridicule an old farmer for not enrolling in the government's literacy program for adults. The audience laps it up, but I find myself speculating that I could have seen a similar entertainment a few hundred miles north, in China, during Mao's Great Leap Forward.

None of the Bhutanese I talk with seem unduly bothered by this. Their faith in their leaders is at times awe-inspiring, at times scary. "Our hope is that Bhutan will not be unique but will set an example for the rest of the world," the *lyonpo* had said to me. Implicit in his hope was another: that Bhutan—or at least the government of Bhutan—can set its own terms as it opens to the world. It has already achieved this in the first wave of tourism. All visitors have to go through a government-approved agency and must spend a minimum of two hundred dollars a day. But the economy needs a second wave of tourism. One day, I fall into conversation with an official from the World Bank, which is heavily invested in Bhutan. He paints a less rosy picture than does the Bhutanese government: The hydroelectric deal with India is so in India's favor that Bhutan won't benefit for at least a decade; the much-touted philanthropy of foreign nations is usually less in the actuality than in the announcement; and even the green policies are threatened unless tourism revenues grow significantly.

And so it is that in the bars and restaurants of Thimphu, where Western-style entertainment (and its corollary, Western-style boredom) fill the evening hours, every Bhutanese I meet introduces himself or herself as a travel agent. It becomes a running joke—we estimate that travel agents now outnumber local deities. The nightly conversation turns around Christina Ong, the Hong Kong billionaire who is opening a luxury hotel in Paro, and Amanresorts, the ultraluxe Asian chain that is building six boutique hotels across the country with the idea that guests will spend a couple of nights in each and travel by foot and in a fleet of SUVs between them. Out in the Phobjikha Valley, where black-necked cranes migrate for winter, we had watched the bulldozers lay foundations for one of the Aman hotels, Paro's now-completed Amankora, with beautiful views of a restored temple and an ethereal landscape beyond. This may be a lovely way to see Bhutan, but it could also mark the beginning of the country's transformation into an upscale Dharma Disneyland. Or perhaps that's too easy an assumption. The lesson of every nation's history, and a vital tenet of Tibetan Buddhism, is that thinking you know what comes next is the pinnacle of folly and delusion.

2004

Force of Nature

by

WADE DAVIS

Olayuk Naqitarvik is a hunter. At twelve he killed a polar bear at close quarters, thrusting a harpoon into its underbelly as it lunged toward him. That same year he took his first whale. In the winter darkness he leaves his family each day to follow the leads in the new ice and hovers motionless, for hours at a time, over the breathing holes of ringed seals. The slightest shift in weight betrays his presence; in perfect stillness he squats, knowing full well that as he hunts he is hunted. Polar bear tracks run away from every hole.

Ipeelie Koonoo is Olayuk's stepfather, second husband to his mother. Revered as an elder, he too is a hunter. When he killed his first bear at nine, he could not stop smiling. His first seal was taken when he was still too small to lift it. But he knew that the animal had chosen to die, betrayed by its thirst for fresh water. That's why he followed his uncle's teachings and dripped fresh water into its mouth to placate its spirit. If animals are not properly treated, they will not allow themselves to be taken. But if they are not hunted, they will suffer and their numbers decrease. Thus the hunt is a reflection of balance, a measure of the interdependence of all life in the Arctic, a polar desert cloaked in darkness nine months of the year and bathed in intense luminosity for the short weeks of *upinngaaq*, the summer season of renewal and rebirth.

Simon Qamanirq is both artist and hunter, the youngest of the three men and the nephew of Olayuk's wife, Martha, the matriarch of the extended family. On his accordion he plays Scottish reels adapted from those of ancient mariners and whalers, and with his firm hands turns soapstone into exquisite figurines of animals. "You can't be a carver," he explains, "if you are not a hunter." For some time Simon lived down south. But he grew tired of the confused ways of people whose "heads were full of a thousand words." So he returned north. "I got nothing more interesting than hunting," he says. "Down [in Canada] I'm always cold. My body needs blood. Even their meat has no blood."

For most of the year these three hunters and their families live in the small community of Arctic Bay, a fiercely self-sufficient and independent clan. But for a brief time in June, a fortnight leading up to the solstice, they make camp on a gravel beach at Cape Crauford, on the western shore of Admiralty Inlet, the largest fjord on earth, a vast inland sea that clefts the northern shore of Baffin Island five hundred miles north of the Arctic Circle. There, beneath the dark cliffs of the Brodeur Peninsula, on a promontory overlooking Lancaster Sound, they invite outsiders into their world.

The journey north begins before dawn in Ottawa and ends nine hours later on the seasonal ice off the shore of Olayuk's camp. It's a five-hour flight just to the weather station and settlement of Resolute Bay, the highest point in the Arctic serviced by commercial jets, where we switch from a 727 to a deHavilland Twin Otter. North of Resolute are another thousand miles of Canada. It is a place, the pilot remarks, where Canada could hide Britain and the English would never find it.

We fly across Barrow Strait, then over Lancaster Sound. From the air the ice fuses with the snow-covered land. Ringed seals appear as dark specks on the ice. At the mouth of Prince Regent Inlet, east of Somerset Island, the ice gives way abruptly to the black sea. Beyond the floe edge, scores of white belugas move gracefully through the water. A small mesa-like island rises out of the sea. The plane banks steeply past the soaring cliffs, and in its wake tens of thousands of birds lift into the air. The Prince Leopold sanctuary is just thirty miles square, but on it nest nearly 200,000 pairs of migratory birds. Baffin lies ahead, and within minutes the plane roars over the beach at Cape Crauford, turns into the wind, and lands on skis on a smooth stretch of ice half a mile offshore.

In brilliant sunlight we stand about, nineteen strangers drawn together by the promise of the journey. As an anthropologist, I want to take a firsthand look at ecotoursim in action. The leader of the expedition is Johnny Mikes, outfitter and legendary river guide from British Columbia. It was Mikes who first encouraged Olayuk's family to establish a guiding operation. On a warm day in September 1989, while on a kayaking expedition in Admiralty Inlet, Mikes stumbled upon a bay where hundreds of narwhals were feeding. On the shore was an Inuit encampment, with narwhals hauled up on the beach. Olayuk's brother Moses had just killed a bearded seal, and in the bloodstained waters Greenland sharks hovered. Mikes had never seen the raw edge of nature so exposed. As he spent time with the Inuit, he came to understand that for them blood on snow is not a sign of death but an affirmation of life. It was something he thought others should experience. And then Moses introduced him to Olayuk, and Olayuk told him about the floe edge and the ice in June.

There are places and moments on earth where natural phenomena occur of such stunning magnitude and beauty that they shatter all notions of a world of human scale. It is such an event that draws Olayuk and his family to their June camp at Cape Crauford.

Every winter in the Arctic, virtually all of the sea between the islands of the Canadian archipelago lies frozen, a single horizon of ice that fuses to the polar ice cap and eventually covers six million square miles, twice the area of the United States. As temperatures drop to as low as minus seventy degrees Fahrenheit, of marine mammals only the ringed seals remain, dependent on breathing holes scratched through the ice. Polar bears survive by stalking the seals throughout the long Arctic night. Other marine mammals—belugas, bowhead whales, walrus, and narwhals—head out through Lancaster Sound to the open waters of Baffin Bay and Davis Strait, between Canada and Greenland.

In spring the animals return, wave upon wave, hovering against the retreating ice edge. The winter population of 100,000 mammals soars in the summer to seventeen million. Feeding in the rich waters, they await a chance to disperse throughout the Arctic. In the long hours of the midnight sun, brown algae bloom beneath the ice, billions of shrimp and amphipods flourish, and millions of Arctic cod thrive upon the zooplankton. A quarter million harp, bearded, and ringed seals feed on the fish, as do thousands of belugas and narwhals. They in turn fall prey to roving pods of killer whales. A third of the belugas in North America gather here, and three out of every four narwhals on earth.

By June, the waters of Lancaster Sound are free of ice. But those of Admiralty Inlet, thirty miles wide at the mouth, remain frozen. From the camp at Cape Crauford, using snowmobiles and sleds, it is possible to travel along the floe edge, where the ice meets the sea, and listen as the breath of whales mingles with the wind.

Snowmobiles and a dozen Inuit kids descend on the plane. An old Inuk motions us to split up and pile our gear and ourselves onto one of the sleds, which he calls *qamatik*s. He speaks no English, and the soft sounds of Inuktitut, the Inuit language, delight and astonish.

The camp is a line of canvas outfitter tents, arrayed with military precision along the high shore. At one end is the cook tent, at the other the guides' tents. The foreshore is a clutter of sleds and snowmobiles. Tethered on the ice are three dog teams. They yelp and howl, and the air is pungent with the faint scent of seal meat and excrement. One of the young Inuit, Olayuk's son Eric, explains his preference for snow-mobiles: "They are fast, they don't eat meat, and they don't stink."

We divide two to a tent and stretch our bedrolls on caribou hides on the ground. Johnny Mikes then distributes insulated boots and bright orange survival suits. They are awkward and stiff, but essential. Chances of survival in Arctic waters plummet after a minute of exposure. In the cookhouse, we are introduced to the Inuit—Olayuk, Ipeelie, Simon, Olayuk's brother-in-law Abraham, and, most important of all, Martha and her older sister Koonoo Muckpaloo, who run the kitchen. Both are beautiful women, especially Martha, whose face is radiant and kind, quick to laugh. Someone asks Olayuk how many children they have. He looks pensive and begins to count on his fingers. "Ten," he concludes. Martha elbows him and spits out a quick phrase. Olayuk looks sheepish. "Eleven," he adds.

Over a dinner of bannock and Arctic char, caribou meat and narwhal soup, I learn that Olayuk and Martha were the first of their generation to marry for love. They planned to elope and were willing to court death by setting off over the ice, but finally the families agreed to the match. They are still in love. One sees it in their every gesture. Martha is asked whether it bothers her to be cooking dinner at such a late hour. "I am used to it," she responds. "My husband is a hunter."

There is no night and no morning, only the ceaseless sun. At some point we sleep, with blinders and earplugs. The camp never rests. Winter is for sleep, and the summers are ephemeral. We wake and head off in five sleds, traveling south up Admiralty Inlet to get around a body of water and return north to reach the edge of the floe. The ice by the shore is a tangle of pressure ridges, but farther on it becomes smooth, glass-like. The spartan landscape rolls on, empty and desolate, and all one can think of is survival.

A dense fog descends, muffling the roar of the engines as the snow-mobiles drag us, three or four to a sled, over the ice. The drivers push on, watching for patterns in the ice, small ridges of hard snow that run parallel to the prevailing winds and reveal where you are. When clouds obscure the sun, Simon explains, the Inuit study the reflection of the ice on the underside of low clouds. Open water appears black, the sea ice white, and ground covered in snow and traces of open tundra appears darker than the sea but lighter than snowless land. Upon the clouds lies a map of the land. Not one of our guides can remember ever having been lost.

A pair of ringed seals are killed for the dogs back at camp, and moments later we reach the edge of the floe. Olayuk peers out over the water, sensing the wind in his face. It's from the north, which is good. Should a fissure appear in the ice behind us, a southerly wind could push our entire party out to sea, without our knowing it.

The only sign of life here is a cackle of glaucous and Thayer gulls, fighting over the carcass of a narwhal killed by a hunter. Suddenly, a shout from the floe edge. I look up to see the marbled backs of four female narwhals barely breach the surface before slipping once again into the dark sea. As we wait, hoping the animals will return, Mikes asks Olayuk to say a few words about his life. A thin, somewhat reluctant account follows. Clearly Olayuk finds the moment awkward. Later Abraham, university educated and remarkable in his ability to move freely between worlds, explains Olayuk's reticence. "In your culture the goal is to excel and stand out, flaunting your excellence in public. Here, you must never reveal what you know, for knowledge is power. If you step forward, you show yourself to your enemies. In the old days, it might be a shaman who waited outside a camp and watched before casting spells on the strongest man. This is something the whites have never understood. The only time you can reveal your stories is when you no longer have the power. In old age."

The next evening we encounter a polar bear and give chase on the ice. After long hours of searching in vain for wildlife, the drivers are eager to get as close as possible to the animal. The bear is run ragged. No one objects. For a brief moment, each client succumbs to the thrill of the hunt. "If you think that was fun," Abraham later told the one vegetarian on the trip, "you ought to try it with a tag" (that is, a hunting permit).

When asked who had first seen the bear, Abraham replied, "Simon did. Well, actually, it was Olayuk, and Simon saw it in his eyes. Olayuk said nothing."

There are ancient graves above the camp, stone mounds erected centuries ago. The bones from those that have been breached lie covered in lichen and moss. Around the graves is a circle of life—purple gentians and dwarf willows, small plant communities established long ago on the rich nutrients of the dead. A ring of flowers around an eider's nest, a seedling growing out of the droppings of a gull, lichen slowly eating away at rock, an inch of soil taking a century to accumulate. One marvels at the art of survival. Bears hunting seals, foxes following the bears and feeding on excrement. Inuit cutting open animal stomachs, feeding on clam syphons found in walrus, lichens and plants concentrated in the gut of caribou, mother's milk in the belly of a baby seal (a delicacy much loved by the elders).

Beyond the graves, half a mile from the shore, the land rises to a high escarpment fifteen hundred feet or more above the sea. An hour of scrambling on steep scree takes one to the ridge and a promontory overlooking all of Lancaster Sound. The sense of isolation and wonder is overwhelming. Gravel terraces on the shore reveal the beach lines of ancient seas. Icebergs calved from the glaciers of Devon Island, and the sea ice covering the mouth of the inlet, are awash in soft pastels—pinks, turquoise, and opal. On the underside of distant clouds are streaks of dazzling brightness. Every horizon shimmers with mirages. Low islands seem towering cliffs, ice floes appear as crystal spires. The land seduces with its strange beauty. In the entire annals of European exploration, few places were sought with more passion, few destinations were the cause of more tragedy and pain.

The Northwest Passage, which begins at the mouth of Lancaster Sound, was always less a viable route than an illusive dream. Hopes of fame and riches drove those who sought it, and certain death found the many who came ill-prepared for the Arctic night. By 1631, the voyages of Martin Frobisher, John Davis, William Baffin, and Luke Foxe had made clear that no practical commercial route to the Orient existed south of the Arctic Circle. Incredibly, by the early nineteenth century these journeys had passed into the realm of myth, and the discoveries had become suspect. Brilliant feats of navigation and cartography were supplanted by fantasies of a northern polar sea, ice-free water at the top of the world.

The real impetus for seeking the Passage was provided by Napoleon. In the wake of his defeat, the British Navy reduced its conscripted force from 140,000 to 19,000. But it was unthinkable in class-conscious England to lay off a single officer. Thus by 1818 there was one officer for every three seamen. The only way for advancement was to accomplish some stunning feat of exploration. And so they sailed for the Arctic. Edward Parry and John Ross's was the first of dozens of expeditions, each met by Inuit who spoke to the ships as if they were gods. The entire endeavor, which lasted the better part of half a century and culminated in the search for Sir John Franklin and his gallant crew, was colored by a single theme: Those who ignored the example of the Inuit perished, whereas those who mimicked their ways not only survived but accomplished unparalleled feats of endurance and exploration.

The British mostly failed. They wore tight woolens, which turned sweat to ice. The Inuit wore caribou skins, loose, one with the hair toward the body, the other turned out to the wind. The British slept in cloth bags, which froze stiff with ice. The Inuit used the heat of one another's naked bodies on sleeping platforms of ice covered with caribou hide, in snow houses that could be assembled in an hour. The British ate salt pork and, to prevent scurvy, dispatched lime juice in glass jars that broke with the first frost. The Inuit ate narwhal skin and the contents of caribou guts, both astonishingly rich in vitamin C. Most disastrous of all, the British scorned the use of dogs. They preferred to harness their young men in leather and force them to haul ridiculous sleds made of iron and oak. When the last of Franklin's men died, at Starvation Cove on the Adelaide Peninsula, their sledge alone weighed 650 pounds. On it was an 800-pound boat loaded with silver dinner plates, cigar cases, a copy of *The Vicar of Wakefield*—in short, everything deemed essential for a gentle traveler of the Victorian age. Like so many of their kind, they died, as one explorer remarked, because they brought their environment with them. They were unwilling to adapt to another.

At one end of camp is a recently erected wooden cross marking the grave of a woman who died delivering a child in the midst of winter. Asked about her fate, Olayuk responds, "She decided to have a baby." This lack of sentiment confused and horrified the early British explorers. To them the Inuit were brutal and callous. How else to explain a language that had no words for hello, good-bye, or thank you? Or a people who would abandon an elder to die, or allow the body of the newly dead to be dug up and gnawed by dogs? What the English failed to grasp was that in the Arctic, no other attitude was possible. The Inuit, a people of patience and resilience, confronted tragedy with fatalistic indifference because they had no choice. Death and privation were everyday events. In our camp is an old woman who remembers the last time her people were forced to eat human flesh. It occurred in the late thirties, during a season when "the world became silent." All the animals were gone. So one of her extended family had designated himself to die, and he was killed. "Someone must survive," she said, "and someone must die." After the event, the women in the group cut off their long braids, a symbol for all others that they had been obliged to sacrifice their kin.

Fear of going native, of succumbing to such impulses, blinded the British to the genius of the Inuit. In dismissing them as savages, they failed to grasp that there could be no better measure of intelligence than the ability to thrive in the Arctic with its limited resources. The Inuit did not endure the cold, they took advantage of it. Three Arctic char placed end to end, wrapped and frozen in hide, the bottom greased with the stomach contents of a caribou and a thin film of ice, became the runner of a sled. A sled could be made from the carcass of a caribou, a knife from human excrement. There is a well-known account of an old man who refused to enter a settlement. Over the objections of his family, he made plans to return to the ice. To stop him, they took away all his tools. So in the midst of a winter gale, he stepped out of their igloo, defecated, and honed the feces into a frozen blade, which he sharpened with a spray of saliva. With the knife he killed a dog. Using its rib cage as a sled and its hide to harness another dog, he disappeared into the darkness.

I thought of the Inuit's ability to adapt early one morning as I sat with Ipeelie by his tent. His gear was scattered about, some of it draped over the cross of the young mother who had died. He was cleaning the motor of his snowmobile with the feather of an ivory gull. Earlier that day his clutch had failed on the ice, and he had needed to drill a hole in a piece of steel he intended to use as a replacement. Placing the metal on the ice, bracing it with his feet, he took his rifle and casually blew a circle in the steel.

Gradually and effortlessly we work toward a nocturnal schedule, when the light is soft and the animals more active. Out on the ice by late afternoon, long pounding runs in the sleds across the edge of the floe, midnight by amber sea cliffs on the far side of the inlet, where northern fulmars nest by the tens of thousands. Breakfast at noon, dinner at 4 A.M., a few hours of sleep in between. There is a hallucinatory quality to the endless sun. All notions of a diurnal cycle of light and darkness fade away, and everyone is cast adrift from time. By the third morning, not one of my companions is certain of the date, and estimates of the hour vary to an astonishing degree.

The wildlife sightings are far fewer than expected. In the first seven days of a nine-day sojourn on the ice, we see birds and ringed seals by the score, but only one other polar bear, four narwhals, one bearded seal, and a fleeting glimpse of walrus and belugas. The numbers are there, but the landscape is so vast that it absorbs the multitudes. The other clients don't seem to object. A psychiatrist from Seattle speaks of the land in religious terms and is content to sit on his collapsible seat for hours at a time, glassing the sea for birds. Others are brash and irritating and find it impossible to be quiet, a trait that makes them appear willfully dense. At one point, during a discussion of Inuit clothing, Martha passes around a dark sealskin boot with a beautiful design of an eagle sewn into the hide. One especially garrulous woman examines the stitching and asks, "How do you find fur with such an interesting pattern on it?" Later in the evening, talk passes to all the places she has been—an impressive list that includes the Amazon, the Galápagos, Nepal, Antarctica, and now the Arctic. When she mentions Borneo, a place I know well, I ask what she did there. After a confused moment, she says, "I don't really remember. But it was all very interesting."

Such conversation is discouraging. One has the impression of travel reduced to commodity, with the experience mattering less than the credential of having been somewhere. By the economics of our times, anyone can purchase instant passage to virtually anyplace on the planet. Ecotourism has become a cover for a form of tourism that simply increases the penetration of the hinterland. But have any of us earned the right to be there? Whatever one thinks of the early explorers, they gave something of themselves and paid a real price for their experiences.

One night I escaped the camp shortly after midnight and returned to the mountain ridge, where I walked for several hours. Peering out over the sound, I thought of some of the early explorers and what they had endured. One who stands out is Frederick Cook, an American physician and explorerer who tried to reach the North Pole. In 1908, lost in the barrens, he and two companions walked five hundred miles, living on meat scraped from the carcasses of their dogs. When forced to winter on the northern shore of Devon Island, a mere hundred miles from our camp at Cape Crauford, he had only four rounds of ammunition for his rifle left, half a sled, a torn silk tent, and the tattered clothes on his back. For five months of darkness they lived in a shallow cave hollowed by hand out of the earth. Using tools forged from bone, they killed what they could, using blubber to fire torches to thrust into the jaws of the bears who stalked them. With the first sign of light in February, they made their escape. Living on rotten seal meat and gnawing the skin of their boots, they managed to walk some three hundred miles across the frozen wastes of Baffin Bay to rescue in Greenland.

One evening, after a long day and night on the ice, there is a demonstration of dogsled-mushing. Everyone is to have a ride. Though the sound of runners passing over ice and snow is sublime, the event is a fiasco. Harnesses become tangled, dogs bellow and snarl at their drivers, and riders are left behind on their duffs as sleds dash off in all directions. It is a far cry from the days when a dogsled musher, with a quick snap of the whip, would cut off the tip of a stubborn dog's ear and bring the team into line. On the way back to camp, some of the clients grumble about "loss of tradition." One asks Abraham if the people ever wear their traditional clothes. Abraham gestures to the modern coat on his back. "Yes," he says pointedly, "I wear my parka all the time."

For the Inuit, the first fundamental break from their past occurred in the early years of this century. Along with European diseases that left only one in ten alive came missionaries whose primary goal was the destruction of the power and authority of the shaman, the cultural pivot, the heart of the Inuit relationship to the universe. The missionaries discouraged even the use of traditional names, songs, and the language itself. The last avowed shaman in Olayuk's community of Arctic Bay died in 1964.

By then the seduction of modern trade goods had drawn many of the people from the land. As Inuit concentrated in communities, new problems arose. In the late 1950s, the wife of a Royal Canadian Mounted Police constable was mauled and killed by a sled dog. Henceforth all dogs had to be tethered outside the settlements. Any dog found without a vaccination certificate for rabies was summarily shot. A distemper outbreak rationalized wholesale slaughter. In exchange, the RCMP offered snowmobiles. The first arrived in Baffin in 1962. No technology since the introduction of the rifle would do more to transform Inuit life.

In 1955, the decision was made to screen all Inuit for tuberculosis. Medical teams whisked away every man, woman, and child for a compulsory X-ray examination. Anyone who showed signs of the disease was immediately sent south to sanatoriums in Montreal or Winnipeg. One out of five Inuit suffered such a fate. Although the intentions of the medical authorities were good, the consequences for those ripped from their families were devastating.

Other initiatives were less benign, even in conception. As recently as the 1950s, the Canadian government felt compelled to bolster its claims in the North American Arctic by actively promoting settlement. Inuit were moved to uninhabited islands. Others found work constructing the DEW (Distant Early Warning) Line and other Cold War installations. Family-allowance payments were provided but made contingent on the children attending school. Nomadic camps disappeared as parents moved into communities to be with their young. Along with the schools came nursing stations, churches, and welfare. The government conducted a census, identified each Inuk by number, issued identification tags, and ultimately conducted Operation Surname, a bizarre effort to assign last names to individuals who had never had them. More than a few Inuit dogs were recorded as Canadian citizens.

After half a century of profound change, what, indeed, is tradition? How can we expect a people not to adapt? The Inuit language is alive. The men are still hunters. They use snares, make snow houses, know the power of medicinal herbs. They also own boats, snowmobiles, television sets, and satellite phones. Some drink, some attend church. As anthropologist Hugh Brody points out, what must be defended is not the traditional as opposed to the modern, but, rather, the right of a free indigenous people to choose the components of their lives.

Canada has at long last recognized this challenge by negotiating an astonishing land-claims settlement with the Inuit of the Eastern Arctic. On April 1, 1999, an Inuit homeland known as Nunavut will be carved out of the Northwest Territories. Including all of Baffin Island and stretching from Manitoba to Ellesmere Island, with a population of just 26,000, the area will be almost as large as Alaska and California combined. In addition to annual payments of $840 million over fourteen years to fund start-up costs and infrastructure and to replace current federal benefits, the Inuit will receive direct title to 136,000 square miles, an area larger than New Mexico. Within Nunavut, all political control will effectively be ceded to a new government completely staffed and administered by Inuit. It is arguably the most remarkable experiment in native self-government anywhere to be found.

Day by day the ice melts. Blue pools yield to a dark bay, the bay fills with broken ice, and the leads in the ice spread to broad channels. The airstrip where we landed but a week ago is open water, and it is here, a day before our scheduled departure, that the narwhals and belugas finally arrive. Olayuk sees them first, and Abraham rustles up the camp to a fever pitch of excitement. Movement over the ice, first by sled and later on foot, is precarious. Olayuk walks ahead, testing the path with a harpoon. It is at precisely the time when the ice is most dangerous that the Inuit hunt narwhal. As we move cautiously forward, with a blazing noonday sun overhead and the ice bending under our weight, someone asks Simon what it is like to camp out on the floe for days at a time when everything is in flux. "You wake up in the morning," he replies, "and run like hell."

A hush falls upon the group as we hear the first sighs of the belugas as they breach and see the vapor of their breath. There are hundreds of the beautiful creatures, white as pearls, moving in small groups, ebbing and flowing with the current. The narwhals swim among them, diving in unison to great depths, driving schools of cod to the surface at such a rate that the fish lose consciousness and lie stunned upon the surface of the water. A feeding frenzy is under way, though it occurs in slow motion, as each massive animal rises and falls with astonishing agility and grace. Only the frantic flight of gulls as they dip and dive toward the water betrays the excitement of the hunt.

A smile comes to Olayuk's face as the tusk of a male narwhal breaks the surface at our feet. It appears like a creature from a bestiary, and in an instant one understands how it inspired the legend of the unicorn.

Throughout the Middle Ages narwhal ivory sold for twenty times its weight in gold. In all of Europe, only fifty complete tusks were known, and they were a source of endless mystery and wonder. The beautiful animals still are. Nearly blind, their entire sensory world is based on sonar reflection, a clatter of clicks that allow them to communicate. Of their behavior and ecology, the patterns of their migration, we understand little, for they live most of the year beneath the polar ice. No one knows where they go or what they eat in winter. There is something wonderful in this, a chance to be with a creature that has defied science and all our obsessions with systematizing the world.

Olayuk knows only that the narwhals come in the spring, as they always have and always will. From him we have learned something of a hunter's patience and are grateful to encounter the animals before leaving. Patience is perhaps the most enduring trait of the Inuit. There is a story from Greenland about a group of Inuit who walked a great distance to gather wild grass in one of the few verdant valleys of the island. When they arrived the grass had yet to sprout, so they watched and waited until it grew. I see patience now in Olayuk's face as he watches the arrival of the first wave of a migration that is one of the highlights of his life. I ask him if he will hunt tomorrow, after we are gone. His eyes sparkle. "Oh, yes," he says. "We will be here."

1998

Some Like It Not Hot

by

CALVIN TRILLIN

"But haven't you been there before?"

That's what people tended to say when they heard that I was about to spend a week or so in Cuenca, the third-largest city in Ecuador. "Funny, I never get that sort of response with Paris," I would reply. If I mentioned that I was about to spend a week or so in Paris—the opportunity to do that has appeared all too rarely, I regret to say—I doubt that anyone would reply, "But haven't you been there before?"

Truth to tell, I'd been to Cuenca twice before, although I'm not sure the first trip should count. In 1995, through a logistical mishap, I arrived in Cuenca, a city known for its solemn observance of the Roman Catholic calendar, the day before Shrove Tuesday. There was so little open and so few people on the streets that I was moved to comment, "This must be what Ecuadorean Yom Kippur looks like." I did stay for Shrove Tuesday itself—actually, there was no choice, since the airlines were among the commercial ventures not operating—but the Mardi Gras celebration in Cuenca turned out to consist entirely of people throwing water on each other, a spectacle that is, I must admit, somewhat less exciting than, say, Carnaval in Rio. Still, I loved being in Cuenca, even when it was closed.

Considering the pleasure I've taken in visiting various parts of Ecuador, in fact, it has always seemed strange to me that so many American travelers use the mainland as a transit point to the Galápagos, without bothering to stop. On a Sunday, when motor traffic is banned from the old town section of Quito, I've spent a glorious afternoon strolling from one magnificent church to another. At an open-air restaurant called La Lojanita, in the beachfront town of Salinas, I've eaten bowls of Ecuadorean seviche so good that the populace was moved to elect the proprietor mayor. I've looked for rare birds in the Ecuadorean rain forest. At a variety of Saturday markets, I've purchased any number of sweaters I didn't need. Outside Otavalo, which has one of the great markets in South America, I've relaxed between market days at Hacienda Cusin, which I once described as the rare example of a seventeenth-century hacienda "that has been restored into complete comfort with no accompanying glitz." In Cayambe, a dairy town north of Quito, I once attended just about the best local festival I've ever been to; on Halloween these days, I wear a mask I brought back from there, even though it doesn't make me as scary as the Cayambe celebrants who were masked with what seemed to be actual cowheads. And, yes, on the Galapagos, I've picked my way carefully along a beach full of sunning sea lions that stared off obliviously while I heard myself murmuring, "Excuse me . . . pardon me . . . terribly sorry."

But I'm particularly attracted to Cuenca. A colonial city that was not connected to Ecuador's other urban centers by a usable highway until the 1960s, it is considered the cultural capital of the country, Quito being the political capital and Guayaquil the center of commerce. But by themselves those facts can be misleading in picturing Cuenca's *centro*. It doesn't look like a sixteenth-century city that has been preserved; it looks like a city that has been in use since the sixteenth century. Most of the buildings do indeed have a colonial look— two or three floors, whitewashed or pastel walls, red tile roofs—and the streets are indeed narrow. Some of the churches do conjure up visions of colonels attached to Spanish gold-snatching expeditions making their confessions to priests who had just arrived on galleons from Galicia. But there are also some recently constructed buildings and some strangely altered buildings and some buildings that appear to have been built in the late 1950s, when there might as well have been an international conspiracy among architects to ugly up the world. Cuenca has the imperfections of a place that is being lived in.

In other words, it looks like what I think of as a walking-around city—the sort I like going back to. That impression is heightened by the climate, which the guidebooks tend to call "eternal spring" and I would call perfect walking-around weather. In walking-around cities, I like browsing the local markets to inspect the variety of vegetables and make certain that the fish are properly aligned. I have been known to drop into office supply stores to see what the notebooks look like. Walking-around cities are often short on well-known sights. I don't mind. For one thing, that makes them less appealing to gaggles of people who follow the checkoffian approach to travel—a reference not to the Russian writer but to their custom of checking off certified sights as they go. I mean no disrespect to world-famous travel destinations. I am grateful for the opportunity I've had to see, say, masterpieces of art in Florence. But when I yearn for that part of Italy, I think of Lucca—a walking-around city that has no world-famous attractions, unless you count the olive oil. I like to walk around.

That's why, ten years after my first visit, I returned to Cuenca to make one of my occasional (and invariably unsuccessful) assaults on the Spanish language—assaults I usually picture as looking like drug raids in which I'm helping to swing a battering ram against a door while wearing a windbreaker that says, instead of DEA or FBI, "Yo Hablo Espanol." In the spring of 2005, I took Spanish lessons and I walked around. I covered most of the streets of the *centro*. I walked along a path next to the Tomebamba River, a fast-flowing stream that separates the *centro* from the modern city that begins on the south bank.

I spent a lot of time at the markets, where, at the prepared-food stalls, vendors come out from behind their whole roasted pigs—pigs that are stretched out like sunbathers trying to get a little color on their backs—and offer passersby a sample of pulled pork or of pork skin that's as crisp as a cracker. I shopped, without ever closing the deal, for what people in other parts of the world call a panama hat and Cuencanos call *un sombrero de paja toquilla*, after the sort of straw it's made from. (If credit were handed out fairly, a panama hat would be called a Cuenca hat: Cuenca has been the principal exporter of such hats from the beginning, while Panama was simply a distribution point—as any Cuencano can tell you at the drop of a, well, a *sombrero de paja toquilla*.) By design, I was doing my Spanish course during Holy Week, traditionally the only time of year that Ecuadoreans serve a spectacular soup called *fanesca*, and I ate nearly my fill of *fanesca*.

"But not my fill," I said to my older daughter, Abigail, last winter when she informed me that she and her family would be going to Cuenca during Holy Week to visit some friends who were spending a sabbatical semester there. Joining Abigail and her family—her husband, Brian, and their girls, Isabelle and Rebecca—would mean repairing a five-year *fanesca* deprivation. It would mean a return to eating *tostados*, which are what, in an ideal world, corn nuts would taste like. It would mean a return to hunting for the best *humitas*, which are like tamales made by someone who simply can't shake off her years of training in soufflé-making. It would mean an opportunity to do a lot more walking around. I figured that Holy Week rituals—which in Cuenca, as in some other Roman Catholic communities, include the obligation to visit seven churches on the evening before Good Friday—would provide just enough spectacle. (We walking-around types like public manifestations of any kind.) Furthermore, I'd been given a more sincere answer for those who said, "Haven't you been there before?" I could say, "Yes, but this time my granddaughters will be there."

As I poked around the Internet, I found to my surprise that my choice of Cuenca as a place to return to was not as eccentric as some people might have thought. According to a blog called Cuenca High

Life (presumably a reference to the altitude, which is 8,200 feet), the magazine *International Living* recently named Cuenca the world's top retirement city—an honor the expatriates already in residence did not necessarily greet with unalloyed enthusiasm. (One of the bloggers was quoted as saying he didn't want Cuenca to become another San Miguel de Allende—a city whose colonial buildings I've always thought of as having achieved a level of Mexican authenticity available only to rich Texans with Italian decorators.)

Toward the end of my Spanish language school visit in 2005, I'd had the good fortune to meet Berta Vintimilla, who, along with her sister Patricia, runs what is considered the premier upmarket restaurant in Cuenca, Villa Rosa. (Upmarket in Cuenca usually means that the entrées run around eight or nine dollars. Since 2000, Ecuador has used the American dollar, and not a whole lot of them. Outside restaurants throughout the *centro*, it is not unusual to see the daily "executive lunch"—say, potato soup, breast of chicken, salad, and dessert—advertised at two dollars.) On the Wednesday of my latest visit, I went with Berta and Patricia to the Feria Libre market, a vast retail and wholesale market on the edge of the city, to shop for dinner. A lot of people were there shopping for ingredients needed to make *fanesca*, which requires salt cod and twelve different kinds of beans and grains. There were a couple of stands that had such a thorough inventory of ingredients that a merchandising consultant from North America might have suggested a sign saying "One Stop Fanesca Shopping Here."

I've spent a lot of time walking around the markets of Cuenca—mostly the two indoor markets within the *centro*. The vendors are mainly *cholas cuencanas*—women from the surrounding countryside who wear white blouses and pleated skirts of bright colors and stiff, high-crowned straw hats. The hats are often worn at a jaunty angle, and that combines with the bright skirts for a look that often leaves me with the impression that the woman I see walking down the street toward the market is about to start jitterbugging—although it would not be easy to cut a rug with thirty pounds of potatoes on your back. Berta bought, among other things, fruits we wouldn't be familiar with—some *zapotes*, which look something like hand grenades, for instance; and some *acho-tillos*, which appear to be the result of crossing a large strawberry with an exceedingly small porcupine. When we were finished, her market basket looked almost too heavy for one person to carry, but suddenly, we were joined by a tiny *chola*—a woman so old and frail-looking that, in my Boy Scout days, I might have offered to help her across the street. Without a word, she whipped off a long scarf, wrapped it around the basket, pulled the scarf tightly around her narrow shoulders, and trotted off to the car. When I expressed my astonishment, Patricia told me the bright side: *Cholas*, for obvious reasons, practically never get osteoporosis.

I saw some goats at the market, and at first I thought that the man holding them was offering them for sale to anyone who wanted to raise goats. What he turned out to be selling was goat milk, which some Ecuadoreans believe has health-giving properties—but not from bottles, from the goats. He would produce a clean paper cup, hold it underneath one of his goats, squirt the milk into it, and hand it to the customer.

Before our dinner at Berta's, she and a grandson launched several celebratory *globos*—large balloons, three or four feet in diameter, that are open at the bottom except for struts that hold some fuel which looks like a large version of a Sterno can under a chafing dish. The fuel is set on fire with a burning newspaper, and the *globo* rises swiftly in the thin Andean air, floating off above the neighboring rooftops. I told Berta that if Abigail and Brian decided to try that in San Francisco—sent balloons with fire in them up in the sky—they might, with a good criminal lawyer and some aggressive plea bargaining, get away with only six or eight months in the slammer.

When the Vintimilla sisters were children, their grandmother dressed in black during Holy Week. No music except religious music was al-lowed in the house. According to an old superstition in Cuenca, if a child took a bath on Good Friday, he or she would turn into a fish, or maybe a mermaid. (The latter sounded rather glamorous to the sisters.)

Some Holy Week customs remain strong. *Fanesca* is still made in huge quantities—to take to people who are living alone, or to give to the poor, or just to have around in case friends drop by. The symphony orchestra still presents requiems during the evenings leading up to Easter. Other Ecuadoreans still think of Cuencanos as devout and traditionalist and rather formal. But Cuenca has loosened up a bit. That may be the result of Cuencanos having been exposed in recent decades to somewhat looser societies: Many of the Ecuadoreans who work in New York are from the Cuenca area.

Still, on the evening before Good Friday, the center of the city was packed with people carrying out their obligation to visit seven churches. Some people say that the custom is connected to the magical properties of the number seven. Some say that it comes from the fact that Jesus said seven words on the cross. (By my count, it was ten, but, then, I can't count in Aramaic.) A Cuencano who is now in his seventies told me that when he was in high school, boys his age looked forward to the Thursday night of Holy Week because, in an era when strict separation of the sexes was observed, it presented a rare opportunity for casual interactions with girls. It's true that even the particularly somber events of Holy Week give the *centro* an almost celebratory air. On Palm Sunday, on the long wall of the cathedral where *cholas* sell palms woven into crosses and other designs, I'd seen two bands—an Andean band and, just out of earshot of that music, a band in cowboy hats playing the music that Ecuadoreans call the *pasillo*. Outside the churches, vendors sell not just religious pictures but balloons in the shape of cartoon characters and shish kebabs and *tostados* and cotton candy and empanadas and *humitas*. An expatriate I met said that the custom of visiting seven churches was to him "a sort of pub crawl."

It's also an opportunity to see the churches of Cuenca. We started with Cuenca's vast and imposing New Cathedral, which would be even more imposing if an engineering error hadn't necessitated tucking its blue-and-white-tile domes almost out of sight. From there we went across the street to El Carmen de la Asunción, a church connected with cloistered nuns, where the religious statuary in the alcoves is shielded from view by purple drapes during Holy Week and where, in a side room, honey and jam and sacramental wine are sold through a wooden turntable that allows you to purchase items from a nun who can be heard but not seen. Outside El Carmen de la Asunción, we grabbed some *zeppole*-like doughnuts that Ecuadoreans call Chilean eggs, to hold us the block or so to San Francisco, a lovely church from which the domes of the cathedral can actually be seen. Just before going in, I had a fantastic dish (if you can call something that's served in a plastic bag a dish) that consisted of combining new potatoes, plantain, hard-boiled egg, *chicharrón*, and hominy. Then, as the crowd seemed to grow, we made our way to Santo Domingo, a Dominican church, where I scored some particularly good *tostados*, and then to San Alfonso and then to Las Conceptas—which was so crowded that we basically just got ourselves inside and out, like a cricketer edging his bat over the crease and hurrying back toward the wicket he came from. Finally, almost back at our hotel, we entered La Merced, our seventh church. I felt virtuous, not to mention full.

"Don't worry about me: I have plans," I said to Abigail one day, after I'd told her that I would not be accompanying them on an outing to a waterfall an hour or so away. My plans were these: I would visit the Casa de la Mujer, a crafts market where the day before we'd purchased a flute that an instrument maker named Luis González had fashioned from the femur of a turkey. Mr. González makes all the instruments he sells, and he can also play them—as he'd demonstrated by picking up a beautiful panpipe and knocking out the opening bars of the Andean classic "El Cóndor Pasa." The mouthpiece of the flute had gotten lost, and I figured that having it replaced might give me the opportunity to hear Mr. González demonstrate a few more instruments. We walking-around types don't need the bright lights. After I had completed my business with Mr. González, I intended to visit the 10th of August Market, nearby, where I needed to make certain I had found the best version of the roasted pork that the vendors pull off the carcass of their hog and serve with hominy and a cousin of potato knishes called *llapingachos*. Also, I had previously spotted a bench outside the *centro's* other indoor market, the 9th of October, that looked like a perfect vantage point for watching a goat owner dispense milk in paper cups. On the way, I intended to stop by a small shop on Hermano Miguel to confirm my impression that its proprietor makes one of the best *humitas* in Cuenca. *Humitas* are slightly sweet, and Cuencanos like to eat them in the middle of the morning with black coffee. I eat them all day long.

My plan was to watch the goat-milk man for a while, and then walk to the Parque de Madres, just on the other side of the river, where there is a statue honoring mothers but a much larger statue honoring Jefferson Perez, described on the base as the greatest Ecuadorean athlete of all time. A race-walker, Perez is the only Ecuadorean to have won medals in the Olympics—a gold and a silver—and I'd been told that at certain times of day would-be Olympic racewalking champions trained in the park. But I'd found myself mesmerized by the goat-milk man. It occurred to me that if leaders of the locavore movement witnessed this process—no middlemen, no waste of irreplaceable fossil fuels in shipping, no bottles or cans to overburden landfills—they might decide on the spot to hold their next world conference in Cuenca.

By the time I was ready to leave, Cuenca's customary afternoon shower had begun. I couldn't get to the park. I'd also have to put off stopping in a sporting goods store to see if I could find some Ecuadorean soccer shirts for my grandsons. And I'd have to wait for another day to check out what I'd heard about a street called Las Herrerias's being famous not only for its iron smiths but for its *humitas*. I realized what the checkoffian tourists mean when they complain sometimes about simply not having time to do everything they need to do.

2010

The Peak of My Desire

by

RUSSELL BANKS

Two days and three nights in Quito adjusting my sea-level cardiovascular and respiratory systems to the 9,300-foot altitude, and I was out of there. Enough already. Enough hanging around the crowded, noisy New City cafés on Amazonas; enough window-shopping and strolling the jammed, narrow streets of the Old City; and enough already of the international cadre of mountain climbers—those slender, tanned, superconditioned young men and women in hiking shorts and T-shirts, those jaded connois-seurs-of-climb lounging around the patios of the hostels and outfitters on Juan León Mera, like Aussie surfers waiting for the perfect wave. It was not what I had come to Ecuador to see or do. I was headed into the mountains, traveling the way I like best—alone, by public transport, riding the packed Latacunga bus south from Terminal Terrestre to El Chaupi.

It was a bone-clear morning, cool and dry, with an endlessly high sky above the mountains that ringed the city like Inca ruins. I gaped at the otherworldly scenery from the open window of the bus, while the rest of the passengers—men, women, children, and babies alike—stared up at the dubbed *Star Trek* rerun on the TV screen at the front. In minutes, the top-heavy bus lost its signal and then chugged its way up and out of the congested bowl of downtown Quito onto an arid ridge, where it lumbered along the potholed Pan-American Highway. Scrawny, blond dogs trotted purposefully along the median strip as if late for an appointment, while huge, smoke-belching trucks and rattling old cars fought each other for the right-of-way in a mad, mechanized, sixty-mile-an-hour rugby scrum. At the edge of the road, thousand-foot cliffs dropped through scrub and eroded, bloodred arroyos to the vast, tin-topped barrio spreading along the broad valley south of Quito like an effluent.

I had come to Ecuador to climb in the Andes, like those elegantly tanned athletes back in Quito—although they all appeared to be twenty-five to thirty years younger than I and had the body fat of ten-speed bicycles. Even the ponytails on the men looked functional. The women in their nylon short shorts, mesh T-shirts, and running shoes looked as if they were built to rescue men like me from ice crevasses and had been taught by counselors how to do it in a nonthreatening way. I'm in my mid-fifties and for more than six months had trained in pain for this, and it did not comfort or reassure me to see people who seemed genetically programmed to climb these eighteen-to-twenty-thousand-foot peaks between workouts. I was glad to be away from them, at least for the day.

Most of the year, I live in the Adirondack Mountains in upstate New York, where for exercise I take occasional day hikes and play a little tennis—aging boomer guy stuff, nothing strenuous. It was my good friends and neighbors, Laurie and George Daniels, who first signed on for this trek with Rock & River Guide Service and talked me into joining them. They are wonderful, intelligent people, owners of a small, independent bookstore and health food store in Keene Valley; but they, too, are twenty or more years younger than I, built like ga-zelles, and they're experienced climbers. Laurie does triathlons and is a rock-climbing guide. George has a ponytail. I was, therefore, secretly relieved that on this first climb, my test run at altitude, they had decided to stay in Quito. If I had made a serious mistake and had wasted six months of nonsmoking, lung-bursting, muscle-developing daily exercise, not to mention several thousand dollars in transportation and equipment costs, I preferred to find it out alone.

An hour out of Quito, the bus shuddered to a stop and dropped me and my backpack off at the side of the road. I was suddenly the only human being in sight, and except for the steady rush of the wind, it was absolutely silent. The sun was shining brilliantly, and the air was desert-dry but cool, barely fifty degrees Fahrenheit. Across the highway was the entrance to Cotopaxi National Park. A dusty, rutted track led through eucalyptus trees and over humpbacked ridges, where it wound across the plain toward Mount Cotopaxi in the distance—the highest active volcano in the world and the object of all our desires on this trek. In nine days, after several preliminary conditioning climbs of somewhat lower mountains and a day of "snow school" (learning how to climb a glacier), we were scheduled—Laurie and George and I; our guide, Alex Van Steen; and the four other yanquis in our group—to climb to its 19,342-foot snow-covered summit.

Not today, however. Despite the blue sky overhead, I couldn't even see Cotopaxi. It was shrouded in clouds—a vast, white, shapeless mass that rose like a storm from the altiplano in the east and blotted out the horizon. For some reason, I had started thinking of the mountain as "she," as the mother of all volcanoes in Ecuador's fabled Avenue of the Volcanoes. Chimborazo in the south, at 20,697 feet, was the slightly taller father, an extinct volcano nicknamed El Viudo, "The Widower." Cotopaxi ("La Viuda"), however, still boiled beneath her snowy cap, and long plumes of steam rose regularly from the crater. The last time she erupted was in 1942, and the slopes and plains that surround the mountain are covered for miles with ash and room-size ejecta from that eruption.

Today I was after smaller game—the three twelve-thousand-foot peaks of El Chaupi. Lomas, they're called, "hills," towering behind me in the west and tied together by a seven-and-a-half-mile, scalloped, narrow ridge. I turned, grabbed my day pack, and started walking. A mile or so ahead of me, the land rose abruptly from the valley to the first of the lomas. Soon, I feared, my body would tell me that I am a vain, deluded, middle-aged fool and should have stayed home.

It was not so much the climbing that had made me anxious. It was the altitude. Over the years, I'd hiked long chunks of the Appalachian Trail and climbed most of the higher Adirondacks and the White Mountains in New Hampshire, but this was the first time I'd ventured this high. I'd heard and read too many stories of perfectly fit climbers of all ages getting to twelve and fourteen thousand feet and succumbing suddenly to altitude illness—nausea, blinding headaches, disorientation, hallucinations, and even unconsciousness and permanent brain damage.

I didn't want to get overconfident—this was the first real test of my training program, begun halfheartedly eight months ago, in February. A half-pack-a-day man, the first thing I did was quit smoking. Then, to the boom box throb of alternative rock, I began lifting free weights three afternoons a week, and on the other days I rode my bicycle. Despite a spare tire around my waist, I wasn't terribly out of shape—your typical middle-aged, moderately exercised ex-athlete, I guess. But I hadn't tried to put myself into condition for serious, sustained athletic activity in decades.

In May I got serious. Five mornings a week, I climbed one hour steeply uphill and one hour down on a two-mile forest path, gradually reducing my time to an hour and forty-five minutes, then an hour and a quarter, and finally less than an hour, practically running the whole way. Once a week, sometimes twice, I took a daylong hike up one of the higher mountains in the region. Three afternoons a week, I bicycled for two hours, logging more and more miles each time, taking on higher and longer hills, until by late August, as I made the long, steep, five-mile ascent through Cascade Notch to Lake Placid, I was drawing incredulous stares from passing motorists. Who is that gray-haired idiot? By mid-October, it was dark from 5 P.M. till 8 A.M., and the snow had started to fly, so I had to switch from hiking shoes to snowshoes and put my bike away. But no matter: I was as ready for the Andes as I would ever be—as ready, at least, as I was willing to be.

All the way up the winding trail to the summit of Loma Sal Grande, I'd been unavoidably facing away from mother Cotopaxi; my view had been mainly of the three linked peaks ahead. The path through shiny tussocks of ichu grass was smooth enough, thanks to generations of donkeys, milch cows, goats, and their keepers; but the trail was narrow and vaguely defined, and several times I wandered off it onto a dwindling tributary and had to clamber over tipped, hummocky fields of the tough, knee-high grasses to get back on route. The solitude was splendid. I met no other climbers—no humans at all since the three native women who had given me directions to the path and giggled shyly at my broken Spanish.

It had gotten much cooler as I ascended from the valley floor, but I was still in T-shirt and hiking shorts, kept warm by exertion. The humidity was extremely low, and the steady wind blew my skin and clothing dry. I knew that I was losing a lot of moisture and was glad that the heaviest item in my day pack was two liters of water bought at a bodega in Quito. I was also carrying rain gear and a fleece jacket (in case the weather changed), extra socks, an emergency medical kit, a chorizo and chunk of hard cheese for lunch, and several Reese's Peanut Butter Cups, from the carton I had hauled down from the States.

Finally, I crossed a pocked, stony collar and scrambled to the summit of Loma Sal Grande, a narrow, bony fist of volcanic rock, where I stopped to rest and take in the astonishing scenery. An oval bowl three thousand feet deep opened below the three humped lomas like a pale green fjord. To the northeast, I could make out the black rooster-comb caldera of Pasochoa, and next to it, the rusty crown of Rumiñahui. Then, suddenly, as I turned further to the east, there she was—Mount Cotopaxi, looming over my shoulder as if she'd been following me all along, sparkling white against the deep blue sky, shocking in her immensity and apparent nearness. Almost iconically symmetrical, a nearly perfect inverted cone rising from a vast, umber plain, Cotopaxi dwarfed the lomas of El Chaupi, so that from my little peak, after my first modest Andes ascent, I found myself looking not down at the world in triumph, as I had expected, but up and in awe.

For the rest of the afternoon, except for lunch at the summit of Santa Cruz, the third and highest of the three lomas, I was ridge-walking and keeping a wary eye on a long, low bank of dark clouds rolling across the northern valley from west to east, coming in from the Pacific. By the time I started down Santa Cruz and made my way across its broad, grassy shoulder, descending in the general direction of the Pan-American Highway, it had begun to rain. I pulled on my poncho and rain pants and plodded steadily downhill, chilled and drawn swiftly into my hooded thoughts, for there was little I could see now that was not ten feet in front of me—the next turning in the narrow footpath, a low, slick boulder beside it, the drooping branch of a euca-lyptus tree.

This is how it is when you climb, and I have never gotten used to it: First you expand out of yourself and enter the vast world that surrounds you, and then, just as quickly, you are forced by weather or fatigue back to your secret interior life, and you lose awareness of the outside world altogether. It's a rhythmic, alternating expansion and contraction of consciousness that feels like the creation of mind. More than anything else, this experience, available to me almost nowhere else and at no other time, is what has drawn me back to the mountains all my adult life—not the grand vistas of sky and rock and colliding planes of light, not the rejuvenating solitude, and certainly not the "conquest" of a par-ticular summit, marking another notch on my walking stick.

Back on the highway, I waited barely fifteen minutes for one of the overloaded, Quito-bound buses. It was jammed with people, and I was forced to stand all the way back to the city—a tall, smiling, strangely elated yanqui bent almost double by the low roof. The seated, tired na-tives, returning home from a long day's work in the fields and shops of the hinterlands, studied me with dignified, mild curiosity, as if I had been beamed up to the bus from the surface of a newly discovered planet. This seemed only appropriate: It is exactly how I felt.

The night before, at the Hotel Alameda Real, I had met my fellow trekkers and guide. To give myself a few extra days to adjust to the altitude, I had flown into Quito before the rest of the group. George and Laurie had met up with me the day before, and we'd spent a cheerful weekend wandering the streets and parks of the city, waiting for the arrival of the rest of our group from the States. To my delight, the hotel—filled with intrepid travelers, mostly young, diesel-powered German tourists and American elderlies—had overbooked and put me into a large, luxurious suite at the price of the single I had reserved. I had just crawled sleepily into my king-size bed when there came a sharp knock on my door.

I stumbled in the darkness over my scattered gear, opened the door a crack, and saw a large, drooping, walrus-style mustache. Then I made out the tall, big-faced man wearing it. He was tired and irritated, as was the woman behind him. Coming down the hallway were a young, bearded man and an even younger woman, both wearing loaded backpacks and dragging duffels the size of body bags. Behind them, pushing a cart loaded with at least four more body bags, came a man I recognized: our guide, Alex Van Steen, whom I had briefly met at the Rock & River Lodge in the Adirondacks when I signed on for this trip.

There had been a screwup. I was supposed to be sharing a double room with the young bearded fellow, Mark, an FBI special agent from Westchester, New York, whereas my pleasantly large suite with the king-size bed was supposed to have been held for the mustachioed man, Fred, and his wife, Beth. Fred, I later discovered, had been the headmaster of a private school near Syracuse and was now a househusband caring for his and Beth's new baby. Beth was a pediatrician. The young woman struggling with her duffel and backpack behind Mark was Michelle, a pretty, twitchy physical therapist from Arizona. As the one solo woman in our group, she'd been assigned a single room, while Alex was supposed to share a single with the expedition gear. Laurie and George, of course, had settled into a double and no doubt were deep in sleep by now.

Fred and Beth grumpily agreed to take Alex's single so that I wouldn't have to pack up and move all my gear at midnight—a task I expressed a sharp distaste for—and Alex and I and the expedition gear would share "my" suite. Not an auspicious beginning, I thought, as I settled back into bed. The simplest aspect of our trip should have been these first days in a large, modern hotel in Quito, and somehow we had created complications and dealt with them gracelessly. Or at least I had.

By the next evening, however, following my triumphant climb of El Chaupi, I was confident and anxiety-free. Feeling more sociable, and a little guilty, perhaps, for my lack of consanguinity in the hallway the previous night, I joined my fellow trekkers for dinner at a cavernous Italian restaurant. Alex sat at the center of our long table, and whenever he spoke, the members of the expedition went on high alert. Bright-eyed and tanned, with a movie star's chin and cheekbones and a professional mountain climber's taut, muscular build, Alex was a ready talker, eager to instruct neophyte and expert alike. As the evening wore on, however, I began to think that perhaps he did not have total confidence in this group's ability to climb some of the mountains of the Avenue of the Volcanoes—Pasochoa, Rumiñahui, Sincholagua, and Cotopaxi— for he had a tendency to overinstruct, even to overarticulate, as if we were hard of hearing. Consequently, I too began to lose confidence in our ability—especially mine—to complete our mission. After all, these folks were at least as experienced as I at climbing (more so, certainly, in Laurie's and George's case), and they were all decades younger. Even Fred, who was unusually large and seemed slightly awkward for it, appeared nonetheless to be very strong and brimming with wellness. They had all taken mountaineering classes, and Fred and Beth had let it drop that they were "Forty-Sixers," which meant that they had climbed all forty-six of the Adirondack Mountains over four thousand feet, a club I never expect to belong to. Half of them were serious vegetarians, even. If Alex was sufficiently worried about them that he was giving them breathing lessons, what must he think of me?

Early the next morning, we loaded our small hired bus and eagerly, if a little nervously, set out for the mountains. Eighteen miles from Quito, we turned onto a cobbled, winding track that crossed over rocky streams and passed through the carefully cultivated land of the Hacienda San Miguel. At last we reached the sloping base of Pasochoa, where there was an empty parking lot and a small cinder-block building that housed a rudimentary environmental education center. Pasochoa was described in our itinerary as a 13,800-foot "acclimatizing hike." We disembarked, slung on our day packs, checked our water supplies, rubbed on sunblock, and began to walk through a large forest preserve, where the narrow trail wound like a dimly lit tunnel amid bamboo groves, dense shrubbery, and dripping eucalyptus trees. It was very hot and humid, and as the trail shifted slowly uphill and walking turned into work, I began to sweat and to wonder . . . Where are the mountains? Where are the views? Why am I here?

Soon, however, the forest thinned, and I could see (with the broad fields and hillocks spreading out below and the great peaks of the Avenue of the Volcanoes gleaming in the distance) how high we were and how far we'd come; and up ahead (with the black, spiky caldera of Pasochoa beckoning at the end of a long, narrow, fast-rising ridge) how far we had yet to climb.

As we walked, there was a great deal of energetic, almost obsessive talk about training regimens and equipment, which I'd begun to regard as coded talk about bodies—one's own. It was as if, behind an apparently earnest desire to describe one's backpack, hiking shoes, Stair-Master, reps, gaiters, and crampons, there lurked an almost narcissistic self-absorption. It struck me that I was learning something useful about the younger generation and the true meaning of nineties sports consumerism. On the other hand, I thought, maybe I just don't have the right stuff.

Periodically, Alex would stop the party and instruct us on walking, breathing, and resting techniques—the same little tricks that, without knowing it, I'd been using my whole life. Consequently, I let my attention wander from the lecture to contemplate the awesome, surreal beauty of the Andes. I was feeling strong as a donkey, even stronger than I had on the lomas of El Chaupi. Risking the role of rogue mountaineer, and the loneliness of the *aislado*, I started separating myself from the group emotionally, and physically too, and found myself more and more often walking alone, either at the front of the pack or way at the back.

The hike took more than five hours, and, strangely, the higher and steeper it got, the easier the climb seemed. Was this a sympton of hypoxia, altitude sickness? I wondered. Brain damage already? More likely, it was the simple, clean thrill of reaching the crisp lip of the caldera of an ancient Andean volcano, 13,800 feet up, and the sight of the terraced valley thousands of feet below, the forests crumpled at the base like a dark green blanket and the conifers spiking the higher slopes opposite like the pikes of an advancing army of knights under the cloudless, taut, blue canopy overhead—and in the distance, majestic and serene in the soft afternoon sunlight, the beautiful white cone of Cotopaxi.

Laurie and I were the first to make the top—or as close as we could get to it, since there was a vertical twenty-foot headwall between us and the true summit. We stood dazed with delight on the small ledge, as one by one the others joined us, red-faced, puffing, and thrilled. For the first time, I was happy to see my fellow trekkers and to share with them this hard-won pleasure.

We began the descent, arriving just as the afternoon rain started, then rode on to the town of Machachi several miles southwest. We were tired and wet but cheerful all in all, for no one in the group seemed to have suffered anything worse than the mildest symptoms of altitude sickness.

At Machachi, we put up for the night at a comfortable old mission-style bed-and-breakfast located next to a railroad station and named, appropriately, La Estación. We were the only guests, and after an ample four-course dinner, the group sprawled around the fireplace and listened to Alex's account of climbing the north face of Everest. It was a tough story to tell, and tough to listen to, for the attempt had ended in tragedy for two men, and it had nearly taken Alex's life as well. As he talked, his voice dropping almost to a whisper, I found myself moved as much by Alex's grief and pain as by the story itself. Finally, I was starting to get it, the climber's mentality: one in which mountains are not a metaphor for life but are life itself. As Alex talked on, I felt guilty for not having listened well enough earlier. I saw that for Alex, and maybe even for some of my fellow trekkers, the apparently obsessive concern with equipment and fitness and the techniques of breathing, walking, and resting was like a Puritan's concern with his conscience, a Buddhist's with his koan, or a warrior's with his weaponry—it's what gets him through his life.

The next day found us at the end of a rutted, almost invisible track ten miles out on the desolate pampas-like plateau of the vast national park that surrounds Mount Cotopaxi. We unloaded our duffels and backpacks and watched our bus lumber off for Quito, and then we were alone on the enormous, darkening henna-colored platter—ten of us, including Alex and two Ecuadorians: Colón, a taciturn, wry young man who would help guide the party for the remainder of our trek, and Elias, a sweet-smiling native man who would stay in camp and guard our equipment while we climbed the days away. We all stood glumly in the cold rain at the steep bank of a fast-running, meandering stream, the Hualpaloma. For the next four days this 12,500-foot-high, treeless piece of the *páramo* would be our campsite, before we moved on to the José Ribas Refugio, the base camp at 15,750 feet, just below the glacier on the rounded, north-facing shoulder of Cotopaxi. There were low, rolling, bald hills in the near distance, pitted and cluttered by volcanic rocks like a lunar landscape, and to the north, beyond the hills, the three cloud-shrouded peaks of Rumiñahui, which we were scheduled to climb the next day. To the right, also lost in the mists, was Sincholagua, scheduled for two days later. Behind us, with only her rocky, broad skirts visible, was Cotopaxi, our final goal.

Alex divided us into pairs—George and Laurie, Fred and Beth, he and Michelle, and Special Agent Mark and me—and passed out our two-man tents, and we commenced to struggle in the raw wind to get them pitched. We were all very cold, the rain didn't help, and it was close to dark. It took a while, but finally we had the small tents up and our gear stowed.

This was when I discovered two things that would have a decidedly negative impact on my Andes camping experience. In my hurry to leave home, I'd grabbed a nylon stuff-bag from among several in the hall closet, thinking it contained my almost-new down-filled sleeping bag. Now I found that it contained instead an ancient, torn bag that I'd long meant to toss out. It was half emptied of its down filler, a flattened, moldy sack of loose feathers with a ripped seam at the foot and no zipper along the side. Also, I'd somehow left my new inflatable ground pad in Quito. I would be sleeping in the sorriest imaginable excuse for a sleeping bag, with nothing between it and the cold, damp ground.

Mark, whose duffel was twice the size of mine and whose expedition pack had more compartments, zippers, straps, and bells and whistles than a sport-utility vehicle, blew up a ground pad as big as a life-size inflatable doll and spread his shiny, nearly weightless, elegantly expanding, waterproof, cocoon-like bag over it. I gazed at my tentmate in envy. When he finished, he glanced at my sad sack, politely looked away, and said nothing. I had clearly failed him. Sheepishly, I offered him a Reese's Peanut Butter Cup, but he declined it, opting instead for one of his high-nutrient PowerBars.

Later, half a roll of duct tape from Alex's emergency pack helped patch my bag, but only temporarily. All night long my stockinged feet kept breaking through, and whenever I turned in my sleep and yanked them back inside, I tore the tape, opening the bag to a wave of cold air that inevitably woke me. Fresh feathers floated idly in the dark above my face, while Mark snored peacefully from the warm comfort of his cocoon. It was a long, miserable, freezing night, and I was deeply grateful when, shortly after five, I heard Alex walk from tent to tent, waking his charges like a drill sergeant.

The ichu grass, silver-soldered by frost in the predawn light, crunched underfoot as I walked to a spot a hundred yards downstream from the tents, where I performed my ablutions in the dark. My breath made clouds before my face, and the surface of the stream steamed in the cold, predawn air. In the east, behind the sharply silhouetted horizon, the night sky was fading to peach. Pale swaths of stars fluttered overhead, where the sky was still blue-black, and a chalky three-quarter moon hovered in the west. It was a splendid, affirming moment, and once again, despite my terrible, sleepless night, I was glad that I had come.

One by one, my companions emerged and gathered before the cook tent for breakfast—cold Pop-Tarts, apples, hard rye bread smeared with peanut butter. Another spartan meal. I filled my plastic, insulated McDonald's mug with hot water and made tea. Then I noted that my fellow trekkers were all drinking from high-tech, stainless steel thermoses. These were serious people; I obviously was not.

Today we were to climb three-pronged Rumiñahui, all the way to the rosy, sunlit summit of the middle prong towering 15,460 feet high, its broad base at Lake Limpio Pungo, a four-mile walk across the rolling plateau from our camp.

We hadn't walked more than a quarter mile in the frosty dawn when, as we rounded a long, moraine-like ridge, we interrupted a meditating coyote that darted into the darkness, startling us as much as we had startled it. Then in the distance we began to see horses grazing, semiwild and unbroken, lifting their long, angular heads warily to watch us pass slowly by. They were beautiful, small, thick-bodied animals, the same stock as the horses the Spanish rode in on half a millennium ago. Rumiñahui in Quechua means "Face of Stone" and is named for one of the Inca generals who fought the invaders. Now, like equine ghosts guarding and honoring the old native general's spirit, hundreds of the sturdy descendants of the conquistadores' horses roamed the *páramo* at the foot of his mountain.

By the time we reached the sprawling, shallow lake—more a marsh than a lake at this time of year—the sun had fully risen in a nearly cloudless sky. We marched single file, hopping from dry spot to dry spot, then circled uphill alongside a narrow, fast-running feeder creek. Alex was in the lead, I was at the rear, and one by one the troop crossed the creek fairly easily. Until it was Fred's turn. He had come out this morning carrying two adjustable aluminum hiking poles with nylon wrist straps attached. He was the least conditioned member of the group and tended to drop back, puffing and red-faced. If you got

behind him—which I sometimes did, lagging back to catch some silence and solitude—you had to watch out or you'd get hit in the eye
with one of his flailing poles.

Now, as he rock-walked his way across the stream, he slipped, and
in he went. He was quickly out, embarrassed but hale and hearty nonetheless, striding in wet boots and gaiters as if nothing untoward had
happened. But it scared me, and I think it scared the others, particularly Alex. It was suddenly clear—from the steep ash and soft-rock
slope looming ahead of us and the arroyos that tumbled away on either
side—that a simple misstep could be deadly.

I decided to keep some distance between Fred's poles and me and
moved to the front of the group as we ascended the long, broad ridge
that came off the central summit. About midmorning, clouds moved
in and the temperature was dropping steadily; around noon it began to
rain. We stopped and changed into rain gear and plodded on. After a
while, the rain changed to sleet. Then hail. Then snow—until we
couldn't see farther than a few feet of the trail ahead. Close by, the
crumbly black rock took on an otherworldly look, strangely detailed
and in sharp focus, as in a high-gloss silver-gelatin print. The alpine
flowers at the side of the trail and along the slopes looked like they'd
been candied—*chocho de páramour*, Colón called it, a tender lavender-
blue bud on a tough low bush. Other flowers—named, in Quechua,
chuguiragua—glowed green, blue, and red through the thin skin of ice
and the padding of wet, sticky snow.

The narrow, winding trail was very slick. Also, the pitch of the slope
had increased considerably in the last hour, and we were moving as if in
slow motion. Breathing was difficult and came in short, shallow, rapid
puffs, and my legs felt like iron ingots. This was hard going. But when I
looked back, I saw that everyone in the group was making it—even Fred,
whose decision to lug his sticks along seemed prescient now. No one
looked happy, however, and for the first time, everyone remained silent.

We were slogging across a reddish sandy rise, our boots sunk to the
ankles in powdery ash, and might have been climbing the sifting side
of a Sahara dune, except that it was snowing and we were at nearly

fourteen thousand feet. Suddenly, powerful beams of sunlight broke through the snow, and the clouds swirled and parted. We could see! We were above the storm. This section was probably the toughest part of the climb, yet it seemed almost easy, thanks to the shocking beauty of sky and cliff hovering above and—as the clouds behind us broke and flowed off to the south—the sight of the deep, pale green arroyos thousands of feet below, where the *páramo* spread out like a multicolored map. Halfway between us and the *páramo*, two of Ecuador's seventy-five remaining condors, like black-winged hang gliders, rode the sun-warmed air currents in wide, spiraling loops.

The last few hundred yards to the summit were a hard pull over crumbling, plate-size rocks. Fred, Mark, and Michelle had slowed considerably, evidently suffering from the altitude, but they kept climbing, even if with tiny, numbingly slow steps. They were not to be stopped, not this close to the summit. Alex fell back and watched them intently, checking for signs of AMS, acute mountain sickness. It's the guide's decision, not the climber's, when to descend, and evidently Alex felt that Fred, Mark, and Michelle were not yet in danger. They eventually joined the rest of the group, where we had gathered on a narrow, protected shelf below the table-size summit. Then, one at a time, in the order we had arrived at the shelf, we climbed to the summit itself and stood there alone. Laurie went up first, and after a few moments came down looking stunned with pleasure, as if she'd interviewed a deity.

Then it was my turn. I reached the top crawling on hands and knees, then stood up unsteadily. Despite the cold wind and sunlight blasting my body and face, I opened my eyes wide, and in a rapture that was in every way new to me, gazed away like a blissed-out anchorite. When I could think again, I thought: For the rest of my life I will be trying to regain this feeling.

We got back to the main supporting ridge fairly fast and, at Colón's suggestion, took an easier but longer route down, so that by the time we reached the plateau, the sun was heading toward the horizon. We were exhausted, and camp was still four miles away. Also, to complicate things, a dense fog was creeping in, and before long we couldn't see more than fifty feet in front of us.

Cold, wet, and bone-tired, we plodded in a southeasterly direction, trusting our guides to bring us to our campsite. An hour went by, then nearly two. The fog grew thicker. Once in a while, huge volcanic rocks, like dark gray icebergs, appeared out of the mists. But we might as well have been crossing the Arctic in a blizzard: Everywhere we looked, it was the same. Even Colón and Alex seemed unsure. We were almost too tired to care—in retrospect, a dangerous state of mind—when suddenly, a coyote loped out of a nearby gully and trotted to the top of a low berm, where it stopped and looked back at us. Was it the same coyote we'd seen at dawn? The landscape seemed newly familiar. Twice, then, we had accidentally come upon the same coyote's den. Now we knew where we were and where the camp was. In silence, each of us thanked the coyote for pointing the way.

We were almost too exhausted to complain about a cold supper (malfunctioning stoves) we had to eat in the dark. And after another freezing, bumpy night in my pathetic sleeping bag, while Mark snored comfortably beside me, I awoke at six-thirty determined to enjoy the one free day of our expedition. It was a splendid day, warm and sunny, and after breakfast George, Laurie, and I lit out on a four-hour hike to distant grass-topped hills, where we picnicked and basked in the reflected light of gleaming Cotopaxi. Later, we followed the meandering Rio Hualpaloma out onto the rolling plain, where brown rabbits bounded across our path and disappeared into the high silver-tipped grass. In the distance we saw gauchos rounding up wild horses and moving them to fresh grazing land. We passed several herds of llamas—whose pursed lips and long-lashed, soulful eyes reminded us of Uma Thurman—tended by lone native shepherds who nodded solemnly at us. On our way back to camp, we looped out toward the center of the broad plain and visited an Inca ruin—a long, rectangular mound fifty feet high, with a commanding view of the entire valley.

Later, we went upstream from our camp, bathed under a heavy, cold waterfall, and dried in the sun like contemplative turtles.

Afterward, we changed into clean clothing and aired our tents and sleeping bags. It was a much needed, rejuvenating interlude. The three of us felt pleased with ourselves, for we had grown stronger and more confident with each new day's test. And we were beginning to learn how to look at this landscape, so unlike anything we had seen before, to understand its logic and scale, and thus to anticipate its forms. It did not seem as intimidating as it had.

Roused at 5 A.M. by Alex, I was ready and eager to climb Sincholagua. Our packs were heavier than on Rumiñahui: This time we were carrying rain gear as well as serious cold-weather clothing and gear. At 16,100 feet, the temperature would be much lower than on Rumiñahui.

For days, every time I looked at Cotopaxi, I had traced out the path we would take up its flank, and each time it had seemed inhumanly high and steep, impossible for anyone but a professional climber like Alex. But this morning, finally, I believed that I could do it. I was feeling like a Sherpa. No longer worried about myself—or George and Laurie— I had started worrying some about the others, especially Fred, whose rapid heart rate was alarming Beth, who took his pulse at every rest stop. Michelle was also clearly suffering from the altitude. Her pretty heart-shaped face was taut with strain, and she was walking at a much slower pace than on Rumiñahui. Mark, too, showed symptoms of altitude sickness, moving very slowly and seeming somehow dispirited.

Soon the group was undergoing fission. Alex walked ahead with me, Laurie, and George, at what felt to us a useful, enjoyable pace, while Colón, our second guide, fell back with the others. Whenever we reached the top of a long slope or came to an arroyo or cliff that marked a transition between ascending zones of difficulty, we would stop and wait for the others to join us. Then Alex would discreetly check for altitude sickness and decide anew whether to push on.

We had gathered on a rocky shelf, where the trail dropped down a vertical twelve-foot embankment to a narrow arroyo and led across a dry streambed to the main ridge up Sincholagua. For the last half hour, Alex and I had been chatting optimistically about my joining him next year, perhaps with George and Laurie, and climbing Rainier. I, too, was now yakking obsessively about equipment, training regimens, and mountains other than the one we were on—a result, I suppose, of my growing confidence and pleasure in my ability to meet this challenge, and perhaps the vanity of a middle-aged man surprised to find himself keeping pace with people in their twenties and thirties. It was a pleasant discovery, and I was savoring it.

First Alex went over the embankment and swung down to the rock-strewn bottom. Mark followed, making it to the bottom safely but with difficulty. Handholds and footholds were hard to locate without help. Michelle went over next, with Mark and Alex spotting, and made it safely down. Then it was my turn. I proceeded exactly as the others had. I got halfway down the wall, so that my head was at the level of the shelf, with my weight held solely by my grasp on the crumbly rock there, while my feet groped blindly for a hold. Finally, my left foot managed to find a cleft in the wall. Then, just as I transferred my weight onto that foot—off balance, due to the pack—the cleft gave way, and I was falling. I remember turning, watching the rocks at the bottom speed toward me, and I remember rolling in midair to avoid hitting my head and spine, hoping instead to land on my shoulder. Then I remember a sound that I recognized as the snap of bone. I was flat on my back, looking at sky. A second later, Alex's face, dark with fear, heaved into view. I knew at once that my trek to Cotopaxi was over.

Epilogue

My right collarbone was broken in two places. On the sloped shoulder of Sincholagua, Doctor Beth and Alex fixed me up with a homemade clavicle splint, and I walked slowly back down to the camp, four hours below, lugging my pack on my left shoulder, while the others continued on. Depressed and slightly disoriented from the fall and the pain, I had a hard time grasping what had happened—and, maybe more important, what wouldn't happen. I might just as easily have fallen and broken my collarbone while stepping from the shower—my accident was in no way a consequence of the difficulty of the climb or of my being out of shape or ill-equipped. Right stuff or wrong stuff had nothing to do with it. Bad luck was all. Okay, maybe overconfidence had made me slightly less cautious for a few seconds than I should have been, but still, it could have happened to anyone, especially me, anywhere.

Given what I'd set out to do—climb at high altitude in the Andes—I'd succeeded. I'd made myself fit enough to keep pace and sometimes even to exceed the pace and endurance of serious climbers. In the last few days, my fellow trekkers, affectionately and without irony, had taken to calling me El Bruto, "The Beast"—no small compliment for an aging boomer.

The greatest disappointment, of course, was that I would not make it to the summit of Cotopaxi, which had become my heart's desire. But the distinction between failure and disappointment is important. I had not failed; I was disappointed. I'd learned, certainly, that I was more than capable of doing this extremely difficult thing, but I had not been able to do it.

A strange mix of melancholy and elation accompanied me as I made my slow way back down the side of Sincholagua and plodded across the plain toward our tents. At the camp, I rested awhile, eventually setting myself the task of gathering firewood, so that when my companions returned, cold and exhausted, they'd be greeted by a blazing fire. They were back by nightfall, a thoroughly dispirited bunch, having been forced to turn back well below the summit. My fall had left the group depressed and discouraged, and several of them were still struggling with altitude illness.

The next day we broke camp—although I could but stand and watch—and drove to the foot of mother Cotopaxi. From there, it was a steep two-thousand-foot hike up to the hut, the *refugio*, located at 15,750 feet, where the glacier began. Determined to make it at least that far up the side of a mountain that I had come to love, I walked ahead of the others, whose climb was slowed by the weight of their packs. It was a sad, lonely walk.

Afterward, I descended alone to the bus and rode back to Quito, where I spent the night at the Hotel Alameda Real. The next day I hired a car and traveled for three days—until my scheduled departure for home—in the Indian villages of the north, day-hiking through twelve-thousand-foot-high lomas and spending my nights in small hotels. It was interesting travel and solitary, the way I usually prefer it, but anticlimactic and lonely. My broken collarbone hurt. And I missed my fellow trekkers—bumptious Fred and his walking sticks; Special Agent Mark, whose love of equipment was exceeded only by his surprising love of seventies quasi-metal music by groups like Rush and Pink Floyd; Doctor Beth, calm and disciplined and thinking constantly of her new baby at home; Michelle, anxious and fatigued and suffering from altitude illness but courageously continuing; my old Adirondack chums, George and Laurie, who would tell me everything I missed; and finally, our garrulous guide, the incomparable Alex, whom, if he learned to cook or hired someone who could, I would follow anywhere. But most of all, I missed the mountain, Cotopaxi, looming over my shoulder, blocking the sun, and, like a grand seductress, inviting me to come back, come back and try again.

1997

Oxford: The Class of 1250

by

HENRY SHUKMAN

It is late January. Park Town, an elegant Italianate development built in the suburbs of North Oxford in the 1850s, looks as graceful as Bath. The curves of its long terraces fronted with Cotswold sandstone catch a sun hanging just above the rooftops and glow a faint, edible orange. Nos. 37 and 39 Park Town are two halves of a house called the Clarendon Villa. I notice that the lace curtain in No. 37's window hangs a foot too short, and realize with a shock that I remember its being too short from long ago. I haven't seen it in twenty years, but there it is still, that ungainly skirt not quite reaching the ornate railing at the foot of the window.

Then another shock: In No. 39, where I lived until I was ten, there is a NO NUCLEAR POWER sticker in the top bedroom window. I put it there myself when I was eight. In twenty-two years, no one has removed it. Nor, for that matter, has anyone fixed the gate. It still leans, rusted and bent, with its black paint peeling, among the leaves of the laurel bush. Is this 1976 or 1996? Does nothing change here?

A man comes out of the door. I introduce myself. He is a builder, in white overalls speckled with plaster and white paint, and has a terrible stammer. He explains laboriously that the new owner is having the central heating redone—finally, thirty years on. Then he introduces me to his foreman.

The foreman is a small, wiry man with a mop of fair hair and ruddy cheeks. He scowls at me as I explain who I am, that I just happened to be walking by, that I grew up in the house and have been living in America.

"That's the place to live," he interrupts. "America's a decent country. Not like this god-awful place."

He speaks in a sardonic lilt, and at once I recognize the typical Oxford accent. It is a strange mix of three distinct regions: a faint nasal twang from the Midlands, the breeziness and glottal stops of the Cockney (*bu er* for *butter*), both of which finally are softened by the rustic *r*'s and *oi*'s of the West Country (*loik* for *like*). It is in fact a perfect gauge of Oxford's place, right in the heart of southern England, at a crossroads between the metropolitan southeast, the rural West, and the industrial Midlands. I also sense a certain familiar angry hardness that at first I take to be merely typical British moaning about Britain (for only in tourist brochures and tabloid newspapers is there such a thing as British pride). But then it dawns on me that there is more to it.

"But Oxford's a nice place," I say lamely.

"Wouldn't live here if you paid me," the foreman spits out.

I laugh, because presumably he does live here. He glares at me. He is not joking. "Well, where do you live?" I offer.

"Northmoor. Out in the sticks," he says proudly.

It's a village not far from town.

Here, then, is another thing that hasn't changed. The foreman is suffering from a peculiar Oxford phenomenon, a specific brand of dis-gruntlement that no other city kindles in quite the same way, a par-ticular kind of latent anger, of smoldering resentment. Its source is the long-ingrained hostility of the "town" to the "gown." For centuries, ever since the medieval riots when the townsfolk and the students peri-odically slaughtered one another, the city has barely tolerated the privi-leged university in its center. Even today, when the university is no longer the bastion of aristocratic youth it used to be, the old resentment, more or less bereft now of its cause, lingers on. It is bred into the genes of Oxford.

But then the foreman tells me with a faint smile of pride that the new owner of the house, for whom he is working, is the bursar of Nuffield College. It is a complicated thing, the town-gown relationship. For it is tinged also with a reluctant admiration.

"Where are you?" he asks me.

He means which college. Since I am wearing neither overalls nor a suit and tie, I can only be a university man. "Nowhere," I tell him, and the disappointment is briefly but unmistakably visible in his face. Perhaps he hoped to have an excuse to resent me, or else he assumed I was yet another clever scholar. "I went to Cambridge," I add.

"Ah." His face lights up. "I've heard that's a decent place."

Cambridge may or may not be a decent place. A porter in an Oxford college once asked a student who had just visited it what it was like. "Something in the Keble line?" he suggested. Keble is unquestionably Oxford's most—perhaps only—hideous college, a depressing place of variegated Victorian brickwork that visitors used to be taken to to laugh at.

Cambridge certainly has its beauty, but the porter was right in one sense. Cambridge, like Keble. is an isolated place. You get the feeling that the real engines of the nation are turning elsewhere. Oxford, on the other hand, has always been both literally and figuratively right in the center of Britain. First of all, it stands at a point as far from the sea as you can get—seventy miles in any direction. The nation's great river flows through it, and it is at Oxford that the canal networks of the Midlands and the North finally join up with the Thames. Oxford has produced twenty-four prime ministers and scores of other politicians. The number of writers and famous men of British history who passed through it are beyond counting. Cambridge has had its share too—Byron and Darwin and Newton spring to mind immediately—but of the two, Oxford seems the place where the bulk of England's history was forged.

Not only that, but Oxford is unquestionably a more interesting town. In Cambridge the colleges and the city are more or less separate, and the city is just another dim market town of the East Anglian fenlands; but in Oxford, with 131,500 inhabitants, the university and the town grew up inextricably intertwined, and the result is one of the loveliest cities in Europe. As you walk around its ancient streets, everything—the busy shops, the hooting traffic, the bustle on the pavements of the High Street, the old stone facades of the colleges with their forests of pinnacles and finials above, the spires of the many churches, the big red buses jostling for the stops, the London-style taxis lining up in the middle of the grand boulevard of St. Giles—tells you that you are in a place that matters.

Oxford is neither an ivory tower nor a dull market town, but a microcosm of modern England. From the haute bourgeoisie leading lives of pseudo-Proustian elegance to the Irish laborers digging the roads, from Welsh car workers to Pakistani shopkeepers, West Indian bus drivers and Indian restaurateurs, the whole modern demography is represented. Until recently, academia was only the third-largest employer in the city. Second was the printing and publishing industry, first the Morris auto-manufacturing works out at Cowley. From the thirties to the sixties, Morris Motors was the biggest car plant in Europe. For years visitors were greeted at Oxford station by a sign saying WELCOME TO OXFORD: HOME OF PRESSED STEEL—Pressed Steel being a company that supplied Cowley with car bodies. But so interwoven are the lives of the city and the university that William Morris, who started out fixing bicycles, is said to have amassed the capital he needed to get going in the automobile business by renting out ladders to undergraduates who returned after lockup and needed to scale the college wall.

But this interweaving has had a price. Oxford may be a prosperous place. It may save more money per capita than any other town in England and be full of interior design boutiques and restaurants serving the latest nouvelle cuisine. At four in the afternoon, the curbs of such smart North Oxford streets as Park Town may be lined bumper-to-bumper with the Volvos and Range Rovers of Oxford mothers waiting for the private schools to let out. Even such old working class districts as Jericho and St. Clements, neighborhoods of small attached brick houses, may be gentrifying—ground floors get opened up into single big rooms, lace curtains come down, and trim venetian blinds go up. Yet tensions smolder. Oxford town has always had its reasons to be proud of itself. It is famous for Frank Cooper's marmalade, for Morrell's beer, for its various printing presses, for its prime importance in the old wool trade, and for its vast car works at Cowley. It has given the world Oxford bags, Oxford brogues, Oxford marmalade, and Oxford English. But by and large, the world knows Oxford for one thing only. It is as if there were a smart little provincial city here bursting with civic pride that has too long been frustrated. For in its midst, like a cuckoo overshadowing its hosts, nests the university.

It is a rainy lunchtime. I duck into the Rose & Crown, a tiny pub on the little lane of North Parade, to get some lunch and to meet two men who know a great deal about the history of Oxford.

One of the great delights of Oxford is its pubs, many of which date back to the Middle Ages. Their walls, their fabrics, their very air, all seem steeped in centuries of comfort found in tobacco smoke, nutty brown English ale, and inspired conversation.

Professor X arrives quietly, coughing as he closes the door. He shakes the rain off his fur-lined coat and checks the time on the pocket-watch hanging from his waistcoat. "Good, good," he mutters by way of greeting. "You're already here." He orders two half-pints of beer for us, pushing his round glasses up his nose and sniffing.

Professor X has a reputation for being one of the wittiest men in Oxford. He is said to have turned down numerous offers of professorial chairs, preferring to keep his desk free of administrative papers, although a few years ago he served as a Proctor, a university post more or less equivalent to a police inspector, and got to know the antiquated workings of the university intimately.

"Have you seen the statute book?" he asks. It is a kind of rule book for Oxford academia. "It's seven hundred pages long. Have you any idea how complicated the university is? How many committees and boards and councils there are? I doubt anyone really knows. Certainly no one knows even a quarter of the statutes."

He tells me an anecdote of an undergraduate who demanded a bottle of red wine in the middle of his final exams. Somewhere lost in the pages of the statute book he had discovered a long-forgotten rule stating that during examination, a student had the right to a flagon of claret. After much consultation of the book, the examiner refused the demand on the grounds that the examinee was not wearing a saber. According to another ancient statute, he was therefore not properly attired.

Just then, Professor Y arrives, another famous Oxford man, notorious for his incisive writings and for the lavish, star-studded parties he used to throw in his North Oxford home. Andy Warhol, Mick Jagger, Sir Georg Solti—all kinds of unlikely people are said to have attended his bashes.

"Of course Oxford is still important," he declares, pitching into the talk about the current state of the university. "Name the last prime minister who wasn't an Oxford man."

"Or woman," Professor X interjects.

"Half the bloody government went to Oxford. And always has," Professor Y continues. "This is the early stamping ground of the establishment. Bankers, publishers, politicians, media types—they all went to Oxford. And that's part of the town-gown rivalry, I suspect. I mean, if you'd just been laid off at Cowley, how would you feel about the Bullingdon?" He means the Bullingdon Club, an elite student dining society immortalized in *Brideshead Revisited* and for which a private income is a mandatory prerequisite for membership.

"But it is changing," he insists, a little querulously. "Now it counts against you if you went to private school. But if you go back far enough, to medieval Oxford, it was probably the other way around. The town didn't like the gown because the students were the oiks. They were the sons of poor artisans and the like, who went to Oxford to escape menial work."

A gust of wind outside suddenly blows a smattering of raindrops against the windowpane, and the barman comes around to throw more coal on the fire.

Oxford began, presumably, as a place where oxen forded the River Thames. In the tenth century it grew into an ecclesiastical center. Throughout the Middle Ages, learning and religion went hand in hand. (As late as 1871, undergraduates still had to study theology and take Christian vows, and dons had to be celibate.) By the twelfth century, Oxford had become a center for learning. Young men— second sons who would inherit nothing, or bright children of artisans and tradesmen—came to study with the learned men of the day.

They lodged in "halls," which were effectively inns for long-term boarders, where they would pass rowdy, beery nights (one of these, St. Edmund Hall, founded about 1220, still survives), but it wasn't until about 1250 that the first three real colleges were founded. By then, Oxford was already a thriving guild town. It had all kinds of tradesmen and artisans, and even though the university inevitably brought more trade—today there are still stores specializing in gownmaking and thesis-binding—the yeomen and aldermen of Oxford resented the bands of boisterous youths in their prosperous little city.

Moreover, the university had privileges and powers that set it apart from the town. It had its own court (the Chancellor's Court) and its own police force (the Bulldogs, supervised by the Proctors), and it even had the right to carry out its own hangings—in theory, right up until capital punishment was abolished in Britain. There were town churches and gown churches, town pubs and student drinking halls—even as late as the sixties, one of the chief tasks of the Bulldogs was to patrol the city's pubs, since undergraduates were still not allowed in them. Fights would break out in the streets between the youths of either side, the most famous and lethal of which was the 1355 massacre of Saint Scholastica's Day, in which sixty-three students were killed.

During the Civil War of the 1640s, the university served as the headquarters of the Royalist cause, while the town supported Cromwell and the Parliamentarians. In the nineteenth century Oscar Wilde and Max Beerbohm changed its image, and the university became the playground of the *Jeunesse Dorée* and, later, of Evelyn Waugh's Bright Young Things. The distinction between the two sides of the city could not have been more pronounced.

Even today, when the university has democratized its admissions policy and thoroughly de-aristocratized itself, you can still see young men in black tie being chased along Cornmarket by angry louts in boots and jeans late at night.

But the same alloy that creates the tensions of Oxford also engenders its charms. The covered market in the middle of town is an eighteenth-century structure with a glass roof, like a great conservatory, and paved avenues of small shops—florists and tea shops and luggage-traders, and a saddler, a secondhand-record dealer, a cheese shop selling ten kinds of goat cheese, along with hundreds of others.

Fellers the butcher has twelve venison carcasses hanging in his window.

"Can you really sell so much venison?" I ask, amazed.

"I go through two hundred carcasses a year," he tells me, red-faced under his straw hat, his blue apron bulging.

"Who buys them?"

"Colleges, for their feasts. I sell fifty-odd thousand brace of pheasant too. Not to mention the rabbits. That lot there . . . ," he waves at a heap of bloody gray fur, "I shot 'em all yesterday, Sunday. Thirty rabbits. They'll be gone by Wednesday."

A butcher who goes out shooting in the woods around town, a city that buys from him alone a hundred thousand pheasant each year—I have forgotten just how traditional Oxford is. It's still like a medieval city, where the countryside interpenetrates the urban scene. You half-expect to see flocks of sheep being driven down the High Street.

When you wander along Broad Street—with Balliol on your left, Christopher Wren's Sheldonian Theatre up ahead, with its busts of Roman emperors, two somewhat shabby rows of eighteenth-century shops facing the classical facades, and the street wide and spacious and cheerful—you can still easily imagine it cobbled. When you make your way along it on a sunny morning, it is the mix of commerce and academic grandeur that creates its bustling charm.

Even in Queen's and New College lanes, where among all the late medieval stone you feel you could be in Venice or Padua, or in the great quadrangle of Tom Quad in Christ Church, with its raised pavements the length of small boulevards, the whole place seeming like the setting for an Italian comedy by Shakespeare, like some grand city of the Cinquecento—for above all else Oxford is a Renaissance town—even here you always know that just beyond the smooth stone walls wait the streets of the town. You know that the ivory tower has been erected in the middle of all the bustle, and therefore hardly seems an ivory tower at all.

Nor can the buildings ever become museum pieces: They are too crowded by the rest of town life, too integrated into the network of labyrinthine alleys and lanes (Oxford is so intricate, so Escher-like, that only the college porters know precisely where the boundaries of their individual domains lie). Merton, for example, has the oldest quad in Oxford. Its library was constructed in the 1370s and houses, among other relics, an astrolabe of the kind upon which Chaucer based his famous treatise: Its ancient oak boards may creak, but it still contains current books and periodicals, and researchers still use it.

Oxford is home to the offices of all kinds of strange societies, such as the Royal Microscopical Society and the British Elastic Rope Sports Society. Only in Oxford could you find a subsidized housing project known as the Aristotle Lane Industrial Estate. And where else a dodo's remains, Pocahontas's father's mantle, and the very lantern with which Guy Fawkes planned to ignite his gunpowder and blow up the Houses of Parliament? Or a collection of shrunken heads from around the world that is second to none? Or, for that matter, a house where John Wesley preached, before launching a major new sect, the Methodists, into the world? Not forgetting the *Bay Psalm Book*, the first English book published in America, in 1640, nor the room in Balliol College where coffee was first drunk in England, by a student from Crete in 1637.

Alice in Wonderland is perhaps the quintessential Oxford work. For it seems to embody all the bizarre conjunctions of the city, its dreaminess and crazy adherence to old traditions and its architectural intricacies and surprises. You can hardly turn a corner in Oxford without being confronted by a doorway, and no sooner do you pass through it, into some yard or loggia, than another door appears, leading into a little garden overgrown with buddleia, from which a footbridge takes you over a stream into a private Fellows' Garden full of mazes of hedges and exotic borders. It is easy to imagine the mathematician Charles Lutwidge Dodgson, better known as Lewis Carroll, wandering the city's alleys and gardens, among all its contradictions and eccentric appositions, his mind full of mathematical formulas and dreamy plans for the future, and giving birth to his opiate masterpiece.

It is a rainy Thursday morning, a typical January day in Oxford. The clouds have been low for two days now, and a mist hangs in the air, but so faint you know it is there only because you can't see the hospital on Headington Hill. The Cowley Road in east Oxford has never looked drabber: the discount supermarket; the truck outside the pub delivering kegs of beer; the straggling shoppers with umbrellas and scarves tied tightly over their heads; and the giant old brick theater of the Star Bingo & Social Club all closed up.

This is the other side of Oxford. The drabness, the flatness, the sense of dismal, ever-perpetuating sameness. Here in east Oxford you remember why you left the city, if you grew up in it, and why you left England, if in fact you have. Nowhere in the world can match England for plain old dismalness. Bosnia may have its atrocities,

India its calamities, and Africa its tragedies, but only England knows how to be thoroughly depressing, how to be the spiritual homeland of Philip Larkin and Lucien Freud. Here you understand why the British moan endlessly (which we still do) about Britain.

Farther out, at the end of the Iffley Road, you can find the little Norman church of Iffley standing on a rise above the River Thames. Its carved doorway is guarded by rank upon rank of beaked birds' heads. They are superfluous now, since the vicar keeps the door locked. A little note kindly explains that the incidence of theft from churches makes it necessary. And the church remains an entirely unchanged piece of Norman architecture, built in the 1170s.

But at the end of the Cowley Road, on the other hand, you reach the vast industrial city that goes no longer by the name Morris Motors but by Rover. You feel you are in a brave new industrial world here. One truck confidently promises FLAT ROOFS FOR THE 21ST CENTURY on its side. Everywhere there are giant chimneys, stained, with smoke trailing up into the cloud cover.

Nearby, a meadow has been flattened into a great rectangle of red mud, soggy now in the rain and trundled over by yellow bulldozers and trucks, all busy laying the foundations of a new piece in the jigsaw of modern commerce. Men in hard hats walk about with surveying sticks and clipboards, tramping through the drizzle. Here Oxford is still growing: The mud sticking to the soles of the surveyors' boots is the very clay of the future, which they are molding.

And in the end it is a relief. Without its modern life, Oxford would be cloying, too rich with its own past—all yolk and no white. Even though it expands into a concrete and steel future on one side, in the center it remains its own unparalleled blend of the medieval and the Victorian, the rural and the urban, the grand and the intimate. But it is good to be able to emerge from the time capsule and come up for the air of today. Soon it only makes you want to go down again anyway.

1996

Corroding in the Keys

by

JONATHAN RABAN

 The Dutch engineer had been living on Key Largo for a month, and he was sweating badly in the steam-bath heat, his face a bunched fist as he struggled to repair the faulty depth finder on our rented boat.

"Corrosion!" he said, making it sound like lust or avarice, a celebrated deadly sin. He exposed the remains of a vital electrical connection. The wires were flaky white with mold. "See? Dust on my fingers! That's the trouble with this climate. *Everything*—every *damn* thing—corrodes here."

I knew what he meant. I had come to the Keys to corrode a little myself. I liked the rusty morals of this scapegrace archipelago, its air of having seceded from the rest of the United States on the conscientious grounds that none of its inhabitants can bring themselves to believe in the Protestant ethic. Five years before, I'd gone into temporary hiding in a run-down trailer park on Key Largo and had been powerfully impressed by the genial loucheness of the place: its bars so dark that you couldn't identify the face of the man on the next stool; its clandestine economy, for which the New York street price of a line of coke was the

Keys' own Dow industrial average; its ruffian wildlife of turkey vultures, rattlesnakes, and barracuda.

This time I had come with my wife, Caroline, and like most people who seek out the Keys, we were on the lam, evading the hard labor of an English Christmas. The idea was simply to go with the wind, drifting from island to island on a thirty-two-foot sloop, to live grubbily in cutoff jeans and gimme caps, to catch lunch over the stern, to see the roseate spoonbills, and to fall in with as many disreputable characters as we could find.

You need a boat to see the Keys. Motorists, tailgating down U.S. 1 past the condo blocks and Burger Kings, never properly get the hang of the place. It is the ospreys, the fishermen, the delivery skippers on the dope passage from the Bahamas, who comprehend the Keys as they really are—an impossibly intricate tessellation of land and water, far wilder and more beautiful than you could ever guess from the highway, and full of secrets, some of them unprintable.

Our boat was snug and simple. A mile and a half offshore, it was sailing itself sweetly down the Hawk Channel. The northeast wind was brisk enough to keep it slicing through the waves on the foresail alone. I tied a length of elastic cord around the spokes of the wheel and looped it around the compass binnacle; it worked as a serviceable autopilot and left us free to lounge and stare like a pair of lazy passengers.

We were afloat on the Atlantic, but the Keys are sheltered by a barrier reef of coral that stops the ocean swell and turns the sea into a milky-green lagoon. Despite the stiffish breeze, the waves broke harmlessly like spitting kittens, and the boat's motion was just a gentle lollop as it seated itself comfortably among these miniature breakers. We overtook a fleet of Portuguese man-of-wars running before the wind under their gelatinous, electric-blue sails and trawling for fish with sheaves of poisonous tentacles. A young dolphin broke the surface beside us and went squirming under our bow, then gave us up as too slow to be worth playing with.

Seen from the sea, the Keys lay as low on the water as rafts of floating weed. No motels, condos, shopping malls—the mangroves had swallowed them whole and made the Keys miraculously green again. The only giveaway signs of civilization were the high bridges spanning the islands, with cars crawling across them in the sun like bugs with shiny wings.

I headed the boat for the narrow gap between Windley and Plantation Keys, and suddenly the mangroves revealed what they'd been hiding, as strange things began to emerge piecemeal from the undergrowth—patches of cinder block, glass, concrete, and aluminum that slowly grew until the green was almost gone. As the Snake Creek drawbridge tilted politely skyward to let us through, we sailed clean out of an idyll and into what passes, in these parts, for the real world.

Somewhere out of sight, a public address system was delivering a choral rendition of "Jingle Bells" at full blast. It's hard enough to match the joy of riding in a one-horse open sleigh with a temperature of eighty-five degrees and a school of angelfish under one's keel; and harder still when, at the same time, you're navigating a tricky course among Swiss chalets, Mexican adobe ranches, Lincoln log cabins, Moorish temples, Chinese willow-pattern pagodas, Doric-colonnaded villas, New England clapboard cottages, and palm thatch pavilions that are a subtle mix of Tudor and Hawaiian. Our untended boat slewed on the running tide, its loose sail thunderclapping in the wind. Drifting slowly backward, we narrowly avoided a collision with a Kentish wooden oast house on concrete stilts.

Under way again, I took a second look at this eccentric village and saw that at heart it was as rigidly conventional as a respectable Boston suburb. An enterprising developer had gouged a grid of canals out of the mangrove swamp, and each custom-built dream house had been constructed around the same organizing principle—same mosquito-screened sun deck, same picture window, same private dock, same white, twin-screw cruiser with a dizzying tarpon bridge. Clad in palmetto, hibiscus, and bougainvillea, with sprinklers playing on freshly seeded lawns, the houses wore a suburbanly anxious look, as if each one were gazing at its neighbor and fearing that next door might be getting a fraction more fun, more fantasy, for its money.

Then, as quickly as they'd opened, the mangroves charitably closed around the houses like a curtain. Even at a sedate speed of about four knots, transitions on the Keys happen at a breakneck pace. Minutes before, we'd been on the Atlantic; now we were in Florida Bay, part of the Gulf of Mexico. We'd been in town, and now we were deep in a wilderness of floppy yellow butterflies, pelicans falling out of trees, egrets stalking prettily on wire legs, and narrow, dark barracuda torpedoing away from the encroaching shadow of the boat.

This sea was very different from the one we'd just left. It was disconcertingly shallow. We needed four feet of water to stay afloat, but the seafloor of what looked like coral silt seemed only inches deep. It was like sailing in a tropical aquarium of the kind that dentists keep in their waiting rooms to soothe their patients' nerves. It didn't soothe mine. More than a mile out in the posted channel, the depth sounder was still flickering between 4.6 and 5.8 feet, and I kept on waiting for the crash as our keel ground into an uncharted coral head. It failed to come, though I watched the stone crabs burying themselves hurriedly in the silt as we slipped past.

As far as one could see, mangroves were busy adding more keys to the archipelago. The sea was riddled with shoals where the rising mud showed purple, like a bruise, and wherever a shoal touched the surface of the water, a mangrove had seized on it. First an arch of root, then a sprig of green—and a fresh island was started. The National Oceanic and Atmospheric Administration charts couldn't keep up with this polyphylogenitive urge of the mangrove. There were dozens of small keys as yet undiscovered by the surveyors—tangled islets of virgin land, still waiting for names. I christened a few of them as we sailed past: Osprey Key, Cormorant Key, Michelob Key—someone ought to honor the mangrove. As fast as the developers and real estate agents work down the main spine of the Florida Keys, so the mangroves are making up for their depredations by building more wild islands far out of reach of the highway and the men who think that every scrap of unspoiled green would be enhanced by a nice big condominium.

There were few other boats about. Far inshore, a pair of commercial crab and lobster fishermen were winching up their traps. The wind had dropped to a warm dog's breath, and we ghosted along in a rapt silence, broken only by the riffle of the pages of Roger Tory Peterson's *Eastern Birds*, as we tried to resolve the spoonbill-flamingo problem. Whatever it was, the handsome bird in question was certainly pink. Ahead of the boat, a submerging turtle left a momentary hole in the water the size of a large dinner gong.

It was dusk when we closed with the shore again, to anchor in Lime Tree Bay and row the dinghy back into the United States. On the highway, things were hopping: Everyone was switching on Christmas lights, and giant illuminated Santas were lurking behind the palm trees, their beards and nightcaps flashing. No one here seemed to have heard of zoning regulations: It was an improvised, ad hoc, happy sprawl of houses living cheek by jowl with the bar, the restaurant, the gas station, the Mr. Grocer, the Bait 'n Tackle shop, the RV park. Everything looked tinker-built, in the careless, hammer-and-nails Keys vernacular style of architecture, in which "pecky cypress," a wood consisting more of holes than grain, plays a central part. With a pile of pecky cypress, you can knock together a shop or a bar-restaurant in a couple of minutes. It will last until tomorrow, or the day after, or until the next hurricane, which is as far ahead as anyone on the Keys can bear to think. These are good-time buildings, and they don't give a damn.

In a restaurant in Lime Tree Bay, a ginger-bearded hulk was demolishing a small mountain of french fries while pursuing a conversation with a friend at the bar.

"You got new people moved in where you are, I hear. They *white*? They *Americans*?"

"Yeh. I ain't seen much of 'em, though. But they're *white* enough."

"Me, I had to move out. *Cubans*. I had Cuban kids wandering in my front yard, Cuban dogs shitting in my backyard. . . . I got *sick*."

We rowed back to the boat. Even on the darkened water, I could hear the voice of the complaining hulk—gravelly, bullying, indignant. Escaping reality can be hard work.

At dawn the next morning, I suddenly jerked awake. I identified the noises that had woken me: surf on a nearby beach and crickets fiddling in the brush. During the night, the wind must have changed and the boat dragged its anchor. I was half out of my bunk when I listened again and heard the noises differently. The crashing surf was only the early traffic on U.S. 1; the crickets were the humming power lines that march on high pylons down to Key West. It was a mistake that anyone could have made: On the Keys, nature and culture get hopelessly mixed up.

The guidebooks make far too much of the "Conchs"—the born-and-raised natives of the Keys. You might as well go in search of Golden Orioles as track down Conchs in Monroe County. For the modern Keys are a creation of the North. It's in the hardworking, cold-winter states like Ohio, Michigan, and New Jersey that the essential character of the Keys has been forged—as a northern dream of sunshine, easy living, easy money. So the founding fathers of the place came streaming over the bridge at Jewfish Creek, where Key Largo is lightly attached to the Florida mainland, in pursuit of a new kind of manifest destiny. Some merely wanted to put their feet up, to emulate the peaceful manatees and dolphins. Some saw a fruitful future in trapping tourists, peddling real estate, or loading cigarette boats with cargoes of white powder, taking their cue from the vultures and sharks. What they shared was a common faith in the teaching of Matthew 6:28—Like lilies of the field, they saw no special reason either to toil or spin.

The closest Keys equivalent to the Puritan township of New England is the trailer park, where the Winnebagos lie hull to hull on rented plots, with shingles hanging over their doors saying THE SCHMIDTS—BILL AND VERA, and good old boys putter around the dock and grumble about the impeccable weather.

We tied up at the Jolly Roger Travel Park on Grassy Key, where a man of about my own age, but in far better physical shape, took our lines. We talked for a few minutes, and I asked him what he did. "Do?"—he looked puzzled; then his face cleared. "Oh, I ain't *worked* since 1969," he said with pride.

A barefoot boy of eleven or twelve was fishing from the end of the dock. He put his rod down to come over and inspect the boat. He was from Manchester, New Hampshire, he said, and he was here with his mother. I thought that, like me, he was on a Christmas vacation. "When did you come down here?"

"Seven years ago," the boy said.

The trailer parks are friendly, improvised, close-knit communities. On the Keys, people have time for each other. They borrow each other's bicycles to get to the store, and each other's boats to go out fishing. At the Jolly Roger I saw the handicapped and the retarded being gentled along by their neighbors with a civility and concern long gone from the average American or European small town. It was thought unneighborly to lock your car, your front door, or your boat. The Christmas lights and strings of tinsel were looped from trailer to trailer in a shared celebration. For as long as we were docked, we had neighbors too: They dropped in to see how we were, drove us out to the local restaurant and the supermarket, and after we'd left, called us on marine radio to ask where we were sailing and whether we were okay. They were refugees from northern cities, and in the trailer park they had managed to reconstruct the self-contained, intimate village life that is now usually confined to nostalgic movies and period novels. It was a man in his seventies who, late in the afternoon, stared at the reddening sea and told me: "I'm dying here. I made up my mind. I ain't moving from where I am. I'm dying here."

I was sad to see the mangroves close in over the Jolly Roger. For the next few miles I was fantasizing about my own Winnebago, its handkerchief-size garden of bright flowers, its carpentered porch with a rocking chair facing the Gulf, its inviting shingle—THE RABANS. . . . But no. I concentrated on steering clear of the crab and lobster traps that dotted the water ahead. Their marker buoys looked like nodding dolls' heads, and there were hundreds—even thousands—of them, many spaced barely a boat's width apart.

There are supposed to be millions of traps set between Key Largo and Key West, and I reckon that I saw at least a million and a half myself.

By the lazy standards of the Keys, trapping crustaceans counts as hard labor. But the sea is warm and calm, and the pickings are easy by comparison with the grim fishing grounds of Maine or Long Island. On the Keys, two men in a boat will tend about two thousand traps, lifting maybe three hundred traps in a working day. Stone crab claws fetch five dollars a pound, lobster tails about twice that price. On an average day, each boat will come in with about a hundred pounds of stone crab claws—a comfortable living, as well as a good front for other, even more profitable activities.

The long city shore of Marathon sped past us like a cruise ship on the beam. The wind was getting up. With a cold front lying from Tallahassee down to the Yucatán, we were in for a "norther"—a modest gale that rakes the Keys in winter and turns the sea soapsuds white. On one sail, we scudded ahead of the wind, with our lines as rigid as iron bars and the water hissing under the hull of the boat. The chart, weighed down with binoculars, a winch handle, and a three-pound sounding lead, was trying to take wing from the cockpit floor. We nipped under the central span of the Seven Mile Bridge, went briefly out into the tame Atlantic, and headed back northeastward to the shelter of Hog Key on the ocean side of Marathon. I had never sailed quite so fast with so little fright: Within the comfortingly safe ambit of coral reefs and mangrove islands it was easy to play the windswept hero, and—just ten minutes before the end of happy hour at Bacchus by the Sea—we entered Marathon like swaggering Athenians. Caroline threw a line from the bow; the bartender caught it, in a nice illustration of the special relationship that exists on the Keys between the land and the water. Tying a round turn and two half-hitches around a post, I ordered up a vodka martini and dislodged a brown pelican. It fell into the sea like a bundle of old clothes.

Robert Dustal had bought his restaurant and "tiki bar" in May; now, in the wake of the October crash, he was anxiously waiting for the "season." "Look at my sunset!" he said. It was a sunset worth looking at, too: as bloodily colorful as a major intestinal operation. "In the summer, it goes down on the Gulf side, but in the winter it plops down right there. *My* side. You come back next week, there'll be folks standing in line to see my sunset." But there were no folks as yet. At the tiki bar, two professional fishermen and a traveling salesman were drinking beer, and drinking very slowly.

Dustal was from New Jersey, a lean, brown, soft-spoken man, with suggestions of the status he'd once enjoyed as a pitcher for the Detroit Tigers. He'd drifted down the Keys, managed Key West's ailing baseball team for a while, and settled in Marathon. "Now . . . well, take a look at me. I'm in paradise!"

He was nursing Bacchus by the Sea much as he must have managed his team. There were no profits yet, but he was building up a clientele of locals. Sweat-suited, spry, and smiling, he introduced everyone to everyone and ran his tiki bar as a private party to which we'd all had the luck to be invited.

Dustal pointed out the "drug boat" moored alongside ours; a beautiful forty-foot wooden ketch. It had been impounded by the Coast Guard and sold off at auction up in Jacksonville, where its new owner had paid $7,500 for it—a fraction of what I guessed it must be worth. My interest in the ketch attracted the attention of a gimme-capped and parka'd "liveaboard," who said I could see *his* drug boat, too. His boat, though, had made a *successful* run, landing seven hundred pounds of cocaine somewhere in the mangrove fringes of Marathon. After that, it had become valueless to its owners, who had sold it for a nominal $5,000 to my parka'd friend. "Full electronics, solar panels—*everything*!" The only snag in the deal was that he'd had to rip out the secret compartments to make the boat legal. It had a false waterline, false cabin floor, false bulkheads, false fuel and water tanks. "It was damn hard *work*," he said, pronouncing the Keys' least favorite word. We couldn't visit the boat yet because he was waiting for his girlfriend to return from her job in the town; then we'd all go over in the dinghy, he promised.

"So *she* works," I said. "I've seen a lot of women around here working. Not many men, though."

"You got it. We have a club down here. The KYWW Club—you know about that? Keep Your Woman Working."

The drug trade distorts the prices of boats, just as it distorts the price of labor in the Keys. A deckhand on a run from the Bahamas, whose job it is to help hide the cargo, tend the ropes, and watch the compass, earns, I am reliably told, $10,000 for the forty-eight-hour trip. At $208 an hour (with several of them spent asleep), it makes waiting on tables look a shade dull. Though Fat Albert, a blimp loaded with surveillance devices, keeps a baleful watch over the Keys, most drug boats still get through. One common cause of drug arrests is not Fat Albert's vigilance but rewarded tip-offs to the Drug Enforcement Administration by the coke suppliers. Around Marathon, where the DEA is known as "Bush's Racket," this is thought unsporting. "What kind of a government is it that puts money in the pockets of Cuban *drug* barons?" complained one injured bum.

Corrosion. It spreads in complicated ways down on the Keys. A few yards up the highway from Bacchus, I looked in on a vast and empty restaurant-bar called the South Seas Lounge, whose bartender was fresh from a suburban country club in Indiana. She was precise about figures. She was "almost twenty-nine-and-a-half years old" and had been living in Marathon for "just three-and-a-half weeks." She couldn't contain the current big excitement in her life: Next Saturday she was off on a "*gambling* cruise" from Key West to Miami. I asked her what she was going to play. Blackjack? Craps? Roulette? "I don't know. All of them, I guess. I mean, they don't *have* nothing like that in Muncie, Indiana," and she named her hometown with all the scorn that the truly corroded have for the cold and proper life they've left behind them.

We were corroding nicely. With the norther still blowing, we'd set off to sail to Key West, but the boat had heeled over on its beam with the force of the wind, and the short, steep seas were difficult to ride. I listed all the things I couldn't face in Key West—historic markers, "Conch houses," gift shops, Hemingwayiana—and turned the boat around to go back to Bacchus. Mrs. Dustal helped us dock. "So you got the Keys disease already?" she asked.

From then on, I stopped ruling long straight courses on the chart, with legends on them like "20.5 miles at 252 degrees." Instead, we began to imitate the flight of the turkey vulture, circling and perching, circling and perching, without plan or destination. Days later, floating lightly along the Everglades after a long and voluble night at Alabama Jack's, I thought that my mind, like the mind of the man at Jolly Roger Travel Park, was almost made up to die here, too. I know a gap in the mangroves where . . . I know a man who . . . The rust was eating into my head. With what little resolution was still left, I got out the ruler and plotted a course that would eventually lead back to the cold, northern city where I'm afraid I belong.

We work hard here. Our afternoons are dark. My chief distraction lately has been a poorly printed color magazine called *The Real Estate Book of the Florida Keys*. I think the corrosion is malignant, for I have spent the past half hour staring at an indecipherable photo involving palm trees and pink cinder block and reading the caption as if it were poetry:

'TROPICAL PARADISE'—2 Br, 1.5 Ba. 60' concrete dock on clean wide canal. Strg shed, scrnd Fla rm. Very well kept mobile w/unusual trees and flowers. $25,000 dn long-term mort. $99,000 . . .

1989

Isn't It Romantic

by

CRISTINA NEHRING

 The hall is sumptuous, the audience in stitches. The actor on the stage—octogenarian Michel Bouquet—is a national celebrity. Yet Molière's *Imaginary Invalid* is absurdly dated.

I shift restlessly in my red-velvet loge at Paris's Théâtre de la Porte Saint-Martin and gaze at my neighbors—two svelte young lesbians with a preschool-age boy between them, and a gorgeously clad fifty-something lady with a gold-and-silver coiled-serpent necklace descending suggestively into her bodice. "You can curl and uncurl it," she tells me during intermission. "Here, try!" She places my hand on her bare bosom.

What could these all-too-contemporary persons find in this story of a seventeenth-century hypochondriac in a pointy white nightcap who hires doctor after doctor to administer oversized enemas? They roar with laughter. They stand up and demand another round of bows from Monsieur Bouquet. And they whisper to me that they will return the following weekend. (The play's run has been extended several times.) Moreover, this is not the only work of Molière's on show in

Paris. Flipping through the city's culture calender, *Pariscope*, I see that there are no fewer than seventeen Molière productions being performed this day, including a second and third *Imaginary Invalid*.

"What's the story?" I ask a French friend over a plate of shaved foie gras drizzled with caramel after the show. It's 1 A.M. and my favorite local restaurant is jammed. "The Paris art scene is tame!" he tells me, looking up and down the candlelit tables at Comptoir de la Gastronomie. "Parisians are too busy dining and drinking and trying to seduce each other to pay serious attention to it."

A cliché, but a cliché with a scrap of truth to it. The French I see around me are not home funneling their vital energy into some artistic pursuit. Much as they may hope that their nation excels at such endeavors, what they reserve their real attention, ingenuity, and passion for is not the art of writing or composing, painting or philosophizing, but—quite simply—the art of living.

You need only pick up a French newspaper to discover that, while other papers in the West offer book reviews, the French offer book raves. Parisian reviewers have mistaken promotion for reflection, commerce for analysis, Serge Halimi, editor of the political journal *Le Monde Diplomatique*, tells me as we wander down a bustling boulevard near his home. The art of criticism is defunct. So, too, is the art of philosophy. Where once the Left Bank intelligentsia rallied around ugly little Jean-Paul Sartre, with his big and disturbing ideas, today it idolizes the tousle-headed millionaire Bernard-Henri Lévy—beautiful to look at but distinctly vapid and unchallenging: a cheerleader for power in all its motley manifestations.

Where has all the French genius gone? Into café life, I decide, as I peer over my paper at the swiftly maneuvering tuxedoed waiters at Le Buci, near my hotel in St-Germain-des-Prés. It has gone into conversation and seduction, into bistro witticisms and strenuous vacationing. It has gone into the French people's zealous pursuit of "quality of life," their almost unseemly *savoir-vivre*.

Just beyond the windows of Le Buci are cratefuls of delicate almond pastries being sold on the street—pastries such as those of us raised in proximity to Dunkin' Donuts cannot imagine unless they are in front of our eyes. If purchased, they will be individually wrapped in a small pyramid-shaped parcel—a bit like the Imaginary Invalid's nightcap—and bound with a brightly colored ribbon fastened into a loop for dangling from one's wrist. Next to the pastry crates is a butcher selling—I counted—twenty-three different products made from duck: *magret de canard, rillettes de canard, pâté de canard, foie gras de canard, pâté de foie gras de canard.* A few steps farther along is a wine salesman pouring samples of dry whites and mellow reds, as his patrons swirl the sparkling fluids while sparkling at one another with smiles of recognition and attraction.

And this daily celebration is not just in St-Germain, admittedly one of the posher parts of town. It is at least as conspicuous in my own borderline-gritty neighborhood between the Place de la République and the Marais, and in the still grittier immigrant neighborhood of Belleville, home to the Tunisian director who made the award-winning *Secret of the Grain*, a film about—what else?—food. It has taken over every one of Paris's arrondissements—from the Louvre on the Right Bank to the Observatoire on the Left.

I know this because I decided, this past winter, to become a tourist in the city where I've lived for several years. I moved out of my tiny apartment in the outer Marais and into a series of hotels in neighborhoods with which I'm much less familiar—the better to dine in their restaurants, visit their museums, attend their theaters, poke a nose into their churches and synagogues, and observe their inhabitants. The mayor of Paris, Bertrand Delanoë, did something of this sort before assuming office. He moved—or so he told his fellow Parisians—into every one of the city's twenty arrondissements in succession. He shopped in their bakeries, talked to their artists and housewives and chefs, and committed to memory their particular savor. If it was good enough for the mayor of Paris, it was good enough for me.

Unlike the mayor of Paris, whose charm, imagination, and wit I like to think I share, I have a seven-month-old daughter—and no regular sitter. So where I go, she goes. Not that I'm complaining. I tend to have a better time when Eurydice is propped up at my side, gazing curiously into the eyes of whatever waiter or actor or restaurateur is in the room with us. She has been nicknamed "Dice" for this reason: Prematurely corrupt, she's a player, a bar hopper, an inveterate flirt. I decide early on that I will use her as a barometer of French hospitality.

Once upon a time, a woman with an infant would have been routinely rejected in the temples of Parisian nightlife. Staff would have thought: big bother, small tip. The French are infamous, as everyone knows, for their intolerance of children. Unfairly so. "Look at that adorable girl!" exclaimed the chef at Les Terrines de Gérard Vié. "Do you have milk for her? May I warm it?" I relinquish the bottle camouflaged in my backpack and turn my attention to the half-dozen terrines perfected in this charismatic—and exceptionally carnivorous—restaurant on the rue du Cherche-Midi.

Walking here from my hotel on this night was unusually sensual. The rue du Cherche-Midi cuts straight through the heart of St-Germain—beginning a stone's throw from Paris's second-oldest church, the Église de St-Germain-des-Prés. As we passed, organ music seeped out of its enormous double doors, and Eurydice and I slipped in for a spell of sonorous ecclesiastical music and an intoxicating amount of incense. The Église de St-Germain has a young and plainspoken new priest who draws unusual crowds of revelers in their twenties and thirties. Its painted oak pillars and oddly woody interior bring to mind an Alpine lodge as much as they do a church; it is easily the coziest religious structure in town. Outside its doors are storefronts still cozier, their inhabitants selling cuckoo clocks and colorful sweaters.

We wound our way past the Café de Flore, where Sartre and Simone de Beauvoir did much of their best writing—each stationed at one end of the second floor and ignoring the other, one of many examples of innovative French love affairs. From there we passed onto the stately rue de Rennes, overhung tonight with millions of twinkling blue lights in the form of galactic spheres. I remembered the slogan of a recent exhibition on the death of God at the Centre Pompidou, Paris's premier museum of modern art. "Eat the Sky," read the posters. "Eat the Sky," said the T-shirts. It struck me at the time that this captured handily the worldview of the Parisians I knew: God is dead; cuisine is king! Heaven's passed onto the dinner plate.

On this evening, at least, the firmament indeed looked good enough to eat. I wished for a knife and fork to plunge into the cool candy planets, the vast blueberry orbs. Everything in Paris seems to glow blue this season. The Eiffel Tower, too, shines sapphire after dark—when it does not glitter, as it does once an hour, a starry white.

The quotidian beauty of Paris is the reason I resolved to live here years ago. I came for a love affair with a Frenchman, but I stayed for the geography of inspiration. It struck me that a city can offer little better than aesthetic arrest every time you traverse it. Whatever the state of French politics, for a person like me—a writer, a romantic, a loner—beauty has no equal and no price. And between the cobbled stone underfoot and the flickering light show above, the spired churches and the lanterned stone bridges, the jewel box–like boutiques and the wonderful fish and fowl and meat terrines awaiting us for dinner, beauty was all too much in evidence.

The people of Paris are part of its beauty. My nearest neighbor at Les Terrines de Gérard Vié is a knockout: black-haired, porcelain-faced, as thin and curvy as a reed in the wind. I'd have thought her a fashion model. She laughs: No, she's a mother—of three. Where are they, I ask, the three? Day care, she says. At 8 P.M.? Sure, many day cares remain open till nine or nine-thirty; hers is right next door. Paris is jam-packed with day care centers. State-supported and inexpensive, they are available to many.

It occurs to me that this is part of the reason French women enjoy the reputation they do—for sexiness, coolness, confidence. It's not just a matter of personal temperament but of public policy, the fruit not only of individual style but of country and culture.

"A toast for the baby girl!" exclaims a man at the table opposite. "What would you like to drink?"

"A kir?" I offer, thinking it a modest suggestion—made as it is with crème de cassis and a simple sauvignon blanc.

"But it has to be with Champagne," he hollers—and presently the waiter delivers a bubbly glass of pink.

In America, I think, I would have been ignored, sitting as I am with an infant. At any moment, after all, I might suddenly have spit-up on my shoulder. "But even President Sarkozy picked a woman with a child for his new bride!" says the beauty next to me, when I offer this remark to her. "It's true," I say. "If he were a public figure in the States and the sort of man people claim he is—vain, a show-off—he'd have picked a twenty-year-old trophy girl. As it is, he chose a fortysomething with an eight-year-old boy in tow."

"And the woman he really wanted," my neighbor says snidely, "has three kids—two of them in their twenties!"

I hope for Sarkozy's sake that he no longer pines for Cécilia, the ex-wife who left him. That having been said, there's not a Frenchman around who blinked at the fact that the femme fatale of France's most powerful citizen is the mother of two adults.

Women age better in France, and they are better admired as they age. One worries about being objectified by pornography, but the danger of being objectified by maternity is far greater, it seems to me. Hidden behind Hummer-size baby carriages and camouflaged in color-less sweat suits, mothers can become shadow people. Americans go for books like Amy Richards's *Opting In: Having a Child Without Losing Yourself.* The French have such books internalized.

"What a lucky man!" exclaims the waiter, as the mother at my side relishes the last of her cheese platter and reclines into the arms of the man I assume is her husband. "He in no way deserves you."

I flinch in spite of myself. "Of course I don't," rejoins the man. "No one here does. That's why she's settled for me"—he beams at his wife—"at least for tonight, *n'est-ce pas?*"

"For tonight," she says coyly. The two reach for coats and scarves, plant a hasty kiss on Eurydice's nose and my cheek, and dash like inter-lopers into the night.

Were they illicit lovers after all? I wonder. "That was Madame *et* Monsieur Dauteville," says the waiter, as though reading my mind. "My son plays with their kids every Saturday."

Climbing up the thick-carpeted red stairs later that evening to my high-ceilinged room at the Hôtel Relais Christine, I muse about the magic of all this sexual ambiguity. Waiters routinely make gallant remarks to taken women—thus reminding their partners of their perpetual appeal to rival suitors. What would be counted an insult in more macho countries, like Greece or Italy or the United States, is considered simple civility in France. Sexual relations in this country are fluid and unregulated; you are not out of the dance just because you have children, or indeed because you are married. Moralists can argue that this is a problem—but I wonder if it's not also, in some ways, a solution. The members of long-standing couples in France flirt with each other. They labor to impress one another. They seem to understand that love is complex; it is free; it answers to no law, however reasonably imposed. Relationships, therefore, become balancing acts, feats of imagination, works of art. Nothing is taken for granted, so everything is earned.

Just how seriously Parisians take love emerges in the shows they attend and the museums they frequent. Ninety percent of theater in Paris is about the life of couples. This includes some very silly stuff. *Ma Femme s'appelle Maurice* ("My Wife's Name Is Maurice") is not an unusual title for a long-running French play. *Ma Voisine ne suce pas que de la glace!* ("The Girl Next Door Only Sucks Ice!") is playing in a fashionable theater in the nineteenth. Leery of this knee-jerk contemporary comedy and bored of the perennially revered Molière, I settle on a series of semi-classics: Stefan Zweig's *24 Heures de la vie d'une femme* ("24 Hours in the Life of a Woman"); *Victor Hugo, mon amour*; Beethoven's *Fidelio*; Milan Kundera's dramatization of Diderot's *Jacques le fataliste et son maître* ("Jacques the Fatalist and His Master"); and—in honor of my daughter—*Orphée et Eurydice*, the opera by C. W. Gluck.

Every one of these works is about *la vie à deux*—the life of couples. *24 Heures de la vie d'une femme* (which is playing in Paris's prestigious Théâtre Petit-Montparnasse and stars the admired French actress Catherine Rich) involves an English widow who saves a gambler from suicide, sleeps with him against her principles, and prepares to surrender her lifestyle and reputation in order to follow him—only to learn that he has returned to poker and curses her as a nuisance. From the looks on the faces of the audience members, one would think every woman here knows what it means to throw her lot in with a man she hardly knows, a man she has no reason whatsoever to count on.

The woman who loved Victor Hugo did just that, as I learn at *Victor Hugo, mon amour*. An aspiring actress and extraordinary beauty, Juliette Drouet became the mistress of the nineteenth-century novelist—and remained so for fifty years. She could count on him, it turns out, if not for fidelity—he had several affairs during their relationship, as well as a wife—then at least for love, support, and an electric correspondence that lasted until her death. The feminist Simone de Beauvoir pitied Drouet, thinking her a woman who did nothing in her life but wait for the Great Man. The author and star of *Victor Hugo, mon amour*, Anthéa Sogno, sees it differently. For her—as she told me after the performance—Drouet is the ultimate hero because she is the ultimate lover: creative, passionate, and intensely verbal, as well as intensely sexual. Who cares if she didn't succeed at her own career? She succeeded at life.

"If only you could be on the stage exactly what you are in life, the world would . . . marvel," Hugo once wrote Drouet. It is a sentiment that might be addressed to Paris itself.

I am standing on a narrow patio on the fourth floor of the Timhotel Montmartre. It is the only accommodation located on the side of the famed hill rather than at the bottom, among the strip joints and cancan clubs and the Musée de l'Erotisme. I visited the museum earlier today, along with the Musée de la Vie Romantique—the former a dizzying collection of sex toys and *Kama-sutra* images, the latter a handsome villa devoted in part to the nineteenth-century love affair between the novelist George Sand and the poet Alfred de Musset. Not surprisingly, Sand and Musset are the subject of a long-running play in Paris (*Tout à vous, George Sand*), in much the same way that Hugo and Drouet have a museum that commemorates their relationship (Maison de Victor Hugo). The French love their lovers. They are as in love with love as they are in love with life. Museums of daily life like the Musée de l'Erotisme and the Musée de la Vie Romantique—as well as that most Parisian of museums, the Carnavalet, which documents the life of the city itself—reward discerning visitors as much as the Louvre.

The closest my own Parisian friends have come to the Louvre in recent years is the luminous restaurant at its center, Le Saut du Loup (The Leap of the Wolf). Sitting in the courtyard, with the ghostly glass pyramid glowing to the left and the giant Ferris wheel of the Tuileries spinning to the right, the Musée d'Orsay across the river, and the Eiffel Tower just beyond, it has one of the most astonishing views of the city.

Possibly the most astonishing view of all, however, is mine in Montmartre. On one side of my little hotel patio—almost close enough to touch!—is the resplendent white dome of Sacré-Coeur. On the other is all of Paris, spread like a lover's body before my outstretched hand. All the numberless dips and curves and crannies and projections. It is midnight and the Eiffel Tower is shivering into action for the second to last time of the night. I watch it spew glittering star fluid into the darkness, and I am transported.

Two midnights ago, I came home with Eurydice from a performance of *Orphée et Eurydice*. Infants are not, as a rule, welcome at operas. But this was a small production, by a young group, in an intimate theater on the curving, cobbled rue Mouffetard. I had been before with my neighbors and, indeed, my visiting parents. I knew the show was spectacular, my favorite in Paris—and not just because of its name. But because of its name—and its terrifically affecting music and myth—I wanted my little daughter to witness it.

I offer this as proof of how much Paris has changed since the olden days of high noses and withheld hospitality: They let me in. They let in an American with a seven-month-old. I'd contacted the opera company—called Manque Pas d'Airs (Lack No Airs), with *airs* meaning both artistic pretension and melodies. I'd told them Eurydice wished to see Eurydice. "Make yourself at home," said the usher as I settled into the back of the theater with my girl on my knee.

The performance was utterly arresting. A single piano echoing in the darkness replaces the orchestra. The curtain rises and a fluorescent-lit black-and-white set emerges. Orpheus, a straitlaced young man with a striped shirt, is mourning the death of his bride as a wedding camera continues to flash meaninglessly and drunken guests loiter over bottles. Soon, the striped-shirt is fighting the four guardians of Hell: They are spitting and barking at him (spitting and barking never sounded so good). Ultimately, they allow him to pass in search of his beloved.

He arrives in the bowels of the Underworld, where the atmosphere, shockingly, is sensual, misty, ecstatic. The four Furies (here, exquisite long-haired narcissists) are gazing at themselves in mirrors and fondling Eurydice's bridal veil. She refuses to leave with Orpheus—on the surface because she is hurt by his failure to look at her, but actually (one senses) because the Underworld is more beautiful than her earthly home, the inhabitants of Hades more appealing than her bridegroom.

Orpheus breaks the Love God's command not to look at Eurydice as he leads her away. He rightfully fears losing Eurydice—and therefore does. The main license Gluck took with the Greek myth comes at the end, when the Love God declares that "Orpheus has proven himself a loyal lover so he will have his girl regardless." A paean to the power of love closes the opera.

Eurydice in arm after the performance, I asked the cast whether I might interview them. To my delight, Orpheus agreed. "I am so glad." He smiled at Dice and quoted his signature song, "that I have not lost my Eurydice."

The following afternoon, various cast members met me at a café and explained their goal: to wrest opera from the clutches of the elite. "People used to break out and sing on the street," said Cecil Gallois, one of the Furies. "They don't do that any longer. Since the song isn't coming back to the street, we want to bring the street back to the song."

I picked my child up at day care in the company of the Orpheus group that evening (at six-thirty, not nine). And under the wooden beams of my tiny Marais apartment, Cecil sang to her a great part of the opera. A countertenor, he can do all the voices. Eurydice smiled, transfixed. Life had become art again. We were in Paris.

2009

The Greatest Show on Earth

by

GUY MARTIN

 Quick story out of Berlin's celebrity wars: Last February, the American songstress Britney Spears somehow finds herself in town with not enough to do. It's nighttime. She decides to go out. This is a very unextraordinary decision here in Berlin, where it's possible to find cabinet ministers rolling out of restaurants at three in the morning and the clubs don't close until six, by which I mean the regular clubs.

Young Britney avails herself of what she thinks is her worldwide fame and heads down to Dennewitzstrasse, in Schöneberg, not far from the courthouse steps where JFK gave his famous *Ich bin ein Berliner* speech. She wants to check out 90 Grad (literally Ninety Degrees), Berlin's premier watering hole, the very dagger point of, well, hotness. It is a regular night. It is not, for instance, Crippled Dick's Hot Wax Sexadelic Dance Party, Crippled Dick being a rowdy Berlin record label whose most recent party was hosted by DJ Mingo-go, a frontally naked female South Pacific islander. Britney arrives, expecting to be swept into the club with the usual popping of corks and flashbulbs in the VIP enclosure. Instead—it's precisely these nightmarish moments that send our more emotionally fragile pop stars straight into Betty Ford—the doorman stares at her . . . the pout, the bad dye job, the humdrum disco gear, the increasingly frantic claims that she's a pop idol . . . *and he just says no.*

For a long time—the duration of the Cold War, to be precise— Berlin's brooding glamour was an acquired taste. The diplomats knew about it (it helped them make excuses to drink); the students knew about it (it helped them drink); the Russian Army knew about it (they didn't need it to help them drink). But really, that ugly-looking *Todesstreifen,* or Death Strip, coupled with the unquenchable thirst East Berliners had for running across it—actually getting themselves killed or at least badly shot up and thrown in jail—this was a little bleak, not to mention in bad taste, shooting defenseless people out in the open like rabbits.

What was this town? It was a macabre cartoon with little bits and shards of death trailing along behind the big death left over from the big war. The Cold War itself was relatively simple compared with the other layers of history immediately under it: Frederick the Great's unrequited love for Voltaire, Hitler's bunker, Bertholt Brecht's house, Mies van der Rohe's house, Hermann Göring's hunting lodge, the Russian soldiers' graffiti inside the Reichstag, the odd mass grave under this or that construction site, Albert Speer's design for Tempelhof Airport as a mile-long Nazi eagle. Here's the thing about Berlin: You have to be a grown-up to get it. If young Britney ever actually succeeds in checking into Betty Ford, even just for the weekend, she'll get into 90 Grad the very next time she tries. The door people here can smell this sort of thing.

In the last decade, arguably the city's best in the twentieth century, Berlin has been lifted up and polished to a strange and contradictory brilliance. It's wrong to compare this Berlin with that of the 1920s, those roller-coaster years before the Nazis arrived, when—mostly out of a sense of impending doom—a modern energy last bloomed here. There is certainly, as then, plenty of naked tabletop dancing, and all of

Berlin still gets excited when a new transvestite revue hits town, but it doesn't cost three million marks for a bowl of pea soup, brown coal heating has been outlawed, and xenophobic lower-middle-class Austrian politicians do finally seem to be staying home. Instead, Berlin is playing host to an absolute boom in politics, film, the literary and performing arts, food, and nightclubs—a sort of high-low chain detonation that started a couple of years back and shows no signs of slowing. It is not a finished process so much as a lively and occasionally violent public debate framed by a central question: How, in the harsh light of history, do you make a capital of Germany?

Fifteen years ago, during my first diplomatic dinner party at an American general's villa in what was then the American sector, the lieutenant taking my coat at the door said, "Welcome to Berlin, the only town in the world where it's still important to have a really big hat rack." The Russian, British, American, and French military chapeaus did, in fact, take up a lot of room that night. The point is that after the war, Berlin operated on the thin gruel of nineteenth-century convention and hidebound postwar protocol, requiring lots of hat racks. Since the former Allies were now basically at war with each other without admitting it, the idea was to keep the field uncluttered by preventing "Germany"— whatever that was—from having any authority here. Over the course of forty years, Berlin shriveled. Ten years ago it received permission to become itself again, but by that time, nobody knew what that was.

Americans might want to imagine the Berlin of today undergoing a process akin to our taking Congress, the attendant lobbyists, the think tanks, the State Department, the White House, a bit of the Pentagon, and a few cabinet posts and jamming them into the area between 42nd and 79th streets in Manhattan. Berlin's need for definition has real, physical force. The tidal wave of newcomers is endless, and it's not just the onslaught of government: It's as if somebody threw a switch and instantly reversed the historical polarity—all of the strange and horrible *emigration* caused by Berlin in the last century has now metamorphosed into mass *immigration*. The city's oldest university, Humboldt, is seeing a rise in its applications. During the first third of this year,

1.39 million tourists descended on Berlin, an increase of thirty percent over 1999. Its image has been buffed internationally as well as intramurally within Europe: The number of overnight stays by Italians, for instance, is up by sixty-eight percent this year.

Construction sites appear suddenly, like big, unimaginably violent canyons that then wreak havoc on the traffic, which in turn causes the people moving through the Fritz Lang–like matrix to fibrillate more furiously, which finally just seems to generate more building. The construction brings special sorts of chaos to the streetscape. Because the water table is so close to the surface of the Prussian plain, foundations of any size become lakes. The early work on the big sites has to be done by platoons of underwater welders and concrete specialists in scuba gear. On their cigarette breaks, the divers stand around on the street corners at the edges of the traffic jams or hang out on barges that float in the lakes of the foundations.

Nobody anywhere in town is getting what they think of as "enough" done. Director and adoptive Berliner Wim Wenders, responsible for the city's most poetic pre-1989 film portrait, *Wings of Desire*, explained the effect to me a couple of years back, as all of this was starting. "I wake up, it's morning," he said. "I make a few calls and look around. Then it's ten at night."

Exactly.

The center of real estate gravity in the city has shifted, violently, from the heart of what was West Berlin to the middle of town. Both East and West Berlin had turned their rumps to the Wall, utterly devaluing the land inside the *Todesstreifen*. The Death Strip was a couple of hundred yards across in places, considerable acreage in light of the fact that the Wall itself was 155 miles long (including the section around the back of West Berlin). This is now the city's most drastically revalued real estate. Potsdamer Platz—with Sony and Mercedes-Benz lording over it—which lay largely within the Death Strip, is now the most expensive commercial parcel in the city, bar none.

The buildings on either side of the Wall also had a minuscule pre-1989 value. The nice people in the West didn't want to have to look at a hundred-yard gauntlet being run through land mines and trip-wired machine guns, so, being Westerners, they moved away. Kreuzberg, the West Berlin neighborhood just south of the East's fat middle, became the devalued haven for Turkish families, squatters, dopeheads, and permanent students. Now it is just a stone's throw from the two-thousand-dollar Margarethe Ley dresses in the renovated Friedrichstrasse—rents rising, its post-hippie idyll slowly breaking up into a new, higher, and much less comfortable tax bracket.

Mitte, or Stadtmitte (literally City Center), the old heart of imperial (Hohenzollern) Berlin, is the site of the most wrenching and exciting turnaround. Mitte contains Unter den Linden, Alexanderplatz, the New Synagogue, the State Opera, Friedrichstrasse, the Gendarmenmarkt, the German Cathedral, Humboldt University, Museum Island—in other words, the city's highest concentration of monuments, tourist attractions, and government buildings. It was taken by the Russians—and thus landed in East Germany—precisely because it was the heart of old Berlin. It died in their hands. Friedrichstrasse was a desert. There were People's Army soldiers goose-stepping down Unter den Linden, a few heavily miked guest rooms at the "new" hotels, and, if you were lucky, you could take a dour tour through the Pergamon, where the guards acted as if you were going to steal a few tons of stone.

"It was clear even ten years ago that the center of town would fill up," says Roland Mary, a restaurateur from West Berlin who dropped his lease in 1989 and moved to a space in Mitte, off the Gendarmenmarkt, a year later. The Gendarmenmarkt is a grand square presided over by the French Cathedral, just south of Unter den Linden. At the time, with Friedrichstrasse stone dead, Mary looked the fool. Now, ten years later, his restaurant, Borchardt, hosts the chancellor and his advisers for lunch a couple of times a week, and at night one is liable to see battalions of the great and near-great—George Clooney, Mel Gibson, Goldie Hawn, Boris Becker, Ben Kingsley, John Cusack, Roland Emmerich—lining up at the trough. The Hilton, the Four Seasons, the Grand, and the Adlon are all within spitting distance, and the State

Opera is around the corner. Half a dozen other restaurants have opened up nearby. "My colleagues who have stayed in the West are sitting around nothing," Roland Mary says. "The scene has moved."

It was always the case that Berlin was much more serious about its carousing than your average middle-class West German town—Berlin has something fundamentally imbalanced and headlong about it, something Slavic and not quite fully Western. It served the same steam-vent function in Germany as New Orleans or New York do for Middle America. But Berlin's famous, age-old licentiousness has undergone a truly impressive deepening of purpose.

The word *party*—used only *auf Englisch*, even in the listings magazines—can mean a) a street festival, b) a theme night at a nightclub, or c) any gathering of more than two people for any purpose whatsoever, but definitely requiring alcohol consumption. The array of choices is staggering: There are trance, house, big beat, acid jazz, industrial, and— patented by Berlin and Detroit—techno parties. There are fetish parties (leather and rubber only, and they mean it); *Saturday Night Fever* parties (Travolta white disco suits); a semiregular Booby Night (all women topless, and they mean it). There is the newly opened Kranken house party at which the barmaids are clad as slightly sadistic nurses and serve fruit smoothies to the overly addled. The ecstasy-fueled touring set will certainly not want to miss the weekend-long raves at nearby abandoned atomic bunkers.

Private parties also play off the bones of the Cold War. The East German sculptor Olf Kreisel recently hosted a party for the opening of his exhibition at the Kunsthalle Karlshorst, an art space near the former Soviet military HQ, at which all guests were invited to assemble model Soviet military planes at large tables while two women played *bottomless* Ping-Pong. *Nebenan trainieren die Mädchen*, Kreisel's rather dry invitation read, "Nearby, the girls will be practicing."

Then there is the Love Parade. Seven years ago a DJ named Dr. Motte—who's given to utterances like "We are occupying the morphogenetic field"—got the notion to lead a summertime parade of (yes, again mostly naked) ravers and clubgoers from the Brandenburg Gate and Ernst-Reuter Platz to the Tiergarten traffic roundabout called the Great Star. Of course, the monument at which the millions congregate—and from which Dr. Motte delivers his annual rave-on/love-on propaganda without so much as a whiff of acknowledgment to Joseph Goebbels—is a monument to the victory in the Franco-Prussian War (1871), which Hitler and Albert Speer had moved to its current location before World War II. But Dr. Motte doesn't seem to mind, nor do the two million attendees. *Speer . . . is it a special party juice?* Over the years the party has grown into a five-day dance orgy, a kind of mid-summer carnival, including this year for the first time—in an unholy confluence of what can only be described as the rave elements of German government and Dr. Motte's dance monkeys on ecstasy—a five-day disco on the roof of the Reichstag.

In short, it's insane, but the insanity is instructive—now Berlin is partying forward, without the millstone of history around its neck. Which, in turn, means that anybody so inclined can reach back into the big, ugly grab bag of German history and pull up a charred chunk for reexamination. In film, Jean-Jacques Annaud has just wrapped the largest film production in Berlin and in Europe to date ($80 million, for Paramount): *Enemies at the Gate*, a story of Stalingrad, with Ed Harris as the Nazi sharpshooter, Jude Law as the Red Army sharpshooter, Rachel Weisz as the Soviet babe, and Bob Hoskins as Khrushchev. The historical irony here is almost too great: A film about the beleaguered Russians breaking the German Army's back in the winter of 1943 was being made within a stone's throw of the former Soviet Army headquarters in Germany, not far from the hotel where Stalin and Truman sat down to divide up Berlin for what turned out to be the Cold War.

Enemies at the Gate would not have been possible without the steadfast, decade-long intervention of director Volker Schlöndorff (*The Tin Drum, Circle of Deceit*), who convinced a consortium of French and German investors to take over and renovate the storied Studio Babelsberg, the original home of Lang, von Sternberg, Billy Wilder, and of course La Dietrich. What happened to Dietrich and Wilder (not to mention Einstein, Brecht, Weill, Lotte Lenya, Mies, or Walter Gropius) during the war is clear—they all came to America.

What happened to the studio is less well known. Like Berlin itself, it bounced from hand to hand. Goebbels took it over and cranked out every propaganda film he ever made, then the Russians took it and gave it to the East Germans, who used it to crank out every piece of propaganda *they* ever made. Once East Germany faded into its amazingly weak sunset, Schlöndorff, mindful of his forebears in prewar German cinema, pulled the consortium together. Today it's among the largest studios on the Continent, with more than a hundred independent contractors, a film school, studio tours à la Universal City. Since Schlöndorff was there at the creation, he's exercised his droit du seigneur and named all the streets after the rebels and castoffs the Nazis and the Soviets and the East Germans didn't want to hear from, namely, Dietrich, Lang, Wilder, and von Sternberg.

"I didn't really do anything," he demurs. "It was fun to remember some of the filmmakers with the streets."

Schlöndorff has just finished a final cut of his latest film here, *The Silence After the Shot*, a witty, chilling examination of West German terrorists—the Red Army Faction—and the support they received from the East German Secret Police in the 1970s and 1980s. The Secret Police, or the Stasi, sheltered a number of Red Army Faction members in a sort of ad hoc terrorist protection program, and allowed a few still-active members to drop through East Germany and practice for some of their future assassination attempts. Schlöndorff shot *The Silence After the Shot* in and around East Berlin, re-creating down to the cheap cigarettes and bad vodka a luscious, Eastern grittiness through which his characters move. It's his most explicit examination of ideology gone haywire. In one of Berlin's more colorful expressions of free-floating historical bile, Inge Viett, a surviving Red Army Faction member who was convicted and imprisoned for her role in some of the murders referred to in the film, has decided to sue Schlöndorff for what she claims are "inaccurate" representations.

"Inge is a difficult person," Schlöndorff says equably. "We offered her a consultancy, of course, before we even started the shoot, which she turned down. Not that the murders were a problem. She'd already done the time for those. It was our rendering of the ideology that angered her most.

"In other words," the director said, smiling, almost able to savor it, "we're being sued because we didn't put the Red Army Faction point of view across quite *forcefully* enough."

Amid its whalelike thrashings for identity, Berlin is attempting to resuscitate the premier cultural legacy it so forcefully discarded. This reembrace of Jewish culture and Berlin's own Jewish legacy is, to say the least, fraught. But if it succeeds—and there are signs that it will—Berlin stands a chance of building a lasting bridge to and of coming to terms with the very blackest part of its long past. It's the critical bit of reckoning that needs to be done for the city to become whole, and it is going to take a very long time.

As it did with so much else, the Cold War froze this process. Two of Berlin's key Jewish landmarks, the New Synagogue in the Oranienburger Strasse and the gloriously bemarbled Weissensee cemetery in what was once a neighborhood filled with the East German political elite, lay for the forty years of the GDR under the moss of neglect. Interestingly, although they were quite assiduous at rooting out all sorts of really nonthreatening expressions of Jewish culture, the Nazis hadn't had the will or, really, the guts to destroy the cemetery. Weissensee is currently in the best shape it has been in for the last half century, since with the fall of the Wall the descendants of its families can now actually get to the graves.

Berlin's venerable Jewish community has made two critical bridge-building moves: The Hans Arnhold family donated its soaring lakefront family mansion on the Wannsee to become the American Academy in Berlin, with Henry Kissinger as honorary chairman (and currently acting chair until a successor is found for Richard Holbrooke, who moved to the UN as U.S. ambassador). Hans Berggruen, a staggeringly wealthy WWII refugee, donated perhaps the finest collection of Expressionist paintings outside Paris toward the founding of the Berggruen Collection here. These acts of generosity have raised the bar on intellectual and artistic debate in town, quietly stunning Berliners into an awareness of exactly what sort of cultural riches the Holocaust eradicated.

The year 2000 is the centennial of Kurt Weill's birth and the fiftieth anniversary of his death, which, although the composer was born in Dessau and died in exile in New York, has given the new Berlin a chance to allow its famous Jewish prodigal son to return. For the Weill centennial, the Academy of the Arts put on an exhibit directed at the composer's life, and there are dozens of concerts around town. The radical French-German chanson singer Dominique Horwitz launched a ripping three-week run of songs from the *Threepenny Opera* in the Hebbel Theater—designed in 1908 by the Hungarian architect Oskar Kaufmann, who was also, incidentally, run out of town by the Nazis.

Horwitz, small and wiry at forty-three, with enormous *Segelohren* (literally, "sail ears") jutting out from the side of his head, has the agile looks and the stinging physical quickness of a grown-up ragamuffin—in other words, he's a twenty-first-century incarnation of a Bertolt Brecht character. His trick is that he doesn't sing "Mack the Knife" but turns several of the women's songs in the play—"Pirate Jenny" and the "Ballad of Sexual Dependency"—into the spine of the performance.

"Look, I think you can do this with impunity as long as you don't insult the audience," he says. "They're grown-ups. They know the play. They know I'm a man. They know what Jenny is supposed to sing." He pauses to pull on a fresh shirt before throwing himself at the women outside the dressing room door. "I think the key here is not to be afraid of singing it."

Weill and Horwitz are easy for Berlin to love, a baby step in readopting its Jewish orphans; the bladelike irony, the sexiness, the raw political allegory, are well-loved stage commodities here. Berlin's ability to embrace the Holocaust directly is, however, a different thing.

If there is a kind of hunger driving Berlin, it's the hunger to emerge from the leg-irons of parochialism to which both sides of town were doomed from 1933 to 1989—in this sense, the fifty-six-year chunk from the advent of Hitler to the final death rattle of Stalinism can be seen as a single continuum of mute, ideologically contorted ignorance. It's painfully slow for the town to unkink this posture. Two structures— the National Holocaust Memorial, designed by Peter Eisenman, and the Jewish Museum, designed by Daniel Libeskind—have been the focus of ferocious public debate, and, simultaneously, can be considered the cornerstones of the city's attempt to address its lost past.

Eisenman's monument remains unbuilt. Construction was postponed pending a feasibility study of putting the attached information center underground—in other words, yet another groundwater assessment and the possible recruitment of many scuba divers. It will get built, but will inevitably require still more debate.

Libeskind's Jewish Museum, commissioned in 1989 and completed in 1998, is easily the most soulful architectural accomplishment in Berlin, and this in a city that in the last decade has engendered more architectural competitions than any other city in the world. Libeskind began the process a decade earlier than Eisenman, which is to say, the fight to build the building was eight years longer than that over the memorial.

Berlin is only beginning to realize what an asset Libeskind has delivered. Bluntly put, his building is staggeringly popular. Fifteen thousand people visit it a month, non-Jewish Germans, Jews of the diaspora on pilgrimages to Berlin, student groups, random tourists. It has had to stay open seven days a week to handle the load. It has no exhibitions in place yet—it's completely, sumptuously empty. Once the permanent exhibition is installed, conservative estimates of the annual number of visitors hover at the half-million mark—a figure so high that the official installation has been postponed until next year, pending the addition of extra toilets, rewiring of the exhibition space, and changes in the climate controls. Libeskind himself is staying in Berlin to supervise the refit.

No one expected it would make such a splendid *grand jeté* into the popular imagination. Here's why it did: It is not an angry, didactic, preachy, or brittle structure. It is enormously grand and open and sad, rather like a later Brahms symphony, very much of the Central European ground. The building wants people. It's also a brilliant maze, with a very direct Libeskindian logic: The three-story, zinc-clad museum is built in a jagged rip along a series of axes punctured by what Libeskind calls voids, which cut through all three floors. They allude to the absence of Berlin's Jews, whose presence the rest of the building celebrates. It's this fundamental tension that makes the museum such a draw, and *that*, ironically, is best seen now, before the permanent collection is installed.

"You're gonna do a museum, in Berlin, about the Jews of Berlin and Germany, so inevitably the remembrance and the Holocaust are all part of it," Libeskind says evenly. "But you cannot disconnect the high points of the Jews here—Albert Einstein, Moses Mendelssohn, Max Liebermann, Schoenberg, you know, the millions of luminaries in Jewish culture were also Germans. And the future of this city is always going to be intertwined with what happened to them. The building takes the Jewish dimension of this city across all these gaps, rifts, and fatalities, but goes on into the city in an emphatic way. I never meant to make a building which speaks only to the past."

Libeskind is a fiftyish man, with blond hair, a cherubic face, a black leather jacket, and a bouncy, rapid-fire way of speaking. Polish-born, he emigrated with his parents to New York, where he attended architecture school at Cooper Union. His Berlin atelier is in the courtyard of a light-industry building in Charlottenburg. It's a friendly jumble of rooms with models splayed out over every available surface. At the same time that he's overseeing the design modifications of the Jewish Museum here, he's designing the San Francisco Jewish Museum, and the addition to the Victoria & Albert Museum in London. His is a family firm, with co-workers and exchange students running the gangways, all of it presided over, loosely, by Nina Libeskind, his wife and the mother of their three children. It was she who suggested that they move here to build the museum when Libeskind won the competition in 1989.

"Berlin is not an innocent place, you know," Libeskind says brightly. "Not innocent at all. An architect said to me at the start of all this that if I could see this through, here, in Berlin, that the rest of my life would be easy. Berlin stands for so many things. It has such a peculiar power—even in its devastation and emptiness, it was still the focus of what the world really looks like. I always thought that when Kennedy said, *Ich bin ein Berliner*, that it was true, that everybody is a part of this city, even if they've never been here."

The full insanity of Berlin's renaissance has yet to be attained, mainly because the identity of the town is not fully realized, or, put another way, the sheer heat given off by Berlin is the by-product of the town forging its new identity. One man responsible for establishing, regulating, and coaxing out this new identity is Michael Naumann, Schröder's cultural minister. Naumann entered the government two years ago from his post as publisher of Henry Holt books in New York, and has been making page-one news five days out of seven ever since.

"How long is becoming the capital going to take?" he says, raising an eyebrow. "A while. Some parts of town are ready. What's gone and what has survived affect the way things will be. Wehrmacht Headquarters: Why, of all the buildings that were bombed in Berlin, did that one survive? If you take the horrible GDR buildings on Alexanderplatz, it's going to be another fifty or sixty years before we'll have the idea that we might want to rip those monstrosities down and make Alexanderplatz into an approachable, human place to be. You and I won't be alive to see it."

Berlin is forever in the process of chewing over, celebrating, destroying, and inhabiting every part of its history at once—Soviet, American, Nazi, imperial, and anything in between. The city has had a cargo cult not just to one conqueror—it has a cargo cult to all its conquerors. It's why the official portraits of East German party chief Erich Honecker now look so fresh in the trendiest bars, why there is an American lacrosse league, an American Little League, and a semiprofessional American football team; it's why Oleg from St. Petersburg,

Berlin's favorite DJ, made a special trip to town to introduce his new CD, on which he samples Prokofiev, early-sixties Soviet propaganda-film soundtracks, and Disney's *Cinderella*. It's also why, in 1992, Mayor Eberhard Diepgen refused to celebrate Marlene Dietrich's funeral here in any official way—she did, after all, return to Germany, traitorously, in an American uniform. It's also why, in 1999, for the Berlin Film Festival, under the same mayor, the city named the place in front of the main cinema Marlene-Dietrich-Platz.

Some days in Berlin it's as if people wake up and, one at a time, do one more-than-slightly-wacky, counterintuitive thing. The directors of Hoppegarten, Berlin's 1868 thoroughbred track, decide to put on an elephant race with circus beasts from around the country. *What?* The annual Whore's Congress, an organization claiming to represent the rights of Germany's prostitutes, cuts a deal with the congregation of the Emmaus Church, a Lutheran congregation in Kreuzberg, to hold its year 2000 plenum in the sacristy. *What?* Fans of the Berlin Polar Bears, the East Berlin semiprofessional hockey team, develop the halftime habit of leading cheers for Erich Mielke, the recently deceased minister of state security for the GDR. *What?*

Finally, Berliners are nothing if not prepared to get tough with each other. It's part of the game. For weeks after the 90 Grad doorman had given Britney Spears her walking papers, the debate raged: Did he do it because he *didn't know* who she was, or did he do it because he *knew* who she was? Which was more insulting? Berlin was unanimous in its approval of his having struck the blow against mindless pablum as personified by Ms. Spears. Not so, of course, Ms. Spears's management, who, it is to be assumed, reached out to the management of 90 Grad, who in turn fired the door dude. This was met with howls of dismay citywide. The staff of a local biweekly, *Prinz*, hosted a party called The 100 Most Embarrassing Berliners. Among those being especially celebrated for their miscreancy were the management of 90 Grad.

And the venue? 90 Grad.

2000

Love and Haiti and the Whole Damned Thing

by

AMY WILENTZ

This is a love song. It's a Haitian love song, played on three drums and an electric slide guitar that never sounds quite on key. No question, you can dance to it.

I'm writing this song not just for me but on behalf of the thousands who have come to Haiti over the centuries and been touched by it, moved by it, even changed forever: the writer Zora Neale Hurston and the abolitionist Frederick Douglass, who was the first U.S. ambassador to Haiti. The actors John Gielgud, John Barrymore, Richard Burton; and, more recently, Danny Glover, Julia Roberts, Matt Damon, Brad Pitt, and Angelina Jolie. I'm writing for rock stars Mick Jagger and David Byrne and for rapper Wyclef Jean (who's actually Haitian-American, and who introduced some of the aforementioned to his homeland), and for the great anthropologist, physician, and author Paul Farmer.

I'm also writing this love song for Maya Deren and Katherine

Dunham, both of whom documented traditional Haitian dance and were bitten by the Haiti bug. This song goes out, too, to director Jonathan Demme, whose son was named after a Haitian shantytown, whose walls are covered with Haitian art, and whose films always have a Haitian touch. In this eclectic group are other writers, also: William Styron, Lillian Hellman, and Haiti's greatest foreign fictionalizer, Graham Greene.

Let's not forget eternally optimistic Congressman Dick Durbin, longtime lover of Haiti, or Bill Clinton (the third U.S. president ever to visit—and now the UN's special envoy to the country), or Jimmy Carter, who came to monitor elections, or possibly the grandest of foreign dignitaries who fell for Haiti, Franklin Roosevelt, who drafted one of the country's many constitutions (that's how we conducted foreign policy back then) and was the first U.S. president to visit—in 1934. Hats off, too, to the late pontiff Jen-Pol Dè, as we write his name in Creole; he came to Haiti during the time of the dictator Jean-Claude "Baby Doc" Duvalier and said that things had to change.

Not to be too arrogant, but I am also writing this song on behalf of Christopher Columbus.

Haiti is not a place you just visit, as Columbus would surely have told you (he shipwrecked there in 1492). It's not a stream into which you just dip a toe. Here, you dive in headlong. It drives you crazy—with love, with anxiety, with desire. You fall into its arms as if it's been waiting forever to receive you.

It hasn't. And as with any great unrequited love, Haiti's indifference only makes you crazier for the place.

Haiti is the Cleopatra of countries, a destination unparalleled on so many levels. It has eccentric history and a tri-continental culture. Its syncretic art is singular and explosive, tender and transcendent. In Haiti, even a pile of garlic for sale, a row of plastic bowls from Taiwan, a display of brassieres (locally manufactured), black bags of charcoal standing at drunken angles cheek by jowl, can be a delicate, devilish masterpiece. There is an ethos of making do with what you have that leads to an ability to make much out of little, to make magisterial statements out of the least materials: With two or three beans, a chicken feather, an old rag of worn-out satin, and a hollowed-out gourd, a voodoo priest can make a whimsical charm that wards off evil.

For sheer unspoiled physical beauty, no place can beat Haiti—from white cliffs that rival Dover's to untouched islets, from the fertile Artibonite Valley to cresting emerald mountains like brawny-shouldered Herculean brothers one after another, and from long white beaches to blue pools set improbably in a crackling-dry forest. To say nothing of its handy location: The Pearl of the Antilles, as travel agents called Haiti in its tourist heyday back in the 1940s, is just a dropkick off the coast of Florida. Yes, of course there is deforestation, and desertification, and all sorts of problems, both ecological and man-made and often both. But if you travel to the magical, transforming heights of the piney forests of the mountain above Port-au-Prince—the capital city that's speckled with slums and racked by occasional unrest—even it looks like a sparkling fairyland.

Which it's not. Downtown is like this: You can't tell what's old or new because everything is crumbling, and—as in other developing nations—new two- or three-story buildings sometimes get only halfway constructed before the workers leave because the builders ran out of money. Low buildings often have hopeful rebar sticking out toward the sky like exposed bone. Overnight, it seems, entire new slums receive people moving into town from the countryside. Here's one climbing up a crevasse like a Cubist canvas being painted before your very eyes. Like guardian angels, two inflatable Santas stand in a broken corner of a new wall—for sale, of course—and look out impassively at the standstill traffic.

On another corner, two African officers from the United Nations Stabilization Mission in Haiti (known as MINUSTAH) stand a different kind of watch. It is MINUSTAH's job to keep the peace, although Haitians complain that the UN officers have come down selectively on certain political elements. The two officers peer inside cars as the traffic inches by. Formed in 2004, after the rough ouster of the democratically elected but controversial president Jean-Bertrand Aristide, MINUSTAH has been begrudgingly tolerated by some as a bulwark against crime. MINUSTAH soldiers can also be seen tootling around Port-au-Prince in pickup trucks—two guys in the bed pointing a very serious piece of artillery out at the Haitian population. This, as many have noted, makes it hard to distinguish whether you're being threatened or protected. In Haiti, this kind of ambiguity is pervasive.

The best-kept and most beautiful wall, gate, and garden belong to Haiti-Securité Assurances, a company that provides vehicles, drivers, and armed bodyguards for visitors and locals, from dignitaries to just plain Haitians who come back for vacation. Not everyone hires protection: I did not—I hired a driver who knows the place well and left it at that. Wyclef does use security, of course. Clinton does. Ban Ki-moon does. For a normal trip to Haiti, Wyclef hired 120 security people.

Pétionville, just a few thousand feet above the bewilderment of downtown, is a traveler's dream in many ways. Although this wealthy suburb seems cut from another cloth, it retains enough that's authentic to keep it interesting. Here's where the fancy restaurants are and the good boutiques. The dazzling art galleries are strung out in the blocks around the central intersection, Place Boyer, named after the president who signed Haiti into debt for a century. There are electronics stores, big supermarkets, and small specialty shops, as well as crafts stores like Gingerbread and Men Nou, which do business with Haitian artists who create the most beautiful things, among them radiant sequined voodoo flags big enough to fill a wall, featuring the gods of marriage, the seas, agriculture, love, and the cemetery, and detailed like a Hieronymous Bosch, as well as baroque found-object sculptures from a school of Dickensian sculptors—both grown-ups and children—who live and work in crowded conditions down on Grande-Rue, next to the old market and the slums.

One day I go to lunch at La Coquille, in Pétionville, with Jean Cyril Pressoir, who runs Tour Haiti, a small company he founded in 2004. La Coquille is so Haitian that it's almost too much. As Cyril says with a shrug, "It's very typical." The chairs are wooden and painted blue. On the tables are bright cloths, the walls are pink and blue, the windows framed with shutters. Lunch, served buffet style, might be *riz nationale*, which is rice cooked with red beans; *tchaka* soup (with corn, beans, and pork or oxtail); *poulet kréyol*; *poisson gros sel* (fish with onions, herbs, and salt); *griot* (super-fried marinated pork bits), and many other traditional dishes. The crowd is plump, local, prosperous. The hot spices make you a little warm, but a nice breeze is wafting in, and Prestige beer is flowing. It's all *très* Caribbean.

Cyril is running tours around Haiti. He's setting up his own fleet of *tap-taps*, the colorful Haitian buses, and has hired local artists to decorate the vehicles. He wants everything very real. On one tour, he'll take you and your group in his *tap-taps* down to the southern town of Aquin. You'll stay at a small hotel ("Clean and basic," he says, "not fancy") and eat marinated oysters, then go down to the town square to a place where you can drink and dance. The next day, the tour will take you to Morisot Beach, and you'll go island-hopping by boat.

"We do a major stop at a deserted beach," Cyril says. "We bring a cooler and water, and we have a totally local lunch on a fishermen's cay, with plantains and boiled or grilled fish or lobster. Then we go to a bird-watching cay. At the end of the day, we look back from a high point down onto the cays we've visited." He takes people to nightclubs in the provinces and to play cards and dominoes, and then to a cemetery to see a voodoo ceremony, or to a cockfight or a *bassin*, one of the inland pools that dot the island. "Then we walk back to a creek and have a picnic under the mango trees." He sounds as if he's fantasizing, but it's all real.

I find myself longing for a trip like this—all pleasure, sand, and sun. The problem is that the hard life of Haitians interferes with my enjoyment of the country's beauty. When I'm having a dish of *poulet kréyol* in Jacmel, or a big bowl of *tchaka* with Cyril, I can't help but be disturbed by the idea of all the Haitians who are not having this meal. Who are not having a meal. Who maybe haven't had a meal in twelve hours.

But as Cyril points out, one of the fastest ways to create jobs and help people in Haiti is to spur tourism, especially the nonexploitative, socially friendly tourism that Tour Haiti envisions.

There's a stop on a Royal Caribbean cruise that's called simply Labadee®. The real name of the place is Labadie, a fishing village on the northeast coast of Haiti, but the cruise line has registered the name in the Anglicized form. Although Royal Caribbean now acknowledges that Labadee® is actually in Haiti, when they describe it in their literature and on the cruise, they say only that it is on Hispaniola, the cartographic name Columbus gave to the island that includes both Haiti and the Dominican Republic. At Labadee®, everyone gets off the ship and spreads out over a gorgeous white beach. Royal Caribbean even offers a drink called the Labaduzee. Many cruisers never realize they are in Haiti.

Haiti, the birthplace of black power, is unique in the Caribbean. In 1791, Haitian slaves, led by Toussaint l'Ouverture, rose up on sugar plantations throughout Haiti against Napoleon and their French masters. After a protracted and bloody war, the former slaves declared independence from France in 1804—a year after Toussaint died, cold and alone, in a French prison in the Jura Mountains. The French withdrew. Just a year earlier, this by now more than a decade old military engagement, so costly and distant, had forced Napoleon to sell the enormous Louisiana Territory to the youthful United States. With one elaborate stroke of the imperial quill, the First Consul turned the United States, a former British principality, into a continental and world power. In a very real sense, America owes its greatness to a courageous band of eighteenth-century rebel slaves.

As for Haiti, it fell into poverty and remained economically isolated. France did not recognize its independence until 1825, compelling Haiti to pay 150 million francs (about $25 billion in current U.S. dollars) for damages incurred during the revolution. This agreement to pay reparations, signed by President Jean-Pierre Boyer, contributed to Haiti's impoverishment well into the twentieth century. It is argued that the already strained Haitian economy never overcame the crushing weight of that debt.

Because of its revolution, and consequent pariah status among the white nations of the world, Haiti has remained largely undiscovered, known only to a few elite outsiders (artists, dancers, writers, anthropologists, journalists, businessmen, free spirits, diplomats, development workers, missionaries, and adventurers) willing and even eager to brave the country's centuries-old reputation to find out what lies beneath.

"I mean, Haiti has culture, it has music, it has white sand beaches that have barely been touched," Wyclef Jean says. "But nobody knows this yet." Jean is at Platinum Studios in New York, eating his dinner and chatting on the phone. But as ever, he's thinking about Haiti. He knows about its poverty because he grew up in a village outside Port-au-Prince, but he also knows Haiti as a playland because when he goes down to visit—he does concerts where tens of thousands come out of the shantytowns to listen to his music—he takes time off to fly out to the spectacular islets scattered around the coast like sparkling little satellites: Île à Vache, La Tortue, and even, he points out, the larger La Gonâve, which is very poor and very beautiful.

"The future for Haiti, for tourism there, is very bright," he says. "Once it's discovered."

He laughs.

One day, early, I set out for Ranch Le Montcel, a new hotel described as a vacation horse ranch—a new concept in Haiti—located on the mountain that crouches over the capital like a vigilant guard, wearing a hood of clouds and fog in almost all seasons. Farm people from the interior are finishing their long march from on high to the markets of Pétionville. As I ascend in my giant, noisy, white four-by-four, they descend on foot in silence as if headed for a funeral. One woman, a tall person with a somber regard and a woven basket on her head, wears a T-shirt that reads, EASILY DISTRACTED. T-shirts almost always provide unintended commentary here, where cast-off clothing from the United States is sold by the pound and many of the people who buy it are illiterate.

The Baptist Mission in the town of Fermathe, farther up the hill, where there are bunches of very white visitors on religious mission, is a pleasant place to get a snack and use a rare bathroom. With a jar of mamba (Haitian peanut butter—I like the one with hot pepper mixed in) in my bag, and a cup of strong Haitian coffee in my bloodstream, I proceed up to Fort Jacques, sister of the more legendary Citadelle La Ferrière, which is up near Labadie. These mountain fortresses, scattered around the country in various states of renovation and disrepair, show how frightened Haitians were about a return to foreign control and enslavement. The walls, made of fitted masonry, are several feet thick and come complete with secret passageways, soldiers' barracks, cooling water systems, and of course dungeons. Fort Jacques looks down over Port-au-Prince, its twelve cannons aimed at Haiti's greatest harbor and the surrounding countryside. But for more than a century after the revolution, no foreign power came by sea to retake Haiti.

Out again on the winding dirt road on the way to Le Montcel, I feel—even in my bulky four-by-four—as if I'm climbing stairs rather than riding on tires. I pass the Glory to God depot and the Red Pelican Bazar, a general store housed in a cast-off freight container with a door cut out of the side. Around and ahead of me are trees, ghostly in the cloud cover, and down below is sunshine. As in a Haitian painting by the master Préfète Dufaut, people in bright clothing dot the roadside nearby and far off, walking single file. The fog opens for a moment—on terraced hillsides, coffee plantings, and a tiny village with more people walking—and then closes again. I put on my sweater. A boy with a bag of rice on his head wears a T-shirt that says, LET'S PUT ALZHEIMER'S BEHIND US. Down the road hurtles a red-and-green *tap-tap*; its name is *To Be or Not to Be*. On the back, as it fades into the fog, I see written the words, as on so many of these chipper, death-defying jitneys, MESI JEZI ("Thank You, Jesus").

When I arrive at Le Montcel, it's closed. It is Thursday, and Le Montcel is more a weekend place for Haitians than a resort for weeklong vacationers from abroad, but that should change. After declining for the past twenty years, tourism in Haiti is on the upswing. The World Travel & Tourism Council predicts that over the next decade, tourism will grow from its current 6.9 percent share of GDP to 7.1 percent. That's not such a big leap, obviously, but an upward trend is, in Haitian terms, a remarkable thing, and cause for moderate optimism.

Le Montcel is unbelievable, unthinkable. It looks like an Adirondack resort: Amid lush greenery are tennis courts and lovely, simple wooden cabins with long balconies. Le Montcel has its own reservoir, stables, and a great house built of stone with a peaked red tin roof, ivy-covered walls, dormers with paned windows. There's also a game room and a soccer field as well as Ping-Pong tables, wine caves, big fireplaces, conference rooms. It's unlike anything you can find at sea level, in the heat and sun of the tropics.

"Either you hate Haiti from the first time you come, or you love it," Christophe Lang says. He's thirty, and he and his family have run Cyvadier Plage, a hotel on the outskirts of the beachside town of Jacmel, for at least fifteen years. "If you love Haiti," he says, "you can't get it out of your skin."

We're sitting on the terrace of Cyvadier's restaurant, watching the sun set over the Caribbean. A TV is on over the bar. Some inane Haitian show is on; the television hostess is wearing red sequins. I ask Lang what kind of people come to Haiti.

"Oh," he says, "people who used to go to the D.R. and are sick of it. Germans, Englishmen. Beyond your nice hotel room, Haiti is a strong experience. Possibly it's not quite ready for average tourism. The culture shock can be hard on people." Lang is a real son of Haitian tourism. His father was a German who led charter tours to Jacmel from the Dominican Republic and the United States in the 1970s, and his mother was the head waitress in a popular restaurant called The Pub. He grew up near Frankfurt and studied cooking in Hamburg.

The beach at Cyvadier is in a little cove at the foot of a set of stone stairs. At sunset, the water is pink and gray. A woman has parked herself here and laid out jewelry across a bit of old stone: Now the beach is a shop! The rocks that surround the cove are tattooed with bad

Haitian art for sale—pictures of fat peasants (of which there are virtually none in Haiti), pictures of wild animals (ditto) in abundant jungles (ditto): Now the beach is an art gallery!

On the sand nearby sits a small blue-and-red fishing boat called *Victwa Malerèz* ("Victory of the Poor"). A silent fisherman sits on the gunwale, wearing the bleached-out gray T-shirt and gray shorts of poverty, with a fishing net slung over his shoulder and a machete in his hand, the tip of the knife touching the sand. From under the brim of his gray baseball cap, he watches the fiery sunset.

It's a trademark of Haitian tourism that you are never far from the Haitian people, whether they are sad and quiet, like this fisherman, or squawking and riotous, like a gaggle of market ladies, or simple and dignified, like the pedestrians up near Le Montcel. You're on a beautiful beach near Cap-Haïtien, say, stretching out, recovering from the potholed trip north, imagining yourself to be on just any old beach in touristland, when out of the trees wanders a bunch of stick-thin kids to surround you and comment on your bikini while asking for a buck or two.

"Haiti has been a problematic destination since 1791," says Tourism Minister Patrick Delatour, referring to the revolution. "You know: 500,000 Negroes running naked in the woods and claiming to be free." He cackles. "Oh, man, how could they? And speaking French!" He's sitting in his office on Port-au-Prince's main governmental square, at a round table strewn with tourism brochures, maps, and blueprints; the tourist magazine *Logo Plus* (motto: "*un concept, une aventure, une découverte*"); and documents of all kinds. Outside, in the park below, is the statue of the Unknown Rebel Slave (like the Unknown Soldier in the Western world), who is blowing on a conch shell to summon his comrades to revolution. There is nothing wild or revolutionary about Minister Delatour, however. He is affable, businesslike, a tall, athletic man in a suit.

In the late 1990s, Delatour tells me, he developed a master plan for tourism in Haiti. (He's been minister of tourism before, and is an architect by trade.) He likens the Haitian situation after the ouster of Aristide to that of Jamaica after another popular leftist president, Michael Manley, lost power.

"After Manley, no one came to Jamaica anymore," Delatour says. "So the travel business there began to develop local destinations, and when those became somewhat known, they attracted an international clientele. And then it got bigger and better known, and then they could say: 'Come back to Jamaica!'" This, he says, was how the Jamaicans began to cultivate well-known spots like Negril—places far from Kingston, Jamaica's famously tough and fractious capital. First bring in local traffic and islanders living abroad, and then, *voilà!*

"This is what we want to do," he says. After the locals, Delatour hopes to attract Haitians living abroad, of whom there are about four million, and add to that what Delatour calls "ethnic tourism," the larger African diaspora. But with each of these steps, Delatour acknowledges, tourism infrastructure, attractions, and accommodations must also advance several notches.

Right now, Delatour is working with Royal Caribbean on a project in the north that is to include dredging a harbor and building a port and new roads—one of them a highway to be made in part from locally available shells, another example of Haitians making do with what they have. By December of this year, Royal Caribbean will be bringing in some six thousand visitors at a time on the *Oasis of the Seas*, which Delatour describes as "the biggest boat ever built as a cruise ship." That's more than twice as many as currently come into Labadee®. The Haitian government is investing fifty million dollars to ready a port at Baie d'Acul, near Cap-Haïtien, to receive the larger vessel. Royal Caribbean is lending half the money to Haiti, and the government intends to pay it back with revenue from tourism taxes. This way, Delatour says, Royal Caribbean gets paid, Haiti gets tourists, and the Haitian people get jobs and money and development.

The new ship will mean a different kind of tourism for Royal

Caribbean and for Haiti. "Labadee® is basically a beach concept," Delatour says, "and a beach concept cannot receive six thousand people at a time and reasonably expect to make them happy. We have to diversify the tourist product. . . . We want to make it possible for people to visit the Citadelle, Sans Souci, and Cap-Haïtien, the second-largest French-designed city in the Americas, with the biggest collection of gingerbread houses. . . .

"Sure," he concedes, "Cap-Haïtien is something of a wreck. It could use some paint. But on the other hand, you can sell 'wreck' as a tourist product," Delatour says, ever honest, ever the optimist. "How many people in Sweden have ever seen a city in wreck?"

This may be a kind of "poorism," but Haitians will always make do with what they have, always make the most of what's available.

Wyclef, *au contraire*, is having none of it. He is not selling "wreck."

"Sure there's poverty in Haiti," he says, "in Port-au-Prince. But the best white sand beaches in the Caribbean are in Haiti. When people see them, they think they're on another island—but they're in Haiti. This is where Wyclef Jean comes in, who's proud of being Haitian." Wyclef has plans to involve himself directly in Haitian tourism. His investment company, the Jean Group, is developing business models for tourism in Haiti.

"We want to build a great resort in Haiti," he says. "The country needs good branding. It needs to be branded with its culture, its art, its music, and its history." Haiti has waterfalls that are reputed to cure all maladies, he points out. It has beaches from which the buccaneers set sail in the 1600s.

"What could sell better than that?" Wyclef asks. "The original pirates of the Caribbean. . . ."

It's true that Haiti's beaches are very attractive. And Wyclef's emphasis on art and music is not surprising to anyone who's looked at the patterns of Haitian tourism. Every time Haiti has experienced a tourism uptick, it has been art, music, and traditional culture that have led the way—those attributes of the country, plus a moment of political stability. Thus, from the 1930s through the 1950s, when the economy was expanding, Haiti began to fascinate the leaders of the Harlem Renaissance, and dealers and collectors began to purchase its naive art. Then the dictator François Duvalier came to power, and many of these successes fell apart. When Duvalier died in the early 1970s, people began to come to Haiti again, even though he left the country's rule to his son, Jean-Claude, another dictator but with a less bloody reputation.

Today, Delatour and others are clearly counting on another period of stability to warm the tender shoots of tourism that are showing in Haiti's rocky soil. Perhaps now, with Obama in the White House and Clinton as the UN's special envoy (an entirely new post), the American relationship with Haiti will be less toxic and good things may come of it, as opposed to the usual inebriating but poisonous brew of political repression, rebound revolt, and unrest in the streets. Certainly things have been relatively calm since Aristide was shoved out, but no one is sure whether it's an artificial calm created by MINUSTAH's presence or something more enduring.

Celebrities with deep pockets and big ambitions may be of some use in a country like Haiti at a moment such as this. A group headed by Wyclef, for example, is doing relief work in Gonaïves. The project should give about five hundred Haitians food in exchange for work removing mud from the hurricane-plagued town. With the mud, Wyclef's people plan to construct a huge concrete concert platform outside Gonaïves, where Wyclef, among others, can perform, and which would also, it is hoped, serve as higher ground during storms.

MINUSTAH is playing volleyball on the beach. The peacekeepers like to party. It's sunset at Club Indigo, on the sandy western shores, just off the road between Port-au-Prince and Gonaïves. Formerly the Club Med in Haiti, the hotel is now privately owned by Haitians. It's a little down-at-heels, but the open-air construction, spacious walkways, and huge pool make it seem luxurious. So much space for so few people! After an early dinner, I'm perched on a low wall between the pool and the beach. The beach is wide and pink in the setting sun. It sends up little sparkles; I can almost confuse it with the shimmering stretch of pale water that separates the mainland from the dark hills of La Gonâve, the island looming like a brooding behemoth between me and the horizon. There could be a famine unfolding on La Gonâve right now—there have been in the past—and I would never know it, sitting here. As usual, I can't keep the rest of Haiti off my mind in these situations. Relaxing on the beach, I think of disaster. I recall that Wyclef always mentions this big island when he talks about locations for future resorts. To my right, a man and a woman have pulled their beach chairs close together. They are drinking tall drinks and whispering, their heads bent toward each other as if contemplating conspiracy. She's in a bikini. He's smoking a cigarette.

The game unfolds enthusiastically before me in a mix of languages—English, French, Nepalese. . . . The volleyball players are wearing bathing suits and T-shirts and seem as clean-cut and cheerful as a bunch of surfside Californians. "Okay!" I hear one shout. The sun is sinking behind La Gonâve. A man approaches to sell me some cheap homemade jewelry dangling from his hand—a conch necklace, something made of coffee beans—but I wave him away with a shake of my head and a *non, non* motion with the right index finger that, I've learned from French friends, is very effective. It works!

I find myself wishing, suddenly, achingly, for a Labaduzee, whatever *that* may be.

2009

The Taj, the Tiger, and the Treepie

by

E. L. DOCTOROW

Morning at the Oberoi hotel in New Delhi. Breakfast in the room—croissants and watermelon juice and the teapot in its cozy. We are in India to see the great Bengal tiger. But to see the tiger we will have to see India.

We have a look at Delhi, which, perhaps from its heritage of discordant rulers, is a spread-out low-rise city of no visual distinction. It is a city of wealthy green enclaves, polo clubs, and former British mansions, bejeweled in metropolitan catastrophe. There is lassitude built into the constructions going up. Older buildings, monuments of tenuous, half-assed business ambitions, are falling to rubble at their edges. . . . Ditches and empty lots are strewn with garbage. . . . Every imaginable kind of vehicle crawls along, honking, pressing its advantage by inches. The buses can't accommodate the crowds waiting at the bus stops.

The air is fetid. Families of squatters living in open lots rise from

E. L. Doctorow

their sleeping bags to make their morning ablutions at hydrants. They cook their breakfasts on makeshift stoves assembled from the bricks lifted from nearby construction sites. Delhi is supposed to be one of the better-off cities in India. The squatters are internal refugees—rural people moved off their land or flooded out: A network of dams is being constructed peremptorily across the subcontinent. Apparently in this nation of one billion, the Indian government is willing to sustain losses.

As tourists, we courteously attend to the architectural relics of the ancient rulers. At each historic site—Humayun's Tomb, the Red Fort of Shah Jahan—we are assailed by peddlers and importuned by beggars, some of them severely disabled. One man scuttles like a crab in the dirt at our feet. Small children run alongside us with their hands out saying "hello, hello!" as if this achievement of the English language will release rupees into their palms. There are no fat people in the streets of Delhi. The only fat people are in the Oberoi. We are back in our rooms watching the cricket matches on television.

We board our train early in the morning and head southeast, clacking along the route that will take us through Agra, Gwalior, the Bhopal of the infamous toxic petrochemical disaster of 1984 that killed almost four thousand, and on to Gondia, where we will disembark for the road trip to the tiger reserve. It is a journey of about six hundred miles, an overnight ride.

Our train is known as the *Palace on Wheels*. It is a modern take on the original accommodations, presumably by divine right, of a raja of Rajasthan: fourteen air-conditioned cars, or saloons, each containing four staterooms with twin beds and private bath and a small sitting room at one end; a pair of turbaned attendants to see to the needs of the travelers in each saloon; two dining room cars, the Maharaja and the Maharani; a bar and lounge with upholstered seating; and a beauty parlor and spa car whose staff includes a masseuse.

Our party of friends is a fraction of a larger group of American birders and nature lovers traveling under the aegis of Victor Emanuel, the youthfully white-haired, passionately idealistic, natural-world tour operator who has serious ornithologic credentials and a loyal cadre of

182

conservationists and earth-loving adventurers along with him on this expedition. All told, there are about sixty of us, travelers and guides.

Our destination, the Kanha National Park, is the home of Bengals, leopards, several species of grazing animals, wild dogs, monkeys, and innumerable birds of the kingdom. Something for everyone.

As spoiled Americans, we are pleased with the service, particularly of our car attendants, who are sweet tempered and accommodating; less pleased with the food, which is indifferent Indian; and disappointed in the condition of the train, having noticed about our luxurious *Palace on Wheels* that the lounge furniture is sprung, the wall-to-wall carpet has never known a vacuum cleaner, the baths are tiny, the fixtures temperamental, and the white towels gray. But we are not inclined to criticize: In the middle of the day, with the sun at its height, our train pulls into a provincial station. On the adjoining track is a train of the India Railways, its ancient coaches packed tight with citizens who sit, stand, and hang out the windows to breathe, while the importunate sway en masse at the coach steps, attempting to board with their babies, bundles, and bags, all of them heedless of the train whistle blowing and various officials running along, shouting at everyone. We see this from the coolness of our interior.

We are traveling a route through the state of Madhya Pradesh never before undertaken by the *Palace on Wheels*, which heretofore had been restricted to the state of Rajasthan. Schedules have been rearranged in our favor up and down the line. Strings have been pulled by Raj Singh, Victor Emanuel's Indian counterpart, an amiable, elegant, mustached fellow in his forties. Raj, the author of a book on the birds of the subcontinent, is a graduate of the Scindia Public School, founded in Gwalior in the 1890s for members of royal families. Scindia's graduates, of whatever generation, need no introduction to one another. They move as if by inheritance into positions of influence and know how to get things done.

If we needed to be confirmed in our postcolonial guilt, people drawn to our mysterious train rush across the platform to peer in the windows. They catch a glimpse of a polished wooden headboard or the portrait of an ancient Moghul, but it is enough. They shout and slap the sides of our car until they are shooed away by the local police.

The long day's journey is enlivened by lectures in the bar lounge. K. David Bishop, a ruddy and voluble Australian naturalist and an expert on the birds of the Pacific region, takes his charges through their *Birds of India* book: how to know the white-rumped needletail, the shikra, the greater racket-tailed drongo, the yellow-wattled lapwing, the jungle bush quail. I suppose I am at this lecture under false pretenses, since I do not qualify as a serious birder, being usually content to observe the common varieties at home when I happen to see them. I'm more interested in a bird's character than I am in its plumage or its rarity, which means I can make do with your ordinary thieving blue jay, feisty white-throated kingfisher, operatic mockingbird, or clinically depressed green heron. But now I hear from Bishop that among the Indian birds we are bound to see is the rufous treepie! What couldn't the poet Edwin Arlington Robinson have done with a name like that:

> *Whenever Rufous Treepie came to town*
> *Everyone cheered, and shouted out his name.*
> *And Rufous, aflush from clavicle to crown,*
> *Wheeled right around and went the way he came.*

Needs work. Besides, it's too early for the drinking hour. The birders are bent over their books. They keep life lists, they circumnavigate the globe to notch their sightings. They're building their birder reputations. Most of them have the money to do this. They are either coupled-up lawyers, doctors, educators, or single pilgrims, women mostly, of a certain age.

It is easy enough to make fun of birders. Coming out of a nation of broncobusters, steer wrestlers, deer hunters, and meat eaters, birders ask only to see something. Not to shoot it, not to touch it, feed it, cage it, mess with it in any way. To see something and give it a name. That's all. Birding celebrates nonpossession. At this time in the history of a planet dammed, deforested, and drilled to its deepest dingles, isn't this a blessed thing? It is the practice of reverence. It is knowledge for its own sake. Here are these birders traveling halfway around the world to amaze themselves with what is left of the winged life of God. Or of Darwin. What does it matter—it's a holy fool's calling either way.

So I decide I am fond of these studious middle-aged Anglos palace-wheeling down the subcontinent. Birding is the solemn engagement of the short-lived relationship. It makes do with the fleeting glimpse, a blurt of color, a call, the bend of a branch. It makes a sacrament of inconstancy. Is there not wisdom in that? Most of the people on this trip are the remarried, divorced, or widowed.

Of course, my primary interest, the Bengal tiger, is another creature you don't want to ruffle. My friend Peter Matthiessen, a great, widely known naturalist who has trekked all over the world to see its manifold creatures and has written beautiful books about the creatures he has trekked the world to see, has my full attention for his tiger talk. I am gratified to hear that the Bengals at Kanha are not known for eating people. The known maneaters are mostly down south in the Sunderbans, the tropical Ganges delta. They're swimmers. They like to slip into the river and come up behind a paddler in his canoe. Realizing that this was the modus—the assault from the rear—the locals down there took to wearing wooden face masks on the back of their head, and for six months, they were able to paddle about with impunity. Then the tigers caught on.

Nobody knows for sure where the tiger originated. Maybe Siberia or western China or Java. The current population of the Siberian tiger is down to about four hundred. This makes them far more rare than the Bengals, which number two thousand or so living in different habitats on the central highland plateau that includes Kanha. But in terms of survival, the Siberians may have a better chance in the long run, because in that vast inhospitable land they range freely, while Bengals live where humans intersect their habitats. The pocketed Bengals will of necessity inbreed, which is genetic disaster.

After the lecture, another of our band, the inimitable writer of self-deprecating personal-risk adventures, George Plimpton, himself a dedicated naturalist, tells me the following story. One day not too many years ago, a British ornithologist named David Hunt impetuously jumped out of his jeep and trekked into the bush, going after something he'd heard or sighted. This was at Corbett National Park in the foothills of the Himalayas. His guides shouted for him to come back—and then heard a harrowing, hideous scream. Hunt had found a tiger. And you know, Plimpton says, when tigers man-eat, the first thing they consume are the genitals.

Meanwhile, the train has been clacking along. The countryside from Delhi to Agra plays out the breadbasket to the north, the alluvial Indo-Gangetic plain of the Punjab and Haryana that is replenished perpetually by the nutrients washed down from the Himalayas. From the window of my car lounge, I see the sort of wheat fields that enticed the Moghuls to invade India. But south of Agra, the farmland gives way gradually to the scrappy, unproductive terrain, stony hills, and sal forest of the Deccan plateau that dominates central India. Central India, I am told with political incorrectness, is Kipling country. More accurately, it is the country from which he made his fortune with the "Jungle" books. The truth is that Kipling lived up north, in Lahore, spending summers in Simla, as far from Kipling country as you could get in those days and still be in India. And by the age of twenty-four, having made a name with his *Plain Tales from the Hills*, he left India to spend the rest of his life in England and the United States.

As the sky bleaches out and the land turns sere and scraggy, we pass villages that look like flea markets. Cows, oxen, and people move along in a casteless mingling. Homes with corrugated-tin roofs are held up by poles. In what looks to be a cinder-block room with one side open, three molded plastic tables with chairs make a restaurant. The proud, poor women in bright saris carry baskets on their heads. A camel pulls a wooden-wheeled cart. A man soaps up out of a bucket. At the edge of town is an old woman goatherd watching her one goat feed on the nubs of dead grass at the foot of the railroad embankment.

Central India is either parched dry or under water, depending on the time of year. We are in the dry. We rack up mile after mile of dirt rice paddies. There is litter in the fields, urban litter. An old man draped in white homespun walks with the help of a stick along a road scratched into the land. He takes small shuffling steps. Where has he come from? Where is he going? The prospect as far as the horizon is of flat, sun-baked land. Here, if you want it, is a vision of unmediated life.

The next morning, when we arrive at Gondia Junction, the jumping-off point for the road trip to Kanha, something is not right. A crowd is waiting for us at the station. They are held back by soldiers with rifles. We step down from the train at the far end of the platform and gather there. Helen, my companion, is alarmed. Raj Singh has a big smile on his face. It's all right, he says waving at us, come along, come along. We move toward the crowd. I take Helen's elbow. Yes, come along, I say. It's justice, after all. You believe in justice, don't you?

But now we hear the strains of martial music. A band is playing. And as we approach, the surging crowd separates and makes a path for us. They are men and boys mostly, smiling at us intently, or staring, or reaching out to shake our hands. Suddenly, a woman rears up and mashes her thumb on my forehead. Another adorns me with a neck-lace of orange marigolds. I look at my fellow travelers: We all have the vermilion thumbprints, the flowers. We are being honored, celebrated, we overfed, dumpy Americans with our backpacks and water bottles walking into the station, up the stairs to the street, every step lined with incredibly hospitable Gondians, a whole townful, apparently, who have seen our arrival as reason to stop whatever they were doing. And by the time we reach the buses, we've gotten into the spirit of the thing, strutting along and smiling and accepting homage, like a drove of Bill Clintons.

Later, I hear from Raj that he happens to know the mayor. And so the word went out that a team of world-renowned American tiger experts—guests of the state—were coming to examine the specimens at Kanha.

We ride away in the buses, the people waving. What a send-off. I am wondering what it takes, really, to be a tiger expert. Tiger worship exists in northern India and Malaysia. Maybe the priests of the tiger cults are the true experts. Or maybe the fellow who wandered into the bush to be eaten, testicles first.

It is a long, torturously slow four-hour bus ride to Kanha. First through Gondia, a busy city of clay-roofed mills and factories, sprawling warehouses, tar-paper shacks, the incongruous signs of international business—IBM Computers, Prestolite!—and streets glutted with trucks, motorcycles, and camel-drawn carts. Then we're into the countryside, and gradually we begin to climb an ascending terrain of stony hills, with valleys of shallow lakes in the distance and roadside villages with oxen lying around under the trees. I find that we are on a winding one-lane cliffside road deemed sufficient for two opposing lanes of traffic. I am impressed by the confidence of Indian drivers, who have so little shoulder to resort to as they contrive to slip their lumbering vehicles past one another at only the most precipitous spots. Somehow they understand one another, I tell myself, though I keep my eyes trained on the road ahead and each huge truck or fat local bus heading toward us.

But the birders around me are otherwise engaged, peering out their windows over the smoky river valleys and calling out their sightings: "Sarus crane at two o'clock," one shouts. "Indian roller!" "Lesser flameback on that tree!" With each sighting, the birders rush to one side of the bus or the other, binoculars at the ready. I imagine our bus slowly toppling over the mountainside. Helen speaks of the romance of an obituary in which we are said to have perished in India.

But finally we are here at Kanha, the seven hundred or so square miles of national park in the Central India Highlands where live, in precarious safety from creatures like us, the birds and beasts of the Indian animal kingdom. We drop our gear in our assigned cottages at the Royal Tiger Resort, a spartan but clean and well-run accommodation, and set off in our convoy of jeeps. There is still time for sightings—late afternoon as well as early morning is the time to be on the trail. Each jeep, driven by a local guide with another lookout riding the tailgate, carries three or four of us, including one of the tour leaders. The drivers peel off, each one choosing this or that fork in the road according to his best instincts.

And suddenly we are alone. We round a bend and find ourselves out of the forest and running in the sun abreast a lush meadow of high, golden grass. In the middle distance is a shallow lake where several animal species and various birds are taking the waters. As the road bends and grows closer to this sunlit watering hole, we make out a variety of deer grazing and drinking: the petite barking deer; the more numerous socially inclined and lovely spotted deer, or chital; and standing absolutely still in a sedge deposit in the middle of the lake, as if wondering how they got there, two brown sambar, the largest of the Asian deer (about the size of a cow). But there are ducks paddling around in the lake—and the birders are now standing in the jeep, binoculars at their eyes—for it's not only ducks but egrets, stilts, a painted stork stepping along prettily at the water's edge, and, festooned in a tree along the far edge of the lake, a populous colony of black fruit bats. When evening comes, the bats will yawn and stretch themselves and rise from the branches in such numbers as to suggest that the tree itself is levitating. But at the moment they are still. They hang there, looking from this distance like eggplants.

In fact, everything about the scene is pacific—our jeep motor has barely raised the heads of the chital, and the creatures who graze are as unconcerned with the creatures who swim and fly as the creatures who fly and swim are with them. There is a kind of forbearing multiculturalism on display here, if you ignore the absent predator cats who live regally at the top of the food chain.

A feeling comes over me—a joyous longing, if that's possible, or an exhilaration that twists into a sort of smiling anguish. This bipolar mental state only increases in the following two days as we range over the meadows, past the bo trees like the one the Buddha sat beneath, into the valleys and over the roads winding through the forests. Peacocks are common here, scooting across the road as we approach or pulling their blue-feathered train into the brush. My rufous treepie is everywhere overhead, a lovely, long-tailed bird with a rufous belly and back, dark-gray head, and blue-gray wings. We stop to observe a small herd of gaur, incredibly massive buffalo-like bovids, their pale, curved horns pointing laterally at each other like calipers. They are quietly eating the leaves off the trees, the grass from the ground, bamboo shoots, seed pods—they are not picky eaters, the gaur. They move with ruminant efficiency through the thickets, their horned heads lowered, their massive necks and shoulders suggesting the difficulty a tiger might have in bringing one of them down, although our guide says that this sometimes happens. Pound for pound, the gaur would make more tigerish economic sense as a kill than any of the deer species. There seem to be several calves and cows in this group and perhaps, judging from its blacker color and larger size, a bull.

I see through my binoculars, at the muddy edge of a water hole, what appear to be a couple of cast-off, flattened tank treads. On closer examination, they are crocodiles taking their ease. Ignoring them, though not getting too close, are various plover, stilts, and egrets bobbing and dipping at the water's edge. Ducks that look familiar enough to me paddle around, and a small herd of barking deer are wandering along the shore, stopping every now and then to stare into the nearby forest, their ears at the ready.

In the trees, as we go on, a troop of langurs fling themselves from branch to branch. Langurs, pale-gray monkeys with round black faces framed in gray fur, live in great numbers at Kanha. They are scrawny things, about a foot and a half to two feet in height, with thin limbs and long, snakelike tails of great versatility. They move quickly. I see one mother with a tiny, hairless, wide-eyed baby clutched to her meager breast. The two of them, mother and child, stop to consider just what sort of life-form I represent. The mother clutches her baby more tightly to her with one hand and, with the other, grabs a vine and sails off, apparently not as willing as I am to acknowledge our primatial relationship.

Later, I see langurs convened in a meadow in the bright sun, sitting up, alerted as our jeep passes. Nearby, their symbiotic companions, the chital, graze. Here and there, rising from the dry patches of barren ground, are rocklike termite mounds three and four feet high. Other jeeps cross our path or meet on the dirt roads. The drivers tell each other what they know and speed off. No tigers yet, but the birds of India are everywhere—in the forest glades, at the lakes, every conceivable terrain offers its winged glory. Jungle babbler, brown crake, jicana, blue rock dove, Indian river tern. The birders are having—yes— a field day. In a small river vale lush with foliage, overhung with a canopy of tree branches, and alive with bird calls, a particularly beautiful vivid-blue bird the size of a robin alights on a branch above my head—just for a moment, for the intake of my breath, and then it's gone. A Tickell's thrush, someone in my jeep says, and writes the sighting down in her notebook. A gift, I think, and write nothing down. That is the inescapable conclusion: A consequential gift has been casually bestowed. I am beginning to understand the peculiar quality of my feelings in this park.

Now all the jeeps are gathered here in this glade so rich with bird life, and the birders are up on their feet, binoculars to their eyes, turning one way and then another as the sightings come thick and fast and the birders call out the names of what they see. We are getting noisy. Victor Emanuel, who organized this trip, has a portable tape recorder slung like an AK-47 over his shoulder. He's heard the call of something. He plugs in a microphone. "Taping, taping!" he calls out in his commanding baritone, and all at once the birders hush, and it's like the silence of a cathedral here in this sheltered vale, with only one faint but pure piping sound to be heard, like the earth itself singing.

But then later—is it this day or the next?—our driver pulls up at the intersection of two dirt roads in the forest and points wordlessly to the left. I see nothing, but I hear the langurs in the trees and they are putting up a terrible ruckus, a chorus of chipped-off growls, a kind of barking. Then it occurs to me that the woods are empty of any other sign of animal or bird life. Nothing flies, nothing grazes. And now I see him: out of the woods, indifferent to the fanfare, the orange-and-white black-striped monarch, shoulders bunching and head swaying as each footpad touches the ground—he is in a world he owns, he has more attitude than a rapper, he is more insolent than a rock star. And omigod, the size of him: As he crosses the road, he spans it.

Now he slips into the forest once more, disappears, is seen again through the brown tree trunks and yellowing brush for a second, and then seems to evaporate into thin air. I understand now why the tiger has stripes.

I expect our driver to follow slowly on a parallel along this road in hopes of another sighting. He doesn't, but backs up a few yards and turns off the ignition. Moments later there emerges, from the same woods that the tiger has come out of, an elephant driven by her mahout. They are plodding along on the trail of the beast and lumber across the road and into the woods after him.

Tigers and elephants get along because neither of them is on the other's menu. The mahout patiently tracks the tiger and comes upon him taking his ease in a sunlit glade. This is what all the guides have hoped for. Within minutes, everyone in the park knows about it and the jeeps convene at the roadside nearest the tiger's encampment, where three elephants are ready to shuttle our party into the brush for a close look.

Ladders are placed against an elephant's side, and we climb up to the howdah, a kind of saddle of old blankets folded on a wooden frame. Two of us sit on the huge back with our legs dangling to starboard, two more are on the port side. The mahout straddles the elephant's neck, directing her with a bare foot behind each of her ears. Riding an elephant through the brush makes Moghuls of us. The dun creature doesn't follow a path, she is the path. The tree branches slapping at us are our responsibility. But the rhythm of this rolling hill, the animacy of the ride, and then the stolid halt before the lazing cat give me an acute reprise of that joyful longing, that dark, shaded excitement I felt in my first minutes here.

Our tiger lies in the sun on a patch of dead leaves. He is in his brilliant array, regal, indifferent, his forelegs stretched out before him as he suffers himself to be gazed upon. Beside him, the remnants of a gaur. The elephant stands impassive. There is some mute understanding between them. The sun shines through the trees. And it comes over me how everything here is poised in beautiful equilibrium. Every creature in this preserve has everything it needs to live. This is not India, this is not any country, this is a realm, a kingdom not of our making. And my smile, with its twist of anguish, acknowledges that once we were part of it—that we belonged here too, once upon a time.

Yet it was predictable that India, with its culture of reverential respect for animals, would provide, from its populous self, room for the preservation of the natural world. We see this respect in the conscientious demeanor of the park wardens, indigenous locals who live in some isolation in various corners of the Kanha reserve to discourage poaching, now the major cause of tiger depletion. (Ground-up tiger bone is used in traditional Chinese medicine, and the male organ, from which a soup is derived, is assumed to convey virility.)

We see that characteristic Indian devotion too when, having reboarded our *Palace on Wheels*, we journey back up north through Agra. And after a day at the Taj Mahal, where the birders turn their backs on the most beautiful building in the world to train their binoculars on whatever bird happens to be darting by, we swing southwest overnight to Sawai Madhopur, to burrow into the haven for wildlife known as Ranthambore National Park.

Ranthambore is a smaller park than Kanha, perhaps 160 square miles of rugged terrain, access to which is via a canyon at the bottom of a cliff dominated by a tenth-century Chauan fort. The topography is desertlike, with stony ridges, murky water holes, washed-out roads, looming cliffs, volcanic rock, and fields of sun-bleached grasses. We see wild boars snouting around in the shadows of lakeside groves, flashes in the browned-out trees of the bright-green alexandrine parakeet. Ranthambore is not far from Jaipur and, for that reason, is more heavily visited by tourists than Kanha. Perhaps, as a result, the tigers that live here are more accustomed to a human presence and so more easily seen. Our driver stops the jeep and shows me pugmarks in the road. A female, he informs me with a smile. "I know her," he says, "she has two cubs."

A while later we see the cubs atop a ridge, half-hidden among a tangle of brush and fallen tree branches. They are large cubs, perhaps three-quarters grown, but they will stay there, where their mother has put them, until she returns. We are on her track now, our guide as excited as we are, but it is Helen who spots her, pointing but not saying a word: The tiger is loping through a rocky arroyo, not after a kill at this point but without question in the hunting mode, moving along briskly, parallel to our road, deftly leaping from boulder to boulder, sidling among the trees, and finally disappearing behind a ridge.

This is the world as it once was, with langurs *chok-choking* in the trees and peeling fruit on the rock abutments, and the brown crake and the black-headed ibis in deep study at the lakeside, and the tiny spotted owlet lurking in the knot of a tree trunk. Just before sunrise, we see the outlines in the mist of two handsomely antlered Barasingha, standing poised, attentive near the ruins of an ancient temple. I will, before we leave Ranthambore, pose for my picture under what I am told is the second-oldest banyan tree in India, without realizing that only a few hours earlier, the tiger and her cubs were posing here for their picture. Afterward, they climbed to the top of the arched stone gate leading to the yard where the jeeps are parked, and there comported themselves, tigers at the gate, to the astonishment of the birders.

And now we are entrained in our moving palace on the way back to Delhi, where we will have a final dinner at the Oberoi and congratulate Victor Emanuel and Raj Singh and their cadre of guides for having brought off a true adventure.

At the provincial railroad stops, squatters seem to be living on the concrete station platforms. They sit or lie about in family groups with their belongings spread out around them. They are people accustomed to the ground.

In the countryside, we see the tenacity of subsistence life . . . in the women scratching away at the baked-out rice paddies, the boy droving an emaciated white cow with its ribs showing, the open-air store with mostly empty shelves but with three bottles of Coke lined up on the counter.

We are back in India.

But now the *Palace on Wheels* does what trains all over the world do—it stops in the middle of nowhere for no apparent reason. As we look out the window of our saloon lounge, we see three children—two boys and a girl. The girl, perhaps eight or nine years old, is in costume, a blue outfit with Persian-style pantaloons tied at the ankles, ballet slippers, and a face rouged and lipsticked and eye shadowed as if for the stage. And this is her stage, this stretch of embankment in the sun just below our window.

The elder of the two boys, a thin, solemn child of about twelve in a white shirt and dark pants, beats a bass drum he carries by means of a rope tied around his neck. The younger boy, no more than four or five, hits a tambourine with the heel of his hand. And the girl dances. Her dance is circus-like, an acrobatic thing of cartwheels and somersaults and handstands and back flips. Between maneuvers, she smiles and flings her arms out wide while the boys scan the impenetrable car, waiting for a door to open.

We call our turbaned attendants. They open the door and press our rupees into the hands of the children. Moments later, the train begins to move and is soon chugging full speed toward Delhi.

The child's smile in the shockingly made-up face of that girl remains in my mind. She is India, of course, tauntingly amused by my clumsy effort to understand her.

2001

Maximum India

by

PICO IYER

There were fires, six, seven of them, rising through the winter fog. Groups of men, scarves wrapped around their heads, eyes blazing in the twilight, were gathered barefoot around the flames, edging closer. A near-naked man with dusty, matted dreadlocks down to his waist was poking at a charred head with a bamboo pole. There was chanting in the distance, a shaking of bells, a furious, possessed drumming, and in the infernal no-light of the winter dusk, I could make out almost nothing but orange blazes, far off, by the river.

How much of this was I dreaming? How much was I under a "foreign influence," if only of jet lag and displacement? Figures came toward me out of the mist, smeared in ash from head to toe, bearing the three-pronged trident of the city's patron, Shiva, the Ender of Time. In the little alleyways behind the flames was a warren of tiny streets; a shrunken candle burned in the dark of a bare earth cavern where men were whispering sacred syllables. Cows padded ceaselessly down the clogged, dung-splattered lanes, and every now and then another group of chanters surged past me, a dead body under a golden shroud on the bamboo stretcher that they carried toward the river, and I pressed myself against a wall as the whisper of mortality brushed past.

It was hard to believe that, just three days before, I had been in California, marking a quiet New Year's Day in the sun. Now there were goats with auspicious red marks on their foreheads trotting around, and embers burning, and oil lamps drifting out across the river in the fog. Along the walls beside the river were painted faces, laughing monkey gods, sacred looming phalluses. The shops on every side were selling sandalwood paste, and clarified butter oil for dead bodies, and tiny clay urns for their ashes.

Imagine finding yourself in a Hare Krishna celebration as populous as Philadelphia. All around you, people are shaking bells, whirling, singing joyfully, though their joy has to do with death, as if everything is upended in a holy universe. At the nearby Manikarnika Well, the god Shiva is said to have met the god Vishnu, usually an occupant of a parallel world. The result of this propitious encounter is that bodies are burned in public there—as many as a hundred a day—and the most sacred spot in the center of Hinduism is a smoking charnel-ground.

On paper, Varanasi is a holy crossroads, a place of transformation tucked between the Varana and Asi rivers, along the sacred Ganges. It is, many will tell you, the oldest continuously inhabited city on earth, as ancient as Babylon or Thebes. Because the city, now housing as many as three million (half a million of them squeezed into the square mile of the Old City), has never been a center of political power or historical conflict, it has been able to continue undisturbed, and fundamentally unchanged, as the most sacred citadel of Hinduism and a cultural hot spot. Bathe yourself in its filthy waters, devout Hindus believe, and you purify yourself for life. Die or be burned along its banks and you achieve *moksha*, or liberation, from the cycle of incarnation.

But if Varanasi means anything, it is the explosion of every theory and the turning of paper to ash. The heart of the city is a chaotic three-mile stretch of waterfront along Mother Ganga on which there are more than seventy ghats, or steps, from which the faithful can walk down into the water. At the top of these steps stand huge, many-windowed palaces and temples that are all in a state of such advanced decay that they seem to speak for the impermanence of everything. At this very spot, the southeast-flowing Ganges turns, briefly, so it seems to be flowing back toward the Himalayas from which it came, and bathers on its western bank can face the rising sun. Varanasi's original name, Kashi, means City of Light, although millennia of dusty rites and blazing bodies and holy men showing no interest in normal human laws have also left it a city of shadows or, as the wonderfully obsessive Varanasiphile Richard Lannoy writes, a "city of darkness and dream."

The son of Indian-born parents, I am (in theory) a Hindu, and though I have never practiced the religion, I was finding Varanasi to be more a mad confusion than the sublime order that a good Hindu would see. Yet in the months before I made my first trip to the city, everywhere I turned seemed to lead there, as if by magnetic attraction. Writing on Buddhism, I was reminded that the Buddha delivered his first discourse at Sarnath, six miles from Varanasi. Meeting a professor of Sanskrit in California, I was told that Shankara, the great Hindu philosopher, had accepted his first disciple in Varanasi and was said to have met Shiva there, in the disguise of an untouchable, more than a thousand years ago. This was where Peter Matthiessen began his epic Himalayan quest, recorded in *The Snow Leopard*; this was where Allen Ginsberg was shadowed by local intelligence and confessed, of the city's residents, "They're all mad."

Varanasi seemed to mark the place where opposites were pushed together so intensely that all sense gave out. Its holy waters flow, for example, past thirty sewers, with the result that the brownish stuff the devout are drinking and bathing in contains three thousand times the maximum level of fecal coliform bacteria considered safe by the World Health Organization. Those old collapsing buildings along its banks, suggesting some immemorial pageant, are in fact not old at all, although they do confirm the sense that one has entered less a city than an allegory of some kind, a cosmogram legible only to a few. Everything is constantly shifting, flickering this way and that in the candlelit phantasmagoria, and yet the best description I found of twenty-first-century Varanasi—"There is movement, motion, human life everywhere, and brilliantly costumed"—was penned by Mark Twain in the nineteenth.

A city that is truly holy is as contrary and multidirectional as any charismatic human, and draws people almost regardless of their faith or origins. So perhaps I should not have been surprised that, the minute I landed following the fifty-minute flight from Delhi and set foot in Varanasi, which was shrouded in a miasmal early-January mist, I ran into a Tibetan incarnate lama, an American Tibetan Buddhist monk I know from New York, and a ninety-one-year-old Parisienne I'd last seen attending teachings of the Dalai Lama's in Dharamsala.

"Oh," she said, unsurprised, "you are here too."

The Dalai Lama, I gathered, was giving his only official teachings of the winter and spring in Sarnath, right there, that very week.

The living capital of Hinduism is home, too, to fourteen hundred mosques and shrines, and every religious teacher from Jiddu Krishnamurti to Thich Nhat Hanh has spent time here; it was here that Mohandas Gandhi entered Indian political life in 1916 (when, at the inauguration of the local Banaras Hindu University, he spoke out against the filth of the city's holy places), and it was here that the French explorer Alexandra David-Néel received lessons in yoga from a naked swami before heading to Tibet.

I got into a car and entered the swirling river of life that in Varanasi reflects and flows into its central symbol. India specializes in intensity and chaos—part of the governing logic of Varanasi is that it is crowded with traffic and yet there are no traffic lights—and very soon I was careening through the crush (a riot in search of a provocation, so it seemed): Here and there an elderly policeman with a mask over his mouth held out an arm, and cars, cows, bicycles, and trucks crashed past him, willy-nilly. Dogs were sleeping in the middle of a busy road—Varanasi's Fifth Avenue, it might have been—and men were outstretched (sleeping, I hoped) along the side and on the pavement. I dropped my bags at my hotel, The Gateway, and in the course of the twenty-minute ride to the river, I saw two more jubilant corpse processions and two parades of children—in honor, I could only imagine, of the God of Mayhem.

"This is a very inauspicious time," my guide warned me from the front seat. "It is called Kharamas. Everyone stays hidden; no one talks about weddings, things like that. Everyone is silent. It is like a curse placed on the city."

I could find no mention of any such observance, but if this was Varanasi at its most silent, I thought, I couldn't imagine it on one of its frequent festival days. "The curse lifts on January 14," my new friend told me. "Then we celebrate." This was not cause for celebration to someone due to depart, as I was, on January 13.

At a Christian church, we got out and joined the crush of bodies pushing toward the Ganges. We walked along the path to the river-bank, dodging the refuse and excrement of centuries, and passed an almost naked man, staring right at us, sheltered by a small fire inside a hut.

"He's meditating?" I tried.

"Everything for him is ashes," came the reply. Philosophy is ceaseless along the Ganges, and usually causeless. Holy men sat on the ground under umbrellas, chanting and smearing paste and ash on their foreheads. "These sadhus, they like very much to live with cremation. They don't wear clothes as we do. They don't do anything like people who are living in the material world. They want to live in a world of ash." To come here was like entering one of the narrow, winding old cities of Europe—my birthplace of Oxford, in fact—in which you are back in a medieval mix of high scholasticism and faith.

A huge, bloated cow floated past us, and we climbed into a boat as five handsome young boys in elaborate gold pantaloons held up five-armed oil lamps in a glossy fire ceremony along the river. Fires were blazing to the north and south, and the air was thick with the smell of incense and burning. "Only in this city, sir, you see twenty-four-hour cremation," offered the boatman, as if speaking of a convenience store.

In other cities, cremation grounds are traditionally placed outside the city gates. Here, they burn at the center of all life.

The next day, a little before daybreak, I walked out of the gates of my hotel to visit the river again. Only one man was standing there now, under a tree, with a bicycle-rickshaw—his eyes afire in his very dark face, and what looked to be a bullet hole in his cheek. We negotiated for a while and then took off into the penumbral gloom, the previously jam-packed streets under a kind of sorcerer's spell, quite empty.

To travel by bicycle in the dawn is to feel all the sounds, smells, and ancient ghosts of Varanasi; for more than a week, the bicycle-rickshaw man would become my faithful friend, waiting outside the gates of the hotel, ready to guide me anywhere. The winter fog only compounded the half-dreamed air of the place, as figures loomed out of the clouds to stare at us, and then vanished abruptly, as if nothing was quite substantial here, or even true. *"Unreal City,"* I thought, remembering a boyhood ingestion of T. S. Eliot. *"Under the brown fog of a winter dawn . . . I had not thought death had undone so many."*

On the Ganges, a Charon pulled me soundlessly across the water, past all the broken palaces, the huge flights of steps, the men and women walking down to the water, barely clothed, dipping their heads in and shaking themselves dry, as if awakening from a long sleep. "In Varanasi," said the ferryman, "thirty-five, forty percent is holy men." In another boat, an Indian man with his young wife and child had his laptop open in the phantasmal dark. Cows, pariah dogs, and figures in blankets appeared in the mist, and red-bottomed monkeys ran in and out of the temples. "Sir," said the boatman, and I braced myself for an offer of young girls, young boys, or drugs. "You would like *darshan*? I arrange meeting with holy man for you?"

All this, of course, is the Varanasi of sightseers, the almost psychedelic riddle at the eye of the storm that entices many, horrifies others, and leaves most feeling as if they are losing their mind. But part of the power of the holy city is that it is shaped very consciously—like a mandala, some say, a series of concentric sacred zones—and as you move away from the river, you come out into a world that is India's highest center of learning and refinement, home to its greatest scholars for as long as anyone can remember.

"It is such a beautiful city," said Pramod Chandra, an elegant soul who comes from a long line of Varanasi thinkers and writers (and who is a professor emeritus of art at Harvard). We were seated in his large, bare family home not far from the burning ghats and the crumbling palaces. "If they did it up, it could be like one of the great cities of Spain or Italy. The tall houses in the Old City? If you go inside, you find abundant worlds there—courtyards and inner spaces, everything. But the problem in India is always bureaucracy. It's deadening." There was now, he said, a plan for creating a futuristic overpass around the Old City, so as to turn the maze of ill-lit alleyways into a kind of inner suburb.

Because the buildings of Varanasi are only about 350 years old, the city has always had to sustain its traditions in human ways, through rites and ideas; it is not the stones or monuments that give Varanasi its sense of continuity, as in Jerusalem or at Kailas, but the unchanging customs passed down from father to son to grandson. The professor recalled for me, over a long evening of talk, the days when educated boys here learned Sanskrit from pandits who came to their homes, committing to memory huge swatches of holy text.

So part of the deeper fascination of the City of Light, beyond the visceral shock, is the way it brings together back-lane black magic and high-flown speculation and, in so doing, serves as India's India, a concentrated distillate of the culture's special mix of cloudy philosophizing and unembarrassed reality. Spirituality in Varanasi lies precisely in the poverty and sickness and death that it weaves into its unending tapestry; a place of holiness, it says, is not set apart from the world, in a Shangri-la of calm, but a place where purity and filth, anarchy and ritual, unquenchable vitality and the constant imminence of death all flow together.

In Varanasi, as everywhere in India, the first rule of survival is that getting anywhere at all—from A to B via T, Q, and Z—is an ordeal;

but settling into some quiet corner and joining in the rhythm of life around you can make for one of the most cozy and companionable stays imaginable. The center of life is Asi Ghat, at the southern end of the line of ghats, which has now turned into a foreigner-friendly neighborhood of eco-institutes and Salsa Dance Aerobics classes, pizza restaurants and compendious bookshops. And the epicenter of Asi Ghat, for the fortunate few, is the Hotel Ganges View, an unassuming-looking place whose thirteen rooms are usually filled with some of the most interesting Varanasi watchers you will ever meet.

Here you can find yourself sharing a table on a candlelit rooftop with a Danish psychiatrist working with trauma in Iraq, Rwanda, and Bosnia, and a German scholar of Hinduism. After dinner, the low-ceilinged dining room was turned into a backdrop for an intimate concert, and as I sat there, being whipped up into the ether by two sarangi players and a tabla virtuoso, a gnomish man with tufts of white hair and a tweed jacket came in. He looked back at me and casually nodded, and I realized that it was a German singer of Sufi *ghazal*s whom I had last seen in the Tiergarten in Berlin, talking of Ethiopia and Mali.

Varanasi has at times this feeling of being an insider's secret, marked on the invisible map that certain initiates carry around with them, and as the days went on, I came to see that the constant back-and-forth—the advance into the intensities of the river, the retreat to a place from which to contemplate them all—was part of the natural rhythm of the city. Every time I stepped out of my hotel to be greeted by my loyal friend with his rickshaw, I was pitched into the Boschian madness of a teeming, pell-mell cacophony in which, amid the constant plodding of beasts, I saw ads for an Institute of Call Centre Training, notices for "radio jockey certificate courses," signs for those dreaming to become "air stewardesses." The promise of the new India is that even the poorest kid in the slums, if he applies himself at a Brain Gym, can make it not to the NBA but to an MBA course, and to the once-unimaginable world marked out by the shining new malls and ubiquitous signs for McVeggie with Cheese. Such is the inclusiveness of

Varanasi and the hundreds of gods it houses that the new is taken in as readily as the old.

We would clatter through the mob and arrive at the river, and I would be reminded how and why members of my own (Hindu, India-dwelling) family would often tell me, "Don't go to Benares [as Varanasi was long known]! It's just stench and crooks and dirt. Only tourists like it." In Aravind Adiga's Man Booker–winning first novel, *The White Tiger*, the narrator declares, "Every man must make his own Benares," a way of saying that, for the upwardly mobile and up-to-the-minute creature of New India, the old city stands for all the ageless hierarchies and ancient rites that have to be pushed aside. Varanasi is the home of your grandmother's grandmother's dusty superstitions, and the new global Indian purports to have no time for it.

At the river itself, on the rare day when the fog lifted, men were blowing conch shells to greet the dawn, and women were pounding clothes upon the stone steps to wash them. Saried figures were stepping into the surging brown, and others were lifting their cupped hands to the rising sun. Varanasi, I thought, was a five-thousand-year-old man who may have put on an FCUK shirt and acquired a Nokia but still takes the shirt off each morning to bathe in polluted waters and uses his new cell phone to download Vedic chants.

There is another sight that helps to underline this ancient dialectic. Indeed, Sarnath, more or less a suburb of Varanasi these days, is to some extent the product of the same back-and-forth. Born into the higher reaches of Hinduism, the young prince who became the Buddha walked away from all the abstraction and ritualism of Brahmin priests in order to find his own truth, just by stilling his mind and seeing what lies behind our pinwheeling thoughts and projections. After he came to his understanding in the town of Bodh Gaya, he traveled to Sarnath's Deer Park and outlined his eightfold path for seeing through suffering.

To travel from Varanasi to Sarnath today is to undertake a similar journey, and one that retraces a central shift in the history of philosophy. As soon as you move out into the country fields and narrow roads on the way to the little village, the roar and tumult of the holy city begin to vanish, and you see Buddhist temples from all the traditions—and buildings with names like the Society for Human Perception—peeping from behind the trees. A beautiful museum houses Buddhas excavated in the area over centuries. One minute you're in the midst of the whirligig shock of crackling flames and darkened lanes, and thirty minutes later you are in a large, quiet park where monks in yellow and gray and claret robes are seated silently on the grass, meditating before the Dhamekh Stupa, originally set up here by the emperor Ashoka 249 years before the birth of Christ.

Because the Dalai Lama was about to offer teachings nearby, the pleasant park around the 143-foot stupa had been transformed into a busy, merry Tibetan settlement. As I looked out on the park, some Vietnamese nuns in triangular bamboo hats joined the Tibetans to pay their silent respects, while a Mongolian—striking in topknot and beard and rich silk robes—roared out his prayers. I went to listen to the Dalai Lama talk about the bodhisattva way of life, and when he was finished, the little lanes of the settlement filled with so many red-robed monks that it felt as if we had all ended up in Lhasa when it was a center of the Buddhist world.

On my arrival in Varanasi, it had seemed impossible to pull myself out of its hypnotic spell, its constant movement, its air of danger around the flames, where so many men (and it seemed to be all men) were waiting in such a state of restless energy that I could feel the sense of violence just below the surface of the Indian communion, in which a spark of misunderstanding can quickly turn into a blaze. On my third day in the city, my bicycle rickshaw ran right into a procession for the Shia festival of Muharram, in which thousands of bare-chested Muslim boys were waving swords, shouting slogans of defiance, and carrying through the narrow, jam-packed streets ten-foot poles and silver-tinseled shrines that looked certain to collapse on us all at any moment. Two days later, the monthlong period of mourning was still blocking traffic.

But as the days went on, I realized that all I really had to do was sit and let life along the riverbank unfold around me. A crow was perched on a placid cow, now and then pecking bits of seed off the animal's cheek. A holy man fielded a cricket ball in the river and flung it back to the boys who had set up a high-speed game along the banks. Gypsies from the backpack trail drifted by, swathed in scarves and shawls.

I had been determined not to fall under the city's spell, nor to repeat the lines that so many millions of visitors have uttered, changelessly, for more centuries than I can count. I knew that Varanasi—India to the max—would stretch credulity in every direction, and I told myself to stay clear and alert, on the throne of pure reason. A part of me, lapsed Hindu, longed to stand apart. But as I kept returning to the ghats, I found myself thinking along lines I'd never explored before. Standing by the bonfires, suddenly noting how silent all the men around me were—the clamor was coming from elsewhere—I started to imagine what it would feel like to see a lover's body crumbling and crackling before my eyes, the shoulder I had grown used to holding every day for twenty years reduced to ash. I started to think about what one does with remains, and what exactly they mean (or don't). I felt the truth of the Buddhist exercises my friends sometimes spoke about, of seeing in every beautiful model the skeleton beneath the fancy covering.

I began to walk south along the river then, till I came to the other burning ghat—orange flames lighting up the surrounding buildings with their glow—and as I kept walking, the path grew deserted and dark till the only light came from far above, where a candle was flickering inside a rounded shrine. I walked on and on, deeper into the dark, knowing the steps and walkways of the city so well by now that I could dodge the areas where the water buffalo were wont to relieve themselves, and knew how not to get tangled in the kite strings of the little boys who raced along the riverbank in the uncertain light as if to tangle us all up in Varanasi itself. The decaying palaces up above, with their hollowed-out windows and interiors stuffed with refuse, or with huddled bodies, looked, when a light came on, like the homes of cele-brants at some great festival who had long passed on—ghost houses.

That death could be a shrine before which everyone pays homage; that holy things, as a tour guide says in Shusaku Endo's haunting Varanasi novel, *Deep River*, do not have to be pretty things; that all of us are flowing on a river in which we will be picked up and brought into a larger current; and that there can be flames marking the fires of heaven as much as of hell—all played havoc with what I thought I knew.

A crossing ground, I began to think, is not just where the dead move on to something else but where the living are carried off to another plane, and where thought and sensation themselves are turned around. "For Hindus," I had read in the work of the great Varanasi scholar Diana L. Eck, "death is not the opposite of life; it is, rather, the opposite of birth"—akin, perhaps, to leaving a cinema by a different door than the one you came in by.

The following morning I ran into my guide from my first day, always so eager to show visitors the beauties of his city.

"How are you, my friend?" I called.

"So good, sir. It is a beautiful day. More warm. No fog. Visibility is good."

"So you think the curse is lifted?"

"Oh yes, sir. This all means it is the coming of spring."

The next morning, my last, I awoke to find the whole city covered in a pall of mist so thick that the ghostly towers and palaces I could see from my room seemed to have unmade themselves in the dark. Planes would not be able to take off or land. Trains would be delayed twenty hours or more. Vehicles would crash into one another, with fatal results. Down by the river, I could not see thirty feet in front of me, so that the smoke from all the fires—and winter fog and pollution—made every figure I saw look like a visitor from another world. It could seem as if we were all trapped now, spellbound in this sleeping world, and that the dense, feverish, self-contained model of the universe was inside our bones and had become our destiny, our home.

2011

Love by the River Liffey

by

EDNA O'BRIEN

 Dublin has many names. In Gaelic she was Dubh Linn, or the Black Pool, and Baile Atha Cliath, the Town of the Hurdle-ford. Then Strumpet City and Dear Dirty Dublin; and Anna Livia after the River Liffey, which among other things is famous for the unique flavor it once imparted to Guinness, the "gargle" of Dublin, which as the author Brendan Behan once said to me, has "atin' and drinkin' in it."

There are many things about this "gallant venal city" to beguile you: There is the wide sweep of the bay, green, bottle green, and scowling black; the sky ever changing, great trammels of cloud marching overhead; the sound of gulls and pigeons swooping in and out of the coves; and beyond, ranges of mountain, friendly, engirdling, purple and deep blue. It is a city buttressed and battered by nature. And a city battered by invasions, having been occupied in the ninth century by Norse Vikings, who built a fort across the river, installing themselves in their mud huts, a safe haven for piracy and commerce, their sway unchallenged, despite skirmishes with Irish kings, until they were defeated by Brian Boru, a Munster king, at the battle of Clontarf in 1014. Roughly one hundred years later came the Norman invasion and conquest, which penetrated beyond Dublin into the country proper, and Ireland fell under British domination, which was to continue for almost eight hundred years. England forwent her sovereignty, and the keys of Dublin Castle were handed over by the British to the new republic in 1921, when some animated young men led by Michael Collins tumbled out of two taxis "to take over the Devil's Half Acre."

The rebellion of 1916, which was the direct cause and catalyst of the 1921 treaty with the British, comprised a handful of volunteers who occupied the General Post Office in Dublin for a few strategic days and eventually surrendered, partly out of fear of civilian casualties. The rebellion was brief, but the flames soared so high that Sean O'Casey said "the heavens looked like a great ruby hanging from God's ear." Most of the leaders were executed in the yard of Kilmainham Jail—the Irish Bastille—and buried in lime-pit graves on Arbour Hill. Much of Dublin Castle and all of the Bank of Ireland (once the House of Parliament, until the Act of Union with England in 1801), the Customs House, Trinity College, and the remaining Georgian squares with their Corinthian pillars, great staircases, beautiful plasterwork, stucco, tracery, and allegorical images, all carry the vestiges of that eighteenth-century grandeur when for the landowners and gentry Dublin was a round of balls, routs, and suppers, and when for the natives in the slums, ragged and destitute, it was, as one visitor described it, "one of the infernal regions." It is said that the Irish should forget their history and the English should remember it, but the City of Dublin is impregnated with her history—political, religious, and literary. It is this sense of the past, however transmogrified, that gives her such verve, such vitality, and an innate sense of, as the song says, "The Rare Aul Times," the very title encompassing the city's tragedies and her glitter.

Last October, standing on a mound of granite rocks in Bullock Harbour and none too steady on my high heels, being photographed by the great but exacting Helmut Newton, I was conscious yet again of the timelessness that Dublin emanates, a timelessness engendered not only by nature but by the people, a sense of laissez-faire. For instance: A young woman called Dolores who looked after the moored boats in the harbor was bailing out water with a bucket, just bailing, and when I asked if I could come back and have a chat with her, she said, "I'm here always—winter and summer—me and the dog." A few lobster pots bobbed idly about, a steamer moved in the distance, recalling Joyce's image of "steamers lowing out like sea cows," and the smell of the seaweed and sea air brought to my mind his more mischievous image, "the gay aire of my soul troublien salt, troublien bay and the race of the say wint up me ambushare."

Last year the figure that commemorates Joyce's Anna Livia, an ample woman recumbent on pillows of water, had been nicknamed "The Floozy with the Jacuzzi," but this year the joke has escalated to her being "The Whure with the Sewer." Thomas Davis, the poet and patriot who wrote "A Nation Once Again," not unsurprisingly has had his statue rechristened "Urination Once Again," and Molly Malone, she who was famous in song for wheeling a "wheelbarrow through streets broad and narrow" as she sold cockles and mussels, is named in some quarters "The Tart with the Cart" because of her big boobs, and in others "The Hag with the Bags." The housing estate where newly-weds live is called Pill Hill, while older people occupy Menopause Mansions. Glasnevin, the principal graveyard, is of course The Dead Centre, and getting a move on is "On your trotters." And on it goes. In order to bring home to the psyche of the plain people of Ireland the fact that tomatoes were homegrown, a government minister a year or so ago allowed himself to be pelted with ripe tomatoes next to the said Molly. Protocol is not the Dublin way. Instead, there is mirth and debunking, and both private and public figures are subject to a bit of ego-bashing. Dr. Johnson once said that he had a great respect for the Irish people, as they always spoke ill of their own.

In many cities—London, for instance, where I live—you get a feeling of shutters drawn—human, physical, and metaphysical. But the opposite is true of Dublin. Here they welcome strangers with an embrace that borders on the atavistic. H. V. Morton, describing the three great feminine capitals of Europe—Paris, Vienna, and Dublin—said that "the first two have all the lure of woman and the last has all her charm and spite." Visitors and scribes have tended either to fall under her spell or to treat her with disdain. A certain Dr. Twiss who went there in 1700 and who disliked the place had, for his spleen, his likeness engraved on the base of chamber pots.

At the beginning of last year I arrived and found Dublin in fine and buoyant mood. It had been snowing, and in the outlying fields on the way in from the airport, the clumps of gray-white snow looked like leaking sods of turf.

"Unbelievable, unbelievable altogether," was how the taxi driver deemed the weather. There was snow elsewhere in the British Isles, but to Irish people, all things, even a snowfall, have a phantasmagoric quality. The driver was not a Dublin man but a "Culchie" (from the country), and he went home to the foot of the Galtee Mountains once a month to renew his accent. Over at Phoenix Park, a Mayo woman named Robinson had taken up residence as the first female president, surrounded herself with female staff, and was as yet, in a complimentary way, "The Bauld Mary with no warts." Meanwhile, the charismatic and volatile prime minister, Mr. Charlie Haughey, often referred to as Charlemagne, had a government building restored for himself and his parliamentary staff to the tune of seventeen million pounds—carpets, stained glass, paneled walls, and a helicopter pad. "Charlie's Palace" was quickly being renamed "Charlie's Phallus." If any city deserves an encomium for comedy, it is surely Dublin, because nothing or no one goes unscathed.

Mr. Haughey, as it happened, gave me a lavish dinner that night in a private room in a beautiful restaurant, Le Coq Hardi, whose owner, John Howard, hailed from my own county, Clare. Ireland being Ireland, I was able to converse with Howard as readily as with any of the guests. He had always had "a feeling for food," and as a young lad

Edna O'Brien*

with no shoes or stockings he went to work as a potboy in a hotel in Lisdoonvarna. One Sunday, with the owners gone to a hurling match, some famished guests arrived, demanding sustenance and allowing him the chance to cook his first meal, which was "a multifarious mixed grill" followed by jam pancakes. He decided he was going to be a great chef, and with hard work at Swiss restaurants he achieved it. Last year he was chef for the heads of Europe when Mr. Haughey was the host president of the EC, and at Malahide Castle the dignitaries had Claren-bridge oysters, salmon in watercress sauce, saddle of lamb with wild mushrooms, and an Irish Mist soufflé. He had grown the watercress himself and had gone to Wicklow in person to dig up the wild mush-rooms. Always among the Irish you get a sense of largess, as if the specter of the famine still remained. Indeed, they use the phrase "a feast or a famine." Mrs. Delany, one of the great hostesses of the eigh-teenth century, gave four people the following fare: "Fish, beefstakes, soup, rabbits and onions, Fillet Veal, Turkey Pout, salmon grilde, pickled salmon, quails, little Terrene Peas, Cream, Mushrooms, Apple Pye, Crab, Leveret, Cheese-cakes, blamange, cherries, Dutch Cheese, Raspberries and Cream, sweetmeats and jelly, strawberries and cream, almond cream, currants and gooseberries, Orange Butter."

The dinner with Mr. Haughey, and indeed, each dinner that I had during my visit (though not when I worked in Dublin in the 1950s as a chemist's apprentice), was lavish, racy, and, in the best sense, intem-perate. Topics ranged from politics to the "troubles" in the North, to the unfortunate twist of fate of the Fianna Fail candidate, Brian Linihan, who through a blunder of his own making lost the presidency to Mrs. Robinson, to the sex appeal of Margaret Thatcher and Mr. Haughey's cherished dream of making a part of Dublin, Temple Bar, a replica of the Left Bank of Paris, with artists, ateliers—the lot. Dublin-Paris-Bonn, he believes, is the new axis of Europe. Conversation was, as always, spiced with song; and before the evening ended it came around to James Joyce, a discussion as to which chapter in *Ulysses* remains the most memorable, the women plumping for the Molly Bloom soliloquy and the men recommending the piquance of the Sirens chapter. There

212

was, I should add, a poet or two, a beauty or two, and some motley friends; there was also a blazing turf fire, sublime food, and a chocolate dish that even President Mitterrand had requested the recipe for.

"The letters of the name of Dublin lay heavily upon his mind, pushing one another surrily hither and thither with slow boorish insistence." So wrote Joyce about his native city, and now James Joyce, Rolls-Royce, or whatever else he liked to call himself trips lightly and proudly and incessantly on the lips of her inhabitants. Castigated, indeed reviled, in his own time, he has perforce made Dublin immortal, has given her that cosmopolitan aura so dear to the Irish, so dear to islanders, so dear to a conquered race. Even those who have not had the time or the stomach to read him can peruse snatches by simply looking down at the pavement, where plaques containing passages from *Ulysses* are laid into the slabstone, marking Leopold Bloom's juicy peregrinations. In Hodges Figgis's bookshop there is a blown-up poster that reads, "Darkness is in our souls do you not think? Flutier. Our souls, shame-wounded by our sins, clinging to us yet more, a woman to her lover clinging, the more the more." I asked the girl behind the counter which chapter that was from, and she said with typical Dublin piquance, "I haven't a clue."

It so happened that Joyce's material had come out of copyright that week, he being dead fifty years, and, moreover, a box containing minutiae of his life was due to be opened by the curator of the National Library. Dublin buzzed with speculation as to what might be in the box. One strongly held opinion was that it was probably the little mannequin's knickers, which he always carried and which some say was the fetish essential to his genius. Others hoped that it might be a lock of Nora Barnacle's pubic hair, and still others that the erotic letters she wrote to him in 1909 in answer to his avalanche of erotic letters might surface—except that a few thought that, being a convent girl, she was too "cute" to leave any smut lying around for posterity.

Joyce wrote about everything to do with Dublin: the streets, the trams, the brands of soap, the Goerz lenses in a shop window in Nassau

Street that cost six guineas, and above all the sea. It was as if he was wedded to the sea, as if the source of his inspiration lay swaddled in her. "Great sweet mother" was what he called the sea, but he also described it as "snotgreen and scrotumtightening sea." His obsession with womanhood found metaphors in the "white breast of the dim sea." The Martello Tower, that cold, domed room where *Ulysses* opens and which is now a Joyce museum, was closed for winter when I visited, and his words "a shut door of a silent tower" were indeed apt: But the bay, the span of open sea with views of Dún Laoghaire, Sandycove, the various lighthouses, the spires of the city, the wooded Hill of Howth, were all there, subject to the sparkle of a searing winter morning.

One of the traditional sounds of Dublin had always been the nightwatch calling the hour and the weather—"Past twelve o'clock and a cloudy night." Now it is music and the ringing of bells. There are buskers everywhere, and you hear the tin whistle, the mouth organ, the melodeon (squeeze-box) playing Irish, English, folk, punk, American, traditional, come-all-ye—all intermingling with the bells in the various churches, especially those from St. Patrick's, the Protestant church where Saint Patrick himself is said to have baptized pagans in a nearby well. Though now peopled with only a mere scattering of souls, it is beautifully maintained, brasses gleaming, hangings and kneelers without a ravel, and the doll-size chairs smelling of wax polish. It was here that Jonathan Swift, the dean of St. Patrick's for more than twenty years, wrote *Gulliver's Travels* and *Drapier's Letters* and urged the Irish to burn every English thing except coal. He took care of the poor of the vicinity and built an almshouse for widows and a hospital for the mad (he thought no city needed it more). He is said to have loved two women, Stella and Vanessa, but it is Stella who holds a sentimental place in the recesses of Irish mythologizing. He first met her in England when she was eight, educated her, loved her after a fashion, and invited her to Ireland as soon as he returned there. Yet he always saw her in the company of another person, her gentlewoman, Rebecca Dingley. After her death, for several winter nights he sat in the gloom of the cathedral composing the *Journal to Stella*, this most virtuous woman, and adding to the speculations that had arisen about them. It was said—it still is—that they were brother and sister, both being the illegitimate children of Sir William Temple. Or that they were uncle and niece, incestuously connected. Or that they had married, but that Swift, upon finding out the horror of the circumstances, shrank from any physical contact with Stella and on a certain day of each year—the anniversary of the aborted marriage—demanded that they each spend it fasting, praying, and in tears. Not too long ago, when their bodies were disinterred during construction work, they were both found to have in their skull identical and perfectly preserved teeth, which added fuel to the titillating incest story. Now they lie side by side not far from the stands selling tea cloths, shoehorns, and jaunting cars, under the cold coral-and-cream tiles of St. Patrick's, and as the little girl selling tickets said, "Maybe they are dancing around in the Poddle underneath."

Near St. Patrick's you will see Marsh's Library, a beautiful little sequestered building, a scholar's library in a cottage garden, founded by Archbishop Narcissus Marsh in 1701, a man whom Swift hated, claiming "none will be glad or sorry at his death except his successor." The librarian, Mrs. Muriel McCarthy, chuckles with unabashed pride at being the first woman keeper and points to her name on a list composed of men. This is her family, these beautiful, dark oak bookcases carved and lettered and topped with miters, these cages where readers were locked in and where even Joyce spent a time when he consulted the faded prophecies of Joachim Abbas. Here are liturgical works, missals, breviaries, books from the hours of Sarum, Bibles in every language, manuscripts of lute music, Elizabethan poetry, and Mrs. McCarthy's favorite book of all, *Cicero's Letters to His Friends*, printed in Milan in 1472. It is easy to say that a place is haunted, but I believe that in the best sense this little library is. The cream vellum volumes stare back at one with all the startle and softness of doves, and to complete the illusion, Mrs. McCarthy leads you by the arm to one of the very first copies of "Sleeping Beauty."

Walking through the Liberties, one of Dublin's oldest quarters, you walk where Swift walked, being too thrifty to take a sedan, and where he passed the Cabbage Garden, which he renamed Naboth's Vineyard and planted as a Paradise Garden with peaches, nectarines, and apples. Here once were alehouses, slaughterhouses, and dwellings so crammed that one visitor described the area as "one of the infernal regions." Huguenots who had fled from France because of religious persecution settled here and became the city's first weavers and artisans. Swift, ever a friend to the downtrodden, gave interest-free loans from his earnings as a writer to those unfortunates who had pawned or sold their looms. At the time a blind ballad singer in a frieze coat and brogue shoes broadcast their straits with a ditty: "I live in Faddle Alley / Off Blackpitts near the / Coombe, with my poor wife Sally, / In a narrow dirty room." Today a small shrine once again manifests the wit and adaptability of Dubliners. It had been erected there for Queen Victoria's Golden Jubilee in 1887 but in 1929 had a Sacred Heart added to commemorate the centenary of Catholic emancipation and in 1979 was dolled up to mark the occasion of Pope John Paul II's visit. You pass acres of wasteland, small Victorian houses with net curtains, a hostel for the homeless, and a saucy advertisement of three career women proclaiming the merits of lager. Everywhere the smell of roasted barley from Guinness's Brewery, a smell that pervades the city the way the drink from the drawn barrels brims over onto the pub counters, recalling Joyce's "gushy flab of porter." Yes, Joyce holds the keys to the city.

Back on Grafton Street, there are the buskers and batches of students from Trinity College, along with the girls for whom window-shopping is a kind of fetish. Trinity College, which dominates College Green and faces the beautiful Gandon building that was once the House of Parliament, was built on a monastic foundation at the end of the sixteenth century, its purpose, as Queen Elizabeth the First succinctly stated, to serve as "a counterblast to Popery" and to convert the rude Irish to the Protestant religion. For hundreds of years Roman Catholics were prohibited, and street fights between the Fellows and the Catholic mob were a common occurrence. In these ecumenical times it is open to all, and in these materialistic times some of its costs are met by the visitors who come to pace its august precincts and visit the library that possesses Ireland's greatest collection of books and manuscripts, including beautifully illuminated versions of the Gospels. There is a harp said to have belonged to Brian Boru, he who routed the Danes in 1014 but was afterward slain in his tent while giving thanks to God.

Grafton Street has many distractions: a mime artist, white and enameled, impassive to any jibes; a poet willing to recite his own poetry or one of your poems for a stipend; beggars, usually with babes in arms, rattling plastic containers; and a man in a wheelchair, his begging bowl a little flowerpot and his hobby Irish music—he listens animatedly to his cassette while bopping in his wheelchair to keep himself warm or amused. You will stop at Bewley's Oriental Cafe because the smell of coffee will tempt you, and if you go in, you will have to taste Barm Brack, a yeast cake filled with currants, raisins, and lemon peel, as you lounge in the James Joyce Room or in the Joshua Room. A sign invites customers to avail themselves of the turf fire although the café is not officially open until eight o'clock.

No one knows exactly how many pubs there are in Dublin, but the stock answer is that there are more pubs than there is truth. The city has always had an abundance of them, and by the middle of the eighteenth century the count was two thousand alehouses, three hundred taverns, and twelve hundred brandy shops. Now they are simply pubs, each with its own designation, a pub for country and western, a pub for old folks' sing-alongs, betting pubs, literary pubs, and, believe it or not, an ex-pub that is now a modest chapel run by two American priests. Two of the pubs that feature in *Ulysses* are still there—Davy Byrne's and The Bailey—and "to cap it," as the Irish would say, the door of number 7 Eccles Street, the abode of Mr. and Mrs. Leopold Bloom, stands in The Bailey vestibule as a showpiece, a weathered dark blue door with cracks in the paintwork and a split down one panel, as if someone had taken an ax to it. An animated bystander will tell you that it was at this door, legless, that Stephen Dedalus and Leopold Bloom came, minus a key, and had to wake up the plenteous Molly from her reveries. The odd thing is, the impression you get from the telling is that these are not characters in a book but two Dublin poxies out late. Fact and fiction have become one. Your bystander offers you a drink, which you cannot refuse, you return the compliment, some others with stories to tell edge their way over to your table, and a leisurely morning's drinking has just begun.

After The Bailey I went to Cheers, having been told that I would hear some traditional music and meet the doyens of folk. Two young men had commenced playing the bagpipes. They were off the gargle on account of Christmas, so when I offered them a drink, it was H_2O only. Elsewhere, pints were being drawn at a nice pace, and those who were suffering were having a little "hair of the dogma." Two minutes is the accepted time to draw a pint, and there are bets in Dublin as to which pub and which barman draws the best. A customer who had come from a neighboring hostelry, and for no better reason than that it was closed for the Sunday "Holy Hour," said he was surprised that I had come to a pub with an American flavor and American memorabilia on the walls and not to a more literary joint—not, for instance, to the pub, the only pub W. B. Yeats was said to have ever stepped into and where, having had a Guinness, he declared that he did not see the merit in it. No, he was not a Yeats man himself. Yeats was a snob—and, worse, a mystic snob.

"What is a mystic snob?" I asked.

"It's a man who can't pull the girls," he said, and I had a vision of Yeats with his rook look and his black cloak, emptying the contents of something worse than a teapot onto this vulgar Philistine.

Saturday night in O'Donoghue's was so crowded that the orders had to be shouted across the heads of customers to a barman who stood up on the counter; he took the orders and shouted them calmly across to two overworked barmen. "Sairtenly," he said, as if all were calm and the rival singing and instruments were not loud enough to bring the roof down. They're used to it. The Shelbourne bar had to close its doors at four o'clock in the afternoon on Christmas Eve, admitting only as many people as went out, which, as Christie the doorman said, was wicked because who'd want to go home anyway! AN CRAIC AGUS AN CEOIL. So say the old-fashioned posters, and so it lives on: the fun and the music, the barman with his "sairtenly" and "thremendious," the various overheards about everything being "game ball" and "swally that" as you're handed a drink by a total stranger and begged to forget your cares and "submit to the alchemy." I declare to godfathers, as they now say, that you do. Myles na gCopaleen, one of Ireland's most rueful geniuses, has called this transmogrification of the English language "a nosegay of amiable cawboguery."

St. Stephen's Green, a huge ornamental garden, is one of Dublin's landmarks, and its artificial lake, curving, as George Moore said, "like a piece of calligraphy," is a meeting place for locals and visitors (or, as it was more grandly said, for aristocrat and parvenu) alike. Once it was a marshland adjoining a leper hospital, where people grazed their livestock, but in time it became a park where the Bucks and the Beaus walked and watched women in their carriages. (An eighteenth-century writer complained, however, that on Sundays around six o'clock, people of distinction were driven out of the green by milliners, manteau makers, stay makers, seamstresses, and nightwalkers, who came to wash their clothes in a pond.) Ah, wouldn't Joyce have relished that trysting hour.

In 1814 it was made a private park, laid out with walks and accessible only to those who rented keys. There was so much outcry about this that Sir Arthur Guinness, responding to a dream of his early youth, decided that he would do everything to return the enclosure to the public. He paid off its debts and in 1880 had it reopened as a recreation place for all, himself seeing to the design of shrubs, trees, waterfall, rock garden, bandstand, lake for the blind—his return gift to the city that imbibed so much of his family's brew. The green is a landmark for all ages, all classes, and, indeed, all creeds. On the stone gate at its entrance are carved the names of the Irish fusiliers who fought in the Boer War, and inside, along with statues to poets, there are statues to the patriots who led the various futile insurrections. One is of Countess Markievicz, a great beauty from County Sligo, whom Yeats celebrated in a poem and who led her own battalion of volunteers there in 1916 and held out for five days. She was condemned to death but given a reprieve because of being a woman, a concession she loathed. To the park superintendent the insurrection merely meant that they lost six waterfowl, seven garden seats, and seven hundred shrubs. There is a leonine statue to Joyce, his thin legs in a snakelike coil, filigree on the green bronze, and a legend that reads, "He dismantled the English language and put it together again so that it became music."

It being a quiet, snowy Sunday, I had the green almost to myself, as well as a private tour from the park attendant, who cogitated on the various works of art we passed, expressing a fondness for the statue of the poet Mangan, who had Roisin Dhub, Dark Rosaleen, the mythic Irish heroine, in plaster in a niche under his heart. The attendant had a dislike for the Yeats piece by Henry Moore, which in his opinion was not only too bulky but was also where a young crowd assembled to buy and sell drugs. As he put it, they start on cider, develop to taking their first puff, and from then on it's havoc. Asked if there were ever any indiscretions in the green, he insisted for a long time that there were not, and then, yielding to a moment of confidence, pointed to the bandstand, asked if I saw where the snow was melting, and said that last summer in broad daylight he saw a coat flung on the ground, saw some people staring, saw movement, and lo and behold realized that it was shameless lovemaking, whereupon he went across and shouted to the fellow—only to be told they'd be finished in five minutes. So he gave him a sturdy kick and said, "You'll finish now or I'll have the law on you." When the fellow stood up and removed the coat, there was a brazen young one, her jeans down, and all her worldly goods on offer.

Walking along Baggot Street later in the evening, I saw a young girl with dark red hair and greenish eyes, the alternative beauty to those with the blue-black hair and blue-black eyes. She had drawn a chalk picture of a house with a pink roof, a large pink motorcar, and a couple of hearts. She said she was ten, but was probably nine. She had come that morning, as she did every morning, from Inchicore, where her family lived in a caravan, her mother and father and loads of brothers and sisters, some that could walk and some that couldn't. She came because her mother couldn't come to beg, having to mind sick children.

"I goes here and I goes up there outside that pub, and then I goes by them big black gates for a while and then I goes beyond the canal, and when it gets dark I goes to O'Connell Street, and if I haven't twenty pounds when I get home they bate me and put me to bed." Her cousin had taught her to dance, though as yet she had not had the occasion to test her skills, and while she admired her cousin and was thankful to her for the chalks, she couldn't believe that "she's gone twenty and not married." Her own wish was to be married very soon and pack off. Off where? She wasn't sure where—maybe Waterford, it was "on the say."

Dublin's fair city where the girls are so pretty. They have always been renowned for their beauty, their sauciness, and their chatter, and now that they are almost three to one under twenty-five, the city is a promenade of young people freaking it out in street fashion, with ultrapale makeup that gives them a Charles Addams complexion and with adventure written all over their faces.

In my young days in Dublin, the mecca was not the theater or the cinema but the dance halls—pink sanctums with powder-slippery floors over which one floated, smitten as one was, not by one's partner, but by a crooner or a bandleader who was the epitome of sex appeal and no small amount of Brylcreem. In this new acid, post-acid, do-your-own-thing epoch, the young are to be found in the discos along Leeson Street, a sequence of basements lovingly called the Strip. *Strip* has added meaning, because so slashed are their attires, their bodices and blouses cut down, their trousers cut up, that you could easily be looking in on an orgy in latter-day Eden. Being a woman alone no longer holds the stigma it once did, and the fun of going with other girls, sizing up the stuff, daunts no one. The older men, who were once called sugar daddies, are now more appropriately called dirty old men, and the initials *DV*, which used to mean God willing, now are used to mean dog virgin.

The approach of yore was like this:

"Are you dancing?"

"I'm asking you."

"Then I'm dancing."

Things have taken a cooler turn, and eye contact defines whether or not a young lady is willing. As often as not she declines, a matter that raises some eyebrows. A young man home from England because he couldn't stand the boredom of it said that the girls there were the limit altogether—too much lip and too much lib and fond of their drink. By contrast, a young girl had her companions in hoots of laughter describing the DOM whom she had just danced with as having the cheek to ask her if her breasts were real or plastic. "Plastic!" she yelled as more drinks were called for.

Is romantic Ireland dead and gone? In a sense, yes. It is abandon-the-blouson approach for the meaner look, better wear very little, and forget the Catholic Church, Mother Ireland, your actual mother, the nuns and priests, the Holy Joes, and keep on that wild side. Yet scratch the surface and underneath the preen and bravura is the longing for a decent fella, and as a girl said, "He'd have to be good-looking because you'd be spending the rest of your life looking at him." On the inside door of one of the lavatories in Trinity College, I read three graffiti that I think have some relevance to the Dublin Girls of today. Theresa asked for "Abortion info" and had her telephone number scrawled threewise—horizontally, vertically, and slantwise. Another wondered, "Where have all the dykes gone?" A third asked in all sincerity, "Am I a freak because I'm dying for a man?"

Walking past the students and the tackles of bicycles, then past the bronzed figures of Burke and Goldsmith outside the imposing entrance to Trinity College, once the mecca of great orators and thinkers, I recalled that Goldsmith had to carry dishes to the Fellows' dining room and clean the cobbles, and to relieve his poverty he wrote street ballads, then stole out at night to hear them sung. Yet there is a stubborn fidelity to poets in Ireland, particularly dead ones. It was rush hour, with citizens either hurrying to the tavern or the chapel, and stepping on yet another couplet from *Ulysses*, I wondered what Joyce would make of his famous city. I thought that despite the yuppies, the pizza parlors, the property sharks, and the supremacy of rock music above poetry, Joyce would still call himself her son, and for no other reason than that the soul of the city, a most intangible thing, had not died, not dwindled, not by a long shot.

1992

City of God, City of Men

by

PICO IYER

Within eight hours of my arrival in Jerusalem, I was reeling. Or perhaps the word is saturated. I had landed in the Holy City on a Friday morning after two days and nights of travel, and as I walked through Damascus Gate and into the spiced and chattering Old City, Muslims were streaming along the narrow lanes to attend Friday prayers at the Al-Aqsa Mosque on the Temple Mount. A few hours later, groups of Italian and French Catholics were gathering to carry large wooden crosses along the Via Dolorosa, stopping at every Station of the Cross to chant and recite passages of scripture as they reenacted their savior's last walk through Jerusalem on a Friday afternoon two thousand years before. In front of the Western Wall, the great open space was so packed with rocking bodies that I could not enter. Soon the faithful, all in black hats and coats, were singing and dancing in circles, their heads thrown back in joy, greeting the coming of the Sabbath.

I walked to the Church of the Holy Sepulchre—the site where, many believe, Jesus was crucified and buried—and found Chinese petitioners paging through copies of Latin-titled prayer books in

Mandarin, and Russians crowding into a tiny Coptic alcove to kiss an icon. An Ethiopian man in a cavern-like space was reading from a huge Bible as three of his fellow priests wailed with an ancient, haunting beauty. Within the ill-lit church, the old stone walls shook with the chants of Armenian monks—each man in thick dark robes and carrying a candle—while Franciscans led their own candlelit prayers in a balcony above.

Where to turn, what to believe, how to stop? I felt I had landed in a combination of three of the most intense and transporting places I had ever seen—Damascus, Lalibela, and Flatbush Avenue, you might say—and now each of them was raising its own heart-lifting prayers, in part to drown the others out. I would have traveled a long way to experience any of these intensities, but here, where they all converged, it was hard to hear any one clearly for all the others. I stood on a rooftop, bells ringing all around me, the muezzin calling the faithful to prayer from a nearby mosque, the chants of Ethiopians and Greeks mingling on every side, and asked myself where we end up when reason and self-possession give out.

The sun was rising over the desert as I pulled into this city of furious passions for the first time. A shuttle bus from Tel Aviv's Ben Gurion Airport drove a cluster of us across what might have been a stony, broken Southern California, and into the midst of the clamor. Modern Jerusalem had a strikingly unfinished look, as if it were hastily drawn up by some planners who had left in a hurry, and our little vehicle seemed a blueprint for a comical disaster movie. Two earnest Jewish kids from America were next to me, here to reclaim their inheritance. Up front sat a cultured older man in jacket and tie—Philip Roth's older brother, he might have been—and three bewildered Italians. In the backseat, an expansive woman from Queens was eagerly talking to her husband, a white-bearded rabbi who did not seem keen to return the favor.

"So what time is it?" I heard her say from behind me.

"In New York?"

"No. Here!"

"What does it matter? Always you must make a story of it. Enough already!"

"No. I'm just interested. I was wondering."

"So stop it already. Stop it! I'm tired of it."

The other essential sound of the city, as distinctive as its chants and pealing bells—incessant, funny, quick, and inalienably human.

"So look at the light," the lady went on, as the early sun caught the Jerusalem stone and began to cast the golden glow for which the city has long been famous.

"Same light in New York, no?" replied the rabbi.

At which point I was inclined to believe that, in this instance at least, the man of God was wrong.

I knew what I was going to write about Jerusalem before I got there, of course; we all do. It's been the same story for many hundreds of years, irresistible to anyone who seeks to pontificate on human aspirations and the vanity of human wishes: a "City of Peace" that has long been most celebrated for its altercations. Here was a place—*the* place, really— where politics and religion were so tightly wound around each other that you could not extract a single strand without pulling out all the others and ending up with a tangle as large as human history. This was the place where our visions of holiness, our longings for something better, came into daily, hourly, conflict with our humanness, and with the fact that we were still not able to live up to the beliefs that we have divined or constructed.

As I wandered the city on my first day there, however, taking in the jostle and the contradictions, I quickly began to feel that the political tensions were as old as the hills, and seemingly as immovable. The names were particular, but the tones and themes were not so different from what I had seen in Sri Lanka, in Beirut, in Chinese-occupied Tibet. Our hope that religions will rise above our smaller differences and unite us in a common aspiration, our disappointment that religions insist on their own divisions and often seem more political than politics—all this is as much a part of us as breathing. No ancient city is unaware of it.

Yet the spiritual fervor that pulsed around the kids in jackets reading F.B.I., the almost tangible intensity that I felt even among stores called Holy Cave and Christ Prison, the way circumstances had placed the centers of three great monotheisms within a thousand feet of one another and divided even the holiest place in Christendom among six mostly feuding groups—all that was like nothing I had met before. This was not just a place where traditions flowed together, like my parents' Bombay, sometimes harmonious and sometimes contentious; it was not just a site sacred to many traditions, as Mount Kailash in Tibet or Adam's Peak in Sri Lanka are: Jerusalem seemed a kind of map of the human imagination, a diagram of that part of us, subconscious and atavistic, where surrender and fear converge.

At the Bible Lands Museum—a strikingly elegant and lucid collection of mostly Egyptian and Sumerian artifacts—one sign pointed out, a little hopefully, that the star is not just part of Jewish lore; it can also be found in Islam and Christianity. The dove, it went on, is as important to Jewish symbology as to Christian. Even the menorah had been found carved in Christian catacombs in Rome and impressed onto Umayyad coins in Damascus. Not far away from this ecumenical notice, though, another sign explained, in tones I was coming to associate with Jerusalem, "Ancient Egyptians seldom entered temples. Like modern atomic reactors, they were complex and dangerous sources of power, requiring special decontamination procedures for the few people who entered them."

I had already registered that, at the Western Wall, I was not allowed to take notes on the Sabbath. In the Church of the Holy Sepulchre, a Greek woman had upbraided me for holding my hands behind my back. When I'd tried to walk up to the two central shrines on the Temple Mount (Haram esh-Sharif), I'd been stopped by guards and told that visitors can no longer enter (even Islamic visitors are often barred unless they can identify verses from the Koran). Signs all over the Old City reminded Jews that, by rabbinical decree, they should not even set foot on the Temple Mount, so sacred is its soil.

I had thought, before I came, that Jerusalem was a complex model not just of the Israeli tangle but of the entire globe at a time when the very religions that speak for unity are enforcing divisions and war. But now I was coming to see that, for me at least, Jerusalem would be a place not just to experience religion but to observe it in a different way, not simply by visiting the holy places but, more deeply, by trying to see what humans do with and around and in response to holiness. This was where I would make a pilgrimage into the conundrum of faith.

A few days later, I returned to Damascus Gate, leaving the clean, broad streets of the modem city behind to find myself amid an ancient cacophony. Little boys were weaving through the crowded alleys, carrying glasses of tea on trays above their heads, while their older brothers pushed large carts of supplies down slippery ramps in the ill-lit souk. In the morning, most of the shops in the Muslim Quarter were quiet—save for some beautiful Koranic chanting from a scratchy radio in a café—but as soon as midday prayers were over, the area around the gate swarmed with vendors selling enormous pink teddy bears, cell phone covers, bras, and hot ears of corn. There were chickpeas on one side and Nokias on the other.

There was a strong smell of cardamom everywhere—then of freshly baked bread and incense—and as I walked into the Ecce Homo Chapel, suddenly the call to prayer struck up above me and I found myself in an overlapping of chants from mosques on every side. A Coptic priest was walking past, his black skullcap with gold crosses marking him as a visitor from another world, and Armenian priests with dark hoods over their heads, as if descending from *The Seventh Seal*, were turning from Christian Quarter Street onto David Street. Yet among all the shops selling postcards, GUNS 'N' MOSES T-shirts, replicas of pieces of the true cross, flyers had been plastered across the Old City reading, "God won't resurrect those who won't save his creation" (onto which someone had scribbled at the bottom *Mother Nature*).

Later, I listened to a guide near the Western Wall explain to his flock that the stones on which they were standing were 1,700 years old, dating from Roman times (like the original Church of the Holy Sepulchre, first set up 325 years after the birth of Christ). What struck me as I wandered, though, was not how old the place seemed but how alive. A bar mitzvah was being held in the tunnel leading to the Western Wall, and most of the figures vaulting past me wore the long forelocks and high black hats of ultra-Orthodox Jews. "Jerusalem is a burning city," I remembered reading in the pages of its great local son, Amos Oz. "But a closer glance reveals an immeasurable weightiness."

What I took that to mean was that it was a city of fire and earth (water is famously scarce in this desert, and the air is often hot). Yet the flames you see—in eyes and hearts—the stones that suffer everything, speak to something central about a city where, if you look down, you see broken pistachio shells and filth and confusion, and if you look up you see a grid of church towers and minarets (and, it must be admitted, satellite dishes). This was an unusually rooted place, Oz seemed to be implying, that was always about to go up in flames.

I am a dutiful traveler, so I took pains in the days that followed to see Mount Zion and the Mount of Olives, the stylish remembrance of the Holocaust at Yad Vashem, and the Tower of David Museum, near Jaffa Gate. I descended into crypts and tombs beyond number—much of Jerusalem is an underground city, in every sense, since there are burials and buildings two stories below the street—and circumambulated the Old City along its ramparts. I visited hard-hitting political museums (the Museum on the Seam) and historical museums (the capacious Israel Museum); I spent a vivid afternoon in a black-and-white daguerreotype of eighteenth-century Europe, walking through the thin, unearthly streets of the Orthodox Quarter—Me'a She'arim—where black-hatted men pushed babies in supermarket carts and banners stretching across the street announced, in English, "Jews are not Zionists—Zionists are not Jews, only racists. We pray to G-d for an immediate end of Zionism and their occupation."

Yet for all these many seductions, it was the Old City in Jerusalem that kept pulling me back, almost magnetically—as if I had been transfixed along a busy street by a single man with blazing eyes, wearing a torn overcoat, whose crazy disputations I could not step away from. And although there was so much else to see, I very soon came to realize that this was not a place for seeing sights so much as for catching everything that can't be glimpsed or put into a viewfinder. (Everywhere I went in Jerusalem, I carried a camera, but when I got back to California, I realized that I had not taken a single shot.)

I packed up my things, therefore, and left my fancy hotel, unexpectedly soon, for a room in an Old City hospice. The sounds of muezzin and bells were my regular companions as I sat on the sun-washed terrace of my small and comfortable room, and I could buy cups of hot tea and nuts whenever I stepped out. There was the smell of sweetmeats all around, in fact, as if I were living in a ceremonial feast—although such lofty thoughts were soon brought down to earth by men calling from their shops, "Hey, Russka! *Buona sera!* I sell you this for three euros. This is the six and a half Station of the Cross!"

You set your watch to a different millennium in the Old City; you're living in the middle of the bonfire, in effect—waking with the sun and going to bed with the coming of the dark. I rose at 2 A.M. on my first night in my little room and, walking to the rooftop a few steps above, saw a small red cross shining near Damascus Gate, while dogs barked somewhere in the vicinity of the Mount of Olives. A single car was moving along a narrow road below, and the moon hung pulsing behind the gold dome on Haram esh-Sharif. On every side of me, the green lights of minarets marked this as a place of prayer.

The view was so different from what I am used to seeing in almost any city of the world that I just stayed there and stayed there, through the hours when I should have been sleeping. Just before the sun rose, I ventured out into the deserted streets and followed whim down a series of ghostly alleyways. At one point, in the dawn, I ran into a large Greek Orthodox priest—all thick black robes and heavy beard—leading a group of believers around his sanctuary. Hooded figures, hands pushed into their pockets against the cold, were passing under a cobbled archway to attend the day's first prayers at the mosque. In the warm, illuminated cave next to the Western Wall, dozens of Orthodox Jews were already in full chant, banging their heads against the stone and intoning verses from the Torah. One of them, wild-eyed and with flowing ringlets, pushed into my hands a copy of a book on Emunah— an ultra-Orthodox kind of New Ageism, as far as I could tell.

None of this was for sightseers, I realized—and it never stopped. The city was like a man constantly pushing, out of breath and hectic, to get closer to his salvation (and silently—or not so silently—cursing all the other bodies doing the same that were standing in his way).

It's common, almost inevitable, to call Jerusalem a pilgrimage site, since few people ever come here casually and almost everyone is on a mission. The very directedness of their trips leads to the sensation of a thousand burning arrows flying off in different directions. But as I walked past the sign outside the Basilica of the Agony, near the Garden of Gethsemane, aimed at too-voluble tour guides—PLEASE: NO EXPLANATIONS INSIDE THE CHURCH—I came to see that a city of beliefs is a city of exclusions, and that a pilgrim who travels in search of history is likely to be confounded in a place where history is exactly what most people are desperate to awake from.

You really come to Jerusalem, I began to think, as a witness. And the more I traveled among its sights, the more I came to realize that the things to see here were, to a surprising degree, the other visitors. There were few backpackers in evidence—Israel is an expensive place—and the books on offer in the library in my hospice (Orhan Pamuk, Marguerite Yourcenar, detailed histories of the Holy Land) reminded me that the people who came here were rarely typical tourists.

I had already fallen into the habit of returning late every afternoon to the Church of the Holy Sepulchre to watch from its rooftop space as the last golden light caught the Russian Orthodox gable, the Lutheran bell tower, and the crosses of Greece, Armenia, and Rome that filled the immediate skyline. One day, I saw a small woman pressing her ear against the bars of the dome of the basilica down below, to catch the chants faintly rising from the candled space. The thump of Arabic music came from a nearby house. There were the sounds of kids playing in an alleyway, and of a mass of nuns singing hymns behind the walls of a convent. Incense drifted up through the cross-shaped gratings on the small dome, sanctifying us all.

As I walked down the narrow stairs of the Ethiopian chapel, from the roof of the central compound, and past four grave men resting on their staffs, holding candles to their Bibles, I came out into the courtyard in front of the main entrance to what is really a warren of distinct chapels and competing sects. "For me, to be honest," a tour guide was saying, "being here is so foreign. It's not the place but the people who come here who make it."

Jerusalem was the first place I could remember in which most of the foreign tour leaders I saw outside the Garden of Gethsemane, or leading chanting groups into the chapels on the Mount of Olives were priests (or, occasionally, professors), while most of the local tour guides in evidence—generally burly, grizzled men in their late fifties, commanding in cowboy hats—seemed to me more or less lay preachers, as pungent, articulate, and contentious as the streets around them.

"It's dark," a professor was saying of the entire complex, "and smelly and full of dirt"—one reason General Gordon (the doomed British hero from the Siege of Khartoum) had devoted many years of his life to "proving" that this was not in fact the place where Jesus was buried, but that that distinction belonged to the Garden Tomb, a sunlit, lyrical space outside the city walls, next to some dramatic rocks.

"You see, there's a 'status quo contract,' as they call it," someone else was telling his four guests, "which lays down in very great detail the precise laws for this complex. How many lamps each of the six groups can burn. Who owns every piece of furniture. Even the ladder"—he pointed to a hopeless-looking set of steps stranded on a ledge halfway up the building—"that belongs to the Armenians. And if the Catholics are meant to be finished with their ceremony at 2:07 and they're still singing at 2:08, when the Armenians start up, you're gonna see a fist-fight. The holiest Christian place in the world, and that's what you get.

"Oh, and yes," he concluded, with a final flourish. "Who has the keys? The Muslims!" He pointed to two burly, mustached men sitting on the stone steps next to the compound's main entrance and explained how, by Saladin's decree, it was two Islamic families who had been entrusted with official control of the church for more than eight hundred years and who, to this day, locked fifty monks inside the place every evening at seven.

These voices, each with their own theory, many of them dismissing the place for its feuds and its unkempt air, were, I realized, the perfect portal to a complicated web of shrines that is strikingly irregular, musty, and inharmonious. Much like the city around it, it is distinctly less beautiful, less restful, and less uplifting than the places of worship you will find in most cities of the world. Few people even go into the basilica here; instead, most seek out dark corners, crypts with nothing in them, dusty spaces that look the opposite of luminous. "It's filthy and it's eclectic and they're all fighting," a Benedictine monk from South Africa told me before I came. "But it's *primal*."

Indeed it is. One day, there were suddenly large groups of Russians everywhere in front of the compound—the Orthodox Christmas was imminent—kneeling to kiss the slab at the main entrance (on which, some groups believe, Jesus' body was laid), pressing crosses and medallions and talismans down on it. Pasty-faced men who might have been Vladimir Putin's cousins were kissing the cold, thick pillars. Yellow-haired Natashas in sexy tracksuits cut open toward the navel were posing near the sanctum sanctorum. Teenage girls were carrying whole bowls of incense, fanning the dim candles flickering around the darkened space into small flames.

I went into a little room away from most of the main chapels, and as I did so, I saw one tiny candle that someone had placed on a stony ledge. A French girl, perhaps fourteen, with black curly hair and glasses, passed it and then stopped, transfixed. I could see tears in her eyes. The candle looked so frail, so ready to gutter. She stared and stared at it, quite alone, till a friend came and held her close. The friend led her away, but as she did so, the schoolgirl turned around and looked at the candle once more, eyes shiny. It flickered and wavered, as if about to expire.

Everything is personal in the city—famously—and nothing is remote. I found myself on alert every day, as if simply to be here was to be conscripted in some war you cannot begin to understand. A Jewish cabbie picked me up—he had fought in Lebanon in 1982 and still advised the army—and launched into a spiel on peace. "Thirty years ago, Israel was a phenomenon. We were in a desert and we were growing vegetables, everything. People came from everywhere to see us. Now, all the money goes to killing. The desert is eating us." An Arab cabbie gave me a ride and, as he swerved in and out of traffic, started scrolling through his cell phone to show me video clips of his new baby. Another driver consented to allow me into his car and then asked me for directions—"I'm from Tel Aviv"—making up for the confusion by passing freshly shelled nuts back to me to sweeten the journey.

In my final days in Jerusalem, I traveled into the West Bank, and again what awaited me was a reminder of the doubleness within us all. At the Greek monastery carved into the rock of the Mount of Temptation (where Satan is said to have confronted Jesus), only two monks were visible: One was a wild-haired figure in robes who might have been an ancient desert hermit, pottering around in a cell that gave out onto the whole valley; the other was an African-looking gentleman carrying a new Universal toaster up to his space. Some of the mud dwellings around Jericho, I had read, date from long before the time of Jesus; others come from 1948, when residents here could not afford to live in regular houses. The area where John the Baptist is said to have baptized Jesus is now, quite literally, a minefield.

And in early January, on Christmas Eve—as it is for the Orthodox—I went to Bethlehem, passing through the checkpoints that have turned it into a kind of war zone, spotting the twenty-six-foot-high wall, part of the barrier that Israel is now building across the country. Policemen were patrolling the rooftops all around Manger Square, and on the way to the Church of the Nativity, I noticed that Pope Paul VI Street ran right into Martyrs Street. Inside the church, amid great crowds assembled for the all-night vigils, a Coptic monk sidled up to his friend, a pale, shy Franciscan, and commiserated. "You know, I was in America when you had that attack from the Greeks. And I thought, *Idiots! Bastards! They're bastards! What kind of spiritual mission is this?*" The Franciscan smiled weakly.

My last evening in the city, I headed out of the Church of the Holy Sepulchre just before nightfall and went back to the rooftop of my hospice. Walking out into the chill night air was like walking into a sudden stillness. All the clamor and contention of the streets was instantly far below. The call to prayer rose up around me (so close it might have been inside me), and I thought I could hear bells pealing not far off.

From the rooftop, Jerusalem became a spacious place, lit up with holy places and symbols as few cities are, and speaking for something far deeper and more enduring than just the wish to be younger or richer or stronger. If you stood here long enough—though maybe this was just another Jerusalem delusion—you could almost believe that you could bring some of that stillness and collectedness, a little order and beauty and calm, back into the push and swarm of the streets below. I stood in the silence and emptiness, happily affiliated with none of the faiths around me, and thought how chants are sometimes sweetest when you don't know where they're coming from.

2010

The Filthy, Fecund Secret of Emilia-Romagna

by

PATRICK SYMMES

The soil in the Arda Valley was, in the first days of September, already furrowed for a second crop. Everywhere we looked, right beside the roaring A1 or at some forgotten crossroads amid collapsing farmhouses, machines had plucked the harvest and turned the ground. Emilia-Romagna, the flat northern heartland of Italian farming, was combed into neat rows. Everywhere we paused, we stared in disbelief. Finally, outside the supermarket in Lugagnano Val d'Arda, I stepped in among the clods.

If you've ever gardened, you know the feeling I had. The dirt— millions of years of silt, washed down from the Alps and Apennines and deposited into this great bowl by the flooding of the Po River—lay meters deep. It is a rich brown humus, fine, dense, almost chocolaty. This stuff—mere dirt—is the building block of the wealth, strife, and food of the Po Valley, the great plain at the heart of Italian agriculture.

The story of Emilia-Romagna is the story of that soil, which grows the grass that feeds the cows that flavor the milk that makes the Parmesan cheese taste so good just down the road in Parma. This is the soil that sprouts the corn and wheat that fatten the pigs that become the ham that becomes *prosciutto di Parma*. This is the brown muck, fantastically productive, that grows the Trebbiano grapes, cooked down into the aged vinegar *balsamico di Modena*, in the town of that name, just another half hour along the A1. And beyond that, right down the curve of the immense plain—the largest flat place in Italy—all the products of this soil have been gathered into Bologna, one of Italy's great, innovative trading cities, whose nimble-minded gourmets invented much of what passes for Italian food around the globe. Ravioli? Tagliatelle? Lasagna? Polenta? Tortellini? Half of all pasta shapes? All from Emilia-Romagna. If your mouth is not watering, stop reading here.

The soil next to the supermarket in Lugagnano wasn't just brown and rich: It was practically alive, a tightly packed silt that the machines had turned up into chunks the size of dinner plates. I prodded one with my foot. "The size of dinner plates," I said to my wife, awed.

"Bigger," she corrected. Some of the pieces were the size of serving platters.

If you want to know how Emilia-Romagna has conquered the world, one table at a time, you need only look down.

We had rented a stone house in Castelletto, an obscure village high up in the Arda Valley. It proved to be a steep hamlet of stone houses, many empty, and about forty year-round residents, mostly old women. Ours was the only rental property in Castelletto, found online. It had good views, modern everything, and it rattled in the fierce mountain winds.

Our son, Max—a precious bundle, aged fourteen months— attempted his first steps in Castelletto's empty playground. We took our first steps too: awkward greetings in Italian, and a quick scamper to the valley's most famous site, the fortress town of Castell'Arquato. I struggled up the medieval keep with Max on my back, and we surveyed the views up the Arda—an ugly dam, and then the gentle

Apennines, sharing a border with Tuscany. In the other direction was the great flat plain of the Po River.

Our goal was to go local in every sense: language, cooking, daily life. By staying in this small town for a week, we could wander far and wide through Emilia-Romagna but always come back to a single point—depth in Italy rather than breadth. We gathered fallen apples from our yard and fed the baby apple mush that had traveled only a few yards in its life. I studied Italian. We walked, cooked, and made slow but encouraging progress in befriending the town's elderly doyennes, who were enthralled by my son's head of Irish hair. *Il bimbo rosso*, they called him: the red baby. *Che bello.* The village was dying, demographically, but EU money had paved even the smallest roads, flavored the local tomatoes with farming subsidies, and put seven sheep and an Audi in the same yard. The houses were in good repair—the children and grandchildren returned on weekends for the essential rituals of Italian family. Rural life was sustained on this high-fat diet of state support, provincial support, supranational subsidies, and an enthusiastic public willing to pay for good, local, traditional foods.

We followed our landlord's tip farther up the Arda Valley to Cà Ciancia, an *agriturismo*, or farmhouse that takes in guests—an embodiment of the last of these trends. We parked against giant hoops of hay and walked past a small barn full of cows, pigs, and rabbits. In the kitchen—half a dozen local women roasting and knifing—these ingredients were cooked and served a few yards from where they were born. In both dining rooms huge collective meals were in progress, a dozen people at one table, eighteen at the next. The food—truffled anolini, pork loin with crisp potatoes—can only be described by my wife's abrupt declaration, just halfway through, that "this is the greatest meal of my life."

Food has to come from somewhere. Emilia-Romagna has beauty in it, but also more hog processors than ruins, more grain silos than medieval towers (and they have a lot of medieval towers). In the Po Valley, "what you see is what you smell," Bill Buford, author of *Heat*, a tale of learning to cook Italian, explained to me. That can mean foodie bouquets of simmering sauce, rich cheese, and roasted chestnuts, but, Buford noted honestly, "even the fog smells like pig poo."

Ask an Italian where the best food comes from, and he will mention his mother, and then his home region. But if pushed, many will admit, as one Roman told me, "Of course, there is Emilia-Romagna." Why here? Good dirt, to be sure, but also rotten politics that created concentrated Renaissance wealth, and aristocratic rulers like the Estes, a clan that rivaled the Medici, sprinkled castles throughout Emilia-Romagna and practically invented the culture of banqueting and conspicuous consumption.

Then there is what the British explorer Richard Burton, writing in 1876, called *sveltezza d'ingenio*—the mental agility, the inventiveness—that is key to the region. Design and industry are fused in local brands like Ferrari, Ducati, and Lamborghini. Reggio Emilia, a quiet university city in the west, perpetually jousts with nearby Parma for the highest per capita income in Italy.

Yet Emilia-Romagna is a kind of lost region for foreigners, known, if at all, for its gemlike cities—Parma, Modena, Bologna, Ferrara, Ravenna—rather than its awkward hyphenated name, rooted in the ancient disputes of the Gauls and the Romans and pronounced with an almost silent *g*. The various cities have been rivals throughout history, pitted against each other like pawns in war and peace, swapped and traded among dukes, emperors, and popes. Naturally resistant to ag-glomeration, they have preserved and cultivated styles, habits, food specialties, and personalities that are independent of one another (the Parmese are reserved, the Modenese vivacious, and the Bolognese consider themselves the best lovers in Italy, or so the story goes).

As an identity, Emilia-Romagna exists chiefly on maps, which show it as a series of highways and train lines connecting outside places that are more important—Milan in the west to Florence in the south to Venice in the north. Forty million tourists a year come to this nation—two for every three Italians—but typically they just pass through Emilia-Romagna in transit.

So it is overlooked.

Fine. More for us.

What foreigners want from Italy changes over time, as we saw the next day. Having left Castelletto at the crack of noon, we toured Fontanellato, one of the many castles studded through the region by rival dukes, protecting their wealth and status with fairy-tale battlements and moats better suited to fishing than holding off a French army. A church wedding here fascinated us, the young men all in funereal black, the women erupting in purple and red organza, everything scented with Catholic incense. But after a few missed turns we arrived at nearby Colorno, whose vast Farnese palace has been divided into a psychiatric hospital in one wing and one of Italy's most ambitious cooking schools in the other. Called Alma, it was opened in 2004 to train hundreds of international students a year as Italian-speaking evangelists of an Italian cuisine held to the highest standards.

One of the school's star chefs, Paolo Amadori, briskly gainsaid the claims that Emilia-Romagna has the best food in Italy. ("Let them talk," he said of food writers. "We don't make any distinctions.") Italian cuisine as a whole was not respected enough. Amadori cited the "Michelin gap," the way restaurants in a single French city hold more Michelin stars than are awarded in all of Italy. "Bottom line, unfortunately, is that Italian cuisine was exported from Italy by nonprofessionals," Amadori said. He meant the poor emigrants who flooded out of Italy, taking a cuisine of hunger built on the ingredients of poverty that was intended to satisfy need, not Michelin. Italian food suffered from what he called "the *nonna* problem."

"They still think the momma should be in the restaurant," he told me, in his chef's whites and toque. "We have had only twenty years of professionalism fighting against a hundred years of the *nonna*, the grandmother. Why are we always talking about the *nonna*?"

A bold stand to attack the grandmothers. In Parma the next day, we saw the arguments for professionalism. The city is a model of affluent Northern Italian efficiency, and in the streets—as in all

Emilia-Romagna cities, the layout is octagonal, following the shape of a castle designed to deflect cannonballs—we saw only Italians here, as in so much of the region.

Granted, there are greater things in Italy than in Parma alone. But for a first-time visitor like me, this was more than enough. Even for my wife, a jaded connoisseur of European beauty, the constant surprises—Renaissance frescoes, Byzantine mosaics, free Wi-Fi in the Parma town square—made Italy enthralling all over again. Later I would see Florence, the magic Italy, the famous Italy, with everything that Emilia-Romagna had to offer but done on steroids, at much greater scale and at infinitely higher cost, and with greater glory. Yet I would also see Florence amid roaring buses, be elbowed off the tiny sidewalks by beaming Russians, and have my pockets cleaned out by the exorbitant fees for museums and meals that came with free jostling. In Parma, by contrast, we had our own little Italy almost to ourselves. We ate a marvelous meal—practically alone—at La Greppia, on the edge of the city center. This was a restaurant advanced by Mario Batali, the New York–based chef, who had built his career on the pasta secrets he learned from three years in Emilia-Romagna kitchens.

La Greppia lived up to Batali's hype and Amadori's standards. Our lunch, made without a *nonna* in sight, featured Parma's gifts to the world: *prosciutto di Parma*; porcini from the Apennines; fresh, soft tagliatelle like long strips of butter; and what a Baedeker Guide would call excellent cheese. The famous *parmigiano reggiano* appeared three ways, first whipped into a curious and liberating *spuma di parmigiano*, like a savory ice-cream appetizer, an oddity that no grandmother would attempt and only a machine could produce. Then there was *parmigiano* shaved liberally onto ribbons of pasta, and finally it appeared in fat chunks, pried from half a wheel by a waiter taken with our grinning child. Max sat through the meal in his high chair, eating parma from each tiny hand. This habit now costs me $16.99 a pound.

Parmese say you eat twice: first at the table, then by talking about it. The food traditions here are among the oldest and most continuous in Europe, giving people enough time to try and reject every adornment, leaving a plateau of quality, a rare combination of inventiveness and simplicity.

If there is one place in Europe you can tour without a car, it is Emilia-Romagna. Even the second-class Eurostar train is utterly clean, quiet, and stress-free, linking the major cities in a straight line (by October, it should be possible to travel from Milan to Florence, right through Emilia-Romagna, in less than a hundred minutes). Secondary cities, like Ferrara, were served by regional trains, slower and covered with graffiti, but nonetheless reliable and cheap, and filled with the real life of Italy: students, immigrants, even dogs, who can ride if they have their own ticket. This is how we came into Modena, on a twenty-five-minute local run. We plopped Max in his stroller and hoofed it into the center of town, gradually falling into silence. The teenagers leaving a local high school were dressed like Nautica models, their scooters the fanciest available; every building was in a nearly idealized state of repair; and in this, the hometown of Luciano Pavarotti, small shops sold sheet music and instruments to lines of enthusiastic customers.

The Giusti family has run a *salumeria*, a meat shop, since 1605, and had roots in vinegar production before then. Originally, the store sold both pork and duck. "The duck was for the Jews, the pork was for the Catholics," the current owner, Matteo Morandi, told me as he showed me around. The store was still bustling in the Italian way—with a fantastic array of wines, high-end cheeses, and meats—but locked down under shorter hours than a Swiss bank. Starting almost seventy years ago, at fifteen, Matteo's father, Adriano, had come to work here as a shop boy for the Giustis. He eventually bought the *salumeria*, and in 1989 opened Hosteria Giusti, a restaurant that, with just four tables, is among the most coveted in Emilia-Romagna. The place is accessible through a tiny passage in the back of the store that winds past the kitchen to tables in the old storage room where hams had hung to cure (the hooks are still driven deep into the overhead beams). We ate a symphony of al dente pasta and milk-fed veal.

The meal ended with a stunningly simple dish: *gnocco fritto*, or pillows of fried dough topped with a few intense drops of sixty-year-old balsamic vinegar. The *balsamico* was so thick that it had to be coaxed from the bottle. The question of what constitutes true balsamic vinegar is nearly impossible to answer. Many balsamics are produced around Modena with unregulated titles like "authentic," "original," and "genuine," but these can be made from Trebbiano grapes in a few days, adulterated with caramel for color, sugar for sweetening, and flour for thickening. The addition of one spoonful of truly aged vinegar is enough to earn the label "aged." These industrially made vinegars are serviceable—Italians routinely use them to lightly flavor a salad dressing—but the truest, artisanal balsamics are produced under the title *tradizionale*, from nothing but a reduction of grapes and time. With a dozen years and up to seven changes of oak or other wood barrels, they take on a nearly black coloring, a thick texture, and an intense, fruity flavor that mark the best balsamics. Those aged more than twelve years earn the title *vecchio*; *stravecchio* covers the rare brands stored for twenty-five years or more.

The great appeal of these complex, wine-like vinegars—from *vin aigre*, or "bitter wine" in French—is the way they naturally accompany a diet heavy in fats, from olive oil to glistening slabs of Parma ham. The *tradizionale* are not mixed into dressings but are highlighted as a prime feature of the meal—dripped onto the finest cheeses or fried vegetables, used to stain vanilla ice cream or risotto on the plate, sprinkled on sweet strawberries with ground pepper to work strange alchemy.

It may seem odd that such a meal was accompanied by a wine that is mocked by snobs. This is Lambrusco, Emilia-Romagna's curious sparkling red, served chilled in violation of every known rule of American connoisseurship. In America, Lambrusco is trailed by a disastrous association with the 1970s, when sales of sparkling red became anathema to a rising gourmet culture. But it is a light and refreshing drink that seems to cut through the richness of Italian food in the same way that balsamic vinegar is an antidote to the fat. A bottle can be a kind of guilty pleasure, all the sweeter for the disapproval of the erudite.

After the meal, I asked Matteo what I asked everyone: Why here? Why is Emilia-Romagna the center of the food universe?

"It's because of the pasta," he said. "Every region in Italy is proud of its cuisine. But we have the tradition of pasta. It's continuous, unbroken."

Then I asked him if Italian food has a "*nonna* problem," if the cuisine is too closely based on images of grandmothers stirring the sauce.

"But that's our whole idea!" he burst out. Speaking loudly and slowly, to compensate for my bad Italian, he said that *of course* Italian food should be based on what *grandmothers* were cooking. "The cuisine is *of the casa*," he told me. "We make *our mothers'* food." His own mother—the *nonna* to his three children—was in the kitchen right now, he pointed out. I popped over a few feet from where we sat in the alley; there was *nonna*, frying the little pillows of dough I had topped with *stravecchio*.

Score one for the grandmothers.

Like a good detective story, Ferrara benefits from what is missing: The dog didn't bark and the tourists didn't come. Of those forty million annual visitors to Italy, I literally did not see another during five days in Ferrara. Boasting an idealized layout, and claiming to be Europe's first planned city, Ferrara lies on the northeasternmost plain of Emilia-Romagna, alternately bathed in summer heat and winter fog, and ignored by all but the most discerning travelers—chiefly Italians seeking some authentic piece of their own nation that has not been squeezed through a tourism machine.

Ferrara benefits from the quiet: Although it is common in Emilia-Romagna for cities to ban traffic in their central zones, in Ferrara the bent alleys of the entire core are pedestrian-friendly. The clattering of wheels over cobblestones and the polite tinkle of bicycle bells may be the loudest sounds you encounter here. For us, wielding a small baby through the region, Ferrara offered a secure and confident respite, where our son could practice his walking freely, at no risk greater than a bombardment of kisses from neighborhood *nonnas*. (When my wife took him walking outside the hotel at 6:30 in the morning, I could track their progress by the faint cries of *"Bambino bellissimo!"* and *"Che bello!"*)

Since Roman times, a road—the Via Emilia—has run straight through Parma, Modena, and Bologna, to Rimini, but Ferrara lies off this access. Ferrara's relative isolation led to stagnation and noble rot; in 1786, Goethe called the city "lovely great depopulated" Ferrara.

Colomba, the owner of a sleepy and delicious trattoria, told me, "1800, 1900—those were abandoned times here. Only in the last five years has tourism picked up." A Lebanese chef, raised in Nigeria and trained in Italy, he had the kind of mixed heritage often concealed behind Italy's classic facade. He was cooking pastas with *ragù alla bolognese* and featherweight gnocchi in sage butter. Ferrara was once a center of Jewish life in Italy, and we sampled heritage dishes here like smoked eggplant and goose with grapefruit. The lack of industry, modernity, and population pressure has preserved the urban core more perfectly than in nearly any other large city in Italy, leaving a *centro storico* of gently curved pedestrian streets.

Ferrara is a humid city in the plains: hot, frequented by mosquitoes, where the women wave Chinese fans to stay cool. I made a rare nocturnal foray, slipping out on a sleeping wife and baby to walk the streets at 11 P.M. Lovely depopulated Ferrara was suddenly coursing with life, the plazas packed with hordes of beer-drinking young people. While eating pizza I made a naive, if profound, discovery about Italians. Everyone was hugging and kissing, slapping backs, the men holding hands, people in rapt conversations still checking cell phones and looking over their shoulder to miss no opportunity with another person. Personality and human relations lie at the core of Italian identity. I watched in amazement as an Italian gallant, clearly on a first date, abandoned his voluptuous companion to race into the street, hug an acquaintance, log some face time with him, engage in passionate push-me, pull-you argument with the pedestrian, and work hard at persuading his friend of something—and not return to his lady friend for a full fifteen minutes. Personality is an art form to Italians, the purpose of life.

Here is how you make fresh pasta dough: Mix flour and eggs together. That's it. There are some useful techniques and tricks, and you can call this dough *sfoglia* if you like, with a good Italian accent. But that is all that lies at the very heart of the secret of Italy's greatest regional cuisine. In Emilia-Romagna in general and in Bologna in particular, the genius of the table is simply fresh pasta. Once you get something right, the only advance comes from simplifying it, and Bologna is the place that gets things right. The city is known by a series of nicknames that shed some light on its history: Bologna the Fat, for its wealth, especially at the table; and Bologna the Red, originally for the dominant color scheme of its buildings and later for its politics. The city remains a Communist party stronghold, even as it is known as a city with the finest clothes, the best food, and the most beautiful homes in Italy. Medieval arches and porticoes line twenty-five miles of city blocks, and although there are some conspicuous tourist attractions here, like a pair of brick towers from the Middle Ages, the city is more "real" than Venice or Florence, oriented toward regular people and home to 100,000 students and some of the best food markets in the country.

I had a chance to put my high theory of cuisine to the test here—two chances, actually. Determined to have at my fingertips the secrets of Emilia-Romagna, I signed up for a couple of cooking classes. One, conducted in the kitchen of a Bologna bed-and-breakfast called Casa Ilaria, was patronized by several young English couples who had, thanks to the bargains available for European air travel, flown to Bologna for the weekend. This class took a few hours and was taught by Ilaria herself, a relaxed and informal teacher who worked us through the mixing of *sfoglia* dough and the technical challenge of rolling out and cutting the result into wide tagliatelle, while assembling a traditional *ragù alla bolognese* and creating a tiramisu for dessert. Ilaria was in the *nonna* school: Like any Italian home cook, she used *soffritto*—the base of minced onion, celery, and carrots—that came from the supermarket freezer section. Her tips were all practical, like flavoring the sauce with "the wine that's open, red or white," and "pasta feels the weather, so keep some flour back until you see the mix." I left feeling, how easy!

The other class was an altogether more serious affair, a weeklong culinary tour of Emilia-Romagna and Tuscany led by noted foodie Mary Beth Clark, which I joined for a single day. We began at dawn beside Bologna's famous statue of Neptune, where Mary Beth pointed to some mysterious white stones embedded in a wall—signs of the original marketplace that thrived here in medieval times, when illiterate servants had to measure out their orders for bolts of cloth and roofing tiles against these standardized forms. We traipsed across the plaza for some early-morning shopping among the cheese and egg vendors, the makers of fresh pastas and cured meats. Then we crossed a few blocks to enter one of the city's most reserved and secretive institutions, the Club Bologna, in a sixteenth-century palazzo. (Trained among Bologna chefs, Mary Beth is the rare female member of this private entity.)

Forget the *nonna*s. We were greeted by a butler, served coffee by uniformed staff, and issued aprons and recipe collections for what would be a whirlwind effort to cook our way through a dozen classic dishes of the region. Assembling in the club's kitchen, guided by Mary Beth and the club's own chefs, we started with the same dishes I had done the night before: fresh pasta dough and a *ragù alla bolognese*. This is the sauce that conquered the world, at least in theory. Genuine *ragù alla bolognese* is a thick, almost dry sauce made with pork and beef that are coarsely chopped, a little tomato, and no garlic or herbs (salt is also little used, since it is present in so many local ingredients, like Parmesan cheese and prosciutto). True Bolognese sauce is used in baked lasagna, or as dressing on broad pastas that can support the meat, like tagliatelle. A Bolognese would sooner go out for Chinese than eat spaghetti alla bolognese, since the thin noodles leave a pile of meat behind in the bowl. In true meat-obsessed Bologna fashion, we also worked up a roast tenderloin and classic *polpetini* meatballs made with veal.

Mary Beth's theory was impeccable, her process professional enough to please even the doctrinaire chefs at Alma. She minced her own *soffritto* rather than using the stuff from the freezer section; she urged us to "harmonize" the *ragù alla bolognese* by using only the same vintage of wine we would be serving with the meal. A true purist, she even declined to put Parmesan cheese on the dish, which Bolognese regard as an unnecessary improvement. And she confirmed my base instinct about Po Valley soil by noting to the class that "if you understand geography, you understand what forms the people, the way they look, and pardon me, the way they smell."

Among the guests was an amiable gray-haired Italian-born man traveling with his Australian wife. He often served as a kind of translator during the cooking, joking and grinning, but I was struck at one point when a shadow passed over his face. He had been talking to the elderly lady rolling out the pasta dough, and I caught a phrase in their rapid exchange that puzzled me: *figli della lupa*. With my dictionary Italian, I misunderstood this to mean "children of the wolf." Clearly it had nothing to do with cooking. I finally forced it out of him. These two gray-hairs, who lived continents apart for almost their whole lives, had found an instant point of common grief in their origins. What he had told the woman was, "We are both Children of the She-Wolf," a reference to Mussolini's Fascist version of the Boy Scouts, the Figli della Lupa. Here was a jolting connection to the old Italy of poverty and dread, recalled at leisure in a luxurious social club, in the relaxed terminus of long lives.

Emilia-Romagna offers plenty of reminders of this history, too. Although Mussolini was actually born here (in Forlì), the region was an anti-Fascist stronghold, and Bologna was the only city in Italy to liberate itself before Allied troops arrived. Northern Italy paid a steep price for this stubborn independence: In Bologna, Ravenna, and Modena, I had seen plaques listing the partisans who died at the hands of the Nazis, and in Ferrara there are plaques remembering the Jews deported to the death camps. Allied bombing and desperate, last-stand fighting by the Germans flattened some towns in the region. This history, combined with the incredible cruelty of the ruling medieval and Renaissance aristocrats, seemed like an incentive to live well while you could. We are all children of the wolf.

The Adriatic coast has retreated from Ravenna. We blew down the A1 from Ferrara and reached the onetime capital of the Byzantine Empire by midmorning. This drive took us through the easternmost parts of Emilia-Romagna, flat and ugly in a way that only a foodie could love. ("Everything smells of pig shit," the author Bill Buford had said of Romagna, sighing with pleasure. "It's pig shit when you wake up, pig shit when you go to sleep, pig shit all day.") Anyone addicted to the Italian table knows what that stink produces, so buck up and breathe deep.

Romagna has more to offer than pig poo, fortunately. Our day was spent touring some of the world's greatest mosaic work, found in Byzantine churches and tombs dating back to the sixth century. I'd seen Roman and Byzantine mosaics in Syria, Turkey, and Lebanon. But the art of stone tiling reached its zenith here, in glittering works of gold and blue that put even Hagia Sophia in Istanbul to shame. In Ravenna, we devoured the famous portraiture in stone of the Basilica di Sant'Apollinare Nuovo and the tiny but stunning mausoleum of Galla Placidia. Then we finished the day with a sprint into the Romagna marshlands, where the very oldest mosaics lie inside the Abbey of Pomposa. There, in cool shade, I was distracted by the frescoes overhead illustrating Christ's life until I heard a suspicious squeak. I looked down but too late.

Bambino alert. Max was speed-crawling under a velvet rope, making his way onto the oldest mosaic in Italy. It is a section of flooring from A.D. 535, a closed archaeological site. Old stones were suddenly causing me a heart attack. Max four-pointed his way into the center, sat down, and, looking around in satisfaction, said, "Hup-hup-hup." He was drooling on treasures from the first millennium.

In America you might be arrested for this. In Emilia-Romagna they have a different attitude. A gray-haired docent dismissed all of my concerns using three languages (if you count sign language).

"*Kinder* okay," he said, and waved a hand.

2009

The Gods Are Watching

by

JOAN JULIET BUCK

They do not light the ancient monuments at night. The Pantheon, built two thousand years ago, rebuilt by the emperor Hadrian in A.D. 118, consecrated to Mary and All Martyrs in 609, stands in private darkness after midnight in the Piazza della Rotonda. Early in the morning, before the tourists begin to cluster, you can lie on the floor immediately beneath the lunette and see the circle of daylight as the sun itself.

The Romans live among gods and always have. The gods demand something; if not sacrifice, certainly attention. You choose which ones to worship and which to ignore. Mary and Jesus are in churches, and sometimes earlier figures are too: Two floors below the altar of the Church of San Clemente is another altar, to the god of Roman soldiers, Mithras the bull slayer. There are smaller gods: Pan, bearded and rapacious, is usually kept on upper floors, perhaps for good reason. Dionysius, a.k.a. Bacchus, is a long-haired marble youth in museums, or the vapor in any glass of wine. Hercules, only half a god, always has a knobby club in his right hand and a lion's pelt slung over his left shoulder, its hairs carefully incised by the sculptor. After you have seen enough statues of Hercules, the fur coats on the Via Condotti take on some muscle. In a window on the Via Bocca di Leone, a huge photograph shows a model gazing at a handbag in worshipful surrender: to Apollo, for the fashion fame; to Venus, for the shape; to Mithras, for the cowhide itself.

There is something else here. *Fellini Satyricon* plunged fully into the torchlit strangeness of the imperial city, using the alien and the grotesque to summon up something of the gigantic numinous presence that still overwhelms Rome. I used to think the air was thick with ghosts. The air was certainly thick: There was so much traffic, so much exhaust, and fumes so dense that even if nothing ran you over, you were flattened by the environment. The traffic has been drastically reduced; the fumes are gone. But this spring it was reported that the Roman air bore traces of caffeine, cocaine, cannabis, and nicotine, apparently in higher concentrations near the university. What used to choke you can now make you high.

I had known many Romes. The socialite's unstable totter in slim high heels across the cobblestones on the way to dinners where people screamed "Brava!" and made coffee in elegant contraptions while speculating about which women were sleeping with one another (Venus). The privileged ride in the back of the rich person's tiny Fiat 500, chauffeur and bodyguard jammed in front, both armed (Mars) to evade kidnappers (Pluto). The journalist's miserable morning trying to get a package of typewritten text across the Atlantic through the services of a courier who wanted to have some coffee instead (Mercury). Apollonian moments: watching Fellini's casting sessions for *Casanova*, watching Coppola shoot *The Godfather: Part II* on the Janiculum and Bertolucci shoot *La Luna* the day John Paul I died, after only thirty-three days as pope, which led to the alarming headline THE POPE HAS DIED A SECOND TIME. Moments, too, in the underworld: I had lived on a high floor in a palazzo where the feral cries of a disturbed child pierced the air from the far side of an unseen wall, had looked at churches with a man who loved Borromini but also, one May morning, tried to strangle me. And now I was back.

My neighbor in the palazzo on the Piazza Mattei had been Milton

Gendel, a twentieth-century Roman legend who had come to Rome on a Fulbright scholarship in 1949 and never left. Married, for the fourth time, to the artist Monica Incisa, he writes for *ARTnews*, and his remarkable photographs of Romans are regularly exhibited. He's moved his office to the ground floor of the Palazzo Doria Pamphilj, a lofty set of rooms with frescoes on the high ceilings and long windows that open onto a garden. Outside, the foliage shifted as a loud squawking squabble rose up. A riot of chickens, a thousand barking frogs, a million cats in heat? Over the din, Milton shouted, "It's the seagulls!" Rome, fifteen miles from the sea, has seagulls instead of pigeons.

Stendhal, in Rome in 1827, wrote, "Having gone out this morning to see a famous monument, we were stopped on the way by a beautiful ruin, and then by the look of a pretty palazzo, where we went in. We ended up wandering wherever we wanted. We felt the joy of being in Rome in total freedom, without once thinking of the duty to see."

I took his approach. I no longer pretend to like the things that leave me cold. Papal history, the Baroque, the Risorgimento, even the churches intimidate me. The intrigues of contessas and fashion designers have become opaque and useless to me, high heels hurt, Fellini is dead. Freed from the obligations to purr and flatter, freed from heels, I set off on a week of exhilarated wanderings in heavy sandals made for intrepid nuns, and walked for eight hours a day, sustained, perhaps, by those airborne traces of caffeine, cocaine, cannabis, and nicotine. I went to see the gods.

On my first morning, wildly alert with dawn jet lag, I ran past the souvenir vendor asleep in his stall on the Via Frattina, through the deserted Piazza di Spagna, up the empty Spanish Steps to the Via Sistina, to a cappuccino in a barely open bar on the Via Francesco Crispi. Then, still running, I went back down through the empty Via Condotti, along the empty Corso, to the column of Marcus Aurelius.

My first adult reading was Suetonius's gory and wonderful *The Twelve Caesars*. I've only recently come to Marcus Aurelius, a rare wise emperor whose *Meditations* is a handbook of stoic philosophy. He wrote, "Begin every day by telling yourself: Today I shall be meeting with interference, ingratitude, insolence, disloyalty, ill will, and selfishness—all of them due to the offender's ignorance of what is good or evil." He also had a grasp of quantum uncertainty: "Loss is nothing else but change," he continued, "and change is Nature's delight."

And Rome has changed. If I was walking fast, it was because I had to go back to where I used to live. The palazzo is near the Largo Argentina, a sunken pit of mysterious ruins populated by feral cats that used to be surrounded by fierce traffic. Two men were performing complex electronic surgery on plastic phone wires by a hole in the ground. There was almost no traffic, but the cats were still there, and the vestigial temples were still named only A, B, C, and D. A sign warned that video cameras were watching the cat colony to make sure that no new cats were deposited—VIETATO ABBANDONARE I GATTI. I went to the tiny Piazza Mattei, where the tourist attraction is a fountain with four bronze boys and four bronze turtles, but my magnet was the Palazzo Costaguti. The walls of the inner courtyard were cleaner, but the porter, now a young man, assured me that the elevator was still old and difficult. I peered, I gazed, I felt little. It had been decades. I wandered off to Vecchia Roma, in the Piazza di Campitelli. We used to eat dinner there every night—*pollo al mattone*, flattened baby chicken broiled to black. One night someone threw a chicken wing at a passing cat, someone else said that chicken bones were bad for cats, and on cue the cat choked on a bone. I took a table and ordered *pollo al mattone*. "We never serve chicken here," said the waiter. He too is protecting the cats. I decided to let my own past go.

Rome was buffed up for the millennium, and the museums transformed from listless warehouses to places of such coherent intensity that they restore sense to the city. Two new museums have been created—the Palazzo Massimo alle Terme and the Centrale Montemartini—and in the old Capitoline Museums on the Campidoglio (Michelangelo's 1546 square), a confident hand has sliced through the accumulation of centuries to reveal the past as new.

The bronze equestrian statue of Marcus Aurelius on a high pedestal in the center of the Campidoglio has been replaced by a facsimile, with the original moved to its own startling new room in the Capitoline Museums. Set low and surrounded by privileged emptiness under a wide skylight, the man and the horse are almost within reach and glow with gold traces. All other mounted statues of emperors were melted down as pagan idols, but Marcus Aurelius, like the Pantheon, survived because he was thought to be Christian; specifically, Emperor Constantine, who made Christianity the religion of Rome in A.D. 325. The two emperors are here and look nothing alike: Marcus Aurelius has hooded eyes, a curly beard, an inward gaze. Across the room, Constantine's colossal bronze head has the features of a pissed-off Scandinavian and the immense flat eyes of a man staring at God.

Jupiter, Jovis, or, in the Latin spelling, Iovis (they ignored the letter *J*) was the frisky Roman god of gods—his domain, power; his attribute, the thunderbolt; his hobby, the relentless siring of inappropriate children. Every guidebook explains that his temple dominated ancient Rome from the Capitoline Hill, but I never knew where it really was. There were drawings and diagrams, but nothing to touch. Walking away from Marcus Aurelius across the gallery's expanse of new marble and glass, I almost missed a little stairway on the side. What seemed to be an awkwardly placed auxiliary exit took me down to the sudden, overwhelming proximity of thick blocks of stone: the foundations of the Temple of Jupiter, laid 2,500 years ago and uncovered in 1998 beneath the Capitoline Museums.

A dark passage full of tombstones seems to be an unnecessary detour until you reach the end and find yourself in a long loggia with immensely high vaulted ceilings. This is the Roman records office, called the Tabularium; most guidebooks still describe the room, bricked up in the Middle Ages, as closed to the public. A series of arches reveals a vista that was opened only five years ago. There, framed by dark, rough walls, you see the bright, day-lit Forum as if you were floating over it. People hang on to the metal railings, mesmerized. Just down to the left is the arch of Septimus Severus (which Stendhal thought ill-designed), ahead are the three columns of the Temple of Castor and Pollux, who, for the record, were the twin sons whom Leda bore Jupiter after he had come to her in the shape of a swan. (For the record, the two daughters of that union were Clytemnestra and Helen of Troy—no temples to them.) From here, you can see the Via Sacra as it leads to the white arch of Titus halfway up the Palatine Hill, and the parasol pines on the Palatine. You grab on to the railing and fly into the past.

There's another revelation inside this complex of dark passageways. A monumental headless statue of a naked young man is identified as Veiovis. I'd never heard of him. Few have. A French dictionary of mythology says that he is "of essentially infernal character." He was a sort of counter Jupiter, an Etruscan deity whose domain was unstable earth and stagnant water. His animal was a goat. "Veiovis," adds the French book, "has no legend." In the excavations at the base of his temple are fragments of the earliest floors in Rome: red, yellow, and black pebbles set in white limestone. It looks like the plain terrazzo tile on the floor of a bar.

The mundane sets off the gods.

When the renovations started in the Capitoline Museums in 1997, a place had to be found to show displaced statues and ones no one had seen. A temporary exhibition called "Machines and Gods" was set up in an early-twentieth-century power plant called the Centrale Montemartini. Roman gods and archaic Amazons were juxtaposed with machines from 1912: diesel engines, boilers, dynamos, and turbines. The temporary exhibition became an astonishing permanent museum that embodies the sexual fantasies of the Surrealists, from Picabia and Magritte to Marcel Duchamp and Giorgio de Chirico, all of whom were inspired by the relationship between metal pistons and female flesh. On the way to the Centrale Montemartini on the Via Ostiense, you drive past the Roman precursor to Surrealism, a pointed pyramid built between 12 and 8 B.C. for one Cestius. Sometime in antiquity the city wall grew around it, and you never know if it's waving or drowning.

The first jolt inside Montemartini is the sight of a draped woman exposing a breast in front of a round black industrial object—marble against metal, beauty and the beast. A coherent pairing: Venus, goddess of love and beauty, was married to Vulcan, the god of fire and metal. The Centrale Montemartini is a museum of lust.

Maybe it's all the metal that makes the marble look so alive. The archaic statues hit you in the solar plexus: A Winged Victory is so simple that it looks weightless, a kneeling armless Amazon is so full of compact tension that she seems about to unfold. A satyr and nymph are shown grappling; close inspection reveals that the nymph is not pushing away the satyr but holding his hand tight against her breast.

There's a rare and strangely feminine statue of Priapus, made by an unknown master. Each detail on the sculpture produces another surprise. Fringe and ribbons run along the chest of his perfectly sculpted toga; his cape falls in fine folds. His hidden legs and exposed toes are long and slim, and his kneecaps press against material so fine that you can see the outline of gaiters on his calves. Thin marble folds fall from his sweetly protruding penis, and he's crawling with small cherubs, Roman amors—one on each shoulder, another shimmying up his leg. On his left arm is a creature somewhere between goat and sphinx. This is not proud, lewd Priapus. He's sweet. Are all the pretty things on him only there to lure the girls?

Not far away, a naked young man with a duck at his feet stands like a man defeated. His penis, removable, has been removed. "Pothos," I read, "is the third child of Venus . . . the symbol of loving desire towards a distant person . . . the personification of regret and nostalgia."

Many cappuccinos and ruins later, in the window of an ecclesiastical shop called De Ritis, a plaster figure of a young nun with a white coif caught my eye. She wore a nice loden winter coat. Whether it was the pale cast of her plaster face or the stoic lack of mode, she looked unflappable, well on her way to the divine.

That night, Carla Fendi gave a dinner on the bank of the Tiber. Rome, like London, Paris, and New York, has just discovered it has a river. Between a little fake beach set up with sand and folding chairs and an effusive party for something called Roma Fiction Fest—a festival for TV shows—stood a new incarnation of a famous restaurant called Osteria del Pesce. Some kind of trouble had caused it to vanish, but now it was back, with barely dead fish laid out in anodized tubs just beyond makeshift steps, and large tables arrayed on a temporary floor. Important Romans whose biographies I didn't quite get sat looking splendid at a table that grew and grew. Carla, who has the features and bearing of a Roman matron from republican times, made sure the fish kept flowing. Unfortunately, the new fashion in Rome is to eat the fish raw, so that the Venetian on my left and the Sicilian on my right and I all made a noisy fuss of the bread and the tomatoes, and blessed the grilled octopus when it arrived. Silvia Fendi, who designs the handbags that make the world go pagan, sat next to her crutches. A pair of high platform heels had thrown her two days before, and many little bones were broken. "Silvia," I said, "I'm a little worried. I've been staring in the window of De Ritis."

"Nun clothes!" she said. "I love them! It's so not fashion! Let's go shopping tomorrow!"

The crutches helped, and so did my thick nun's sandals. I added dark socks and a baggy dress from a member of the Belgian avant-garde, and kept my eyes down. The backstory, should anyone ask, was lay sisters from Paris, or maybe Nairobi. In the door past the medals and chalices, past pictures of the pope, brocade vestments hung on dummies. Silvia clattered up the stairs, refusing help from the gentle young woman in gray. She had shopped there before, so she knew what she wanted: shirts, cardigans, and sleeveless knitted vests. The shirts were folded, pinned, plain, in dark wooden counters that ran along the mezzanine. The aesthetic of Helmut Lang, I realized, or Jil Sander—Austrian and German, Protestants for sure. We each bought gray polyester-blend shirts and sleeveless vests. Silvia—blond, round, and pretty, just over forty and soon to be a grandmother—asked with gestures if they had very simple nightshirts. The gentle girl in gray took out flowered nighties, as ordinary as housewives. "We can't get things made just for us anymore," she said. We smiled sadly. We were sad.

We'd wanted an alternate reality, no matter how austere. "I'm nostalgic," said Silvia. "I love the smell of mothballs so much I'll follow old ladies in the street if they've just taken out their winter clothes."

To compensate, we went to the place where they make the clothes for cardinals. I cannot say its name, because inside, while I was staring at the rolls of purple wool for cardinals and Silvia was buying the last pair of purple silk kneesocks for cardinals, the owner asked if I was a journalist and I lied. "I hate the press," he said. "They're liars." A bishop's floor-length black dress, edged in purple with a short attached cape and a row of buttons down the front, lay on the counter. "How many buttons do these usually have?" I asked. The salesman looked at me oddly. "It depends how tall the bishop is," he said.

Silvia bought me a length of cardinal-purple wool. She was enthusiastic about Rome's new mayors—"They could have turned it into Venice, but they made the city livable!" We headed back to the Via Ostiense, where she had just acquired a small disused brick factory to convert into a house. Ostiense—full of the charms of workers' housing, a gasworks, and a rough plebeian past—is the Brooklyn of Rome. "I love Ostiense," Silvia said. "I love it as much as I hate Parioli. People don't have books in Parioli."

We drove past the Via del Gasometro; it was 11:30. "I have to show you Al Biondo Tevere!" she said. "Visconti made *Bellissima* there, with Anna Magnani, and it's the last place Pasolini went before he was murdered that night in 1975."

Al Biondo Tevere, so named because the Tiber water turns blond when it rains, seemed to be more terrace than restaurant, a sprawling place just half a block from the Centrale Montemartini. The floor was of course terrazzo tile. Across the street, the former Mercati Generali (General Markets) is being remade into a culture palace by Rem Koolhaas. Giuseppina Panzironi, the owner, took us past the photos of Anna Magnani and Roberto Rossellini and sat us down at a table. Outside the open windows, the Tiber flowed past fields. "The workers would come out of the gasworks and bathe out there, but it's too dirty now," said Mrs. Panzironi. Seagulls, pheasants, and ducks wandered down by the river. "No more shooting allowed." There were sheep, too, she said, until 1975. Pasolini always ate "half a plate of white fettuccine without salt. He said the brain worked better without salt."

"Are you making *suppli* today?" Silvia asked. (*Suppli* are fried balls of rice with a little mozzarella inside.)

"Every day," said Mrs. Panzironi. Bread came out with chopped tomatoes on top, and then the *suppli*, and pasta. White wine was poured. Silvia told Mrs. Panzironi that bamboo shades would be wonderful on the windows.

She and Silvia talked about the food that didn't exist before: "Moravia ordered carpaccio!" said Mrs. Panzironi, appalled.

"What about *penne alla vodka*?" asked Silvia. "Where did that come from?"

"And what about *rughetta*, which used to be *rucola*, a weed that we ate because we were poor?" said Mrs. Panzironi.

Roman food isn't what one imagines: It's plain, rough stuff, mainly starch. Along with the fried-rice *suppli*, it's white beans, boiled pasta, or cold pasta fried with an egg. A tomato is sliced with reverence and laid on a plate like jewelry, every time. The ancient Roman plebeians ate porridge; the patricians had roasted dormouse. They all seasoned food with garum—liquid rotted fish, much like the Vietnamese *nuoc mam*. Today, ladies in light shawls order small portions of mozzarella from different provenances at Obikà, a clever mozzarella bar in the Piazza di Firenze, but the cheapest item in the market, everyone knows, is squid. Cappuccino in Rome is like nowhere else, the foam as stiff as meringue, the coffee underneath a distinct, almost medical, entity.

At the American Academy, built by McKim, Mead & White on the Janiculum in 1914, the food is now nearly as famous as the guests. Alice Waters of Chez Panisse has dispatched Mona Talbott from Berkeley to run the Rome Sustainable Food project, which has transformed the academy's kitchen from an embarrassment of institutional cooking to a model of the new way. The academy's New York president, Adele Chatfield-Taylor, and its Roman director, Carmela Vircillo Franklin, can now invite prominent Romans to eat food grown in the kitchen garden—turnips, radishes, peaches, peppers, celery, and tomatoes, which ripen in a special shed—and prepared with the kind of imagination and attention that changed the way Americans eat. Out in the garden—the highest point in Rome, where Galileo demonstrated his telescope to the pope in 1611—Mona Talbott handed me a fruit I'd only ever read about: a medlar, *nespola* in Italian. It tasted deliciously like a sour apricot. She knows the quality of every bit of land around Rome—that the south is rich, marshy soil and the north is olive oil country, that the nearby hills produce great beans and lentils, and where to get "incredible" anchovies. She had been there four months. The chili peppers had been pressed into oil, and bay leaves will be a liqueur.

"Rome's public school system food," she said with awe, "is already ninety percent organic."

Where did all this enlightenment come from? Who paid attention to Marcus Aurelius when he wrote, "What is no good for the hive is no good for the bee"? Rome used to be a smug, sleepy hell. The old center, the Campo Marzio, was banned to major traffic but strafed by percussive motorbikes, many driven by *sciappatori*, snatchers who knocked women, and men, to the ground and sped off with their handbags. Museums were often closed. The human will flatlined under the weight of history. Rome has become a kind of model of renewal.

Silver buses run on methane; no one smokes indoors, and barely in the streets. Motorbikes are slow, museums are open, films are being made again at Cinecittà. A film festival, the Cinema Festa Intemazionale di Roma, is in its third year.

A new performance space, Auditorium Parco della Musica, designed by Renzo Piano and built five years ago, is used not only for concerts but for colloquia. Colloquia! Adults paying to hear people discuss ideas!

Communism, which used to scare the rich so much that they wore gold hammer-and-sickles from Bulgari on their chains, vanished into a left-wing democratic alliance that called itself La Margherita (The

Daisy), after being called L'Ulivo (The Olive Tree). They were preceded by La Quercia (The Oak Tree). It is now the Partito Democratico.

Two mayors, Walter Veltroni today and Francesco Rutelli before him, decided to have some fun. Rutelli was for years in the Green party; Veltroni dubbed the Italian voice for a character called Mayor Turkey Lurkey in the film *Chicken Little*. Rutelli, Veltroni, and their crew, led by the brilliant senator Goffredo Bettini, are pragmatic Greens with a passion for movies and a compulsion to wrestle Rome into the present.

I went to visit Senator Bettini at home on a Saturday morning. It was a ground-floor apartment on the bourgeois hill called Parioli, where it's said no one has books. A maid let me in and went back to her ironing; I introduced myself to a middle-aged man in the book-filled living room. He took my hand and shook his head: Goffredo Bettini had not yet emerged; he was only the doctor. Bettini, a huge man in his early fifties, entered barefoot and heaved onto a yellow couch with his doctor, to discuss diet.

Bettini has been in politics all his life, as a Communist until 1989, when he joined the Social Democratic party. He's now in the Daisy-Olive-Oak alliance. Three years ago, he and Mayor Veltroni dreamed up the film festival. "It was easy to organize—just and natural. The Auditorium made it possible.

"Rome had only two industries before: construction and civil service," he continued. "We're trying to build a new Rome on culture, with the Auditorium, new museums, the Mercati Generali. It's not enough to rely on the beauties of our past."

The doorbell rang. The maid let in the next appointment, a man in a neat blazer. Bettini talked a little faster. "I have the same passion and desire for change as I did when I was a Communist," said Bettini, "but it's difficult to use certain terms that have been burned by history."

Communism, traffic, and *pollo al mattone* at Vecchia Roma have vanished as if they never existed, and the statues are alive again.

On the way back to my hotel one night after dinner, I stopped to take a photograph of the Pantheon with my digital camera. I was alone in the square. There was a parked car blocking the view. I moved to face the columns of the Pantheon, temple of all gods. When I plugged the camera into the computer in my room a few minutes later, the image on the screen had a strange shape on the right. White scrolls that seemed to make a woman's face, a bird flying toward the dark columns. It wasn't smoke—there was no smoke, and no one was near me at 1 A.M. in the Piazza della Rotunda. I sent the shot to Milton Gendel.

"That's ectoplasm," he said. "Very interesting. I only got it once, in a photo of Iris Origo. Something floating across the room."

I used to think the air was full of ghosts.

2007

My Monet Moment

by

ANDRÉ ACIMAN

 The romance begins for me with a picture of a house by Claude Monet on my wall calendar. More than half the house is missing and the roof is entirely cropped. All one can see is an arched balcony with hints of another balcony on the floor above. Outside, wild growth and fronds everywhere, a few slim trees—palms mostly, but one agave plant stands out—and beyond, along a wide, unpaved road, four large villas and a dappled sky. Farther out in the distance is a chain of mountains capped with what could be snow. My instincts tell me there is a beach nearby.

I like not knowing anything about the house or the painting. I like speculating about the setting and imagining that it could easily be France, Italy, possibly elsewhere. I like thinking that I'm right about the wide expanse of seawater behind the house. I stare at the picture and fantasize about the torpor hanging over old beach towns on early July days, when the squares and roads empty and everyone stays out of the sun.

The caption, when I finally cheat and find it at the bottom of the calendar, reads "Villas in Bordighera." I've never heard of Bordighera before. Where is it? Near Lake Como? In Morocco? On Corfu? Somewhere in Asia Minor? I like not knowing. Knowing anything about the painting would most likely undo its spell. But I can't help myself, and soon I look up more things, and sure enough, Bordighera, I discover, lies on the water, on the Riviera di Ponente in Italy, within sight of Monaco. Further research reveals the villa's architect: Charles Garnier, famed for building the Opéra de Paris. Finally, the year of the painting: 1884. Monet, I realize, was still a few years away from painting his thirty views of Rouen Cathedral.

I know I'm bit by bit demystifying the house. As it turns out, the Internet reveals more paintings of gardens and palm trees in Bordighera, plus one of the very same house. It is a copy of the image on my wall calendar, painted by Monet, not in Bordighera but later that same year in Giverny and meant as a gift for his friend the painter Berthe Morisot. As always, Monet liked to paint the same scene again and again. Sometimes nothing at all changes—just the transit of light spells the difference between impressions of morning and noon.

Monet went to visit Bordighera for the light. His intended visit of a couple of weeks ended up lasting three laborious months in the winter of 1884. He had come the previous year with the painter Renoir for a brief stay. This time he was determined to come alone and capture Bordighera's seascapes and lush vegetation. His letters were filled with accounts of his struggles to paint Bordighera. They were also littered with references to the colony of British residents who flocked here from fall to early spring each year and who transformed this fishing and agrarian sea town famed for its lemons and olive presses into an enchanted turn-of-the-century station for the privileged and happy few. The Brits ended up building a private library, an Anglican church, and Italy's first tennis courts, to say nothing of grand luxury hotels, precursors of those yet to be built on the Venice Lido. Monet felt adrift in Bordighera. He missed his home in Giverny and Alice Hoschedé, his mistress and later wife; and he missed their children.

As far as he was concerned, Bordighera promised three things: Francesco Moreno's estate, containing one of Europe's most exotic botanical gardens; breathtaking sea vistas; and that one unavoidable belfry with its dimpled, onion cupola towering over everything. Monet couldn't touch one of these without invoking the other two. Lush vegetation, seascapes, towering belfry—he kept coming back to them, painting them separately or together, shifting them around as a photographer would members of a family who were not cooperating for a group portrait.

If he was forever complaining, it may have been because the subject matter was near impossible to capture on canvas, or because the colors were, as Monet liked to say in his letters, terribly difficult—he felt at once entranced, challenged, and stymied by them. But it was also because Monet was less interested in subject matter and colors than he was in the atmosphere and in the intangible and, as he called it, the "fairylike" quality of Bordighera. "The motif is of secondary importance to me," he wrote elsewhere. "What I want to reproduce is what lies *between* the subject and me." What he was after hangs between the visible and the invisible, between the here and now and the seemingly elsewhere. Earth, light, water are a clutter of endless, meaningless things; art is about discovery and design and a reasoning with chaos.

Many years after seeing the reproduction on my wall calendar, I finally happen upon Monet's third painting of that very same house at an exhibition in the Wildenstein gallery in New York. Same missing back of the house, same vegetation, same sky, same suggestion of a beach just steps away, except that the third floor, which is absent in the first two canvases, is quite visible here; one can almost spot the balusters lining the balcony. And there is another variation: In the background looms not the snowcapped mountains but Bordighera Alta—the *città alta*, the oldest part of the city—which like so many old towns in Italy is perched on top of a hill and predates the Borgo Marino on the shore. This inversion is also typical of Monet. He wanted to see how the scene looked from the other side.

I want to be in that house, own that house. I begin to people it with imaginary faces. A plotline suggests itself, the beach beckons ever more fiercely. Like a fleeing cartoon character painting escape routes on a wall, I find my own way into this villa and am already picturing dull routines that come with ownership.

Then one day, by chance, I finally find the opportunity to visit Bordighera and to see it for myself. I have to give a talk on Lake Como, so rather than fly directly from New York to Milan I decide to fly to Nice instead and there board a train to Italy. The bus from the airport to the train station in Nice takes twenty minutes, purchasing the train ticket another fifteen, and as luck would have it, the train to Italy leaves in another fifteen. Within an hour I am in Bordighera. The train stops. I hear voices on the platform. The door opens and I step down. This is exactly what I expected. Part of me is reluctant to accept that art and reality can make such good partners.

I don't want a taxi, I want to linger, I want to walk to my hotel. Before me, leading straight from the small train station and cutting its way through the heart of the town, is a palm-lined avenue called the Corso Italia, once known as the Via Regina Elena. I've arrived, as I always knew I would, in the very early afternoon. The town is quiet, the light dazzling, the turquoise sea intensely placid. This is my Monet moment.

I've come to Bordighera for Monet, not Bordighera—the way some go to Nice to see what Matisse saw, or to Arles and St-Rémy to see the world through the eyes of Van Gogh. I've come for something I know doesn't exist. For artists seldom teach us to see better. They teach us to see other than what's there to be seen. I want to see Bordighera with Monet's eyes. I want to see both what lies before me and what else he saw that wasn't quite there, and which hovers over his paintings like the ghost of an unremembered landscape. Monet was probably drawing from something that was more in him than out here in Bordighera, but whose inflection we recognize as though it's always been in us as well. In art we do not see, we recognize. Monet needed Bordighera to help him see something he'd spot the moment he captured it, not before; we need Monet to recognize what we've long sought but know we've never seen.

My first stop, I tell myself, will be the house on the Via Romana, my second the belfry, and my third the Moreno gardens. Luckily, my hotel is on the Via Romana too.

As I walk, I cannot believe what I am seeing: plants and trees everywhere. The scents are powerful and the air pure, clean, tropical. Right before me is a mandarin tree. Something tells me the potted lemons are false. I reach out through a fence and touch them. They are real.

I force myself to think positively of the hotel I booked online. I even like the silence that greets me as I arrive and step up to the front desk. Upstairs, I am happy to find I have a good room, with a good-enough balcony view of the distant water, though the space between the hotel and the sea is totally obstructed by a litter of tiny brick houses of recent vintage. I take out clean clothes, shower, and, camera in hand, head downstairs to ask the attendant where I can find the Moreno gardens. The man at the desk looks puzzled and says he's never heard of the Moreno gardens. He steps into the back office and comes out accompanied by a woman who is probably the proprietress. She has never heard of the Moreno gardens either.

My second question, regarding the house painted by Monet, brings me no closer to the truth. Neither has heard of such a house. The house is on the Via Romana, I say. Once again, the two exchange bewildered looks. As far as they know, none of the houses here were painted by Monet.

Monet's Bordighera is gone, and with it, most likely, the house by the sea. On the Via Romana, I stop someone and ask if she could point me in the direction of the town's belfry. Belfry? There is no belfry. My heart sinks. Minutes later I run into an older gentleman and ask him the same question. Shaking his head, the man apologizes; he was born and raised here but knows of no campanile. I feel like a Kafkaesque tourist asking average Alexandrians where the ancient lighthouse stands, not realizing that nothing remains of the ancient Greek city.

From the Via Romana, I make my way back to the train station, where earlier I had spotted a few restaurants on the long seaside promenade called Lungomare Argentina, probably because Eva Perón loved it. Yet along the way—and I barely have time to realize it—there it is: the belfry I've been searching for. It looks exactly as in Monet's paintings, with its glistening, mottled, enamel rococo cupola. The name of the church is Chiesa dell'Immacolata Concezione, built by none other than Charles Garnier. It's probably the tallest structure in town. How could anyone not know what I was referring to when I kept asking about a campanile? I snap pictures, more pictures, trying to make the photos look like Monets, exactly as I did twenty minutes earlier when I stumbled upon a public garden with leafy dwarf palms that resemble those Monet painted in Moreno's garden. An old lady who stops and stares at me suggests that I visit the *città alta*, the town's historic center. It's not too far from here, she says, impossible to miss if I keep bearing left.

Half an hour later, I'm on the verge of giving up on the *città alta* when something else suddenly comes into view: a small hill town and, towering above it, another belfry with a bulbous cupola almost identical to the one I spotted on the *chiesa* by the shore. I can't believe my luck. Bordighera, I realize, has not one but two steeples. The steeple in Monet's paintings is not necessarily that of Garnier's church by the marina but probably another one that I didn't even know existed. Coastal towns always needed towers to warn of approaching pirate ships; Bordighera was no exception. A steep, paved walkway flanked by old buildings opens before me; I'll put off my visit to the historic center and walk up to the top of this minuscule town instead. But this, it takes me yet another delayed moment to realize, is the *città alta* I came looking for. My entire journey, it appears, is made of uninformed double takes and inadvertent steps.

Bordighera Alta is a fortified, pentagon-shaped medieval town full of narrow, seemingly circuitous alleys whose buildings are frequently buttressed by arches running from one side of an alley to the other, sometimes creating vaulted structures linking both sides. Laundry hangs from so many windows that you can scarcely see the sky from below. The town is exceptionally clean—the gutters have been covered with stones, and the clay-tiled paving is tastefully inconspicuous. Except for a televised news report emanating from more than one window lining the narrow Via Dritta, everything here is emphatically quiet for so packed a warren of homes. As I make my way around the square, I see the Santa Maria Maddalena's clock tower again, and to my complete surprise, once I step into a large courtyard that might as well be a square behind the main square, another belfry comes into view. Then a post office. A church. A barber. A baker. A high-end but tiny restaurant, a bar, an *enoteca*, all tucked away serendipitously so as not to intrude on this ancient but glitzified town. A few local boys are playing *calcetto*, or pickup soccer. Others are chatting and leaning against a wall, all smoking. A girl, also smoking, is sitting on a scooter. I can't decide whether this town is inhabited by working-class people stuck on this small hill all year or whether the whole place has been refurbished to look faux-rundown and posh-medieval. Either way, I could live here, summer and winter, forever.

Once again, through an unforeseen ascent of a hill, I've stumbled upon something perhaps far better than what I came looking for. I find myself suspecting that the humbling, intrusive hand of Providence is arranging events which couldn't seem more random. I like the idea of a design behind my desultory wanderings around Bordighera. I like thinking that perhaps this is how we should always travel, without foresight or answers, adventitiously, with faith as our compass.

As I'm making my way through a maze of narrow lanes, I finally come to an open spot that looks out toward a huge expanse of aquamarine. Straight below me is a marina. I decide to head back down to the Lungomare Argentina and am beginning to leave Bordighera Alta. Because I am already planning my return trip to Bordighera in six months, I stop at what looks like a picturesque two-star hotel. I walk inside and start by asking the man at the desk for the price of a double. Then, as though my next question follows up on the previous one, I ask if he can tell me something about the Moreno gardens. Once again I am given the same story. There are no Moreno gardens. "But Monet—" I am about to interrupt. "Moreno's land was broken up more than a century ago," says a portly man who had been chatting with the hotel's owner and was sitting in the shade. Francesco Moreno, he continues, came from Marseille and, like his father before him, was a French consul in Italy—he owned almost all of Bordighera and was in the olive and the lemon trade. He imported all manner of plants from around the world, which is why Monet tried everything he could to be allowed inside the garden. The estate, however, was sacrificed to build the Via Romana.

Moreno, it appears, did not put up a fight with the city planners, even though he was the wealthiest landowner in sight. He died, probably a broken man, in 1885, one year after Monet's visit. The family sold their land, gave the rest away, then his widow moved to Marseille. The Morenos never returned. There is scarcely a trace of the Moreno mansion or its grounds—or, for that matter, the Moreno family. For some reason no one wants to talk about them.

It's only then, as I leave the hotel and take a steep path to the Church of Sant' Ampelio by the sea, that I finally spot a white house that might very well be the house, or something that looks just like it, though I could, of course, be wrong. A rush of excitement tells me that I have found it all on my own—yes, adventitiously. Still, I could be wrong. It is a gleaming-white construction; Monet's house is not so white nor does it have a turret. But then, I've only seen cropped versions of it. I walk down the path and head right to the house. There is no doubt: same balconies, same stack of floors, same balusters. I approach the villa with my usual misgivings, fearing dogs or a mean guardian or, worse yet, being wrong.

I brace myself and ring the buzzer by the metal gate. "Who is it?" asks a woman's voice. I tell her that I am a visitor from New York who would give anything to see the house. "*Attenda*, wait," she interrupts. Before I can compose an appropriately beseeching tone in my voice, I hear a buzzer and the click of the electric latch being released. I step inside. A glass door to the house opens and out steps a nun.

She must have heard my story a thousand times. "Would you like to see the house?" The question baffles me. I would love to, I say, still trying to muster earnest apology in my voice. She asks me to follow and leads me into the house. She shows me the office, then the living room, then what she calls the television room, where three old women are sitting in the dark watching the news. Is this a nunnery? Or a nursing home? I don't dare ask. She shows me into the pantry, where today's menu is written in large blue script. I can't resist snapping a picture. She giggles as she watches me fiddle with my camera, then shows me to the dining room, which is the most serene, sunlit dining room I have seen in ages. It is furnished with separate tables that could easily seat thirty people; they must be the happiest thirty I know. The room is impeccably restored to look its age, its century-old paintings and heavy curtains bunched against the lintel of each French window. The house must cost a fortune in upkeep.

Would I like to take a look at the rooms upstairs? asks the nun. Seriously? She apologizes that her legs don't always permit her to go up and down the stairway but tells me I should feel free to go upstairs and look around, and must not forget to unlock the door leading to the top floor on the turret. The view, she says, is stupendous. We speak about Monet. She does not think Monet ever stepped inside this villa, but he must have spent many, many hours outside.

I walk up the stairs gingerly, amazed by the cleanliness of the shining wooden staircase. I admire the newly corniced wallpaper on each floor. The banister itself is buffed smooth, and the doors are a glistening enamel white. What timeless peace these people must live in. When I arrive at the top floor, I know I am about to step into a view I never thought existed, and will never forget. And yet there I was, minutes earlier, persuaded that the house was turned to rubble or that they weren't going to let me in. I unlock the wooden door. I am finally on the veranda, staring at the very same balusters I saw in Monet's painting in the New York gallery, and all around me is . . . the sea, the world, infinity itself. Inside the turret is a coiling metal staircase that leads to the summit. I cannot resist. I have found the house, I have seen the house, I am in the house. This is where running, where searching, where stumbling, where everything stops. I try to imagine the balcony a hundred years ago and the house a century from now. I am speechless.

Later, I come down and find the nun in the kitchen with a Filipina helper. Together, the nun and I stroll into the exotic garden. She points to a place somewhere in the far distance. "There are days when you can see the very tip of Monte Carlo from here. But today is not a good day. It might rain," she says, indicating gathering clouds.

Is this place a museum? I finally ask. No, she replies, it's a hotel, run by Josephine nuns. A hotel for anyone? I ask, suspecting a catch somewhere. Yes, anyone.

She leads me back into an office where she pulls out a brochure and a price sheet. "We charge thirty-five euros a day." I ask what the name of this hotel is. She looks at me, stupefied. "Villa Garnier!" she says, as if to imply, What else could it possibly be called? Garnier built it, he died here, and so did his beloved son. The widow Garnier, unlike Moreno's, stayed in Bordighera.

It would be just like me to travel all the way to Bordighera from the United States and never once look up the current name of the villa. Any art book could have told me that its name was Villa Garnier. Anyone at the station could have pointed immediately to it had I asked for it by name. I would have spared myself hours of meandering about town. But then, unlike Ulysses, I would have arrived straight to Ithaca and never once encountered Circe or Calypso, never met Nausicaa or heard the enchanting strains of the Sirens' song, never gotten sufficiently lost to experience the sudden, disconcerting moment of arriving in, of all places, the right place. What luck, though, to have found the belfries and heard the sad tale of the Moreno household, or to have walked into an art gallery in New York one day and seen the other version of a painting that had become like home to me, and if not home, then the idea of home—which is good enough. I tell her I'll come back to the Villa Garnier in six months.

But the nun has one more surprise in store for me.

Since I've come this far for Monet, she suggests, I should head out to a school on the Via Romana that is run by other nuns and is called the Villa Palmizi, for the palm trees growing on what was once Moreno grounds. The school, which is totally restored, she tells me, contains part of the old manor house.

We say good-bye and I head out to the Villa Palmizi, eager to speak to one of the nuns there. The walk takes five minutes. The end of one search has suddenly given rise to another. I knock, a nun opens. I tell her why I've come. She listens to what I have to say about Monet, about the Villa Garnier, then asks me to wait. Another nun materializes and takes her place. Then another. Yes, says the third, pointing to one end of the house that has recently been restored, this was part of the Moreno house. She says she'll take me upstairs.

More climbing. Most of the schoolchildren have already gone home. Some are still waiting for their parents, who are late picking them up. Same as in New York, I say. We climb one more flight and end up in a large laundry room where one nun is ironing clothes while another folds towels. Come, come, she signals, as if to say don't be shy. She opens a door and we step onto the roof terrace. Once again, I am struck by one of the most magnificent vistas I have ever seen. "Monet used to come to paint here as a guest of Signor Moreno." I instantly recognize the scene from art books and begin to snap pictures. Then the nun corrects herself. "Actually, he used to paint from up there," she says, pointing to another floor I hadn't noticed that is perched right above the roof. *"Questo è l'oblò di Monet."* "This is Monet's porthole." I want to climb the narrow staircase to see what Monet saw from that very porthole.

The story of Monet's *oblò* is most likely apocryphal, but I need to see what Monet might have seen through this oblong window just as I needed to come to Bordighera to see the house for myself. A sense of finality hovers in my coming up here to see the town through Monet's window. Same belfry, same sea, same swaying palms, all staring back now as they did more than a century ago, when Monet first arrived.

I begin to nurse an eddy of feelings that cannot possibly exist together: intense gratitude for having witnessed so much when I was so ready to give up, coupled with the unsettling disappointment which comes from knowing that, but for luck and my own carelessness, I would never have witnessed any of this, and that, because luck played so great a part in things today, whatever I am able to garner from this experience is bound to fade. Part of me wishes to make sense of all this, only to realize in a flash of insight as I'm standing in Monet's room, that if chance—what the Greeks called Tyche—trumps meaning and sense every time, then art, or what they called Techne, is itself nothing more than an attempt to give a tone, a cadence, a meaning to what might otherwise be left to chance.

All I want, all I can do is retrace my steps and play the journey over again. Stumble on the image of a house on my wall calendar, spot the same house in a gallery, arrive by train, know nothing, see nothing, never sight the old *città alta* until I come upon it, see the town "with" and "without" the belfry, with and without the sea, with and without the chopped-up quarter of Moreno's house, and always, always chance upon Garnier's home last. I want to restore this moment, I want to take this moment back with me.

Stepping out of Monet's tiny room, I am convinced more than ever that I have found what I came looking for. Not just the house, or the town, or the shoreline but Monet's eyes to the world, Monet's hold on the world, Monet's gift to the world.

2010

A Streetcar Named Sazerac

by

JULIA REED

 In 1942, a man named Robert Kinney wrote a charming little book called *The Bachelor in New Orleans.* Billed as "a handbook for unattached gentlemen and ladies of spirit visiting or resident in the Paris of America," it was apparently meant as a (slightly) tongue-in-cheek response to the more serious guidebooks produced by the W.P.A. Federal Writers' Project. It also turned out to be remarkably informative—even today— and raised an important metaphysical question. "Few bachelors," according to Kinney, "really know whether New Orleans is an alcoholic mirage or whether New Orleans drinks are part of a general illusion, including wrought iron grillwork, impossibly beautiful women, magnolia blossoms, race horses, carnival parades and Mardi Gras, moonlight, and the suggestive music seeping out into the streets from a hundred courtyards. When—if ever—you leave New Orleans for that place you used to call home . . . you only know it was swell, whether it was the drinks that created the city or the city that created the drinks."

It is easy to see how such a conundrum might arise. A great many people, after all, come to New Orleans in order to lose their cares or themselves, overimbibe and overindulge, and generally revel in a lost weekend—albeit one a tad more lusty and uplifting than that of Ray Milland—so that when they wake up, still hung over, back home in High Point, say, or Akron, they are inevitably confused about the solidity of what they experienced.

Part of the problem is that there is very little in New Orleans that is actually solid. The city is located just above the Gulf of Mexico, between a famously unruly river and a forty-mile-wide lake, on land that is not quite land and which is invariably referred to as either pudding or gumbo (a nod to the latter's dark and viscous roux). The ground literally shifts under your feet and is currently sinking at a rate of about a third of an inch per year. Also, even without the benefit of what Kinney calls the "wondrous drinks" constantly on offer, a variety of factors conspire to make the place feel more than just a little miragelike.

The light is often murky, the air can feel like water, and the water table itself is so high that bodies are buried aboveground (and are everywhere visible in gleaming white minicities of the dead). All manner of insects, from mosquitoes to flying Formosan termites, swarm in great clouds; tropical lushness spills out from behind courtyard walls and through wrought iron fences; naked women (and men) spill out onto the stage of Bourbon Street. (Walker Percy once wrote that "the tourist is apt to see more nuns and naked women than he ever saw before"—a typically jarring juxtaposition that understandably might be passed off as yet another optical illusion.)

In such an unsteady environment, one could certainly be driven to "create" a few drinks. In fact, though it is a subject of much debate, the cocktail itself is said to have been invented here, by a pharmacist named Antoine Peychaud who had escaped a slave revolt in his native Santo Domingo with a family recipe for bitters in hand. In 1838, he opened an apothecary shop on Royal Street, where, after hours, he offered friends a mixture of brandy and bitters in an egg cup (hence the theory that a cocktail is a badly pronounced *coquetier*). Thus was born the precursor to the Sazerac, a cocktail now made with American rye whiskey (a substitute for cognac after an attack of the deadly grapevine pest phylloxera made that spirit hard to get), absinthe (which was replaced by Herbsaint or Pernod when it was outlawed in 1912), and bitters (Peychaud's remains the only brand used for a true Sazerac).

In the ensuing decades, an enormous number of additional cocktails were invented in New Orleans: the Vieux Carré, the Brandy Crusta, the Ramos gin fizz, and the Hurricane, to name a few. Last year, the Louisiana legislature wasted an entire month arguing over which one should be named New Orleans's official drink. After no less than ten House and Senate votes, the Sazerac (a cocktail even more "authentic" now that absinthe is again legal) won out over the Ramos gin fizz, an outcome that would have saddened Huey Long, who so favored the latter that he took a local bartender with him to Manhattan's New Yorker Hotel in order to instruct the staff in how to produce a proper one.

The legislature's shenanigans aside, no proclamation has ever been needed to encourage the city's relationship with alcohol—the two have been inseparable from the get-go. In 1718, when Jean Baptiste Le Moyne, Sieur de Bienville, insisted on establishing New Orleans as the capital of the fledgling French colony of Louisiana in the location it still (however tenuously) occupies today, it was over the objections of his own engineer. Barely a year later, a flood wiped out the handful of palmetto huts that had been completed, and, not surprisingly, the first commercial establishment in the rebuilt "city" was a wine shop. A century later, the English botanist Thomas Nuttall wrote, "Time appears here only to be made for lavish amusement. Is the uncertainty of human life so great in this climate as to leave no leisure for anything beyond dissipation?"

It should be pointed out that the uptight Nuttall's previous forays into North America had included Philadelphia, St. Louis, and what is now Oklahoma and Arkansas. He would have been wholly unprepared for a city whose heady mix of French, Spanish, African, and Catholic cultures separated it so profoundly from the rest of the proper old Anglo-Saxon U.S.A. (Not only is New Orleans psychically disconnected but it is physically pulling away from the continent at the rate of a few millimeters a year.) By the time of Nuttall's arrival, New Orleans had been in the hands of America for only seventeen years, having already absorbed the languages, mores, and slave regimes of two decidedly un-American colonial powers. It was also a thriving port through which all manner of contraband moved; Jean Lafitte, the privateer who trafficked in everything from rum to slaves (and whose "blacksmith shop" headquarters/front is still in business as an excellent bar), was a local hero. (He and his men had been crucial to Andrew Jackson's defeat of the British at the Battle of New Orleans.)

New Orleans has little more in common with the predominantly Baptist Deep South than does the rest of the country and even much of Louisiana, where local blue laws still ban the sale of alcohol on the Sabbath. (Another taken-aback Yankee visitor, the architect Benjamin Latrobe, arrived a couple of years after Nuttall to discover not only his dead son's illegitimate children but a city in which "there is no visible difference between Sunday and any other day.") In the next-door state of Mississippi, Prohibition was not repealed until 1966. In New Orleans, by contrast, Prohibition meant very little—not even inconvenience. In the 1920s, when a federal agent named Isidore Einstein traveled the country to test how easily he could obtain a drink, New Orleans placed first among the cities he visited—a scant thirty-seven seconds elapsed between the time Einstein stepped off the train and the moment he held a drink in his hand.

Today, a visitor can be sated just as quickly. Liquor is on sale twenty-four hours a day, seven days a week, somewhere in the city's fifteen-hundred-plus barrooms as well as in liquor stores, supermarkets, and drugstores. When my friend Brobson Lutz arrived by train from dry rural Alabama in 1968, he was astonished to find that not only could he drink legally, "there was an aisle of liquor a mile long" at the grocery store. "I thought the devil himself had something to do with creating New Orleans when I saw that." You can drink and walk the streets of New Orleans (as long as your drink of choice is not in a glass receptacle); you can buy frozen daiquiris at one of the many drive-through windows. Booze is on sale in the lobbies of movie theaters and in stands on the street. One of the most popular parade throws during Mardi Gras is a large plastic "to-go" cup—most households keep literally hundreds on hand.

Thus it is that for some people, drinking is to New Orleans what gambling is to Las Vegas: the point. But there is a more apt analogy, I think, a variation on the slogan, "What happens in Vegas stays in Vegas." What happens in New Orleans stays here too, but it couldn't happen anywhere else, so you have to keep coming back to find it—to somehow reassure yourself that your experiences were in fact real and not part of the "general illusion" that is the city.

Like Kinney's bachelor, I spent the better part of my youth making countless, possibly illusory visits, culminating in a trip to the New Orleans Jazz and Heritage Festival (better known as Jazz Fest) eighteen years ago, when I began the slow crawl toward permanent citizenship. It was sometime in the early morning of the second day, after two sets at the Maple Leaf and many, many drinks, that I heard myself say I was coming back. Ten weeks later, I had taken a tiny apartment, ostensibly to cover an election, but that contest, between a colorful former governor and a Klansman, entertaining though it would prove to be, was not remotely all there was to it. I had danced and I don't dance; I had kissed someone I was not supposed to kiss (and had an idea that wouldn't be the end of it). In the airport, heading home to New York, I encountered dozens of live crawfish, escapees from a seafood store's takeout box, skittering frantically at my feet. Once I assured myself that they weren't themselves illusions, I was wholly sympathetic to their plight—I was almost as desperate not to leave as they were.

When I returned (for increasingly longer stretches), I began a reconnaissance mission of sorts, recovering bits and pieces of my own immediate past and slowly making my way well beyond those first bachelor-like impressions of the city itself. I also quickly came to realize that as such research goes, I could do a lot worse than spend time in the many micro-universes that are the city's bars.

During my first summer in town, I ate lunch every day at the

Napoleon House, the ground-floor bar in a building completed in 1814 by Mayor Nicholas Girod, who offered it as a refuge to the exiled Napoleon seven years later (the story goes that the mayor had authorized Jean Lafitte to send a ship to fetch him). Napoleon died before he could accept, but his presence is felt in various portraits hung on the peeling walls and in the plaster bust atop the now-defunct cash register. No one could explain to me why an English drink—the Pimm's Cup—has long been the house specialty in a place that is a shrine to a French emperor (one who met his literal Waterloo at the hands of an English commander), but I'd been drinking them there since long before I was old enough to do so, and now I sat at the bar with a bowl of gumbo and a Budweiser, reading the local paper and occasionally chatting with the genial but properly taciturn bartender.

After over a decade in the far more intense urban confines of Washington and New York, I found these brief lunches in the upper reaches of the French Quarter a joy, a perfect example of what Walker Percy identified as the city's "peculiar virtue . . . a talent for everyday life rather than the heroic deed." New Orleans, he wrote, "has nurtured a great many people who live tolerably, like to talk and eat, manage generally to be civil and at the same time mind their own business." He added that if a person were to fall ill on the streets of Manhattan, folks would grumble about the inconvenience of stepping around a body. In New Orleans, on the other hand, it is still likely that "somebody will drag you into the neighborhood bar and pay the innkeeper for a shot of Early Times." They will, in other words, take care of you in the same way as Girod had hoped to nurture the down-on-his-luck Napoleon, by giving him a safe haven and a restorative pick-me-up.

In the Napoleon House, I absolutely felt as though I had a safe haven—it served as a timeless midday respite from both the heat (the high plaster walls, the ceiling fans, the cross-ventilation between the courtyard, and an entire wall of French doors ensure that it is surprisingly cool, even in summer) and the modern demands of phone and office. Everything, from the architecture to the cuisine to the music (classical symphonies and opera only), hails from another century; even the apparatus on which the music is played (a stereo with a turntable) is virtually prehistoric. But for the newspaper, I would have been hard-pressed to identify what year it was. And this is the other mirage-like thing about New Orleans, to paraphrase Faulkner, who lived for a time in the Quarter: The past is not remotely past, it surrounds you. "New Orleans is not like most other cities, where history is put in depressing little history zoos, and visitors are invited to gawk," says Wayne Curtis, author of *And a Bottle of Rum: The History of the New World in Ten Cocktails.* "The past is animated and healthy here and, perhaps, even a little pushy."

That first summer, I got used to driving down streets named not just for Napoleon but also for the places at which he was victorious (Valence, Jena, Milan, Constantinople, Marengo), and past an almost entirely black housing project named, ironically, after Jean Lafitte. My first apartment was a block away from the enormous gay bar Lafitte's In Exile and two doors from Lafitte's Blacksmith Shop, which, except for very low lights that allow the bartender to work his magic behind the bar, is lit entirely by candlelight and looks much as it must have when Lafitte himself hung out inside.

In such places time becomes relative, suspended even, as though you were on an airplane—though one with generally better seating and service and more entertaining companions. Tennessee Williams wrote of the city's "long rainy afternoons when an hour isn't just an hour but a little piece of eternity dropped into your hands, and who knows what to do with it?" Williams managed to figure it out, discovering both his sexuality and the subject matter for his finest work. "In New Orleans, I found the kind of freedom I'd always needed, and the shock of it against the Puritanism of my nature has given me a subject, a theme, which I've probably never ceased exploiting." Williams clocked at least some of those rainy hours in French Quarter watering holes ranging from the Hotel Monteleone's Carousel Bar, where the bar itself further erodes one's bearings by making a slow rotation, to the bar at the New Orleans Athletic Club, where old boxing trophies sit next to bottles behind the copper-topped bar, and where it is still possible to get a refreshing screwdriver after a morning workout on the StairMaster.

In New Orleans, Williams found refuge from oppression, Sherwood Anderson found refuge from boredom (he was from Ohio, after all), Faulkner found "a place by and for voluptuousness"—so much so that he couldn't concentrate, apparently, since he wrote his first, and arguably worst, novel here. Like many writers before and since, they were all drawn to a place that, in the words of a *Wall Street Journal* reporter, "refuses the entreaties of the rest of the world to eat less, get to work, stop dancing, and wear clothes appropriate to your gender."

This particular reporter had been sent down several years ago to do a front-page story on the city's famously excessive ways and the citizenry's shorter-than-average life expectancy—an assignment that began, at least, with a slight whiff of judgment. But then the Romanian writer and New Orleans convert Andrei Codrescu spent an evening with him at Molly's at the Market, and the reporter came to understand, says Codrescu, that statistics were unimportant if you "live experientially twice as long" as folks in more "virtuous" places.

The eureka moment happened at about 3 A.M., when a gorgeous tattooed woman clad only in a sarong climbed up onto the bar. One experience in particular seemed to have a significant effect: As she unwrapped herself, "the snakes, beginning at her coccyx, circled flowering vines to descend from her shoulders to her perineum," Codrescu reported. "It was a magical moment, like a door opening suddenly to another world. The inkster of the *Wall Street Journal* was transfixed like a deer in the headlights of the moment, understanding in a flash that the grim statistic he was trying to explain was a figment of time, whereas what unfolded before him belonged to timelessness."

Molly's was founded by another refugee from the Midwest, the late Jim Monaghan, who at one point owned thirty saloons in town. After Katrina, Molly's stayed open, serving as a candlelit beacon to those of us in desperate need of a cold beer and camaraderie during another entirely "out-of-time" moment in the city's history. Monaghan had died four years before the storm, but he was a comforting presence throughout: His son, the current owner, keeps his daddy's remains on a shelf behind the bar, a presence of sorts that reassures the regulars that nothing, neither death nor a hurricane, is going to upset the sanctity of their domain.

Like that of Williams and countless others, Monaghan's is hardly the only ghost haunting a saloon. While it is said the world over that most folks drink to forget, in New Orleans they drink to remember. They toast long-dead emperors or the ashes of proprietors; they sit in chairs where someone else sat a hundred years before. New Orleans is a city of continuity and long-ingrained habit, in which gentlemen go to the same bars as their fathers and grandfathers and great-grandfathers before them—whether it is to the working-class Markey's or the more upscale Sazerac Bar.

The Sazerac, located in the storied Roosevelt Hotel, home of the Ramos gin fizz (the proprietors bought Henry Ramos's formula and the rights to the name during Prohibition) and the New Orleans headquarters of Huey Long, is marked by fabulous Art Deco–style murals of the city's street life and, of course, an exceptional Sazerac. It is also an example of how seriously the locals take their rituals: In a place where existence itself is so precarious, ritual and ceremony (even the ceremony of a perfectly made cocktail) become bulwarks against impending disaster, and when they are tampered with, people get very nervous. So it was that when the Roosevelt was sold and renamed the Fairmont in 1965, the locals steadfastly refused to refer to it by its new name. Such vigilance, ironically, paid off. The hotel, whose luster had dimmed considerably under the Fairmont's management, suffered water damage during Katrina and remained shut. In June, it finally reopened in all its former glory as part of the Waldorf Astoria Collection, which wisely gave the hotel back its original name.

When I first moved here, I thought the refusal to acknowledge the name change of a major hotel was amusing, but now I understand completely. Because New Orleans is a rare American city where the great majority of lives are played out in public spaces, those spaces become virtual temples filled with personal memories, landmark moments, sacred occasions. And when those spaces are ruined or lost, you don't just lose a favorite watering hole, you lose part of your own history as well as the soothing familiarity of an old friend. I reunited with one man I loved at Vaughan's, a former grocery store in the Bywater, and made the excellent decision to get rid of one I didn't at the same place. On the latter occasion I was joined by my friend McGee, who had picked me up in a fit of pique at her own beau, and within the space of five or six hours, we'd ditched both guys, drunk all the dark rum in the house, given the bartender a ride home, and had a surprisingly cheerful and productive time of it. Whenever the bartender, who is moving a bit slower these days, sees us, he reaches for the rum. And now I wouldn't think of drinking anything else there.

2009

A New Yorker in Old Amsterdam

by

JAY MCINERNEY

 The night before departure I found myself seated at a big round table in Elaine's, on the Upper East Side of New Amsterdam, nominal host to a party of some twenty raucous bibliophiles allegedly celebrating the publication of a book and demonstrably sucking down vast quantities of vodka and Pinot Grigio. The group kept expanding—tables at Elaine's, I believe, are made of some kind of space-age alloy, infinitely elastic—and before long I found myself sitting next to a young woman who looked like, and in fact was, a swimsuit model. "Don't let me drink too much," she said by way of introduction. "I have to fly tomorrow."

"Going to Amsterdam by any chance?" I inquired. She looked at me with wonder and admiration. "How did you know?" she asked.

I too was flying the next day, and Amsterdam just happened to be my destination. I immediately felt I was onto something if my dinner companion was typical of the clientele. Otherwise, I didn't know much about the city. I had a few key stereotypes in mind, of course, falling under the headings of Hashish and Heroin, Red-Light District, Squatters. I'd heard that there were canals. I couldn't quite square my separate notions of the Dutch—stolid and bourgeois—with what I hoped was the licentious weltanschauung of Amsterdam.

The next day provided yet another occasion to wonder why east-bound transatlantic flights have to leave in the evening only to arrive at a hideous hour the following morning just as you have fallen asleep on what you thought was the night before. No city in the world looks good under these circumstances. I was greeted by two official escorts representing my Dutch publisher and Dutch film distributor. The women, Charlotte and Paulette, were extremely blond and pleasant. We were rolling along by this time in a big Oldsmobile sedan. From the front seat the driver was giving me a minicourse in local geography and history. One of the best things about Amsterdam, normally, if you aren't craving a little Zen silence, as I was just then: Practically everybody speaks English.

Amsterdam's ugly suburb belt—that inevitable ring of hell between airport and any major metropolis—is narrower and less offensive than any I can think of. The sense of nausea one feels when arriving sleepless into the morning light of, say, Heathrow or Malpensa, is compounded by the aesthetic horrors of an hour-long journey to London or Milan through the billboard alleys and late-fifties housing-project sprawl.

Amsterdam, the driver explained, was built outward from an old center in a series of rings delineated by semicircular canals. The outer ring, the one that looked as if it dated from the fifties and sixties, passed in a flash. Then we were in the center. I was to learn later that all of Amsterdam is called the center. A city of some 700,000 egalitarian souls, Amsterdam has never felt the need to divvy itself up into neighborhoods, which makes things a little confusing for the visitor, who receives the answer "the center" to any question about his current location. Fortunately, the place seems only a little bigger than TriBeCa in New York, so one orients fairly quickly.

The center, to my weary eyes, looked generally pleasing and quaint, canal-riddled, composed largely of narrow four- and five-story brick houses with imaginatively shaped peaks. My hotel was an exception to this rule, a big pile of new brick called the Sonesta. To be fair, it was only eight stories high, but it took up most of the block and looked like just the kind of place a film company would assume an American would want to stay in. I was led up to the Royal Suite, a couple of vast rooms with Euro-modern furniture and a bed several acres in area. I kept meaning throughout my stay to screw up my courage and my prima donna tendencies and demand a transfer to digs more, well, Dutch, but I never got around to it, and I was consoled a couple of days later by the arrival of Bruce Springsteen, who requested my suite and had to settle for the presumably less opulent Presidential Suite on the same floor. For the moment, too jet-lagged to even think of complaining, I collapsed on the big bed and promptly fell asleep.

At 10:30 P.M. I was awakened by a Dutch journalist friend whom I'd met in the States a couple of years back. Ad is a freelance critic and commentator with serious academic and bohemian credentials, the sort of café intellectual that we no longer seem to have in this country.

Fortunately, Amsterdam is the kind of place, though just barely, where you can get fed well after eleven. This is one of my personal litmus tests of a serious city. (Los Angeles flunks this one as well as so many other tests of urbanity.) We went to a bistro in the center of town, the interior of which was rather like the Cafe Luxembourg in Manhattan—streamlined and white. There were two levels, both with marble-topped French bistro tables. My friend Ad and his stunningly blond girlfriend, Miriam, filled me in on their recent adventures over some good French food and white Burgundy while I gradually regained consciousness. After dinner we had coffee at a bar called the Blincker, which is a theatrical hangout Ad described as a white café. "A what?" I said.

The most basic type of bar or pub, Ad explained, was the brown café—an old, cozy establishment with dark woodwork, the kind of place in which an English typesetter or middle manager would feel at home. Back in the late seventies a new type of watering hole had sprung up—the white café, which, as its name implies, is stark, modernist, and mostly white in decor. The newest thing, the late-eighties thing, was the PoMo bar. As in the arts in general, even this far along in the eighties no one was exactly clear on the requirements and specifications associated with the postmodern.

From the Blincker we strolled out into the A.M. Amsterdam is a good city for walking, although the natives favor bicycles. Bikes somehow became a theme of my stay here, though I never climbed onto one. They were everywhere, and as we strolled up a cobbled street, an emaciated man of indeterminate age and ethnic origin who looked as if he needed many good meals pedaled up and accosted us. After a short exchange he pedaled off. Ad and Miriam explained that he was a junkie and that traffic in stolen bikes was a mainstay of the local junkie and nonjunkie economy, part of life in the city. Everyone has a bicycle. The junkies steal them and then pedal around looking for buyers. Since every bike stolen implies a bikeless rider, there is a thriving market. The going rate is about twenty guilders, which is roughly ten dollars, although they start out asking for fifty. Miriam had gone through three bikes in the past year. After losing a few bikes that cost several hundred guilders new, she suggested, one loses one's scruples about the whole process. Everybody plays the game.

"Haven't you guys heard about bike locks?" I asked.

Yes, said Ad, bike locks are standard equipment, but standard equipment for an Amsterdam junkie includes a hydraulic pump device that cracks the toughest locks. Many junkies, I discovered, carry the shrapnel scars of bike locks that have exploded in their faces.

Since we were on the subject, I asked about the heroin situation. Ad shrugged and said there were a lot of junkies in the city. "Many of them are foreigners," he said, "Germans and Italians. They come here because the drugs are the best in Europe. A lot of them OD because the stuff is much purer here than they're used to." He said this, it seemed to me, with a mixture of weariness and pride. Weariness because he and most other natives of the city weren't involved in the drug trade and were a little tired of talking about it. Or tired of losing their bikes. Proud, perhaps, of the tolerance that is one of the city's greatest indigenous virtues. And did I detect a little bit of perverse pride in the fact that the local dope was primo? (Holland is a small country, and every country wants to excel in some area or other.)

Maybe I just have the wrong kind of face, but I was accosted by pedestrian heroin dealers three times during my five days in Amsterdam.

We were ambling up a narrow cobbled street lined with eighteenth-century houses when a sideward glance revealed a black woman of Rubenesque proportions in a Frederick's of Hollywood–style negligee framed in a picture window awash in the lurid glow of a black light. She was perched on a barstool. Catching my eye, she winked and thrust her pelvis in my direction. The ground-floor windows of the next house displayed two more women, one in a G-string and bra and the other wearing a Hard Rock Cafe T-shirt.

Turning a corner, we were on the main axis of the red-light district, divided down the middle by a canal. The picturesque canal houses were the same here as elsewhere in Amsterdam, except that many of them displayed red lights over the doors and seminude women in the ground-floor windows. Drawn curtains were an indication of business in progress. Here and there, illuminated signs advertised SEX SHOP and LIVE SEX SHOW. The pedestrian traffic was largely male, giddy, and nervous. Snatches of cockney and German phrases drifted over the water between the two sides of the canal, voices imbued with the forced bravado of prurient men. You can hear the same translingual tone around Times Square or outside the cabarets in Tokyo's Shinjuku.

It was a little disconcerting, all these sexually explicit women behind glass, just a foot or two beyond the sidewalk. That was my first reaction, anyway.

After a few minutes I began to feel more at ease. In fact, there was something cozy and domestic about the scene, an ambience unlike that of any commercial erotic zone I had seen before. It seemed to me to lack the menace of similar places. Although natives warn you that it's a dangerous place, I think they mean comparatively dangerous. This is not a city that has three or four murders a day. The streets were clean. The canal houses were cute. And the women, for all of their exhibitionism, were behind glass. They were not, as on Broadway and Forty-seventh Street or the Place Pigalle, out there on the sidewalk. It was all very, well, Dutch.

The Dutch have a word that seems to go a long way toward situating an aspect of the national character: *gezellig*, which means cozy or homey. Curiously, the red-light district had this quality.

We ended the night sometime around three at a disco, the name of which I don't remember because by that time I was back in that hyperspace reserved for the severely jet-lagged and mildly intoxicated. The place reminded me of a second incarnation of Danceteria, on Twenty-first Street in New York. The tone was kind of punk, with black walls and dyed hair. A lot of orange hair, in fact.

The orange-hair motif became acute the next day. And not just hair. Roaming the streets I saw faces painted orange, and altogether too many orange shirts. Being of southern Irish extraction, I found this rather disturbing. And strangely, the gray, damp air of June in Amsterdam carried cries of "Olé! Olé! Olé!" This was Holland, wasn't it? Had I taken a wrong turn?

One thing I knew about Holland was that it had produced a disproportionate amount of great painting, and I was keen on viewing the local stock of Rembrandts, Vermeers, and Van Goghs. Charlotte, the publicist, kindly agreed to take me to the Rijksmuseum, the national museum of the Netherlands, which is conveniently located in—you guessed it—the center of town.

The museum is a big neo-Gothic brick pile, circa 1885, turreted and elaborate in exterior detail, one of the most strident edifices in the city. Charlotte dismissed it as a Catholic building, uncharacteristic of Amsterdam, explaining that the architect, P.J.H. Cuypers, was indeed of the popish persuasion. Amsterdam may be as different from the rest of

Holland as New York is from the Midwest, but around Amsterdam the Dutch are generally Calvinists who dislike ostentation, bourgeois who are suspicious of grandeur in either aristocratic or nouveau riche modes. Unwritten sumptuary laws hold sway. Already I'd felt that my standard New York wardrobe was too formal—my linen suit branded me as conspicuous a foreigner as the herds of Japanese following a flag-bearing leader, although everyone was much too nice to say so.

The obligatory stop in the Rijksmuseum is Rembrandt's *The Night Watch*, which, like Michelangelo's *Pietà*, seems to exert a powerful magnetism on the lunatic fringe as well as on tourists: Charlotte informed me that somebody slashes the canvas every five years or so. Nevertheless, it looks spectacular and is still unprotected by glass. Next door are four of the world's thirty-six Vermeers, which I found utterly hypnotic—three interior scenes suffused with a soft gray light that is so ordinary and natural it seems miraculous, and an exterior scene called *The Little Street*, which might be a snapshot of a contemporary Dutch city except that in my experience Dutch women no longer wear silly white hats and bibs. My enjoyment was inhibited by an American tour guide advising his group to "take a deep breath, come on now, through your nose, that's it. In, out, in, out. What do we smell? Who can tell me? Do you smell anything? It smells old, right? That's the smell of culture. That's the dust of the centuries . . . one more time now, breath in . . ."

Breathing normally, we proceeded to the nearby Van Gogh museum, an unfriendly modernist lump designed by the sometimes brilliant Gerrit Rietveld, a founder of the De Stijl movement. The paintings, some eighty arranged chronologically so as to show Van Gogh's development, more than compensate for their setting. Some of Van Gogh's greatest paintings are hanging here. Looking at the bleak *Crows over the Wheatfield*, one of his last paintings before his suicide, I felt a sense of vertigo and disorientation that went way beyond jet lag. And I thought of the last line of Wittgenstein's *Tractatus*: "Of that which we cannot speak we must therefore remain silent."

Emerging into the prosaic daylight, I was once again assailed by cries of "Olé! Olé!" and flashes of orange amid the generally drab tones of the pedestrians.

We strolled over to the Leidseplein, a large square fringed with cafés and fast-food joints, roughly the equivalent of New York's St. Marks Place. The square has a scruffy, youthful vitality and is a favored site for demonstrations and celebrations. Charlotte took me into the Bulldog Coffeeshop, the flagship of a citywide chain and a big destination for younger tourists. It looks and smells like the early seventies—pot, denim, leather, hair. Downstairs, one can order dope from a menu of brands. The government cracked down on these establishments about a year back, hoping to clean up the city's image for a bid on the 1992 Olympics, but when Barcelona won out, the cleanup was quietly abandoned, and it seems to be business as usual, drugwise.

"What's with all the orange?" I asked as we passed a man with a can of orange spray paint tinting the hair of passersby.

"My God, you don't know?" she said. "This is the biggest thing to happen in Holland since Liberation. Today is the finals of the European Cup—Holland versus Russia." She explained that the entire country was in the grip of soccer fever, that Holland had never won a cup. A few days before, they had beaten the Germans in the semis, and there had been a riotous celebration. Like most Europeans, only more so, the Dutch hate the Germans, so the victory had been particularly sweet.

"The Dutch fans had these big signs at the stadium that said stuff like GRANDMOTHER, I GOT YOUR BICYCLE BACK." Seeing my puzzlement, Charlotte explained. "During the war, the Germans supposedly stole all the bikes and sent them to Germany. It's a joke, you see."

"Oh," I said.

Half an hour before the match, Amsterdam looked like a ghost town. No one was on the streets except for a few dazed tourists. Everyone was at home in front of the tube or jammed into the local café. We met my Dutch editor and watched the match in a traditional brown café called the Pieper. The level of enthusiasm was radical. My editor, cosmopolitan and hip, was a little disdainful of the hysteria. "This shows how little sense of national identity we have, getting all excited over a soccer match." Nevertheless, by the second half he was kneeling on a table to see the TV set. I was standing on a barstool. Every Dutch kick was cheered. At key moments the assembled crowd burst into song. There was one song they sang every time the face of the Russian coach came on.

"What does it mean?" I asked Charlotte.

"They're calling him a dog's penis," she said. I was knocked off my perch in the wave of enthusiasm over the first goal, a header by Gullit, the dreadlocked darling of the team. The second goal, an improbably angled shot by Marco van Basten, sealed the victory. Everyone was screaming "Olé! Olé!" Charlotte explained that a couple of years back the Dutch had hoped to go to the World Cup in Mexico City and had taken up the chant "Olé!" in anticipation, though they never made it. Now it was an all-purpose chant in Holland to indicate crowd enthusiasm, whether at rock concerts or soccer matches. Bruce Springsteen was no doubt scratching his head for a while and checking his tour schedule to see where he was.

After the final whistle we walked back to the Leidseplein. From every corner of the city came the same chant: "Olé! Olé! We are the champions, we are the champions." The English phrase was borrowed from the song by Queen some years ago, and I have to say that within a few hours I was getting tired of it, though it continued to echo through the city for days.

Passing the police station, I caught sight of a policeman wearing an orange wig and a false orange nose. Orange smoke bombs were exploding everywhere, and people with cans of orange spray paint were decorating everything and everybody. My editor, who dresses like a New Yorker and was not eager to change the color of his Hugo Boss blazer, led our retreat to a white café called Walem, where the clientele were dressed in black and white, rather like East Villagers, and looked pretty disgusted with their countrymen. But they were a distinct minority.

By dinnertime the revelry had intensified. We ate at Markx, the absolutely up-to-the-minute place, which everybody agreed was PoMo although no one was sure why. Perhaps it was the sponged-bronze paint job—more or less the equivalent of the Canal Bar in New York. The diners were more stylishly attired than your average Amsterdammer, although I got the distinct impression that being hip in Amsterdam was not so competitive and elitist a pursuit as in New York. There were empty tables around us at peak dinner hour. In five nights, I never discovered a bar or nightclub that had an exclusionary door policy.

The menu at Markx was divided into four sections—Szechuan, French, German, and American Southwest. I had a decent fried salmon with black and gold fettuccine in cilantro pesto and felt right at home, except that the service was lackadaisical as opposed to nasty.

Then into the sodden orange night. The entire population seemed to have spilled out into the street, dressed in orange—which, by the way, is the color of the royal family. Remember William of? Pedestrianism was difficult. Strangers kept embracing us and spilling beer on our shoes.

We tried to find refuge in various pubs, but they were all packed to the rafters. My editor claimed to know a quiet place, "a nice cozy little bar." We got there to find a masked transvestite ball in progress. A person in a full leather mask, leather bra, leather G-string, and chains wanted to dance with me.

"Just like home," I said.

"It's not usually like that," my editor said. "Very strange. I know another place. It's sort of a hangout for intellectuals. It's called Schiller." We fought and shoved our way through the streets. It didn't seem possible, but Schiller was more crowded than the sidewalks, and the intellectuals were baptizing each other with Heineken and Amstel between choruses of "We are the champions."

Desperately searching for a haven from all the orange, we pressed on to a nightclub called Richter, stepping over bodies in the street. Richter has been a hot spot for six years, the life span of clubs apparently being much longer in Amsterdam than in New York. The city closed the place down for a few months during the Olympics-courting period because of blatant drug abuse on the premises, but it was thriving now, full of the young and the restless.

The clientele were very good-looking, but something struck me as funny, something I'd been trying to put my finger on for a while about Amsterdam. Toward the end of the night I figured out what was strange about the scene to the eyes of a New Yorker: the absence of libidinous energy. The average Manhattan nightspot is seething with sexual tension, but at Richter the clientele were not visibly cruising each other. There was almost none of that predatory leering or conspiratorial winking that is standard nightclub demeanor elsewhere in the world. And I realized I had also missed this on the street. The Dutch don't seem to spend a lot of energy sending sexual signals out into the world at large or receiving them, as compared with, say, New Yorkers, Parisians, or Romans. The atmosphere even here in the hot nightclub was one in which groups of friends had come to have chummy fun. What they do when they finally go home, I can't tell you.

By 3:30 A.M. the club was still rocking, but we were fading. Out on the street the party continued. I joined in for a few choruses of "We are the champions." Back at my hotel finally, I had an entirely redundant nightcap in the hotel bar, which was called the Boston Club, where I found myself among a group of black men and gaudily dressed Asian women. The women had large hairy hands and Adam's apples. I decided it was time for bed.

Sunday was a day of convalescence and meditation for me, although the party continued in the streets. The revelry looked unrestrained, but by the end of the weekend, according to the *International Herald Tribune*, there had been only three arrests, and most of the injuries were the result of people fainting at the rally. Imagine if the English international team had won. (English clubs are barred from European play because of the tendency of their fans to kill and maim and run amok.) Still, the next day everyone was saying there had been nothing like it since Liberation in '45. At that time, the party had gone on for months. And in fact, I was told by several people, the exuberance of this celebration had almost as much to do with defeating the Germans the week before as with winning the finals against the Russians.

Everyone kept telling the big joke of the match against the Germans, the slogan "Grandma, I got your bicycle back." I was sitting in a white café called the Palace with my friend Ad when he repeated this. "I don't get it," I said. "Did the Germans really steal all the bikes? I would think there was more valuable stuff for them to steal."

"It's a kind of Dutch understatement," he said, looking even more serious and wrinkled of brow than usual. "How can I explain? It's like, the bicycles, talking about the stolen bicycles, is really a way of talking about all the horrible things that happened—the Jews, the murder, all the killing and stealing. It's like a metaphor. We talk about the bicycles, but we really mean all the other things."

A few minutes later we were walking alongside a canal when he stopped me and pointed out the Anne Frank House, an unremarkable brick canal house where eight Jews hid for twenty-five months during the occupation.

Amsterdam is not a city of churches, particularly. There is the Oude Kerk (Old Church, circa 1300) and the Nieuwe Kerk (New Church, circa 1400). The religious establishment I was most interested in seeing was the Church of Satan (circa 1970). Some say that this is not a church at all, that it is in fact a sex club evading taxes under the guise of religion, or antireligion. I heard stories of satanic rites performed by women who are called sisters and nuns. Everyone had heard about it, but I couldn't find anyone who had been there or knew exactly where it was, not even the cabdriver waiting in front of my hotel at the start of my last night in Amsterdam. But he took me and Ad to the red-light district, and from there we started asking.

It didn't look like a church. Like almost everything in Amsterdam, it looked like a house. We had to buy tickets at the door to the tune of about forty dollars an hour, which included all we could drink. We could make special donations to individual nuns once inside if we wished to request particular rites and ceremonies.

Inside, the walls were painted with pentagrams, prostrate nudes, and snakes. There were no other communicants in sight when we stepped into the first-floor nave, which had a bar running the length of one wall. A redheaded white whale of a woman was stretched out along the bar, holding a pose reminiscent of Manet's *Olympia*, although in fact not even Rubens could have done justice to this expanse of flesh. Only Botero could have painted this.

"Welcome, mates," she said in hearty East Londonese.

"Olé, Olé!" I responded.

"What'll it be?" she asked. A smaller, olive-skinned woman in a loincloth crouched silently beside her.

The cheery behemoth drew two beers for us, flesh rippling and un-dulating with her every move. She asked us where we were from and then went back to telling her silent companion about an argument she'd had with her landlord. I was vastly relieved when she turned her attention away long enough for us to escape upstairs, where we encoun-tered three more nuns, languidly reclining, minimally clad. Again, the ceremonial questions about our places of origin and choice of beverage.

"Any snake venom or virgin blood?" I asked, but they were fresh out. A black woman of advancing middle age, who said she was from Brazil, came over to chat us up and tug at our zippers, but her heart didn't really seem to be in it.

Yes, she was a nun, she told me; she worked an eight-hour shift, 6 P.M. to 2 A.M.

"Any satanic rituals coming up in the next hour?" I asked.

"You got forty guilders?" she asked.

We were distracted by a commotion on the stairway. Suddenly the place was full of smirking middle-aged men and English accents. The other two nuns sprang to life, darting in among the boys, tugging and poking and teasing. After everyone had a drink, a collection basket was passed around with exhortations to reach deep and give till it hurt. When the women were satisfied with the take, the ceremony commenced, interrupted from time to time by a pudgy clown who kept trying to do headstands between the legs of prostrate nuns.

"That's my boss," muttered a man hiding in the corner in our vicinity, shaking his head in disbelief.

"What is it that you do?" I asked.

"We work for Whitbred ale. It's a business trip. We've just come from touring the Heineken brewery." His eyes widened as one of the nuns did something fairly remarkable with a hard-boiled egg. In one case, two of the women decorated the body of a third with pentagrams, though the other things you could see in Bangkok or, for that matter, Bentley's in Manhattan on a Wednesday night.

The flavor of the scene was unique, though. Somehow Dutch tolerance seems to neutralize the menace and the squalor and the tension of sin. A curious country, sexual license combined with a sort of asexual national demeanor—politically liberal and emotionally conservative. Nowhere else in the world could a sex show in a place called the Church of Satan seem, well, homey. *Gezellig.* Cozy. The guys from Whitbred sitting on the couches with their beers. A smiling woman in leopard panties saying, "Come on now, who wants to help me with this next one."

In seeking out the Church of Satan, I had imagined that I would finally view the Hieronymus Bosch aspect of the national character— orgiastic revelry and abandon. And indeed, on the face of it the scene had more than a touch of *The Garden of Earthly Delights*. But even so, there was still more than a touch of Vermeer.

1988

Romancing the River

by

PATRICK SYMMES

Maybe I'm crazy, but it took me several years in Manhattan to fully absorb that I lived on an island suspended at the mouth of a broad and powerful river, just where it does battle with the sea. Only slowly did I begin to fathom this natural drama. It was the sight, down a cobblestoned lane, of the wind-whipped Hudson gleaming as a winter sunset gilded every crested and scallop-edged wave. It was realizing, one spring morning, that the tangy scent discernible amid the bus exhaust was that of a fresh salt breeze, ripe with tidal surge and oceanic possibilities. It was learning, eventually, to separate the cry of the nesting cormorant from the angry tooting of a yellow taxicab.

Finally, after much time and consideration, I reached down one Saturday morning in the first June of the new millennium and, hesitantly, touched it. Water flowed over my urban fingers like a wild thing, bracingly cold, surprisingly fresh, and, yes, clean. I was wet only up to my wrists. But that was enough. My love affair began in earnest. Late on weekend afternoons, when skyscrapers throw New York City into shadow, I would stroll from the Avenue of the Americas six thousand feet westward, against the thronging tide of humanity, dressed in ridiculous kayaking costumes or tilting an improbably long fishing pole. And each time I caught that first glimpse of the Hudson and of the openness of the vast harbor, I paused, conscious that I was now joining the nameless throngs who, throughout the ages, have gone down to the sea in ships.

These Homeric reveries, of course, were usually interrupted by a horn blast from an impatient commuter careening toward the Holland Tunnel. But I never let a few problems discourage me. I was learning to love the Hudson, and love is blind.

If you somehow missed the news, as many have, the Hudson is back. Once considered a national disgrace, the punch line to a nasty joke, the river is now cleaner than it has been for a hundred years, the shorelines of New York City have been regreened by new parks, the sport fisheries are exploding, and the Hudson Valley as a whole is reclaiming its heritage as the repository of American grandeur and beauty—and, not least, as the vast playground it once was.

The part of the Hudson I know best is the stretch near my home, Manhattan's Greenwich Village, which just happens to have some shockingly good sportfishing. I've bounced plugs off Governor's Island, drifted hooks deep in the Hudson's rocky depths, hit the beaches of Staten Island at dawn, and even delighted in the way frenzied schools of bluefish part to the charge of the Staten Island Ferry. I have relished the oceanic solitude found just a few hundred yards from eight million people while kayaking against the river's quixotic, sweeping current. I have run a J/24 sailboat aground on Ellis Island. This is a lovely river.

There are problems, of course: More than twenty years ago, the lower two hundred miles of the Hudson were labeled a toxic Superfund site because of pollution far upstate. Between 1946 and 1977, General Electric power plants near Hudson Falls discharged more than a million pounds of PCBs into the river, but this July the EPA ordered the company to begin dredging out the contaminants—a multistage cleanup that will take years and will cost roughly half a billion dollars. And yes, I learned to avoid the river after a heavy rain, when it is often muddy and tree choked. But as the Hudson improves year by year, the insults leveled at it are becoming less a fact than a tactic used by river aficionados to keep other people away. Is the state going to build and open swimming beaches along more than 150 miles of river? Then crack a Jimmy Hoffa's last dive joke.

I saw this strategy employed by swimmers, boaters, fishermen, and people sitting in quiet cafés with spectacular river views. I too could not stand having to share my best fishing hole. I began to dread the morning paper, with its offensive headlines like STRIPERS REBOUND. My whole day could be ruined by the sight of another banner proclamation (CLEANEST WATER OF THE CENTURY). One day, *The New Yorker* ran a cartoon of one striped bass asking another, with a crestfallen expression, "How do we tell the kids we're edible again?"

Yet somehow, despite all this, the Hudson's recovery remains underappreciated and almost ignored. On sunny Sundays, when there are fist fights in Central Park over blanket space, swards of lush grass still lie unoccupied in Hudson River Park. Only a step beyond busy streets, the harbor and its neglected fringes offer the rarest qualities of urban life: space and empty vistas, peace and tranquillity. Smitten with this discovery, I was drawn almost inevitably up the long valley of the Hudson, compelled to measure over the next several months the entire river, all the way to its source, and to see what further treasures were hidden in plain sight.

A journey of 306 miles often starts with a short cab ride, and last fall, it was this familiar conveyance of explorers that hauled me to the Ear Inn, an old sailor's bar on the watery edge of Manhattan's SoHo that has remained staunchly impervious to trends since 1805. A Guinness later, on my way out, I tapped the chalk mark by the front door that declared HUDSON SHORELINE 1797. A pair of naval bollards nearby emphasized the point. After four centuries of human improvements, the

Hudson is a thousand feet west. It is there, at Pier 32, near SoHo's Spring Street, that the latest and most needed of these improvements has begun: the curious aforementioned Hudson River Park. Only a few hundred yards wide but five miles long, the $330 million park is not just the city's newest, but by 2005—the projected completion date—it will be the city's largest, encompassing more open space than even Central Park.

It was the first annual Hudson River Park Day, September 24, 2000, when I arrived, but only the free rides on a fireboat were attracting a crowd. At Pier 40, just north of Canal Street, I found volunteers from the Hudson River Park Trust loaning fishing poles (and worms!), as they do on summer weekends, and made a few uneventful casts before spending a vigorous quarter of an hour as one of six galley slaves on a Whitehall gig, a speedy replica rowboat built by Floating the Apple, a group of volunteers determined to bring back recreational boating in the harbor. The coxswain, a regal seventeen-year-old from the Bronx, had helped build the gig with nineteenth-century techniques. Fewer than twenty percent of New York City students even realize that Manhattan is an island, but this young seaman left me confident that a new generation of New York water rats will eventually rise, their enjoyment of the Hudson its ultimate protection.

Back on dry land, I strolled down to an event that was drawing a slightly horrified crowd. On Pier 26, near TriBeCa, scuba divers were vanishing into the murky Hudson with mesh bags to retrieve garbage from the bottom. The cleanup was intended to prepare an area around the pier for further adventures in scuba.

"I went down there and put my hand in the mud," said Cathy Drew, director of the River Project, a science and education center on Pier 26, "and I couldn't see a thing." Drew has spent more time than most peering into the Hudson. The River Project shed is filled with fish tanks offering thrilling proof of the river's natural resurgence—crabs, shrimp, striped bass, bluefish, and plankton—but birds have been the Hudson's most visible success story: There was not a single cormorant in the harbor in 1985; today there are more than eight hundred. Twenty other species, including herons, have returned over the same period. At a special presentation late that afternoon, Drew and fellow enthusiasts presented data on the improved water quality, discussed plankton counts, planned nesting sites for more wading birds, and talked of rotting piers as "emerging wetlands." A cormorant paddled by, as if on cue, and beneath the gleaming towers of Manhattan, the mile-wide river ran blue and steady. We sat on the pier, watching sunlight slide across the harbor toward us. It was hard for Drew to feel sore about the low turnout. Looking around the empty piers, the quiet park, she could barely conceal her delight. "Great," she said. "More for us!"

The appropriately named *Commander*, a double-decker tourist boat, pulled out of West Point with a passenger list including sixty-eight nuns in disguise (they were dressed in street clothes for a "secret" outing, one later informed me) and two dozen juvenile delinquents on medication. Within minutes, we left behind the gray walls of the military academy that loomed proudly like an American Gibraltar over the tightest part of the Hudson. The *Commander*, oval and lethargic, turned slowly into the current and puttered upstream—heading directly toward a rocky cliff topped with brush called World's End.

When Henry Hudson first ventured to this point in 1609, captaining a tiny barque of exploration for the Dutch empire, he anchored overnight, unwilling to risk his vessel in such an improbable passage. Here, half a mile above West Point, the river twists so sharply that it seems to pour out of the rocks themselves. This abrupt switch in the water's course, the narrowest spot on the Hudson, does serve as a border between one world and another, as Henry discovered the next morning, when he finally rode through the narrows on a flood tide.

Even from the *Commander*'s upper deck, I was too close to the waterline to make out, just before the turn, much of Constitution Marsh, a low-profile favorite of nature lovers along the eastern shore of the Hudson. The marsh, a 270-acre nature preserve, is filled with tawny cattails and twisting water trails perfect for canoe trips. Short of a canoe, the best place to study it is from high above, on the smooth green lawn of Boscobel, the Monticello-like estate of States Morris Dyckman. Dating to 1804, the house, now a museum, has a sublime sense of republican proportion and modesty that is surpassed only by the carefully landscaped grounds, with a bowling green lawn that points toward Constitution Marsh, directly below, and the crenelated battlements of West Point, across the river. There is no finer place for the public to see the river, full of islands and the swirling wakes of speedboats, with the spires of Bear Mountain Bridge, the loveliest crossing point on the Hudson, visible about five miles downstream. As the *Commander* rounded that final bend of the narrows and the great wide river ahead suddenly came into view, with Breakneck Ridge on the right and the round dolomite mass of Storm King Mountain on the left, the nuns burst into enthusiastic applause. Even the juvenile delinquents were drawn to the railings, trailed by their counselors, their uncharacteristic silence a testament to the awesome power of the scenery.

The *Commander* swerved right, passing a few outbuildings of the Army academy, and then headed up the widening stream, past the town of Cold Spring, where George Washington and I have both slept. He even named this miniature community, while headquartered in the area. On an earlier trip, I had eaten here and then checked into the Hudson House, a remnant of the steam age and the hotel with the finest view of the Hudson, period. Sitting on a second-floor balcony at sunset, I watched the sky turn the color of the stone, as men plucked blue crabs from the water flowing past the town's carefully restored old steamboat pier. This is the only spot where the Appalachian Mountains, rich with dolomite and limestone, come down to, and are broken by, the sea: The Hudson was known to Native Americans as "the two-way river," because ocean tides reverse its course twice a day. Brackish water can reach well above Cold Spring, creating a productive estuarine environment where freshwater and ocean species mingle up to 150 miles from the sea.

"In a one-hundred-yard stretch here, you can have blue crabs, brown trout, bluefish, and high-altitude stone flies," said Robert Boyle, the legendary founder of Riverkeeper, perhaps the earliest and most effective organization dedicated to restoring the Hudson. Boyle, a sportswriter and fisherman, lives just south of Cold Spring in a house with a sweeping view of the river that he has known for close to seventy years. The deep and rocky Hudson is "a nutrient factory, a super protein factory," he emphasized. "The lower one hundred and fifty-four miles are a shoestring version of Chesapeake Bay. It is the only major estuary on the Atlantic coast of the United States that still retains all the original spawning populations of all its original species."

Boyle linked the recovery of the river to geographical determinism. Not only is this fast-flowing mountain river able to flush out many pollutants, but the source of the largest quantity of pollution—New York City and its effluent—is conveniently placed at the very bottom of the river. Human effort has also played a major role in cleaning up the river—notably the Clean Water Act of 1972, which banned open dumping of industrial waste. Riverkeeper appointed an individual warden to live on and patrol the river, documenting pollution. Working with groups like Clearwater and the Natural Resources Defense Council, it brought more than a hundred lawsuits against Hudson polluters, generating more than one billion dollars in fines, money that has been used to fund further cleaning of the Hudson.

Humans, however, still remain the greatest threat to the river. Since 1995, twelve new power plants have been proposed for the banks of the Hudson; combined with a new crop of cement factories, this "reindustrialization" is the biggest challenge facing the waterway. Human rivalries have also come to the fore: Boyle left Riverkeeper last year after a bitter dispute with the group's charismatic chief attorney, Robert F. Kennedy, Jr., a prodigious fund-raiser seeking to expand Riverkeeper's purse and profile. The schism was all too typical of the Hudson: There are dozens of environmental groups up and down the river, with little coordination or common agendas, divided in their goals and priorities.

"All of us profit from the ferment, the competition," Kennedy said in a cell phone interview conducted as he drove along the river toward Manhattan. He doubts a unified plan could ever emerge from the di-

versity of interests and jurisdictions along the Hudson's 306 miles—
and that is fine with him. A diverse river needs diverse agendas. "There's
room on the river for everybody," Kennedy said. "The Hudson looks
like America. It has working landscapes, farms and agriculture, large
cities, beautiful river towns like Cold Spring, Kingston, and Saugerties,
and it's got the most powerful city in the world, New York. I love that
about the Hudson."

Kennedy has kayaked, rafted, swum, fished, and scuba dived most
of the river for most of his life, and he relishes the experience of
camping on a pristine island as oceangoing tankers slip past, or
scouting his favorite fishing hole to discover sea-run bluefish, mountain
brook trout, goldfish, catfish, blue crabs, pumpkinseeds, eels from the
Sargasso Sea, tropical sea horses, Caribbean sergeant majors, and cold-
sea striped bass, all intermingled in the cheery chaos of a single Hudson
tributary, the Croton River.

"It's a Noah's ark, a species warehouse," he said, "the last refuge for
many animals going extinct elsewhere." In 1965, when his father first
took him rafting on the Hudson, the water was too polluted to drink
and the river was "a national joke." Now what Kennedy calls "the miraculous resurrection of the Hudson" has inspired sixty Riverkeeper-
type organizations around the country, and the model—water patrols
to track down polluters—is being exported internationally.

It is hard to get Kennedy to stop talking about how much he
loves the Hudson, about his vision for its future. But eventually his
cell phone signal begins to break up, and he warns me that he is
driving into the Holland Tunnel. A moment later, with Kennedy still
discoursing on the pleasures of a life lived on the Hudson, his line
goes dead. Only the weight of the river itself can squelch the man's
enthusiasm.

Despite its deep bed and the twice-daily scouring by a this-way, that-
way current, the Hudson occasionally pauses to rest. Its lingering side
channels, eddies, and marshlands are among the places where it is
easiest to approach the river's beauty. Much higher in the valley now, I

picked my way down through the back streets of Saugerties, left the car in a gravel lot by a Coast Guard marina, and strolled into a swamp.

This required mud boots: The Ruth Glunt Nature Trail, a well-maintained path through a forest, over footbridges, along a sandy beach, and through a bog thick with towering cattails rustling in the wind, takes only ten minutes to cross. At this point, the Saugerties Lighthouse heaved into view, a compact, two-story brick house built in 1869 and topped with a still-functioning Fresnel lens blinking out three-second warnings to river traffic.

Once a navigation hazard, the spit of land on which the lighthouse sits now serves to isolate and protect one of the valley's most curiously charming bed-and-breakfasts, a two-room operation run by the light-house keeper. The half-primitive facilities—showers depend on ade-quate rainwater reserves, and there is but a single composting toilet—have never deterred determined visitors, and rooms are booked months in advance. The reason is obvious: You don't simply get close to the river here, you are literally in it twice a day, when a rising tide closes the boggy path behind you for up to ninety minutes at a stretch. Waves lap against the stone foundation of the lighthouse, boats pass, and a fresh river breeze rustles the cattails behind you. An ample dock equipped with benches makes the lighthouse a popular day-trip, too; I found myself visiting again and again, simply for the sensation of being thrust far out into the Hudson.

As darkness fell on the dock, ending a beautiful afternoon of doing absolutely nothing, I hurried back to beat the rising tide, reached my car, drove back into Saugerties, and settled into Frank's Hunting Lodge, a main street bar featuring bowling trophies and ball games on TV. A glass of Genesee wet my parched throat, and then I ate just up the block at the Café Tamayo, one of the justifiably renowned restau-rants that makes traveling the valley such a dangerous pleasure these days.

After a dinner featuring duck confit and a bottle of pinot noir from Millbrook Vineyards, across the Hudson, I drove twenty minutes farther north, toward the almost silent, eerily preserved town of Athens, hard against the river. There I checked into the Stewart House, an 1883 hotel originally intended for steamboat passengers that now attracts actors. The management and staff are long-suffering thespians, and Uma Thurman and Ethan Hawke have stopped by for drinks under the long bar's pressed-tin ceiling. The hotel itself starred in *Ironweed*, alongside Jack Nicholson and an actress who would haunt me as I slept. "Yup," the manager explained, as he showed me into my corner room overlooking the river, "Meryl Streep died in your bed."

It was a good base. For days, I roamed the banks of the Hudson, visiting glossy river towns like Rhinebeck, stopping to see a production of Shakespeare on the Hudson at a spectacular bend in the river, parading through the immaculately preserved town of Hudson, which has a personality split between sixty-seven antique shops and half a dozen substance-abuse treatment centers. I got lost hiking in the immense Tivoli Bays marsh and, ten minutes below Hudson, loitered at Olana, the Moroccan hilltop palace of Frederic Church, leader of the Hudson River School of landscape painters. Church had been inspired by the quiet of his cosmopolitan redoubt, and I too found myself returning again and again to these few miles of the river. But there was more still.

We hit the trail at 7 A.M., on schedule, for the final leg of this excursion: the approach to the very headwaters of the Hudson, in a remote part of the High Peaks Wilderness of the Adirondack Mountains, more than 250 miles from the sea. I'd recruited a friend to join me in a daylong sprint through the coniferous forest, toward the source. Here, the Hudson shed the lazy peace of the main valley and twisted up through black peat into the foothills. We'd spotted this mountain Hudson half a dozen times, alternating between small stony rapids and flat pools. We stayed in a B&B in North Creek, a town packed with rowdy hikers and kayakers, but dawn found us dutifully sprinting up the southern route to Mount Marcy, the highest peak in New York State.

A hundred yards in and the Hudson was there, roaring alongside the trail, a flume through a rock-strewn ditch. Only moments from its source, it was ten feet wide. Another hundred yards up, we crossed a wooden bridge without guardrails—the last of all the bridges over the Hudson proper—and then saw the stream beginning just above us, at the mouth of Henderson Lake.

The lake was once voted the Hudson's "true" source by an overeager New York State legislature, and this was indeed the first place—this very spot, where water from the lake spilled over a dam—to bear the name Hudson. But further research identified the river's ultimate source—the highest source of the source that fed this lake that launched the Hudson on its way to the Ear Inn in SoHo. That ultima Thule was a small pond high on the side of Mount Marcy, which was promptly renamed Lake Tear of the Clouds. In making this pond our round-trip goal, we were gulled by historical markers along the route. They told of one such forced march on this trail, to the pond and back in one long day. The man who did this was Teddy Roosevelt, which should have deterred us from even trying. Roosevelt was vice president when he started up the trail, and came back down as president on September 14, 1901. Just as he reached his camp on Mount Marcy, a messenger caught up to him with news that William McKinley appeared to be dying. Roosevelt emerged at about midnight, having traveled perhaps fifteen hours, to accept the burden of history.

From Henderson Lake we followed Calamity Brook; from there the Opalescent River led us up. In early afternoon, as we lunched by a lake, the water reflected the rounded peaks of the last and first place that makes the Hudson. A breeze caught the reeds, and in their sigh we accepted that we were no Roosevelt. We were, despite our timely start, way behind schedule. We packed up our things and prepared to turn down current. It was easy enough to do. There will always be something about the Hudson that is unknowable. Not all secrets get out.

2001

Alexander's Lost World

by

WILLIAM DALRYMPLE

One evening late last fall, I found myself climbing up a goat path in Swat, one of the most beautiful valleys on earth. Here, the snow peaks of the Karakorams widen and thaw into a landslide of cultivation terraces. Below, the Swat River—in autumn the color of lapis lazuli—meanders lazily around a green plain of orchards and wheat fields. As you wander past, scenes from an Indian miniature take shape in the fields around you: Men are bent double beneath shocks of grain, reaping with sickles; others carry bundles of branches for feeding to their goats. The sun is sinking, and the sky is as pink as Turkish delight.

The tarmac road had given up far below, and a shepherd boy had offered to lead me. Although he must have been barely twelve years old, he marched on ahead, scrambling up the track at a pace that only one born among mountains could set. I followed in fits and bursts, stopping every few minutes to wheeze and catch my breath. In this fashion, we climbed up past mud-brick farms and through unharvested fields, the track getting ever smaller and steeper. Behind us the dying sun was sketching deep-cut shadows in the hills. We passed a group of hayricks, and above the hayricks a herd of cows chewing their evening cud. In the distance you could hear the ringing of bells as the shepherds led the fat-tailed sheep home for the night. We climbed on; eventually, doubling back up the side of the hill and turning a corner, we arrived.

It was an extraordinary sight. Perfectly preserved in the middle of nowhere—miles from the nearest main road, somewhere in the wilds of the North-West Frontier of Pakistan—lay a sophisticated and beautifully constructed monastic complex. It was built in a style that would not be out of place in Rome or Athens: The ruins had pedimented fronts and were supported by carved Corinthian pillars. Halls, chapels, stupas (memorial mounds)—all were built in a style immediately recognizable as classical Greek; yet these were Buddhist buildings a few miles from the Afghan border, and they dated from the early centuries of the Christian era, long after the demise of classical civilization in Europe.

I stood on top of the highest stupa. A crescent moon had just risen, though it was not yet dark, and the cicadas were singing. Pillars of dung smoke rose from the valley villages. I looked out over the Asian landscape and wondered: What on earth are these superb Greek buildings doing here in this wilderness?

The answer, as I later discovered, was every bit as romantic as the ruins themselves.

In the autumn of 327 B.C., Alexander the Great swept into the highlands of Swat at the head of his victorious Macedonian army. Intending to conquer even the most distant provinces of the ancient Persian empire, Alexander had crossed into the Hindu Kush; and there, high on the Afghan plateau, he had first heard stories of the legendary riches of the Indian subcontinent—of its gold, said to be dug by gigantic ants and guarded by griffins; of its men who lived two hundred years and women who made love in public; of the Sciapods, a people who liked to recline in the shade cast by one enormous foot; of the perfumes and silks (which, the Afghans told him, grew on the trees and even in the cabbage patches of India); of the unicorns and pygmies, the elephants and falcons, the precious jewels that lay scattered on the ground like dust, and the unique variety of steel that could avert a storm.

It was the end of the hot season, the beginning of the rains, and Alexander had arrived at the edge of the known world. Now he made up his mind to conquer the unknown world beyond. Easily defeating the Hindu rajas of Swat and winning a great victory on the banks of the river Jhelum, Alexander prepared to cross the last rivers of the Punjab and conquer the Indian plains. But on the swollen banks of the Beas he was brought to a halt. His homesick soldiers refused to go on; the torrential monsoon rains had destroyed their spirit where everything else—heat, starvation, and disease—had failed. Alexander was forced to turn back, leaving behind a series of garrisons manned by Greek mercenaries to guard his conquests. On the return journey he died—or was poisoned—in Nebuchadnezzar's empty palace in Babylon, and his empire split into a million pieces.

In the ensuing anarchy, the Greek garrisons of India and Afghanistan were cut off from their homeland. Although many deserted, some decided to stay in Asia, intermingling with the natives and leavening Indian learning with Greek philosophy and classical ideas. Over the following one thousand years an astounding civilization grew up in the vastness of the Karakorams, deep within the isolated and mountainous kingdom known as Gandhara. Buddhist in religion, Gandhara's icon was a meditating Buddha—dressed in a Greek toga.

Gandhara survived for a thousand years, long after Greek civilization had disappeared in Europe; and when it died it left behind a legacy of finely constructed monasteries—a fifth-century Chinese traveler counted no fewer than 2,400 such shrines in the plains around Peshawar—and also a scattering of well-planned classical cities, acropolises, stupas, and superb sculptures. Their slowly decaying remains still litter northern Pakistan. Few know of Gandhara's existence, and even fewer have explored this lost world.

There are not many places left where the traveler can still feel like Indiana Jones; think of the ring of tour buses that daily besiege the

Pyramids, Stonehenge, and the Colosseum. But no tour bus has ever been seen in Gandhara; the area is one of the great and best-kept secrets of Asia. Its tribal people have a tradition of hospitality to travelers that is still a real ethic; the Central Asian cuisine of the area is one of the most intriguing in the subcontinent; moreover, this region is now served by one or two first-class hotels, and it is possible to explore it in a fair degree of comfort.

Lahore is a labyrinth, a city of palaces, an open gutter, filtered light through a filigree lattice, a landscape of domes, an anarchy, a press of people, a whiff of spices. It is full of riches and horrors, and it is as dramatic a baptism into Asia as any traveler could ever wish. You can enter Pakistan from a number of different points, but Lahore is always the best. Spend at least a week there if you can; it is not a city that reveals its charms immediately—it needs to be explored.

Getting there is easy; leaving the city is more of a problem. You can always hire a chauffeur-driven car—at barely twenty dollars a day, such luxuries are easily affordable in Pakistan—but *real* travelers always take the train. The catch: You are heading northwest, toward the Frontier, and the best and fastest train, the 71-up Subuk Rafter Railcar, leaves at dawn.

You get up at the fearful hour of 5:45 and take a taxi to the station. Bleary-eyed, you look around in amazement: At home the milkmen are abroad at this time, but no one else. Here the shops are already open, the fruits and vegetables on display, the shopkeepers on the prowl for attention:

"Hello, my dear," says a man proffering a cauliflower.

"Sahib—your good name?"

"Sabzi! Sabzi! Sabzi!"

"Good sir? Only one minute, please—what is your mother country?"

A Punjabi runs up behind your taxi waving something horrible, a wig, perhaps, or some monstrous Indian vegetable. "Sahib, come looking! Special okay shop! Buying no problem!"

Eventually you reach the station and fight your way through the melee of tottering coolies and ragged refugees, past the tap with the men doing their ablutions, over the bridge, down the stairs, along platform 9—and there it is, the 71-up, waiting patiently at the buffers.

Pakistani trains are a good compromise between the dull efficiency of a Western rail network and the exhilarating anarchy of Indian railways: They have the same vibrant platform life as the latter, the same color and strangeness, but in Pakistan you don't have to enjoy it all from your hard-won perch on the luggage rack. If you reserve a seat, the seat will be there waiting for you. Moreover, the train will, probably, leave on time.

Certainly the 71-up Subuk Rafter Railcar pulled out of Lahore Central at precisely 6:15 A.M. We moved swiftly through the freight yards, then swept out across the Ravi, khaki-colored with monsoon mud. We passed by the filigree minarets of the tomb of Jahangir, the fourth Mogul emperor, and beside it a cluster of other tombs, one with a decaying pinecone dome. We overtook a string of swaying camels and a team of turbaned workmen prying up a piece of track. Then we passed out into the flat, fertile plains of the Punjab.

Alexander had passed by here during the height of the monsoon, 2,318 years previously. When he and his army reached the capital of the area, a lost city somewhere in the plains outside the train window, the native king had marched out of the main gate in all his regalia. Rather than tangle with the Macedonian conqueror, he immediately handed over his beryl-studded scepter; the name of his kingdom, he told the Macedonians, was Prosperity. The Macedonians were impressed: The king was an unusually good-looking man, superbly dressed in gold and purple embroidery; and according to one of Alexander's historians, there was a reason for this splendor:

"Among these people, the strangest feature is their respect for beauty: They choose their most handsome man as king. When a baby is born, two months after its birth the royal council decides whether it is beautiful enough to live."

For days, the army feasted while the king entertained them with his ferocious dogs, whose pedigree, so he claimed, included the blood of tigers. Alexander was amazed by their courage—he witnessed a contest in which four attacked a lion—and was well pleased when the king of Prosperity presented him with one.

On the train, no one offered me a dog, but I was besieged with every other kind of gift: cups of tea, biscuits, samosas (spicy batter triangles), and delicious Indian sweetmeats. No other form of transport encourages intimacy so much as a train. In the West, we usually manage to protect ourselves from this enforced chumminess by placing a protective shield of newsprint between us and our fellow travelers. In Pakistan, a newspaper, even if you had one, would be little defense against the generosity—and curiosity—of your neighbors.

Pakistanis are not just generous neighbors; they are also expert inquisitors. By the first two stops, all your secrets are out. Your name, religion, job, salary, and marital status are exposed. When I revealed that I was twenty-five years old but had no children, the possibility that I was suffering from some grave genital defect was discussed and analyzed. Soon my neighbors had extracted all the necessary details and took the opportunity to disperse around the carriage to give a small lecture tour:

Inquisitor: That is Mr. William. He is a Christian from Scotland, which is a hill station near Inglistan. He is a writer.
Chorus: *Ya Allah!*
Inquisitor: But not a famous writer. He is not like Mr. Gore Vidal.

(*Chorus look disappointed.*)

Inquisitor: He has four brothers, and one is a Christian priest. His father has a heart problem, but his mother is in quite good shape. His grandmother is eighty years old. She walks without a stick, and her hair is still its original color.

Chorus: May we be like this lady!

Inquisitor: Mr. William likes wearing Pakistani clothes, and he is fond of Pakistani food. Particularly he is liking *kulfi* (Indian ice cream).

Chorus (*wobbling their heads*)**:** *Kulfi! Kulfi! Kulfi!*

Inquisitor: He speaks a little Urdu, and he once interviewed Imran Khan.

Chorus (*slapping Feringhee on the back, shaking hands, etc.*)**:** Imran *zindabad!* Long live the Feringhee! A hundred blessings on Mr. William's grandmother!

Inquisitor: But he lives in India.

Chorus: Indian pigs! Hindu dogs!

Inquisitor: He says he has a girlfriend, but he has no children, he is probably impotent.

(*Chorus, disgusted, lose interest and drift off.*)

Outside, villages shot past. As you looked out, you caught little glimpses of rural scenes frozen as if in a Victorian album of Indian photographs: a rookery of women sweeping past in black calico chadors; a man leading a dancing bear; goats picking among the graves of a cemetery. Below the embankment, white water lilies glistened on the surface of a pond.

Taxila, my destination, had a quiet and well-loved station. Red flower-pots were lined up along the platform; wire cages containing bowls of nasturtiums hung from a shady line of arches. It looked as if someone had bodily picked up the station from Yorkshire or Dorset and myste-riously transported it into the middle of the Punjab. On some sidings, an old goods train rusted at the buffers; goats grazed beneath an awning. It was a rural scene: There was nothing to indicate that Taxila was once a great cosmopolitan city and the most powerful fortress in Upper India.

I took a horse-drawn *tonga* from the station, and while we trotted through the Punjabi countryside, I opened my bible—*Alexander the Great*, by Robin Lane Fox, the best of the biographies of the Macedonian conqueror. According to Fox, the ruler of Taxila had decided, like the king of Prosperity, against challenging the Greeks. Instead, he met Alexander in Swat and guided him through the forests of rhododendron and alpine clematis to the plains of the Punjab. Eventually they arrived at Taxila, and Alexander's troops were able to rest and take in the Indian scene.

To the Macedonians, familiar with the glories of Athens, Babylon, Susa, and Egyptian Memphis, the buildings of Taxila were unremarkable: The houses were made of mud and uncut stone and were laid out without any central order or plan. But what did amaze the Macedonians were the Indians themselves:

"Physically, the Indians are slim," wrote Alexander's Admiral Nearchus. "They are tall and much lighter in weight than other men . . . they wear earrings of ivory (at least the rich do), and they dye their beards, some of the very whitest of white, others dark blue, red, or purple or even green . . . they wear a tunic and throw an outer mantle around their shoulders: another is wound round their head. And all except the very humblest carry parasols in summer."

Although Alexander stayed at Taxila for only a matter of weeks, his visit changed the course of the city's history. Visiting the museum at the entrance to the archaeological site, I wandered through the rooms looking at the Greek style of the Buddhist sculptures, some of which dated from nearly a thousand years after Alexander's death. Even the Buddha, that symbol of Eastern philosophy, had undergone a process of Hellenization: His grace and easy sensuality were thoroughly Indian, yet the images in the Taxila museum were all defined by Western ideas of proportion and realism; moreover, the Buddha was wearing a toga, European dress.

Most remarkable of all was the coin room. Over one entire wall were scattered the gold and silver coins of a millennium of Taxila's rulers. It wasn't just that the coins were all modeled on Greek originals.

What was amazing were the names of the rulers: Pantaleon, King of North India; Diomedes, King of the Punjab; Menander of Kabul; Heliochles, King of Balkh.

The coins hinted at the strange hybrid world these kings inhabited. They brought East and West together at a time when the British, the only other Europeans who ever attempted to rule India, were still running through cold prehistoric fogs dressed in bearskins. The coins of Heliochles of Balkh were typical: They showed a Roman profile on one side—large nose, imperial arrogance in the eyes—but on the reverse, Heliochles chose as his symbol a humped Indian Brahman bull.

Outside, among the ruins—which are spread over a distance of some twelve square miles and overgrown with hollyhocks and wild foxgloves—it is this strange mix of Europe and Asia that continues to grip the traveler's imagination. At Sirkap, descendants of Alexander's soldiers founded a classical Greek town in 190 B.C. It was to be the New Taxila, a great advance on the Old City, and they carefully laid out the different streets in a grid of straight lines, like a chessboard. As at Athens, a magnificent boundary wall loops around the residential areas and rises up to the fortified citadel, Sirkap's answer to the Parthenon.

My favorite of the Taxila ruins is that of the monastery of Jaulian, named after its founder, an imperial Roman Buddhist. The monastery was always a place of retreat, and today it still retains its original calm. I arrived there late in the evening, just as the smoke from the village fires was forming a perfect horizontal line above the fields. At the foot of the hill, below the olive groves, leathery black water buffalo sat with their legs folded beneath them. Above, there were parakeets among the olives, and as you walked up the hill, flights of grasshoppers exploded from beneath your feet.

I was shown around by the elderly *chowkidar* (watchman). He was a fascinating old man, and as he explained the function of the different ruins, the monastery slowly came to life. Soon I could see the orange-robed monks tramping clockwise around the stupas, or queuing for their food in the refectory, or snuffing out their oil lamps in their austere stone cells.

Best of all, I could visualize the builders. They were men with a sense of humor, for they included in the design a hundred little conceits, all lovingly pointed out by the *chowkidar*. Here were a series of grotesque atlantes—they had narrow Mongol features, muttonchop whiskers, and giant earrings—groaning as they sank under the weight of the stupa that was resting on their shoulders. Here—and this was obviously the *chowkidar*'s favorite—was a scene from the temptation of the Buddha. As he sat meditating under an arch, two girls appeared around the corner flashing their assets at him, trying to distract him from his spiritual quest: "Two nude women showing themselves to Buddha-sahib," said the *chowkidar*. "But Buddha don't like she."

Around the base of the stupa the *chowkidar* pointed out more temptresses—some flashing shapely legs, others baring their breasts, others proffering amphorae of wine: "Girls, dancing, wine, drinking—all no problem to Buddha-sahib. He liking only prayer, preaching, and hymn singing," said the *chowkidar*. "Buddha-sahib is very good gentleman."

At night, Taxila Station took on a different, more Dickensian aspect. The passengers gathered in the main waiting room, dwarfed by the outcrops of huge Victorian furniture—mahogany dressers, and old hatstands originally designed for bowlers by Locke of London. Around the walls there stretched a line of "Bombay fornicators," ingenious wickerwork chairs with extended arms that enabled the British sahibs to put their feet up after a hard day's work among the "natives." Everyone sat around a long dining room table waiting for the train, the 5-up Zulfiquar Express. Some played cards, some smoked *bidi* (cigarettes), some sipped cups of tea. Overhead the fans whirred silently. There was no sign of the train.

"Are you sure this train is coming?" I asked the stationmaster forty minutes after the train was due.

"Oh, yes, sahib. Train will come."

"When?"

"Soon, sahib." Then, a little less confidently: "Perhaps in one hour, *insh'Allah*."

"Maybe longer?"

"Maybe longer."

"Has it left Lahore yet?"

"No, sahib."

"Then it can't possibly get here for another three hours."

"Maybe, sahib. But God is great."

The train did come, four and a half hours later, just before ten at night. "Train is little behind, so now full speed," said the stationmaster, comfortingly, as he waved good-bye.

The slatted seats were painted pea green. At Attock we took on a carriageful of Pathan tribesmen—big men whose long, drawn features peered out from blank forests of facial hair. Many wore bandoliers; as we moved out of the station, turning west along the foothills of the Himalayas, mountainous white turbans gleamed in the platform lights. Then we were out of the town, and the lights were extinguished. In the dark, we rattled across Attock Bridge and crossed over the Indus into the North-West Frontier.

Machismo is to the Frontier what prayer is to the Vatican. It is a way of life, a raison d'être, an obsession, a hobby, a philosophy. Kalashnikovs are taken on shopping expeditions as nonchalantly as a Londoner would take an umbrella. Status symbols here are not swimming pools, Mercedes, or Swiss watches—though there is no shortage of any of these; in Peshawar, you have really arrived only when you can drive to work in a captured Russian T-72 tank.

Travelers are safe here; the Pathan tribal code dictates that strangers must be treated with the same honor as a prophet or a holy man. Americans, moreover, are more popular in Peshawar than they are almost anywhere else east of Israel: After all, it was the CIA that funded the war against the Soviets in Afghanistan, and the Pathans have not forgotten this. They reserve their violence for other Pathans, and, like the

Sicilian Mafiosi, they relish long and indescribably bloody feuds with their tribal rivals.

The people here are as hard as the schist; they have been conquered by no one since Alexander the Great and have seen off centuries of invaders—Persians, Arabs, Moguls, Sikhs, British, Russians. Nevertheless, they are not an isolated race. Peshawar lies at the foot of the Khyber Pass, one of the principal crossroads on the Silk Road, the Times Square of Central Asia. Wandering through the main Peshawar bazaar (one of the most magnificent in Asia and known as the Qissa Khawani, or Street of the Storytellers) you soon realize that, in the wake of centuries of trade caravans, the genes of a hundred different races have met here and mingled.

The passage of Ghengis Khan and his Mongol hordes has elongated many eyes and turned to silky down the normally thick beard of a Pathan chin. Bright Aryan blue eyes flash beneath Himalayan turbans, calling to mind the taste for British memsahibs and lady missionaries that the Pathans developed over the century following 1840. Curly hair and Semitic noses evoke the slightly far-fetched legends which maintain that the Pathans are a lost tribe of Israel that got separated from Moses during the forty years of wandering in the desert; according to this legend, they mistakenly stumbled into the Hindu Kush while looking for the way back to Egypt.

It is just possible to believe the story of the Lost Jews; what is at first much more difficult to understand is how the Pathans could be descended from the gentle Greek philosophers who created the civilization of Buddhist Gandhara. Yet scholars maintain that they are, and if you visit the museum in Peshawar, you can slowly begin to understand the connection that links the warlike tribesmen in the bazaar with the philosopher-soldiers of Alexander's army.

The most obvious link is material. In the wonderful friezes that illustrate the ancient Buddhist scripture, the Gandharan sculptors included details from the everyday life they saw around them, details that one can still see repeated today in the lives of the people of the Frontier. The writing tablet and reed pen that the Buddha used as a child can still

be seen in the Frontier primary schools. The turbans that the Gandharan chieftains sported in the sixth century A.D. have yet to disappear.
The sandals of the bodhisattvas are still worn, their musical instruments still played, their jewelry manufactured today in the silver
bazaar. Even the design of the houses remains more or less unchanged
by the passage of time.

But the link with the world of Gandhara runs even deeper than
this. The Peshawar museum is home to one of the most brilliant collections of Buddha images in existence. Room after room is filled with
black-schist figures: standing, meditating, preaching, or fasting. The
images follow a prescribed formula. The physique is magnificent: Muscles
ripple beneath the diaphanous folds of the toga. The savior sits with
eyes half-closed and legs folded in a position of languid relaxation. His
hair is oiled and groomed into a beehive topknot; his high, unfurrowed
forehead is punctuated with a round tilak (caste mark). His face is full
and round, the nose small and straight, the lips firm and proud.

It is only when you have stared at the figures for several minutes
that you realize what is so surprising about the Gandharan version of
the Buddha: It is its arrogance. There is a hint of rankling self-
satisfaction in the achievement of nirvana; a sneer on the threshold
of enlightenment. This is the Buddha as he was in life—a prince. And
soon you realize where you have seen that haughty expression before—
outside in the bazaar. In other peoples of the subcontinent there is a
tendency toward groveling subservience; the Pathans, on the other
hand, meet your gaze and level their eyes at you in contempt as much
as in curiosity. Hawk-eyed and eagle-beaked, they are a proud people;
and as the Buddha image demonstrates, their poise and self-confidence
directly reflect that of the Greeks who first brought Western civilization to Central Asia more than two millennia ago.

At the hotel, I had booked a car and a driver, and at seven in the
morning, both were ready and waiting to set off.

The driver was an unusually small, round, and somber Pathan
named Murthazar; the car an ancient Morris Traveller. We had gotten

as far as the outskirts of Peshawar before the Traveller began splut-tering: "Car going *ruk-ruk*," said Murthazar, shaking his head from side to side. "Sahib, this *ruk-ruk* is not good noise." It certainly wasn't. But despite the noise, the car jolted grudgingly on, and soon we had moved out of the town and onto the plains of Peshawar.

It was well past noon by the time we arrived at the ruins of Pushka-lavati, the City of the Lotus. Once upon a time Pushkalavati had been a rival of the great Babylon, but its conquest by Alexander began a de-cline from which it never recovered. Today it is a strange and romantic ruin, more like a ziggurat in desert Mesopotamia than the ruins of the one-time capital of the fertile Punjab. The barren gray clay walls rise eighty feet out of the canebrakes, huge and sheer and craggy. Their original shape has been washed away by two and a half thousand years of rain, and all that remains now is a Herculean block of mud, a series of local legends of a "city made of gold," and a lingering impression of strength and antiquity.

Beyond the ruins of Pushkalavati, the first lavender-colored peaks of the Himalayas rose up into the sky. I got into the car, and we set off toward the Malakand Pass, the gateway to Swat.

Here the road rises some five thousand feet in a serpentine ascent of only a few miles. It is a most dramatic drive up a virtual cliff face, un-spoiled by such tiresome impediments as crash barriers or fences to break your fall if perchance you skid toward the abyss. It is emphati-cally not a road to be traveled by anyone suffering from vertigo; nor is it recommended for anyone driving an ancient Morris Traveller—as we soon discovered.

We had just rounded the first of the great U-bends when the car began to shake and rattle like a boiling kettle. "Car going *ruk-ruk* again," observed Murthazar. Two more bends and the car had slowed down to a snail's crawl. Little puffs of steam were billowing out of the hood, and the gearbox was wheezing like a dying asthmatic. Yet the car did not ever quite draw to a complete halt, and over the next hour, it continued to climb the Malakand at its own slow and stately pace.

Below, the fields of the plain of Peshawar receded into a quilt of patchwork squares, broken by seams of poplar avenue. We crawled on, up and up, through a series of cavernous tunnels, and suddenly, to our amazement, we were there, at the top, the summit. The Traveller gave a last metallic groan and turned its nose triumphantly into the valley on the far side. "Olden car is golden car," said Murthazar in a tone as much of surprise as of pleasure. As if to reward the car for its good behavior, he then turned the ignition off and let the Traveller freewheel down the slope to the banks of the Swat River.

So relieved was I to have achieved the top of the pass that it was several minutes before I began to take in the beauty of the valley into which we were rapidly lunging. It was like entering a lost world, a forgotten Eden isolated on its high Himalayan plateau.

We were passing rapidly through the vortex of an asoka avenue, flanked on one side by the blue Swat River and on the other by green orchards watered by bubbling irrigation runnels. There were mangoes and cherries and quinces and apples and apricots and almonds, and beyond the orchards there were thickets of tamarisk and casuarina and groves of mulberry trees belonging to the silk farmers.

Within two hours we reached our hotel, once the marble summer palace of the wali of Swat, the ruler of the valley. It was already four o'clock, but I was determined not to rest before I had seen one final sight: the peak of Pir Sar, the highest hilltop in Swat and once the greatest fortress in Pakistan. It was the site of one of Alexander's last victories before he returned homeward, and the final indisputable proof to the Macedonian troops of their general's divinity.

Aornus, as the peak was then known, was considered impregnable, though it was less its fortifications than its sheer height and gradient that made it invincible. A rumor went around the Macedonian camp that "even Herakles, the son of Zeus, had found it impossible to conquer." Yet it took Alexander less than a week to pry the Swatis from their rocky pinnacle.

The peak lay a full day's trek away from the wali's palace. I was told, however, that it should be possible to see the mountain if I followed a pilgrim's track up the valley for about two hours. Leaving Murthazar with a cup of sweet Pakistani tea, I crossed a stream on a pontoon bridge and headed up the riverbank. The sun was shining, and the stones in the riverbed were speckled with white, like a nest of plover's eggs.

The light was already beginning to fade, and I had no idea whether I was still following the right track. Seeing an old man passing on a path high above me, I shouted the name of my destination. He waved to the left, and I set off in the direction he had indicated. The track turned into a goat path, and the goat path into a track so uncertain that I began to doubt whether it existed at all outside my imagination. But I pressed on, through increasingly thick undergrowth, into a dark coniferous forest. Two hundred feet above me, through the trees, I thought I could see a hint of blue sky.

I pushed on, with thorns tearing at my jeans and twigs brushing my face, wondering whether it would be better to admit defeat and turn back before darkness fell. If I lost the path, I told myself, I would spend the night alone up the hill. In fact, I might never get down. Maybe there were wolves. Bears, even. Holy Mary, Mother of God, pray for me. Saint Christopher, Patron Saint of Travelers, pray for me. Saint Jude, Patron Saint of Lost Causes, pray for me.

Then, just as I was beginning to give myself up for lost, I heard the unmistakable sound of girls giggling somewhere above me. I pushed myself up, and suddenly I was out of the forest and on a wide-open path—the same pilgrim's track I had lost far below.

"Pir Sar?" I asked the girls, who turned out to be a pair of very pretty Pathan shepherdesses.

The girls pointed in front of them. There, rising out of the bottomless depths of the valley, was the dark silhouette of a vast mountain—massive, sheer, and impregnable, the shape of a perfect pyramid.

As I was taking in the towering bulk of the mountain, one of the two girls started gabbling, and though I could not understand her rapid-fire Pushtu, one word repeated over and over again stood out: "Sikander," the Indian name for Alexander. So the local Pathans remembered the battle too.

In the distance there was a loud clap of thunder, and looking beyond Pir Sar, I saw great black cloud banks massing on the skyline. I wanted to stay, but there was only half an hour of light remaining.

It was time to go back. Like Alexander, I had a long journey ahead of me.

1993

The City of Will

by

ROBERT HUGHES

Just as everyone's mental visit to New York begins with the Statue of Liberty, the visitor to Leningrad should begin with the Statue of Tyranny—the figure of Peter the Great, mounted on his rearing horse in Decembrists' Square and shooting forth his absolute bronze hand to the city he forced into being 285 years ago. When Boston and Philadelphia were bustling cities full of carriages and clerks, when Moscow had existed for half a millennium, this spot was salt marsh: flogged by Baltic winds and rigidly ice-cased in winter, humming with mosquitoes in summer, deserted except by Finnish netters and mud-pecking birds. Less than three hundred years old, it is a city made by one man's act of will. On an island in Swedish territory near the mouth of the River Neva, on May 16, 1703, Peter the Great cut two strips of peat with a soldier's halberd, laid them crosswise, and exclaimed, "Here shall be a town!" To build a city here, let alone declare it the new capital of Russia and give it the social character of a real capital, defied all common sense.

But autocracy loves a blank slate. Peter wanted the city because he was bent on crushing the Swedes and ruling the Baltic with a navy he did not yet have. The Baltic was the royal road to Westernization, and Peter I's dominion of it would be secured by this garrison state, even if the Neva was so shallow that warships built in its yards had to be winched across half a mile of mud to be fitted with their guns at the Kronstadt arsenal.

This project, for all its concrete difficulties, had a weirdly abstract air. If Peter had only wanted a strategic base on the Baltic, he could have taken Riga. But no: He had to have *his* city, a bespoke capital whose newness would mirror his dreams of a new Russia. He named it St. Petersburg, after his own patron saint, the key bearer.

More than any church, more even than the Winter Palace itself, the effigy of Peter in Decembrists' Square is *the* symbol of Leningrad. The Bronze Horseman, as everyone calls it, has trampled through the dreams of Leningraders since 1782, the year Catherine the Great erected it. Peter gallops up and over a crest of rock, crushing the serpent of Deviation, and reins in his mount so that its hooves paw at the air above the Neva. The Bronze Horseman's literary associations are immense. Writer after writer—Gogol, Dostoyevski, Herzen—saw in it the epitome of the czarist state, the all-seeing power that dwarfs the "little man," the overreach and ambiguity of Petrine foreign ambitions. "Russia, you are like a steed!" exclaimed Andrei Bely, a Russian precursor of James Joyce, in *Petersburg*, published in 1914. "Do you want to separate yourself from the rock that holds you, as some of your mad sons have separated themselves from the soil?" Its most famous appearance was in Alexander Pushkin's poem on the Neva flood of 1824. At its height the "little clerk" Yevgeny, maddened by fear, imagines himself racing and stumbling through the city, pursued by the implacable Horseman: "O mighty master of fate! Was it not thus, on the very edge of the abyss, that you reined up Russia with your iron curb?"

In Pushkin's time the pedestal rose straight from the granite of the square; today, alas, the prim taste of Russian municipal gardeners has surrounded it with grass and a ring of reddish wax begonias, like a garnish of chopped beetroot around a salad. No matter; in the long "white nights" of the Leningrad summer, when you can still read a book on a park bench at midnight, people drift in twos and threes through Decembrists' Square to contemplate the Bronze Horseman. Sometimes they lay bunches of carnations and lilies before it.

No graffitist has ever touched this statue. It is absolute and inviolate, in a way that no Western monument could be. And over the years, it has ridden down its enemies.

The first modern Russian uprising was that of the Decembrists— liberal, aristocratic army officers, friends of Pushkin and men whom Byron would have admired, who tried to lead an army mutiny against the new czar, Nicholas I. It started and ended beneath the Horseman's gaze on December 14, 1825: Four hundred rebel soldiers were cut down by cannon fire, and their leaders given a show trial and then hanged in the Peter and Paul Fortress. (The execution was so bungled that three of them slipped through the nooses and fell, in a tangle of broken limbs, at the gallows' foot. "Poor Russia," groaned one of them, a hero of the Napoleonic Wars named Sergei Muraviev-Apostol. "She cannot even hang a man decently!" They were strung up again.) Decembrists' Square is the cradle of Russian revolt, as well as the expression of its tyranny.

The traveler to Leningrad, shuffling brochures and not knowing what to expect, meets one phrase again and again: "the Venice of the North." Its absurdity dawns on you after you have cleared customs and the taxi assigned to you by Intourist—a ten-year-old Volga, smelling of brilliantine and exhaust fumes—is rattling past the ranks of giant bronze citizens glaring skyward from the plinths of a monument to the 1941–44 siege, through outlying canyons of Stalinist concrete, into the heart of Leningrad.

Certainly the place *looks* nothing like Venice. It has canals, but not the Venetian bustle of water traffic. They are glazed with a brown, empty calm. You can walk their banks for a week, between the geometrical lines of ice-green and corn-yellow palaces, and see no boats except police launches. Once you are off its spinal avenue, Nevsky Prospekt, which is jammed with people, most of the center of Leningrad on a Sunday evening in June feels like a gigantic empty theater set, with none of the social eddying, knotting, and promenading that fills every corner of Venice. At 11 P.M. the light raking across the *pave* between the Winter Palace and the General Staff Building (a square five times the area of Piazza San Marco) throws into silhouette one lone figure, a faraway boy running wheelies on a skateboard along the shadow line cast on the pavement by the cornice of the mammoth museum. You are not in Venice, but in the world's largest Giorgio de Chirico, a place of endless avenues, glowing walls, aching perspectives, all suspended between the white sky and the brimming mirror of the Neva. "I count fewer men than columns on the streets of St. Petersburg," wrote a French visitor, the marquis de Custine, in 1839. "These squares . . . are always silent and sad because of their grandeur, and particularly because of their imperturbable regularity."

On a less sublime level, one soon finds that while Venice is wholly a service city, Leningrad is wholly not. Tourism, like Napoleon's army, marches on its stomach; and here, eating is not a spontaneous act.

You plan, or go hungry.

Each cheap restaurant, by lunchtime, has a queue that stretches halfway to Irkutsk. All Leningrad bars seem to have been closed by Gorbachev's antivodka campaign. So mostly you eat and drink in the hotel.

Room service does not work on the spur of the moment; at deluxe hotels like the Evropeiskaya and the Astoria you must order hours in advance, through the front desk. Our best meal each day was breakfast in the self-service cafeteria of the Evropeiskaya—boiled eggs, blini, potato salad, grated beetroot, Spam, cheese, black bread. The next best was lunch, same place: black bread, cheese, Spam, grated beetroot, potato salad, smoked fish, pickled tomatoes. This monotony is pleasing, especially if your childhood was spent in boarding school. Mother Russia, foe of choice, enfolds you. But with dinner, there are problems.

The first is getting a table at all. The maître d'hôtel is there to prevent this. At 7:30 the restaurant may look half empty, but it is geared to collective tours and all seats are reserved for what he calls—with a roll—ga-*roups*. The un-ga-*roup* has only one weapon: Fish out a full, virgin packet of Marlboros (it should still have the cellophane on it) and lay it gently but firmly on the maître d's desk. This will free a table at 8:30, unless you have had the bad luck to meet the only maître d' in the USSR who does not smoke. Marlboros cost six rubles (about ten dollars) a packet on the black market, and they are the one cigarette that every Russian wants.

There is no Siberia in Russian restaurants. All tables are equal, in that none receives service. It is vulgar to wave fistfuls of rubles in the air, crying. "This can be yours, *tovarishch*, if you will pull your finger out and bring the cucumber salad!" Put another pack of Marlboros prominently in the middle of the table. Soon a waiter will get the hint. *Do not give him the pack*. You have not yet been served.

And there are times when nothing works.

At 8:00 one evening, on the dot of our reservation, Victoria and I go to the main restaurant of the Evropeiskaya Hotel and are seated. The room is huge. It has a charming, melancholic datedness, redolent of the ancien régime. The whole end wall glows with a stained-glass window of Apollo driving his quadriga of winged horses over the roofs of St. Petersburg. There are towering opalescent lamps of 1910 design, and the tablecloths, though darned, are thick and snowy. All around, long tables are set for groups, with ice buckets in which bottles of wine and the omnipresent Pepsi are cooling.

We wait, watching the waiters come and go. At 8:20 I play the Marlboro gambit.

Response is sluggish, but at 8:30 one of them moves crabwise from his station with a menu. We discuss it in German, which neither of us really speaks. I ask for two shots of vodka and a bottle of Georgian dry white wine. The menu features "Soodak Fish Intourist Style" and "Pâté Surprise." Caviar, the waiter says, is off, but it may be on again shortly. He bestows on the Marlboro pack a stare of such Uri Geller–like intensity that one half expects it to twist into a pretzel.

Twenty minutes pass; twenty more; another twenty.

At 9:30 the waiter reappears with a liter bottle of vodka. It is warm. I wonder what it will do to my stomach, which feels like an empty salt mine.

"*Eis,*" I remind him. "*Und Weisswein, bitte.*"

"*Weisswein kaput. Nicht in Hotel Weisswein.*"

I get up and walk down the hall, to the maître d's desk. "Excuse me," I say carefully, "but I would like a bottle of white wine and the waiter says there isn't any."

He gives me a shifty but pitying look. "In hotel is no white wine."

"All those tables have some."

"Only for ga-*roup* is white wine."

"But I had a bottle last night in the restaurant upstairs."

"The roof-garden restaurant," he says with finality, "does not serve wine."

"But I chose it from their wine list. Could I see the wine list, please?"

"Here is no white wine on list."

"Perhaps I could choose another wine."

"Here is not wine list."

"Well," I croak in desperation, "I could have some beer."

"I am very sorry, sir, but here beer is Russian beer. It is sweet and warm. You not like it."

Defeated, I creep back to Victoria. We make small inroads on the liter of warm vodka and rapidly become plastered. *Fawlty Towers* is one thing; but *Fawlty Towers* backed by the immense, inscrutable resources of the State is another. At 10:00 the food arrives, all together. At 10:45 I catch the waiter's eye again and ask for the bill. It comes at 11:20. In the meantime we catch glimpses of the swelling queue behind the maître d's entrance curtain. Such is service à la Russe: half the diners begging to be let in, the other half beseeching the waiter to let them pay and get out. At 11:45 the waiter brings the change, and we are released. The waiting has taken three hours, the eating forty-five minutes. Back in our room, leafing through a copy of the *Economist*, I read that Mikhail Gorbachev intends to shift 16 million Russian workers out of smokestack manufacture and into service industries by the year 2000. Perhaps then Leningrad really *will* be the Venice of the North: a city of eager waiters.

But they do not all despise the dollar, these heirs of October. Indeed, Leningrad is one of the few places in the world today where the humble greenback is viewed on the streets with eagerness, not disdain. In the Leningrad bank one's dollar is worth sixty kopecks, but on the street it brings as much as 3.5 rubles—a difference of nearly six to one. You cannot stroll on Nevsky Prospekt without running into the money changers in their jeans, blousons, and sneakers. They have their regular beat, and at lunch one recognizes them eating in the cafeteria of the Evropeiskaya. Some ride up and down in the hotel elevator, hoping to nail a deal in the few minutes between floors. You feel a mysterious tapping of a toe on your foot. "Hello, where you from, please?" The question is neither the thin end of a pickup nor an effort to hasten peace through international amity. It is to find out if you are American and have American cash.

It is unfair of Russian banks to want your dollars so badly but give you so little for them. Still, Leningrad shops have little a traveler would want to buy. This even applies to the *beriozka* shops, unless you fancy taking home cans of some Baltic fish that resembles a barracuda, or nesting babushka dolls or, in extremis, red fake-morocco editions of *The Communist Manifesto*. Leningrad seems to have no antiques shops, and nothing you might want, like icons or one of those exquisitely plain walnut-and-ebony neoclassic cabinets, ca. 1825, can be taken out of Russia. You cannot cruise the yellow arcades of the Gostiny Dvor department store, Vallin de la Mothe's great covered bazaar on Nevsky Prospekt that is the Macy's of Leningrad, without feeling depressed at the shoddiness of its goods: ugly pseudo–folk art dolls, shirts that rasp, paper-thin frying pans, costly TVs that sometimes relieve the tedium of state broadcasting by bursting into flames. The Dom Knigi (House of Books, formerly the Singer Sewing Machine Building, a little farther down the Prospekt), which is the chief bookshop in the city of Pushkin and Dostoyevski, cannot offer a complete set of its great sons' works, although the shelves are full of unread, unreadable junk like the collected speeches of Leonid I. Brezhnev.

The dollar confers a decisive advantage in one area: prostitution. Street hookers in Leningrad (*putanochka*) lack allure and rely on maternal appeal—"Ullo, you poor darling," one of them greeted me. "You must be very alone tonight." But at night in the restaurants of the Evropeiskaya and the Astoria, the hard-currency whores come out two by two—not at all the Slavic bagels you imagined, but slender, Paulina Porizkova–like beauties with bad teeth and heavy streaks of rouge on their chiseled cheekbones (the blending of makeup, for some reason, is not a Russian skill), boogying furiously together to the strains of "Rock Around the Clock" as tables of Finns, glazed with vodka, goggle appreciatively.

So there is no point in changing your dollars on the street. It may get you arrested. If not, you will still be left at the end of your trip with a wad of unconvertible rubles whose size, in the absence of stamped exchange slips, may need to be explained to the stony gent with red shoulder tabs at the airport currency-control desk—an East-West dialogue that could continue in a small room for some time after your flight has left.

But you do not come to Leningrad to shop or gourmandize. You come for its cultural frame, the emblems of its past—especially its buildings and art collections, including the Hermitage, the Louvre of Russia, and the Russian Museum, that building storehouse of every kind of Russian visual art. You want the Kirov Ballet, the Pushkin Museum, the palaces—and maybe the symbols of revolution. Leningrad, the capital city for two hundred years, fell from power in October 1917 when the Bolsheviks, led by Vladimir Ilyich Lenin, hijacked the Revolution from the Kerensky government and deprived Russia of the only chance for social democracy it had ever known. Lenin took the seat of power back to where it had been in the days of Ivan the Terrible: Moscow, deep in the geographic bowels of the state. The Romanovs are present everywhere and yet wholly remote, like the ghosts of Ottoman sultans in Istanbul. Generally you can enjoy the architecture without encumbrance, since a few years ago the government took down most of its own mottos, slogans, and other ideological clutter.

A huge bronze of Lenin stands outside the Finland Station, where he arrived in the "sealed train" from Zurich in March 1917 to take command of the Bolshevik party. If you make special arrangements with Intourist, you may be allowed to visit the Smolny Institute, from which the Leningrad Soviet under the command of Trotsky led the rising of October 1917; the small rooms in the south wing where Lenin lived for two weeks after October 27—the desk he wrote at, the chair he sat in, the light he read by—are preserved here, like the cell of a saint, though it is hard to get a peek at the even more sacred lodgings he took for four months after November 10 while organizing the Bolshevik cabinet.

The most accessible Sacred Site of 1917 is a cruiser, the *Aurora*, moored on the north side of the Neva opposite the bulk of the Leningrad Hotel and brought to a dazzling pitch of spit and polish by cadets from the nearby naval academy. Up to October 1917, this old tub's sole distinction was to have escaped the general sinking of the Russian Baltic fleet by the Japanese at the battle of Tsushima in 1905. But in October 1917 she was in St. Petersburg, moored near the Angliiskaya Naberezhnaya, or English Embankment, not far from Sergei Diaghilev's palace. The Bolsheviks persuaded her crew to mutiny, and on the night of October 24–25 they fired one shell, a blank, in the general direction of the Winter Palace. The bang so alarmed Kerensky and the remnants of his cabinet that they walked out, and the Bolsheviks walked in.

The myth of the "heroic *Aurora*," like the "storming of the Winter Palace" (which happened only in the minds of John Reed and Soviet propagandists: Not a drop of Bolshevik blood was lost as they walked up the marble stairs), is believed by every good Russian, and visitors swarm all over her every day, gazing with awe at the famous six-inch forward gun that fired the blank—the penis, so to speak, of the Revolution.

One can more swiftly taste the pharaonic terms of the effort of will that founded the city by walking the Neva quays, with their cyclopean masonry of pink-gray granite, and reflecting that every one of these immense slabs had to be brought from somewhere else: The swamp had no bedrock. Of all Peter's campaigns, the building of St. Petersburg was the hardest, and its labor gangs, raised from all over Russia, died like flies in unrecorded numbers from cold, scurvy, hunger, exhaustion, and the knout: perhaps a hundred thousand, perhaps two, perhaps a quarter of a million—nobody kept count.

At first the workers had no wheelbarrows and moved the mud and rubble from the excavations in old rags, mats, and the skirts of their clothes. By ukase, Peter brought forty thousand workmen a year to St. Petersburg and made it law that no stone buildings could be erected anywhere else in Russia. It was St. Petersburg or starve.

Around 1720 wolves prowled after dark in St. Petersburg and its streets often flooded: Peter once nearly drowned in Nevsky Prospekt. But the walls and ravelins of the Peter and Paul Fortress, his first stronghold, went up in five months flat. Soon after that Peter had a German sculptor, Conrad Osner, carve a minatory relief for its portal, the fall of the heresiarch Simon Magus, cast down by St. Peter, with a message to all future political prisoners from Acts 8:22–23: "Repent therefore of thy wickedness, and pray God, if perhaps the thought of thine heart may be forgiven thee. For I perceive that thou art in the gall of wickedness, and in the bond of iniquity."

Under this arch, in years to come, Russian revolutionaries of every stamp would go to their long entombment. Throngs of visitors now pass inside the thick walls, reading their names: the Decembrists, the Petrashevsky conspirators (one of whom was the future novelist Fyodor Dostoyevski), the anarchist Bakunin, the archterrorist Nechayev (on whom Dostoyevski modeled the hero of *The Possessed*), the assassins of

Alexander II in 1881, the poet Kalyaev, whose grenade blew the Grand Duke Sergei to mincemeat in 1905, and so on to Mensheviks and Bolsheviks. Even Maxim Gorky was jailed here in 1905. Some cells were insulated with felt, like the walls of a recording studio in our own day, to prevent prisoners from tapping messages to one another. Not until the rise of the Lubyanka, the KGB's prison in Moscow, would any building in Russia be more salted in raw fear. Today its evil reputation has dissipated, and sunbathers in odd statuesque poses bask against its red outer walls, soaking up every last wavelet of UV radiation stingily granted by the northern sky: muscular men, women with huge pale breasts and Picassoid thighs. All the Romanov czars except for the last, Nicholas II, shot in a cellar and dumped in a mine shaft, lie inside these walls, in cold white sarcophagi below the golden spike of the fortress's cathedral, presiding in death over the memory of their foes. The only one on which visitors ever lay flowers is Peter's.

The monument of St. Petersburg's strange gestation phase is a log cabin, built in three days (May 24–26, 1703, to be exact) by Swedish prisoners of war—in the Swedish style, with hexagonally adzed logs, not in the Russian manner, with round ones. It was Peter's first house, lovingly preserved by generations of czars and now housed in its own museum building on the north bank of the Neva.

Peter's Cabin is his true shrine. Elsewhere, Leningrad is vivid with Petrine relics and souvenirs. The Hermitage has his life-size wax effigy by Rastrelli, in a faded blue court suit with pink stockings, his death masks at his feet, his glass eyes bulging with febrile energy. It displays Peter's surveying and navigation gear, the ornate carpentry tools this omnipotent hobbyist used in helping build his warships, his surgical instruments, and, scariest of all, the dental kit with which, as a special favor, he would operate on his boyars' rotten teeth. (If you fear dentists, Peter's forceps will pursue you in dreams: All Russia was his surgery, and no patient could refuse treatment.)

But nowhere does the man seem so present as in his log cabin. It is only thirty-five by eighteen feet, and very plain. It attests to the curious relation between log cabins and political virtue, believed in by Russians and Americans alike. It declares Peter to be a man of the Russian heartland, locus of truth and manly simplicity, like the American frontier. So basic is this primal hut to the social imagination of Leningrad that it was the first museum to open as the city was digging itself out from the rubble and misery of the German siege of 1941–44; nothing else in the city had its power as a rallying point. It is the spartan heart of a garrison state. Peter's simple furniture is still there: a small dining table, a cramped desk, a chair he reputedly made himself. Later czars, with their dilute blood—Pushkin was fond of pointing out that Nicholas II was only a hundred-and-twenty-eighth part Russian, the rest of his corpuscles being German—would want gilt consoles with lapis lazuli tops, vast malachite urns, and acres of inlaid floor; not Peter. The long lines of Russian schoolchildren who wind through the museum and around the Cabin all day stare at the rowboat he built, and whisper together at the sight of the toy brass mortar on his desk and the carved lignum vitae pipe with a devil's face, a present from his gross and cunning favorite, Menshchikov, which he used to puff while thinking up St. Petersburg. For their stronger edification there is the spelling book of Peter's only son, the czarevitch Alexei, most wretched of wimps, knouted to death at twenty-eight (possibly with his father's active help) in a ravelin of the Peter and Paul Fortress.

That Peter Westernized Russia, bringing Enlightenment through science to brutish Muscovy, is only a part-truth. He impressed European courts when he went traveling, but at home he was a wild man, a monster of appetite. He would ply envoys with Tokay by the pint until they fainted and then thrust axes into their hands to make them sweat out their liquor cutting down trees on his vast estate, destined to be an imitation Versailles, at Petrodvorets. He liked banquets to begin at noon; the doors were locked and no guest could leave the room until midnight. His butler Wiaschi, who doubled as the State torturer, had leave to go around the room beating guests with his wooden sword until their wigs fell off. They were served roast crow *en croute*, and found strings of live mice squirming under their peas; dead drunk, they would get only one plate for the twelve-hour succession of dishes and have to fight their neighbors for the use of a napkin. If any ruler ever epitomized the demonic infantilism as well as the dynamism of absolute power, it was Peter the Great.

But, as they say, he got things done, which was why Joseph Stalin worshiped him and strove by all the instruments of state propaganda to identify his image with Peter's. He liked a hero who could hang the walls of the Kremlin (after the revolt of the *streltsy* in 1698) with the half-roasted corpses of his political enemies one minute, and create a modern navy the next. When Stalin was up, we saw Peter the Good, the Revolutionary Father, the inspired, unstoppable, can-do genius of Russian history. Now that Stalin is down, a different Peter begins to stir beneath the pages of Soviet historians. How much of the "authentic" Russia did he recklessly throw out, along with its backwardness and inwardness? Were Peter's strategic and cultural achievements worth the deforming tyranny of his effort to reorganize Russia from top to bottom? Granted a different scale of suffering—for Peter did not murder 19 million people—most questions about Stalin turn to interrogate Peter as well. After 250 years he remains the Sphinx of Russian history, but a Sphinx in reverse, with a man's body and a beast's head, hunched over a map of the world in his lair of logs.

If Leningrad's bones, its basic town plan, was Peter's, its flesh of buildings was created by his successors—especially by that acquisitive, domineering, randy, coquettish locomotive of an empress, Catherine the Great. Most of the architects were Italian. Probably none of them would have looked first-rate, or got big commissions, in Italy. But to be the Bernini of Lapland—that was something. Watered by inexhaustible cash and imperial backing, their talents flowered in unpredictable ways. Their Baroque doyen was Bartolomeo Rastrelli (1700–1771), son of the Italian sculptor who made Peter's waxwork. His peak came with the midcentury reign, between Peter and Catherine, of the empress Elizabeth Petrovna. Rastrelli designed the Stroganov Palace, a green ice swan feathered in white on Nevsky Prospekt. His masterpiece is the

Smolny Convent, where the Russian onion dome ecstatically joins with taut Borrominian drums and facade, a fusion of Muscovy and Rome.

But Rastrelli's best-known work by far, the one building that everyone in Leningrad, Russian or foreign, flocks to, is the immense Winter Palace, partly occupied by the Hermitage, one-half by one-third of a mile of turquoise stucco, chalk-white columns, cartouches, writhing pediments, and gesturing comice statues. It absorbs thirty thousand people a day—"Oh, you cannot imagine how I love the museum when it is closed," sighed one of its junior curators to me as we struggled against the hordes of tourists surging through its galleries and backing up, like migrating salmon at a flume, against Rembrandt's *Return of the Prodigal Son* and Leonardo's *Benois Madonna*. At the end of a long, hot day the Hermitage's immense chambers stink like locker rooms. You need a week to grasp the basic layout of this labyrinth, which winds through 1,050 rooms and up and down 117 staircases; a year of daily visits would hardly exhaust its collections of antiquities, paintings, sculptures, gems, coins, drawings, and furniture.

Most foreigners head for the slightly less jam-packed top floor, where the modern art hangs: the expropriated Cézannes, Gauguins, Matisses, Picassos, and other works of the Ecole de Paris that were collected, before the Revolution, by Sergei Shchukin and his fellow enthusiasts. One comes away convinced that no collector of the twentieth century had a greater instinctive eye than Shchukin. Some aesthetic gene, some long-implanted Oriental love of the ecstatically decorative, led him to Matisse. His Russian melancholy chimed with the elegaic sadness of Gauguin's last paintings. But he seems to have been incapable of choosing an inferior work. The Hermitage's 1908 Picassos (such as the stony, red Michelangelesque *Three Bathers* or the astoundingly brusque and intense brown *Nude*) hit you with a wallop that rivals your first sight of *Les Demoiselles d'Avignon,* and they attain a pictorial resolution that *Les Demoiselles* does not. No matter how well you think you know Picasso, you do not know him until you have been to Leningrad. The Hermitage's collection of Matisses is the best in the world, its only rival being the Museum of Modern Art's in New York, and its big decorative canvases—*Dance, Music,* and the double portrait of the pajama-clad artist and his wife in their breakfast room—expand themselves with a mastery as absolute as anything by Rubens or Rembrandt downstairs. One bows before the lost grandeur and historical continuity of early twentieth-century painting.

If the Hermitage is too big to absorb except by repeated immersion, so is the Russian Museum, on Ploshchad Iskusstv, dedicated to painting, sculpture, and decorative arts from within Russia itself. Its range is almost as daunting as the Hermitage's—one skims through galleries of icons that would give a specialist half a lifetime's viewing—and its pictorial scale, once you reach the nineteenth century, is, if anything, more grandiose: The history paintings—shipwrecks, and destructions of Pompeii by academicians like Bryullov and Aivazovsky—make Cecil B. deMille at his most extreme look timid. Downstairs are the most popular of all Russian nineteenth-century paintings, the works of Ilya Repin—*The Volga Boatmen* and the bizarre *Zaphorozhets Cossacks,* engaged in writing their insulting letter to the Turkish sultan, like a conclave of Hell's Angels carousing on the steppes. But what is on view is merely the tip. Vladimir Gusev, the new director of the Russian Museum, elected by his staff (not appointed over them, as in preglasnost days) only two weeks before our visit, says that the museum contains more than 360,000 works—ten times the holdings of the Tretyakov Gallery in Moscow—and only has space to show two percent of them. It gets 1.5 million visitors a year, less than half the Hermitage's gate, but they are almost all Russians and they only come in the warm months: "In winter the polar bears in the streets frighten them away." A brisk, shrewd-eyed man in his mid-forties, with the hair and friendly grin of a country-and-western singer, Gusev sets off at a fast clip through a maze of corridors and stairs toward the rooms where they store the museum's immense holdings of Russian modernist paintings, kept from the public until now by cultural ideology and lack of museum space. This is the fundamental collection without which the full history of Russian Constructivism can never be grasped. There they all are, the heroes and heroines of 1900–1940, their works propped against one another, leaning casually against walls, stuffed in racks—early Chagall, Malevich, Kandinsky, Klyun, Rodchenko, Popova, Goncharova, Lissitzky, Altman, Udaltsova—an entire culture frozen by Stalinism like a mammoth in an ice bog, known only partially in the West and now, at last, thawing out.

One of the lessons of Leningrad is that absolute authority loves absolute architecture. Rastrelli left Russia in 1762, the year Catherine the Great came to the throne. He knew there would be no more work for him. Catherine's iron whim had fixed on a newer mode, the classical revival that was beginning to sweep Paris, London, and Rome.

There is nothing in the world quite like Leningrad neoclassicism. If Hitler had won the war and Albert Speer had kept building, there might be; but probably not, since from Catherine to Alexander I Leningrad had better architects, both Russian (Ivan Starov, Andrei Voronikhin, Vasily Stasov) and foreign (Vallin de la Mothe from France, Carlo Rossi, Giacomo Quarenghi, and Antonio Rinaldi from Italy, and Charles Cameron, a follower of Robert Adam, from Scotland). "The square and the chalk line," remarked Custine with sour Gallic relish, "accord so well with the point of view of absolute sovereigns that right angles become one of the attributes of a despotic people." A melancholy truth, to which the visitor's sore feet bear witness. The masterpieces of Russian neoclassicism, like the twenty-two-meter-high facades of the twenty-two-meter-wide Street of Rossi the Master Builder behind the yellow-iced cake of Rossi's Pushkin Theater that swims in air off Nevsky Prospekt, seem to go on forever. Peristyles and porticoes, orders and Palladian windows, march away in implacable diminuendo. This is purely scenographic architecture and at times it approaches genius, but it is also oppressive; you long for some littleness, the in-out breathing of civic space that makes more organic cities like Venice or Barcelona a delight to walk in. Amid so much gigantism smaller buildings, like the bloodred Beloselsky-Belozersky Palace (41 Nevsky Prospekt at the Anichkov Bridge over the Fontanka River) or Velten's delicious little white-and-blue Armenian church of St. Catherine (40–42 Nevsky

Prospekt), gleam in this Brobdingnagian context. Its crushing nature is summarized in the Admiralty building, which stretches nearly half a mile along the Neva with three giant Soanian arches and, above the central one, a tower and gilded spire some two hundred feet high, which its architect, A. D. Zakharov, seems to have copied from conjectural engravings of the lost Mausoleum of Halicarnassus. Everything in between is yellow-and-white stucco, and because its acreage of wall is so little articulated, the whole thing looks like giant cardboard.

The czars never lost this taste for anti-state architecture. It even extended to repairs. In December 1837 the Winter Palace was gutted by fire. Most of the paintings in the vast collections amassed by Catherine the Great and her successors were saved, but the interior was a total loss. Czar Nicholas I, that most censorious and detail-ridden of autocrats, wanted its thousand rooms fixed up in one year. His aides dragooned ten thousand workmen, and behold, the Winter Palace did reopen to Nicholas's court exactly twelve months later, down to the last inch of gold molding. On opening day the ceiling of the throne room thunderously collapsed under the weight of its new bronze chandeliers, just missing Nicholas and his empress. In 1839, when the Marquis de Custine visited the Winter Palace, he learned the human cost of the deadline. Toward the end six thousand craftsmen were working in rooms heated to eighty-six degrees (with ice packs on their heads) so that the stucco and gold leaf would dry faster; since the outside temperature was down to minus twenty degrees, "a considerable number died each day, but, as the victims were instantly replaced . . . the losses were not apparent. And the only purpose of so much sacrifice was to satisfy the caprice of a man!"

Custine is as basic to an understanding of Russia as Alexis de Tocqueville is to America. Custine may have intermittently exaggerated what he saw in the Russia of Nicholas I, but his book *De la Russie* was so right a prophecy of Stalinism—the secrecy, the surveillance, the murderous primitivism, the orthodoxy, the numbing bureaucratic inefficiency—that it has been banned in the USSR for the past forty-five years. Custine's impressions of the architecture of St. Petersburg can be weighed by any visitor who walks its quays and avenues today. "A city of palaces—it is majestic!" he exclaims, but then dislocation sets in:

> Gilded shafts, fine as lightning rods; porticoes whose founda-
> tions almost disappear under the water; squares adorned with
> columns which are lost in the vastness of the ground that
> surrounds them; statues copied from the antique . . . [that]
> resemble heroes imprisoned in the land of their enemies. . . . It
> is the result of an immense force of will, and, if one does not
> admire it, one fears it—which is almost to respect it.

The interior with the final word on Leningrad's insecure and straining gigantism is that of the Cathedral of St. Isaac, the biggest church in Russia and, after St. Peter's in Rome and St. Paul's in London, one of the largest in the world. It covers nearly two and a half acres. Its dome, adorned with 220 pounds of gold leaf, rises some 330 feet above the flat granite embankments of the Neva. Each of its forty-eight porch columns is a 114-ton shaft of solid Finnish granite. Within are thousands of square yards of rose-flushed white marble, tons of gilded copper, vaultsful of frescoed saints and Pantocrators. Even the Pentecostal dove that once hung from the dome looks as big as a Piper Cub and has a grim scowl on its beak.

Although the cost of this enterprise is not known, the *Blue Guide* estimate is 23,256,000 silver rubles. It monopolized the lives of its makers. One sculptor alone, Giovanni Vitali, made three hundred statues for it; here, one realizes, was the ancestor of those social-realist Russians of the thirties and fifties in their factory studios, with assis-tants jackhammering out white busts of Lenin and Stalin. St. Isaac's architect, a French import named Auguste de Montferrand, was only thirty-two when he won the design competition set by Alexander I's chamberlains in 1818, and he had built next to nothing. The cathedral gobbled up his whole life and he died in 1858, the year it was consecrated, having built little else.

Bog, as he is known in Russia, invented vulgarity by creating malachite, that bright mottled green stone to which the czars were addicted. Anyone who has flinched at the man-high malachite vases in the Hermitage will be dumbfounded by the iconostasis of St. Isaac's, framed as it is by ten solid malachite columns, each sixty feet high and four feet thick, dragged from the Urals. Their hectic green glare, topped and tailed by gold Corinthian capitals and bases, fills the whole church. In between them, all is gold mosaic with holy ones as big as American billboards, modeled to the last hair in millions of tesserae the size of a baby's thumbnail: Christ and the Virgin, St. Isaac and Alexander Nevsky. This is the last blare of Byzantium magnified by the taste of mid-Victorian Munich and Paris. It dazes you with its grossness and elaboration.

In 1931 Stalin declared St. Isaac's to be the State Anti-Religious Museum. Visitors were encouraged to smoke and the vaults were hung with slogans about the opium of the people. The world's largest Foucault pendulum, 305 feet long, was installed in the dome, its tip sweeping an ever-changing arc across the center of the marble floor, to prove that the earth spun on its axis and was not, as priests said, the fixed center of the universe.

All this atheistic piety failed, as it was bound to do: Inside St. Isaac's, no amount of agitprop could compete with the glitter, the gloom, the marble, and the malachite. Defeated, the commissars in 1932 moved their exhibits and slogans to the Kazan Cathedral, nearby on Nevsky Prospekt. The pendulum continued to swing for another fifty years, but then in 1985 it was taken down "for cleaning," and there are no plans to put it up again. The guides who chivy their (mainly Russian) groups across the dark marble lake of St. Isaac's floor, waving their white plastic pointers like ivory wands of office, are Christians as often as not; they reel off building statistics and names of artists, but they have dropped the antireligious propaganda. The only sign of orthodox disrespect is a little boy of four, riding on his father's shoulders and waving a cap pistol at the frescoes. But for most, St. Isaac's relieves

the drabness of ordinary life. Will it ever be reconsecrated? Time, and
perestroika, will tell.

In fact, running a museum of atheism is not so easy. It goes stale,
whereas religion stays fresh. The former Kazan Cathedral has displays
of "primitive" art naively illustrating man's progress from ignorant
savage to transcendent cosmonaut; it shows tokens of religious corruption, satires on lustful nuns, and—a great favorite with the kids—
the chains and plates of gilded penitential iron with which monks once
loaded themselves. The staff have put up walls of icons: Here, they
imply, is what your ancestors were so misguided as to worship. But as
one looks at these stiff, lambent flakes off the old block of eternity, now
arraigned to testify against themselves, a young woman in business
dress darts forward, bends, kisses an icon's *riza*, crosses herself, and
steps back again.

It is common news that the Orthodox Church has made a comeback
in Russia. But to sense the deep anchoring drag of its ritual one should
attend evening service in the Troitsky Sobor, or the Cathedral of the
Trinity, within the Alexander Nevsky Lavra, one of the Soviet Union's
four major monasteries, founded by Peter the Great in 1713. As priests
with oiled beards perambulate its nave and aisles, blessing the crowd
with billows of incense smoke, one feels transported into a Russia
scarcely changed since the time of Turgenev: the deep basso of the metropolitan, the soaring responses of the choir, the ripple of lamplight
across the gold doors of the sanctuary as, with immense theatrical
pomp, they swing open; the shawled women with crumpled faces,
crossing and recrossing themselves under a baldachin before the gold-
lidded ark that contains some bones (no one knows which ones, since
the skeleton was scattered by Bolsheviks in 1918) of Alexander Nevsky.
Religion, it used to be said, is only for old women. But old women, in
Russia, are a renewable resource, and among the young there are no
calls for a "liberalized" Church, as in America—they crave ritual and
transcendence.

At the side of its overscaled and stilted splendors is another Leningrad, the place of liberal instincts and literary associations—the city Pushkin adored, though its rulers repaid him with censorship and vigilance throughout his life, and a secret burial; monuments and museums came afterward. "O gallant city mine and fair!"

> *I love thy chaste*
> *Inclement weather with its bracing*
> *And moveless air, the lusty bite*
> *And pinch of frost, the sledges racing*
> *On Neva's banks, the bloom of bright*
> *Young cheeks, the ballroom's noise and glitter,*
> *And, at a bachelor's get-together,*
> *The hiss and sparkle of iced champagne*
> *And punchbowls topped with bluish flame.*

Not a surviving object touched, used, or worn by Pushkin has failed to be preserved in the museums dedicated to his cult, and his statue lords it over Arts' Square. (It faithfully records the African features of which he was so proud: His maternal grandmother was the daughter of an Abyssinian slave, the real-life model for the fictional hero of Pushkin's *The Negro of Peter the Great.* He attributed his own sexual energies, which were notable, to his black blood.) One could do a Pushkinian tour of Leningrad—or a Dostoyevskian tour or a Gogolian one. It would be full of curious linkages. At 10 Ulitsa Gogolya (Gogol Street), for instance, stands a faded rosy palace, once the home of Princess Golitsina, a formidable gambler. Pushkin knew her, and made her into the ancient card-playing countess whose spirit avenges itself so decisively on her killer, the wastrel in *The Queen of Spades.* Later Peter Tchaikovsky would adapt Pushkin's classic story as an opera—and in 1893 he died in his brother Modest's house, at 13 Ulitsa Gogolya, just across from the home of the long-dead Princess Golitsina.

Russian literature rose with St. Petersburg; its glories begin with

Pushkin and go underground in the 1920s, a span of only one hundred years. After that, it was repression for some Leningrad writers (Anna Akhmatova), suicide for others (Yesenin), or, for the relatively lucky ones like Vladimir Nabokov or Joseph Brodsky, exile. Nabokov in the fifties claimed that, because of its short span, the whole canon of great Russian writing could be fitted into 23,000 pages (an idea inconceivable in France, England, or Germany). Perhaps because the literature rose with the city, the two often seem indissolubly wedded. One thinks of Gogol's sweeping, delicately sarcastic panegyric on the greatest street in all Russia, which was still being built in the 1830s, when he wrote his vision of the avenue as palimpsest of class:

> All-powerful Nevsky Prospekt! The only place in St. Petersburg where a poor man can combine a stroll with entertainment. . . . Here is the footprint left by the clumsy, dirty boot of an ex-army private, under whose weight the very granite seems to crack; and here is one left by the miniature, light as a feather, little shoe of the delightful young creature who turns her pretty head towards the glittering shopwindow as the sunflower turns to the sun; and here is the sharp scratch left by the rattling sabre of some ambitious lieutenant—everything leaves its imprint of great power or great weakness upon it.

It is still true, though the shops are gone, the long perspective is grimed with neglect, the girl-sunflower is more likely to be a student, the ambitious lieutenant has red tabs and no saber.

Relatively few of the sites are marked, though, as they would be in London or Paris. Dostoyevski has his own museum in the apartment where he once lived. The house where Gogol wrote *Dead Souls* has its bas-relief, and its street is named for him. But no plaque beside the third-floor oriel window of the pink granite apartment block at 47 Ulitsa Gertsena (Herzen Street, once Morskaya Bolshaya Street) records Vladimir Nabokov's patrician boyhood there. And it will doubtless be even longer before the balcony on the Dom Moruzy, a big

Dakota-like apartment block opposite Preobrazhensky Cathedral, is publicly identified as the former home of Russia's latest literary Nobelist, Joseph Brodsky.

To persecute a writer while living and deify him or her after death is the Russian way, established long before 1917. For his revolutionary views, Fyodor Dostoyevski had to endure a mock execution by firing squad in Semyonovsky Square, followed by a cell in the Peter and Paul Fortress—whose commandant happened to be Ivan Aleksandrovich Nabokov (1787–1852), great-granduncle of the future author of *Lolita*. But when he got out and began to preach humility, suffering, and obedience, he was attacked by *bien pensant* Russian radicals for the rest of his life.

So there is a special poignancy to the commemoration of the great dead in Leningrad cemeteries. They have paid their dues. Those attached to the Alexander Nevsky Lavra, once visited, are unforgettable; the Tikhvin Cemetery, with its winding paths under dripping plane trees, is the nineteenth-century pantheon, and the crowded graves of the Lazarus Cemetery opposite are mainly eighteenth century. The composers lie all in a row in the Tikhvin—Glinka, Mussorgsky, Borodin, Tchaikovsky, Rimsky-Korsakov. Dostoyevski's bust glowers from its monument. Music, theater, and dance lie farther in among the trees. Marius Petipa, the founder of modern choreography, lies beneath a modest marble ellipse. The tragic actress Anna Esipova sits on her tombstone with a bouquet of dead lilies meticulously carved in their festering.

The most famous inscription, and the most laconic, is on the tomb of General Suvorov, the Wellington of Russia, nearby in the Lavra. As he lay dying in 1800 a poet named Gavrila Derzhavin stood ready to write a fulsome panegyric. No, said Suvorov: Be brief. His white marble slab bears three words, staccato gold notes from the trumpet of fame: HERE LIES SUVOROV. The quaintest tombs in the Lavra are those of Bolsheviks, declaring their faith in science, technology, material progress— Funerary Constructivism. An engineer has a model of an electricity pylon atop his grave. The test pilot Nikolai Gordaev died in 1925 and lies beneath the propeller of his aircraft.

Probably the funniest tomb in the Lazarus Cemetery belongs to a hussar officer, Carl Johann Christian von Kessig. In 1847, the story goes, he was on guard duty when Czar Nicholas I, a demon for discipline, appeared out of the night on a tour of inspection. Presently His Majesty left and von Kessig, reckoning that he would not be back, settled down for a snooze. He was wrong. The autocrat came back and was gazing wrathfully down when von Kessig awoke, blinked, gulped, and died on the spot of a heart attack. His effigy sprawls along his tomb slab, wrapped in his pelisse, head peacefully pillowed on his shako. Von Kessig is still asleep.

Our guide to such arcana of the city was a slender, sandy-bearded young architect, Alexander Kobak, chief historical expert for the Leningrad branch of the Soviet Cultural Fund (SCF).

One of the oddities of casual conversation in Leningrad—for the visitor, anyway—can be its indirection. We had heard, vaguely, of an "underground group" dedicated to the preservation of historic buildings in the city. The idea seemed piquant; samizdat conservation, as it were. Did anonymous idealists scurry to peeling facades at night and patch them up before the authorities twigged what was going on? Even a pair of young junkies we ran across one night in the classical vastness of the Street of Rossi the Master Builder said, between their compulsive babble about smack and German needles, that they knew a café where its members could be found. But no one really knew.

In fact, the guerrilla conservators turned out to have an address at 31 Nevsky Prospekt, a phone number, and official red passes.

The Soviet Cultural Fund is not a government body. It came into being with grassroots support, Kobak explained, mainly from the young, who were sick of seeing Leningrad decay from official neglect and disappear under the wrecker's ball of official "development." The conservation movement had been growing since the sixties, just as in

America, and Leningrad was its center. The city has a listed building system, like the English National Trust, though with less power. The first class, Architectural Monuments, covers about twelve hundred structures and sites from 1703 to about 1820. Most government funds are reserved for them. But there is a second class, Registered Monuments, mainly from the period 1870–1925—eclectic, modern, rarely studied until the late 1960s, saturated in history, but not as seriously treated by officialdom. And there is never enough money or skilled labor to deal with the first, let alone the second. Volunteer groups had sprung up in the eighties. Kobak and his colleagues in the SCF, unpaid, work to coordinate them, to direct lobbying, to propose alternatives to development. Thus the SCF has just finished the first and only documentary archive of significant Russian buildings lost in the twentieth century. Its slender budget comes from contributions, mainly from the unions of writers, architects, and musicians. That it exists at all, on however precarious a shoestring, shows *perestroika* at work.

It will never have the money or the power for large-scale conservation; it can only agitate for it. One of its subgroups, ERA (Ecology of Ordinary Architecture), tries to monitor changes in domestic buildings, old apartment blocks, minor palaces. The two hundred or so members of another group, MIR, do unpaid-labor work on historic buildings in their own time, salvaging fireplaces and cornices, carting rubble. A third, Leningrad Necropolis, keeps track of cemeteries, a vital historic resource. "The Siege killed a million people in Leningrad," Kobak points out. "Stalinism, another two million. There had been enormous emigration as well. So thousands of important family graves go untended."

Finally there is a group studying *toponomika*, or street names. Leningrad conservationists hate the bureaucratic habit of renaming everything as a pious souvenir of socialism. The city is now cluttered with the names of utterly forgotten commissars and apparatchiks of the thirties, forties, and fifties—even Nevsky Prospekt, Kobak points out, was rechristened 25 October Prospekt, but that stuck in the civic throat.

Did they want to go the whole hog and rename Leningrad

St. Petersburg? "Bog, no. Somebody once suggested that idea to Anna Akhmatova, and she hated it. It made her sick. First, it wouldn't be administratively possible. Second, it's been Leningrad for seventy years. A quarter of the history of the city! And a history that includes the Siege! We're historians, Socialists, not nostalgia peddlers."

We are standing on the edge of the square in front of the Smolny Convent. Behind, Rastrelli's facade mounts into the pallid evening sky like a blue-and-white fata morgana. It is miserably dilapidated, the stucco coming off in lumps, the tense rococo whorls of its iron balconies rusting. "But this has to be saved," Kobak says. He gestures to what lies in front of the square: a vast gray plaza of concrete offices from the fifties. "And that," he adds in a mild voice, "must never happen again."

At such moments, the visitor is struck by a paradox about the past: that, while seeming so overwhelming, it is so fragile. In Leningrad, more than in most Western cities (where popular opinion has forced a degree of conservation-mindedness since the 1960s), the iron whim of the wrong paper-pusher can abolish an old building in the name of "efficiency," condemn it or not, or wreck its context. There are still plenty of powerful Russians who equate a concern for the past with a sickly lack of faith in the future. The face-saving argument is that treasures like Leningrad's are the collective achievement of the Russian people— as indeed they are. But as Leningrad gears up for an open mass-tourist future, there is no guarantee that its melancholy grandeur will stay the same. In twenty-five years travelers may look back on it (though not on its food) with the same nostalgia with which one thinks today of Florence in 1960. Best, perhaps, to go now.

1988

L'Afrique, Mon Amour

by

AMY WILENTZ

When you're smack in the middle of the street in Dakar, sitting there with your windows down, and you're watching a traffic cop disconsolately attempt to do something about the developing situation, and the street vendors are proceeding in a line past your window with their wares held up in desultory fashion for you to examine (plastic pink sandals and drinking glasses, hangers, a veritable hardware store of extension cords and wrenches and USB cables, a set of handballs, key rings and watches, clothespins, not-so-new candies of all kinds, penknives and mirrors, a velvet painting of the mosque at Mecca, a pink and purple poster of a Senegalese holy man, individual tissue packets, melting Binto chocolate cookies)—when you've just begun to wonder where it will all end and if you'll ever get out of this standstill and why would they be doing construction right here and how come that bus is on the sidewalk and . . . crazy bus driver, watch out for the sheep! . . . and then suddenly, across the street from your car, someone turns on a radio, and a little boy who's wearing shuffling sandals and a tiny pair of blue jeans starts dancing on the sidewalk like a human rubber band to the almost inaudible music—well, that's the moment you know you've really arrived in Senegal. It's the moment you begin to feel a part of things, and that those things are a part of Senegal, and that Senegal is a part of Africa.

You watch the boy dance; his dancing seems like the only possible reaction to the existential questions posed by the traffic jam. And there he is, so small, so delicate, so fluid, so much in motion, while the rest of us are stalled out, going nowhere. Oddly, he's not going anywhere either: He never leaves his spot, but he's got two arms and two legs and they're all moving at the same time, his knees knocking sometimes, and his feet flying straight up off the ground, while his torso is seemingly stationary—and you're hooked into this kid. Everyone's watching him. He's the only game in town all of a sudden, and you're the audience.

What the kid is dancing to is mbalax, an improbable name (sounding to the Anglophone ear as if it's somewhere between "balance" and "relax") for the national music that keeps Senegal bobbing along the surface of all the jams and standstills and obstacles of life in the developing Third World. The heart of Senegal may remain the same, mbalax says, but in its extremities, the country is always in motion.

Senegal is not safari land. It's not about giraffes and lions but about people. It's not zoology; it's sociology, cultural studies, and art. And despite mile after mile of unspoiled beaches, it's not a Riviera, either. Businesswoman Fabienne Guillabert lectured me on this point when I met her in the French colonial town of St-Louis: "Don't come if you just want a beach, if you want to get a tan!" she said, wagging a plump finger at me. There are European tourists who do this in Senegal, notably the French, on package tours that take them only to resorts on the Petite Côte, south of Dakar. "The beaches are nice," Fabienne says, "but that's not the best of what we can offer. It's our personality that counts. The Senegalese are a welcoming people. You could say we maybe get a little too attached, it can be annoying. We're always looking for contact, community. So you can't come if you're not ready to accept our hospitality. If you want to stay in your room and eat club sandwiches, no! What we offer is our love."

Over the course of my trip, I learned the truth of Fabienne's advice. I visited the historical slave-exporting island of Gorée and graveyards where presidents and poets and Senegalese who fought in the world wars were buried; I went north to the colonial town of St-Louis and the bird sanctuary off its shores, and then looped around down through Kaolack, a crossroads town. From there, we headed over the midlands to the Petite Côte, where finally I did go to the beach. And then up through Joal, the birthplace of Léopold Sédar Senghor, Senegal's first president (after independence from France, in 1960), and back to Dakar. Everywhere I went, from hot sweaty markets to music clubs to the sea, I had a guide or a boat pilot, a librarian or an artist, a weaver or a designer, a mosque assistant or a museum attendant, who was glad to help me, to show me around, to overextend himself or herself for me—and not just for the tip.

Before I arrived in Dakar and after, people told me to beware of pickpockets, and I had heard that there was considerable petty crime, yet not for a minute in the city (much less in the countryside) did I experience even the smallest frisson of fear. Perhaps something about me— jeans, microfiber bag, sneakers, no jewelry, dorky golf hat—made me a nonstarter to the petty criminal. But actually, I ascribe my perception of security to . . . a really secure situation. Although buffeted by the hurly-burly of their open economy, the Senegalese still live more or less according to the customs of a traditional society and are used to respecting rules. They are Muslim and observe proper behavior—for the most part. They may be poor, but they are not starving and they are not angry at anyone in particular, although they have the mental habit, no doubt passed down from the French, of being forever irritated by the political situation. Visitors are not attacked for being French or American or whatever. As Fabienne says, what the Senegalese offer is their love, or something like it. The country is happy and welcoming. The Senegalese tell you that they want to see you dance—and you just have to trust that it's not because they want to make fun of you afterward.

More than most African countries, Senegal, the continent's west-ernmost and always a trading nation, stands at the jittery crossroads where the modern, developed world intersects the traditional universe of Africa and of Islam. It's a place where the free-market economy crashes up against the old African necessities of village life and against Muslim ideals of community and cooperation. This friction makes for an exciting environment where tall, slender berobed Africans mix (and don't mix) with Lebanese and Syrian import-export merchants, Chinese traders and workers, European expats and businessmen and together create an intense microcapitalist environment that is like a twenty-four-hour-a-day work of street performance art.

Cultural combinations are everywhere. The charming wrecks of French colonialism turn up here and there, with columns and gilt clocks and bell towers and New Orleans–style grillwork, and they give the rest of the blocky Third World architecture, with its flat Arabian-style roofs, a historical context whose details echo back and forth be-tween today's world and the past. This is a place where artists like Cheikh Lô and Youssou N'Dour (Senegal's bell-voiced pop musician, whom *Rolling Stone* magazine described in 2004 as "perhaps the most famous singer alive"), along with many others, have created a world music in which Islamic songs and African rhythms meet European sounds from abroad. Similarly, in the 1960s and '70s, tapestries from medieval France fused with traditional African communal weaving and developed into masterful wall hangings, an *artisanat* that persists in various weavers' and designers' ateliers today. And you can even *taste* the grand historico-cultural mélange in Senegalese food—with its creamy, mustardy, onion-and-garlicky French character, its halal mari-nated grilled fish and chicken (to say nothing of its tragic Islamic lack of pork products), and its peppery, peanut-infused, root-vegetable-loving African base.

Still, in the cuisine, as with everything in Senegal, when you get right down to it, Africa predominates. It shows through everywhere, erupting over other cultures, more recent arrivals, flowing over them and making them its own. Plus—to generalize a bit but not much—the women are beautiful to look at, the men are elegant and sometimes jazzy, and there are corners where a painted wall, even though it's made of cement block, will stir you with its raging deep-maroon color, and a single palm tree and a single sheep in a village compound, up against the flat ocher of a quick-falling sandstorm sunset, will make you sigh with poetic ecstasy.

The contemporary, complicated face of West Africa, with all its funny contradictions and its mixture of tradition and modernity, is Dakar. As Senegal's leading edge, at the very tip of Africa's Atlantic coast, it has always been a place that looks out toward the rest of the world. Its openness to new things, whatever they are and whether or not they work for Senegal's betterment, is obvious everywhere you look—from the huge and busy port to the overloaded cargo trucks, the cell phone cards (possibly the street vendors' only worthwhile merchandise), the bars (in an Islamic country!), the fine dining, the pharmacies, the Wi-Fi areas (pronounced "wee-fee," *à la française*), the occasional suits of the men and the Parisian cool of the women, and the *cars rapides* that provide public transport and that, contrary to their name, can often be found in the center of a traffic jam, broken down. Though it is evidently African and much of its life is lived in plain view on the streets, Dakar is still clearly a contemporary creation, a child of the global economy and of the international communications boom.

This means that the city is now go-go-go all the time. The cosmopolitan culture seethes and froths around you, pushed this way and that by foreign influence and international culture-peddling. There is music everywhere, cross-cultural dance in every club (if you want to understand Michael Jackson's moves, watch people dancing to mbalax); there are artists on every corner, selling not just in the streets but at the sprawling artists' village at the edge of town, and craftsmen of all kinds, producing the finest quality furniture, those gorgeous tapestries, and beautiful woven linens. There are bookstores in which full walls are lined with the literature of Senegal, a rarity in the Third World: not just political tracts and photocopied, poorly bound government documents but real works and novels by nationally and internationally known figures, published in Paris or in Dakar.

To find out where you really are, drive out at a non-rush-hour time (though there is actually no such thing) to the old Phare des Mamelles, one of the oldest lighthouses in Africa, built in 1864. It affords a panoramic view of the city and the sea, and gives one a real sense of the hugeness of the African continent. The Phare is also a very fine example of lighthouse architecture, but it's windy up there, so hold on to your hat.

Below, Dakar spreads out like a stain—in fact, the city has already taken up almost every square foot of the Cap Vert Peninsula. There are endless neighborhoods and areas and quartiers, many of which you can see from the lighthouse: the Corniche along the Atlantic, where the hotels and some of the nicest restaurants are located; downtown, where most of the music clubs and the trendy new restaurants have been established, and where the biggest of the markets extend like ramshackle nuclei (the Marché Sandaga, where you can get almost anything, and the Marché HLM 5, the huge cloth market, replete with bolts of fabric and the tailors to turn it into a new outfit while-u-wait); the Medina, a lower-middle-class neighborhood that never sleeps, where you can find anything that you might actually need, like batteries or string or a T-shirt or toothpaste; and Almadies, a fancy residential area on the water where most of the expats live and where there are also a number of good places to eat. When—if—you can turn your back on the fracas of Dakar's daily explosion and drag yourself off to a beach or a baobab forest or a tide pool where flamingos stand at attention, you'll feel pretty much as if there couldn't be a better place in the world, because Senegal has a heady portion of all the things that make travel worth doing.

Early in my visit, to see how the Senegalese feel about the old Africa, I went downtown to visit the imposing art museum of the Institut Fondamental d'Afrique Noire (IFAN). Here, there are *tableaux vivants* of rituals in which very tall men, some on stilts, are wearing very wide raffia skirts and white paint and gathering to worship and appease gods who are very far from Allah, very far from Lord Jesus. Poorly lit and not very informative, the nonetheless stunning exhibits show dancers wearing masks of bulls, rhinos, and mythical hybrid beasts with horns and slits for eyes and gaping angry mouths. The drums have breasts.

Unlike the anachronistic dioramas in the Museum of Natural History in New York, where woolly mammoths loom behind Native Americans, these rituals and gatherings, these masked festivals and dances, were still going on in the 1950s and 1960s, and many of them continue to take place, not in Dakar or in the other cities of West Africa, perhaps, but deep in the countryside. Strange to have in a museum what can still be seen in real life. Yet in West Africa there seems to be a disconnect of history, in which distance serves the same function as time: What is actually happening is seen only by those close by. If you're far away, even things that still happen seem to have happened a long time ago, or they seem not to happen anymore. Dakar's urban worldliness divides it from the deep bush, and it is of today, while the savanna or the distant, divine baobab are from a century or even an aeon ago. Say, a time before the French, a time even before the Muslims.

But Senegal has so many things that make it special and particular, things that you can find everywhere and that do not include indigenous gods, raffia skirts, or chieftains. Everyday things: For example, I ate chicken *yassa*, tasty leg and breast meat in a sauce made of onions, lemon, and mustard, at Metissacana, a neighborhood restaurant downtown, where the tables are made of plastic and a vine is growing over the ceiling, and at every table are big Senegalese men in business suits, their cell phones next to their plates, and everyone is drinking tall glasses of *bissap*, a cold red hibiscus infusion. The restaurant is owned by Oumou Sy, one of Dakar's big fashion designers, and on the walls are posters of the outrageous designs she has done for various festivals, and through a door opening out from the dining room is her boutique.

One day, I drove with my friend Koyo through Sicap, a little residential area in Dakar, to the only place, according to her, where you should ever buy *sow*, a local drink usually made from unpasteurized milk—which happens to be one of Koyo's favorite things. We bought it from a lady who sells it fresh each day out of a refrigerator in her living room; the door to her house is always open, as if her home were a store—and it is. Koyo took our bag of *sow*, and we walked across the street and up a set of stairs to what looked like an apartment. There, Aziz Dieng, a musician who is also, as a sideline, a political organizer, was in his studio, wearing his dashiki and finishing up for the day, fiddling with his computer and his soundboards. Koyo said hi and then headed for the kitchen.

She mixed the *sow* with sugar and put it in a bowl and held it out to me. It looked like bits of cottage cheese sinking in thin buttermilk, but I thought, *I'm in Dakar!* and plunged my spoon in and ate some. Well, I liked it! I cannot claim it is the best thing I've ever eaten, but *sow* is refreshing and strengthening, and just pretty good at the end of a long, hot day. And I believe in the West it must be curds and whey. I felt like Little Miss Muffet then, with my bowl of *sow*, talking to Aziz and Koyo about Aziz's free concerts to benefit street boys, and about the various methods Youssou N'Dour has used to become the richest musician in Senegal.

Mbalax is not just a kid dancing in a traffic jam in the heat of noon. It's also late nights at music clubs like Just 4 U, downtown. I arrived there at a little after eleven one night with a bunch of Senegalese friends. A band called Ceddo was about to go on. Blue lights illuminated the stage; on a wall behind the bar hung a poster for the St-Louis Jazz Festival of 1997. The club attracts an upscale crowd—a mix of races, nationalities, languages—all very well dressed, eclectically got up. A Senegalese man sat alone at one table, his face hidden under a dark fedora, and other tables were reserved, it seemed, for older white men accompanied by elegant, young, long-necked Senegalese women, as if one had suddenly entered a later chapter in a novel by Graham Greene. A white man with Victorian whiskers sat with two Senegalese friends in baseball caps. There was a table of quite correct white ladies. There were bright coral necklaces, backless dresses, pants with silver appliqués, and even sequined boubous, nighttime versions of the bright African wraps that women here often wear.

Ceddo is a roots band, traditional African. *Ceddo* itself is a Wolof word that refers to non-Islamic, traditional Africans (Wolof is the dominant Senegalese language). In Senegal, the cultural rebellion among nationalists is not just against French colonialism (the French ruled Senegal from the late 1700s through 1960) but against Muslim cultural imperialism as well. Because Islam took root in Senegal so much earlier than French culture—in the eleventh century—it is more thoroughly incorporated in the society. It's not hard to see where France ends and Africa begins, but to distill Islam's chemistry from the general Senegalese flow requires great knowledge, intellectual rigor, indeed imaginative historical and cultural leaps.

But when Ceddo started to play, France and Islam went out the window, and only Africa, both the ancient continent and the place as it exists in the modern world, was onstage. The singer was in a dark Western-style suit with his back to the red walls; he had a tremulous tenor, like a Wolof Paul Simon. The drummer was wearing a sweatshirt with the hood up; he was playing three African standing drums with both a stick and his palms. The drums are not just musical instruments but the tools that traditionally summon the gods into the presence of men. Ceddo is not trying to call down the gods, but when you hear the music—lyrical, dancing, quavering, and tragic in a spritely way—you feel that the gods might just come down and join the party anyway. It's not only Just 4 U. It's also Just 4 Them. Although the music was practically begging for it, I refused—out of sheer self-consciousness—to get up and dance.

A huge billboard at the Place de la Gare, downtown, shows the much magnified head of the elderly, saturnine president Abdoulaye Wade (pronounced *wad*) beside the slogan *"Gorgi Dolli Nu,"* which, roughly translated, means "the old man is our favorite." The president's dull mug is looking out at the ornate but dilapidated colonial train station, from which a train that is equally dilapidated leaves once a week for Bamako, in Mali. Wade is at least eighty-one years old, and his political life spans Senegal's history as an independent nation. The political party he heads came into existence only because it was sanctioned by Léopold Senghor, who occasionally regretted his generosity to Wade.

As the first president of independent Senegal, Senghor set the tone for the country's postcolonial success. He was an internationalist and, though a Socialist, friendly toward the West in the Cold War era, when it mattered. An intellectual and one of the first of the *noiristes*, he believed in promoting black African culture and tradition and rejecting imposed colonial norms. He cared deeply about the arts and spearheaded initiatives to encourage weavers, artists, and sculptors. Elected for the first time just after independence in 1960, Senghor was reelected three more times, serving a total of twenty years.

In a way, he was a model first president. His long and fairly stable rule gave his administration a chance to try to steer the country out of colonialism and into the modern age, which he did with some degree of success. Stability is one of his legacies: In the forty-seven years since independence, Senegal has had only three presidents, all of them elected—if all in a heated atmosphere of corruption charges, assassination attempts, and imprisonments. Still, it is one of the rare African countries never to have experienced a coup—although maybe that's just because its political leaders have managed to stuff their opponents into jail before the coups could get under way.

Wade has been both jailer and jailed. A lawyer and an economist arrested once on murder charges and twice for threatening state security, he spent almost twenty years unsuccessfully running for president before—as in so many countries where the political class is small and each man who really tries will eventually get the job—he was finally elected in 2000. His nickname is Wade the Builder, because he loves to create infrastructure; he adores major development projects, with all the money they bring into the country from foreign lenders, and all the jobs and (thus) all the popularity they create. As Landing Savané, another perennial presidential candidate, told me, "Wade loves concrete." (That makes him different from Senghor, who was an internationally respected poet, the first black person elected to the Académie Française, and the first black person to teach French to the French, in France.)

I barreled out of town with Doudou and Arona, two Senegalese friends, in a car big enough to house half a village. I was pleased because it seemed as though we were going to make good time. But we only barreled along for a bit. Then traffic slowed, and every twenty yards or so, Doudou rolled his eyes, because every twenty yards or so, we were in a new traffic jam. At one point, the Dakar–Bamako train passed us at a stately pace. Eventually, though, we escaped Dakar and found ourselves at the Lac Rose, or Pink Lake.

The lake is an ephemeral environmental phenomenon, and, like many ephemeral things, beautiful in a transitory way. It was created in 1970 by high Atlantic waters filling up what's called a sink, and it is quickly evaporating. Salt, other minerals, and microorganisms give the water a notably pink hue, especially when the sun is high. Like many places in Senegal, the lake is the site of intense activity: Where there is a resource, the Senegalese will find it and mine it with a single-mindedness that approaches obsession. Here at Lac Rose, families from the area devote the dry season to extracting salt from the thick waters.

Not far away is the Atlantic, from whose waters the lake arose. Doudou and I got in the back of an open-bed jeep to fly over the high dunes between the lake and the sea. A local driver was at the wheel, very young and enthusiastic, madly shifting, obviously someone who fancied himself an up-and-coming contestant in the annual Paris-Dakar rally, which ends at Lac Rose. The jeep itself was an ancient wonder, and I watched in amazement as Doudou bounced up and down on his flea-bitten seat yet failed to be ejected. We zoomed down steep dunes and stuttered up the next rise, and then suddenly before us was a wide, wide beach and the calm, open sea, and not another human in sight. A flock of gulls swooped down and over and back, and the Atlantic made little lapping waves on the shore. The flat beach wound up and up the shoreline and then disappeared altogether at the horizon. Three wild dogs stood near the edge where the dunes began again. Untouched, I kept thinking. Beautiful and free, and so unlike the scene back at Lac Rose.

The lake's shores were messy with human endeavor. The women, who were wearing sunglasses, slathered their skin with shea butter (available in great beige heaps in every market) to protect themselves from the salt, which they were unloading on the shore. All the men were in the water, waist-deep, loading the salt into boats. The shore was strewn with plastic buckets. As their parents labored under a strong sun, small salt-worker children gathered around Doudou and me, begging cheerfully for candy. One boy pointed at me, laughing, and said, *"Toubab."* This means "white person." The other kids echoed his word.

We continued on down the highway, past aged baobab trees that look as though they grow with their roots in the air, as if they'd been upended and shoved upside down into the earth. This tree is one of the great and enduring symbols of Africa. According to Doudou, the baobab is a miracle tree. Its leaves cure arthritis and, mixed with shea butter, relieve the pains of childbirth. An extract from its fruit—which hangs down from the branches on long stalks the way tossed sneakers hang from street wires in New York City—cures diarrhea; Doudou called this concoction "the national Imodium."

In the old days, the baobab had both medicinal and religious purposes. A tree stood at the center of every village, and not only were sacred festivals celebrated beneath its branches but it also served as what's known in Africa as the "palaver house," a meeting place where the elders would gather to share news, discuss issues, mete out justice, and plan village life—like a combined church, courthouse, and café. After they died, poets and storytellers, called griots here, were buried within the crevices and hollows of its capacious trunk, sitting up and dressed for recitation in all their finery. This custom is now illegal. But if Homer, say, had been an African, a baobab would have been his final resting place.

Youssou N'Dour is from the griot class, as are almost all Senegalese musicians. Both his mother and father were griots. You don't just become a griot because you are personally inclined that way; it's in your blood. And caste will tell. Still today, it is unthinkable for a woman of the aristocratic class—a descendant of chieftains, say—to marry a man from the griot class. "Even as rich as he is," said Doudou, "Youssou would not be able to marry a chief's daughter or granddaughter."

One baobab we stopped to admire was big enough that I could stand inside its open trunk; indeed, I could have stood there with my family of four and invited Doudou, Arona, and a couple of their friends inside, too. Arona estimated the tree's age at around six hundred years—pre-Shakespearean, as I think of it. At the foot of another tree was an enormous *termitière*, an anthill that seemed built of cement and stood as tall as my shoulder—as if some tiny, energetic President Wade had been busy with construction projects there for centuries.

There are other builders besides Wade who've made their presence felt in Senegal. Just off the shores of the continent, across from what is now Dakar, is the small island of Gorée, first settled by the Portuguese in the 1400s. It has a little village, an elegant governor's palace, several imposing old houses, and a wide, fortified building giving onto the sea—this last is the infamous Maison des Esclaves, or Slave House. It's disturbing to see, as you walk up the quay, hundreds of little Senegalese students on a school trip, dressed in their satiny feast-day best, disembarking from the ferry from Dakar, laughing, holding hands, and swinging backpacks as if they were going to a picnic, when really Gorée is, at least imaginatively speaking, the Auschwitz of Africa. But their pleasure and delight in the trip is all of a piece with the disjunctions and bizarre juxtapositions of Gorée.

The island is inarguably one of the prettiest places in Senegal: no cars, no visible garbage, and no ugly new jury-rigged, two-cent cement-block architecture. You can amble down little alleyways festooned with bougainvillea and imagine yourself in eighteenth-century French West Africa. But that's just the problem—although it was lovely and gracious, it was also the gateway to the charnel house of the African slave trade. From Gorée, captured Africans by the tens of thousands, perhaps the hundreds of thousands, were forced onto ships headed across the Atlantic for the work-and-death-camp plantations of the Americas, while slavers and merchants and their Creole mistresses—known here as *signares* (from the Portuguese *senhora*, or "lady")—led a mincing life of high society. In a building like the Dutch-constructed Slave House, the traders would eat, sleep, and socialize upstairs in the airy and graceful living quarters, while below, their cargo was held, sometimes in heavy chains, in inhuman conditions.

Modern-day visitors can see the lovely upstairs rooms, and then below, the dank, dungeon-like cells, the holding pens, the force-feeding cells for those too thin to survive the long trip, the weighing chamber, the tiny cell for rebels. Standing at the foot of the sweeping staircase that leads up from the cells to the traders' quarters, Joseph Ndiaye, the museum's longtime curator, an erect, gray-haired man in a Western-style suit, gave an impassioned speech to Italian, American, German, and French tourists. He conjured up the hideousness of the entire slave trade and placed it all imaginatively on Gorée, although there is some dispute about how important Gorée was as a slave trading port. Ndiaye finds this immaterial: "The Slave House is a symbol of the cruelty of this trade," he said.

You leave the buildings stunned at the global enormity and grotesque horror of the centuries-long commodification of humans. I kept thinking, fifteen million to eighteen million people. So many were "deported from Gorée," wrote the Polish journalist and poet Ryszard Kapuściński, that "the mass abductions and deportations depopulated the continent. Africa emptied out, became overgrown with bush and weeds." The world's first brain drain, in addition to the terrible human loss, was for Africa an inestimable siphoning off of manpower and community strength. As you walk through the ruined but still impressive palace of the Chevalier de Boufflers (a minor French poet who was briefly the colonial governor of Senegal in the late 1700s), it's hard to forget that the fortunes, and the colonial and postcolonial civilizations, of Western Europe, the United States, and Latin America were built on the backs of Africans who were dragged through this island and other places like it.

Stay on Gorée for even a few hours and you see simple things in a new light. The beige Band-Aid on the back of a Senegalese policeman's hand as he directs the students along the quay seems historic, meaningful. The children on the bottom floor of the ferry back to Dakar, filling the windows with their sweet faces, look like Middle Passengers. The Frenchmen in baseball caps and Frenchwomen in shorts, formerly innocent tourists, now appear to be inheritors of an undeserved complacency, as they tool with cheerful curiosity around their former colony. And the quote from Martin Luther King's "I Have a Dream" speech, painted informally on a wall in Gorée, seems no longer like a worn-out cliché but instead like a cry from one generation back over the long centuries to another, from one continent back over the wide ocean to another.

Unlike Gorée, which was settled and run by Europeans from the fifteenth century through independence in 1960, the holy city of Touba came into being just over a hundred years ago, in 1887, at a spot about fifty miles inland from Dakar. It was there that, sitting under a tree, the anticolonialist holy man Amadou Bamba, founder of the Mouride sect of Sufi Islam, had a vision of God-inspired light and decided to build the town.

Touba is dominated by an immense and impressive mosque. Its construction, which started in 1929, has never ended—new sections, walls, and chapels are added on as money permits. As the mosque grew larger, so did Touba, whose population has expanded from 5,000 in 1964 to almost 500,000 today (it is the second-largest city in Senegal after Dakar). Members of the Mouride sect, representing about a third of Senegal's population of 12.5 million, keep Touba afloat. Only a group that can generate stupendous sums would be able to pay for such a large, ornate construction, as well as its upkeep. The Mourides are now led by Serigne Saliou Mbacké, the last living son of Amadou Bamba, who died in 1927, when Serigne Mbacké was only nine. Wielding the clout of his dynastic privilege and religious dominance, Mbacké has become (oddly, at least to the foreign mind) one of the world's largest peanut farmers as well as a powerful Senegalese political figure. Touba is essentially a state within a state, an African Vatican with Mbacké as its pope.

As you enter the city, the first word that comes to mind would not be *holy*. More likely, it would be *bustling*, or *wild*. Small groups of pilgrims in white robes with pictures of Bamba strung around their necks waft across the busy streets. Otherwise, business goes on as usual in any Senegalese city, but more intensely, because the population is bigger and there are always thousands of visitors. Amid the pilgrims, blacksmiths beat metals into shape in their dark, mysterious stalls; boys play *babyfoot* (French foosball); small shops serve ready-to-eat meals; tailors pedal old sewing machines, and street boys sell the usual wares. One big difference: In Touba, no woman goes uncovered. I too ended up under the veil, purchasing a peacock-blue rayon hijab with sequined butterflies. But why, I wondered, was my hijab *still* on my head as I drove out of Touba in the afternoon? To solve this spiritual question, I realized, I needed a marabout.

You may not yet have come to this realization yourself, but you need one too. A marabout (pronounced *MAR-ah-boo*) is Senegal's expansive version of an Islamic holy man (or woman—there are two famous female marabouts in Dakar, an African emendation to Islam) who acts as counselor, leaf doctor, and spiritual adviser. Marabouts combine the attributes of a priest and a traditional medicine man, among other qualities. They understand your spiritual needs, your problems. President Wade has a marabout, and Wade is an intelligent man with degrees in law and economics.

Of course, Wade's marabout is the most important marabout in Senegal, the same Serigne Mbacké of Touba. In Senegal, the marabouts run everything and everyone. The big ones own contracting firms and mosques and thousands of acres in the countryside and have tens of thousands of followers. Little marabouts have a place in the city as well as about twenty young students, known as *talibés*, in their care, whom they run, in the style of Fagin in Charles Dickens's *Oliver Twist*, as beggars. Whatever money the boys manage to amass from begging goes to the marabout, ostensibly for their room, board, and religious education.

When President Wade was elected, before he spoke to the press or the assembly or was sworn in, he consulted with his marabout. He went to talk to his teacher because Mbacké was instrumental in this good *talibé*'s election; a huge number of the Mouride congregation follow the Touba marabout's political, as well as spiritual, direction.

Look at a bumper sticker, a minibus, a store, a house, a market stall, a restaurant, and you'll notice that almost any flat surface in Senegal is likely to have a portrait of a marabout on it, most often that of Amadou Bamba, Mbacké's father. The portraits are often ghostly—old paint applied to bumpy, worn-out cement or concrete walls. From beneath old-fashioned muslin headscarves, the marabouts on the walls were watching over us everywhere, warding off evil spirits, taking care of their *talibés*.

A marabout, I thought as I left Touba, would be just the thing. I needed some guidance. In just one day, I'd come to like my hijab and my new invisible status. I found I could get used to it. I could wear my blue scarf all over the country. But the veil is not common in the rest of Senegal, and I could never learn to wrap a headdress the way African women do outside Touba, with a flourish that rounds the skull and ends with a perky twist rising up toward the skies, beckoning the higher authorities. If I couldn't consult with a marabout, I supposed I would just have to revert to my dilapidated golf hat.

That's what I was wearing as we came into St-Louis (blue hijab folded up and stored away), and it felt all wrong. An exquisite place, St-Louis is the former colonial capital, and, set on the Atlantic at the mouth of the Senegal River, it's dramatically self-important. No doubt its geographical insularity and prominence added, in its heyday, to its political renown. The river—once a major export pipeline from the African interior—is overhung here by a gorgeous seven-arched bridge designed in 1897 by the fabled French architect Gustave Eiffel, eight years after the construction of his legendary Parisian tower. (It was meant to cross the Danube, but that's another story.) Eiffel's bridge runs between the mainland and the narrow colonial island and lends St-Louis a romantic aura at its very heart that the city easily lives up to.

Protected by historic zoning, St-Louis has not been destroyed by the unfortunate architecture that replaced colonial styles in so much of the Third World. The wise Fabienne Guillabert, daughter of a *signare* and the second president of Senegal, runs the Maison Rose hotel here. It's an old house formerly owned by a family from Bordeaux that dates back to the French Revolution, and even though it's a moneymaking establishment now, the Maison Rose is not exempt from preservation regulations. Fabienne complained that she has not been allowed even to "touch" the staircases, although the wood could use renovation. The inspectors would only let her reinforce the stairways' underpinnings. She was indignant yet pleased to be part of preserving the place.

Because of these rules, St-Louis is like a crumbling combination of New Orleans and Venice. The exteriors have a lovely worn warmth. Doudou and I took a horse-and-buggy ride through town one evening. We passed the mosque that the French had built with a bell tower instead of a minaret so that the French governor would not have to hear the muezzin's call to prayer five times a day, which supposedly gave him a headache. We saw the port where ships used to come in from Nantes, Bordeaux, and Marseilles.

There is a charmed feeling of relaxation in the streets of the colonial city in the evening. Girls braided one another's hair, sitting on bright polyester rugs along the sidewalk. In the quiet streets, boys kicked a ball around. Our small horse stirred up dust, and we passed by all but unnoticed. A smell of incense drifted on the cool air. A tailor worked, cutting threads for tomorrow's jobs. In a broad tree-lined courtyard, two soldiers in uniform checked their drying laundry.

We rounded a corner and headed over the Petit Pont to what was known as the African Town in colonial days. The difference was stunning. This is a fishermen's village, and it never stops bustling. All the markets were open at sunset. It felt as if we might be in the countryside; on the ground, a bunch of women were tying together leaves for medicinal cures. Rice filled colorful bags, each color signifying a different type of grain. The palm trees waved in the evening breeze, and local people—not tourists—were taking horse and flatbed buggies home from the market with their purchases. The call to prayer sounded over a megaphone as we clop-clopped past block after block of pungent smoked fish drying in the now slanting sun. The people in their colors looked like a living paint box or a scattering of bonbons wrapped in colored foil. A madrassa master with a cane was striding among his squatting students, the open-air classroom silhouetted against the sun-splashed sea.

At the Maison Rose, Fabienne offered me a marquise, a flavored rum drink. She is both very correct and quite bohemian, in the relaxed yet elite tradition of the *signare*. Plump and sexy, with long soft hair and light skin, she talked about the traditional Senegalese charms for lovemaking—about the *bin-bin*, beads that women wear around their waists and that make a stimulating *ch-ch-ch* noise; and about the *bethio*, a little skirt made of strips that hang from the hips down past the crotch, like a short hula skirt; and about incense ("Every woman does her own," Fabienne said).

In my very pretty room, a painting of a topless *signare* preparing for love hung over the bed. She was wearing the *bin-bin* and the *bethio*, and on a little table, she was mixing her incense. Fabienne had talked about the power of the *signares*: "Having a white father in the old days gave you access and ability. Those fathers always helped the future husbands of their daughters. Some *signares* were also slave owners. But they were very, very sought after. They had all the traditional African allure but with modern features."

We presented an interesting feminine contrast, the woman in this portrait and I. Sitting on a couch in the tiny salon of my room, in jeans, a white polo shirt, and sneakers, watched over by this enigmatic figure of seduction, I was trying to figure out how to dispose of a lump of smelly shea butter that Koyo had bought for me and what to do with the two mangoes I had purchased curbside in Touba that were now rotting in my tiny refrigerator. My *signare* looked down on the scene impassively. Things in her sphere smelled a lot better than things in mine.

One of the most wonderful and underappreciated places in Senegal is Kaolack, a town of about 180,000 and the center of the peanut-processing industry in Senegal (don't go if you're allergic). Downtown, the amazing Alliance Franco-Sénégalaise has a library decorated with zebra striping, indigenous tiles, and vibrant patterns. Serious students sat in the main room under fluorescent lights, and children upstairs were reading the imperialist and racist Asterix and Tintin comic books. The librarian, Amadou Abdoulaye Ba, took me on a tour that ended in the library's small research room, where the twenty or so computers were in almost continuous use and an air conditioner whirred. Out in the courtyard, I drank a cup of espresso. I could have spent a lot of time here.

But most of all, I was transported by the Kaolack market: There's the section for suitcases, the tailors' locale, the area of electric fans, the place of locks and keys, the region of pots and colanders. A dozen eggs in an open carton traveled above the frenzied crowd on a woman's head; likewise a folding cot on a man's shoulders. At the taxi stand, I watched as the collective cars filled up: one lady in blue with orange hair extensions; one tall girl with straightened hennaed hair who was wearing an orange-and-black, two-piece, ankle-length boubou; a young man in a Kobe Bryant T-shirt; and last, a minor sheikh all in white. Men in front, ladies behind, the taxi-packer herded them in and hit the roof, literally—and off they went, only to stop a few feet later in the stalled market traffic. Over next to a blue wall amid the madness, older men played checkers and cards and chatted amicably, as if they were in a quiet living room. Meanwhile, all around, speakers in telephone stalls were blaring music above the traffic. Winding through the labyrinth, a group of about a dozen dreadlocked Sufi mystic youths, in camouflage and khaki, were on an impromptu parade, smoking as they went, seeking alms and playing traditional African drums.

Après tout ça, I was grateful for respite at the Relais de Kaolack. The Saloum River flows by it, gray-blue in the evening light, and the peanut factory fumes smell like childhood. As wind and the sound of the call to prayer rose up, strange river gulls swooped down over the pool, where white men were sipping pink drinks at a blue-tile table.

From Kaolack, it isn't too far to the Siné-Saloum Delta, where the Saloum River cuts into the Petite Côte, which is where the beach resorts are. Filled with lagoons and palms, tide pools where flamingos gather, and mangrove swamps, this vast area is one of Senegal's most impressive landscapes. At Djifer, I rented a pirogue (a local fisherman named Amadou piloted it with one hand while holding his cell phone with the other and talking) and headed out from the fishermen's village to Île Sangomar, a mystical island dominated by three sacred baobabs, about which Senghor wrote some of his most beautiful poems.

The thing I always fantasize about, when I've had a few long days somewhere far from superhighways, First World amenities, and the telecommunications revolution, is a sunny little restaurant somewhere on a beach, with a breeze blowing, white tablecloths, and a plate of poached salmon and a glass of cold white wine. Before I went to Senegal, this had never happened. But in Senegal, it did.

Often, I'd spend the day wandering among villages like a creature from another planet, like a Victorian anthropologist. In the villages that dot the highways between the towns, what the people seemed to want from me was candy for children and prescription drugs for adults, who also happily accepted aspirin and shampoo. Though they cook on the ground and sleep in straw huts, they too have trouble sleeping; they too have headaches. Sometimes after several days, the difficulties of their conditions and the disjunction between their lives and mine made me want to slip away and crawl back into my normal life.

Graham Greene, when he went through Liberia on foot in the 1920s under the harshest of travel circumstances, said that what he always longed for was, simply, an iced drink. In Senegal today he'd be fine. If you're willing to travel hard on the highway, you can spend a day going from parched village to parched village, talking with people who've never traveled more than four miles from home, and then you can get back on the road and end up at a place like Le Royal Lodge, a resort in Palmarin, on the Petite Côte. After you've been thoroughly disheartened in a barren place along the highway where some rich man, with permission from Wade's government, is cutting down baobabs to put up a development, you can go swim in Le Royal Lodge's bright-blue infinity pool overlooking the ocean. It's like my fantasy of white wine and salmon, only more so. There's a cave for wine. There is a clipped green for playing *boules* under the palms. You can have grilled fish for dinner. Or you can stand in the pool and have drinks at the bar, if that's the kind of thing you like to do. Then the next morning, after sleeping under sheets emblazoned with Napoleon's signature bee, you can lie under a baobab on the beach, looking out at a shadowy ship-wreck that has been there for decades. You can eat fresh mangoes and have an espresso.

Just make sure to tell Fabienne, if you stop by her place in St-Louis, that you didn't come to Senegal to get a tan.

2007

¡Olé! The Home of Legend

by

NORMAN LEWIS

Peace, so relentlessly denied to the traveler on the Costa del Sol, descends instantly when just beyond Marbella he turns off north onto the Ronda road. This is marvelously deserted. Ronda—kept short of accommodation, it is alleged, by a hoteliers conspiracy—rids itself of the bulk of its visitors at the end of every day. A few cars passed me on their way downhill to the coast; otherwise there was little sign of life in these splendidly empty mountains.

Five miles short of Ronda I pulled in at a roadside café. It was precariously sited close to the slope of a steep valley, and a previous customer's car, unsuccessfully parked, had rolled fifteen yards downhill into a corral with some donkeys. From the organized life of an area now described as the California of Europe, I had suddenly crossed an invisible frontier into the improvised Spain of old. The man who ran the place made me an omelet of potatoes studded with mountain ham—very dense and dry, to be correctly eaten with the fingers. He poured himself a glass of bluish wine and sat down with me to share the view. A huge bird—eagle or vulture—flapped into sight over a nearby peak and planed down the valley. Why were there no houses? I asked him, and he said it was because this had been bandit country. There had been bandits in these mountains as late as the forties, and one of them had ridden in here one night for what proved to be his last meal before falling into an ambush laid by the Civil Guards.

While this conversation was in progress, a large and handsome nanny goat had stationed herself at the back of my chair, and now with great delicacy and precision, she leaned forward, picked up a piece of my bread, and began to chew. "Hope the goat doesn't bother you," the man said. "She's a friend of the family. Often pays us a visit."

"She doesn't bother me in the slightest," I said. "She's a fine-looking animal. What's her name?"

The man seemed surprised. "Not being a Christian," he said, "she doesn't have one. We just call her 'the goat.'"

I thanked him, patted the goat on the head, and left. Ten minutes later I drove over the top of the sierra and down through the outskirts of Ronda, and the landscape burst into life. There were hens and pigeons and litters of scuttling black piglets in the open spaces. A mother snatched up her baby from the verge of the road, a horseman wearing leather chaps and a big hat galloped after an escaping cow, and a traditional turkey woman controlled her flock with a seven-foot whip.

The great Arab gate called the Puerta de Almocábar barred the way at the entrance to the town. It was flanked by massive towers, and through it a perfect white Andalusian street of matching houses curved up into the heart of Ronda. There are bottlenecks among Gothic and Moorish buildings at the top of the hill, and, after that, a descent to the New Bridge over the theatrical gorge of the Río Guadalevín, and glimpses, through ornamental grilles, of cyclopean boulders rearing up three hundred feet from the trickle of water in the bottom. Across the bridge the town opens into the Plaza de España, a charming, if haphazard, square smelling of geraniums and saddlery, with shops like caverns, a coachman plying for country hire on the box of a vehicle resembling a tumbril, and men with sonorous voices calling the numbers of lottery tickets for sale.

Here, through a fine, ruined archway, is the town's parking lot, with the cars lined up under a backdrop of the old town over the river, its white houses crammed as on a seaside terrace along the edge of a five-hundred-foot precipice. On our side, across the road, Don Miguel's restaurant jutting out over the gorge at its narrowest and most fearsome point recalls a scene in Tibet. I asked the knowledgeable attendant about eating there, and he replied, "You could do worse. Personally, I never set foot in the place. I suffer from vertigo, and it makes my head swim."

In all it was a memorable first encounter. Here was a small corner of Spain miraculously preserved; hardly changed, or so it seemed, since the editor of *Murray's Handbook*, a difficult man to please, wrote of it in 1880, "There is but *one* Ronda in the world," hastening to warn of children "fond of throwing stones from dangerous heights at an unprotected traveller."

By now it was 8 P.M., with the sun waning in power at the bottom of the sky, and an evening relucence diffused from surfaces of bare rock, and a nacreous speckling of clouds to warm the whiteness of the buildings. The best of Ronda, built along the edge of the Tajo gorge, rises to nearly a thousand feet, with the prospect at this hour of a vast amphitheater saturated with fading light, men on donkeys and mules immediately below among ancient, abandoned houses with trees growing through their roofs, a herd of sheep running as nimbly as cats, a threshing floor ringed with stones like a miniature Stonehenge, and in the distance the sierra being pulled apart, range from range, by the mist.

The Tajo provides the reason for Ronda's existence, for apart from this incomparable natural defense, why should it have occurred to anyone to settle here? Only the unreliable irrigation provided by the Guadalevín offers relief in an environment largely copied from African deserts. The cliff abetted the inhabitants in their struggle against marauding armies, but the living was poor. Before the new affluence promoted by tourism, Rondeños picked olives, raised pigs, and cured ham. Until after the war, day laborers might hope to find employment for a hundred days a year, and the daily wage could be as low as three and a half pesetas, at a time when there were nine pesetas to the dollar. The Andalusia of those days has been described as the poorest region in Europe, and there were Andalusians, as reported in the newspapers of the day, who literally starved to death. Hence the chronic and permanent banditry. Hence the garrote set up outside the Chapel of Los Dolores in Ronda, where desperate peasants who had taken to robbery were brought to be strangled in batches of four—as recorded in macabre fashion by the figures carved in the church's porch.

Unendurable poverty, and its long legacy of hatred, determined the atrocious aspects of the Spanish civil war in Andalusia. It is widely asserted that the cliff in Ronda was the scene of the episode described in Hemingway's *For Whom the Bell Tolls* in which local supporters of the Franco revolt were compelled by cudgel-armed peasants to run the gauntlet before being tossed over the edge. There is no clear-cut evidence that this actually happened, and the subject is avoided in local discussion, but it is not denied that many hundreds of civilians were murdered in the town. With its capture by the Nationalists, Republican sympathizers were punished, as elsewhere in Andalusia, with extreme severity. Broadcasting from Seville, the Nationalist general Queipo de Llano had said, "For every person they [the government supporters] kill, I shall kill ten, or perhaps even exceed that proportion." There is no doubt that he meant it.

"Panem et circensis" were the Roman recipes for civil peace, and there can be no doubt that even when bread was in short supply in Spain, fiestas, the Spanish equivalent of circuses, were provided in abundance.

I arrived in Ronda halfway through the annual festivities conducted in September, which, although scheduled in the handsome official program to take place between the eighth and fourteenth of the month, had been inflated by tacking a full extra week of jollifications onto the front. What was on offer was a marathon of pleasure guaranteed in the end to reduce revelers to a state of exhaustion. Every day of the interminable two weeks was crammed with such attractions as displays of horsemanship, shows put on by folklore groups invited from numerous countries, a concert by flamenco singers, pageantry by lovely ladies in old-style costumes, a carriage-driving contest, military parades to the music of stirring bands, a pentathlon, an "interesting" football match, a bicycle race, a procession of giants and "big-headed" dwarfs, a comic bullfight in which aspirant toreros dressed as firemen would squirt each other with fire hoses, a novillada fought with young bulls, and the celebrated annual *goyesca*, in which all participants are attired in the bullfighting regalia of the eighteenth century.

Those who are still on their feet at the end of each long, festive day are expected to make a night of it at the feria outside the town, in operation from 1 A.M. until dawn. Here *casetas* (temporary cottages) are for hire, where families entertain their friends, sherry flows like a river in spate, and professional Gypsy dancers and guitarists can be called in to keep the party going.

Alarm is often voiced at the inroads made by expanding fiestas into the serious business of living. Here is Don Rafael Manzano, a former director of the Alcázar of Seville, on the subject of his city's spring fair—now, according to Don Rafael, completely out of control—which Ronda has set itself to imitate, if not surpass. "Until recently, only rich people with no work could stay up and enjoy themselves all night. Now everybody tries to. If the parents stay up, so do the children as part of their democratic right. The result is my own children fall asleep over their books at school. As a nation we are in danger of forgetting that there is work to be done."

The main attractions of the Ronda fiesta are staged in its bullring— the excuse for the fiesta itself being to commemorate the birthday of Pedro Romero, a Rondeño who became the most famous bullfighter of all time. Romero invented the modern style of bullfighting, conducted largely on foot. At a time when life was notably short and brutish, he lived until the age of eighty-five, having faced his first bull as a boy of eight, and killed some six thousand animals in all. Pedro Romero attracted the attention and admiration of Francisco Goya, and the archaic costumes worn in the annual bullfight in homage to both men are based on the paintings from his *tauromaquia* collection, in which some paintings depict Romero in action.

Ronda's bullring, scene of so many of Romero's exploits, is one of the oldest, the largest, and the most elegant in existence. Its exterior—with the exception of the splendid Baroque main gate, featured in the film of *Carmen*—appears of massive African simplicity, giving the illusion of an enormous white, slightly flattened dome dominating the center of the town.

The museum it contains offers a wide though eccentric variety of bullfighting memorabilia, with occasional bizarre items such as a matador's pantaloons displaying the blood-stained rent through which the wearer accidentally skewered himself with his own sword. Possibly the first bullfight poster to be published advertises the appearance of Pedro Romero, who, it was promised, would kill sixteen bulls with his cuadrilla that afternoon. Could captured Barbary pirates have been forced to fight in the ring in Goya's day? Several prints show dark-faced bullfighters in turbans and flowing robes defending themselves somewhat hopelessly with their swords. These prints, the captions assure us, are based not upon fact but upon the painter's imagination. Nevertheless, one wonders.

Ronda is devoid of self-conscious displays of the trappings of antiquity. The monuments of Roman, Arabic, and Gothic occupation associate in a comfortable and matter-of-fact way with the buildings of our day: the Minarete de San Sebastián next to an ironmonger's shop and facing the bakery at the top of the Calle Salvatierra, and the princely facade of the Salvatierra Palace itself at its bottom in an environment of bars. Everywhere history is taken for granted. The permanently crowded bar called La Verdad ("truth") in the Calle Pedro Romero has an ancient Arabic inscription running all around the doorway leading to the kitchen. It reads, THERE IS NO CONQUEROR BUT ALLAH. A remarkable declaration of an outlawed faith in a town in which the Inquisition once ruled. So much is forgotten, so much overlooked.

José Paez, who has written a book and many newspaper articles about the town, accompanied me on a final stroll through its streets. It was the last day of the fiesta, and there were girls by the hundreds in Sevillian-style costumes roaming in groups, clicking their castanets, dancing, and singing in their high-pitched voices. Sometimes a man went with them, banging on a drum as they passed from street to street, leaving no corner or alleyway unvisited, as if beating the bounds of the town. José agreed that what we were witnessing could only be the vestiges of some bygone ceremony, by which the town had been cleansed of evil influences. The dancers seemed moved by compulsion, communicating a little of this to onlookers in their vicinity. As the current of excitement took possession, women put down shopping bags and abandoned babies in prams to join in, and once in a while, a man correctly dressed for the routine of an office or bank would stop to dance a few steps. It was a moment when one saw the fiesta in a new guise, not merely as the vehicle of popular enjoyment, but—at least in part—as a ritual left over from prehistory, once seen as essential to the well-being of the community.

Our walk ended in the splendid and gracious Alameda del Tajo Gardens, laid out in 1807 by a mayor who hit upon the ingenious and wholly successful method of raising funds for this project by imposing stiff fines upon citizens heard to blaspheme. Ronda is full of wildlife, and here it was present in concentrated form. Enormous diurnal moths hung like hummingbirds in suspension before the flowers they probed with their long proboscises. José, a student of nature, has produced a most interesting theory after a study of the behavior of vultures, which infallibly appear every year at this time to circle in the sky for an hour or so before flying off. It had been at least fifty years, he said, since the horses killed in the bullring were dragged to the edge of the cliff and thrown over for disposal by the vultures. Every year, nevertheless, the birds brought their young here on their first flights, as he supposed, to pass on to them the knowledge of the place where once there had always been food in abundance, which might possibly be provided once again.

We strolled to the edge of the cliff. The sun had just set, and shortly, stripped of its light, the sierra would lose both color and depth. Within half an hour night would suddenly fall, and the mountainous shapes, reduced to a sharp-edged cutout against the still-luminous sky, would come very close to the town, filling the gardens with the hootings of enormous owls.

"I regard this town where I was born as an earthly paradise," José said, "and although I have traveled in many countries, I always return to it with gratitude and relief." After a moment of thought, he added, "People come to this spot to commit suicide. Sometimes I ask myself, Why do they not look at the view and change their minds?"

1993

Spain at the Extreme

by

GULLY WELLS

I have always believed that it is possible to fall in love with a country. Crazily and forever. You can be attracted to a certain part of the world and discover something there that charms you as nowhere else quite can. Places can dazzle your eyes with their beauty and steal your heart with their courage, wit, and intelligence. Just like people. And if a country can be seductive, then it seems only natural that it can also be feminine or masculine. Who would ever imagine that Venice was anything other than a woman? Or Israel anything but a man? Mother Russia has a hard time convincing us of her femininity and comes across instead as a clumsy cross-dresser: a burly, none-too-sober man in ill-fitting women's clothing. London has always been quietly masculine, Paris exuberantly feminine, and Switzerland has carefully avoided the whole messy business by remaining neutral/neutered, stranded forever in a sexless no-man's-land of chocolate, cuckoo clocks, and clockwork bankers. And if France is a woman's country, then Spain is just as surely a man's. And if Spain is a man—*qué hombre*—then the province of Extremadura can lay claim to being

that part where its masculine character is expressed in its most extreme form.

Southwest of Madrid, abutting the Portuguese border and entirely landlocked, Extremadura is remote, both physically and in spirit. It is not on the way to anywhere. Its landscape is tough and uncompromising, and its towns are handsome—even beautiful—but never pretty. There are the ubiquitous ruined castles on top of deserted hills, and empty roads that slice across plains and through valleys and climb mountains, where hawks and vultures perform their aeronautic pas de deux, seemingly for your eyes only. There are cathedrals as splendid as any in Europe, but instead of stained-glass windows (which suddenly seem vulgar, like gaudy costume jewelry), they have translucent panes of alabaster that filter the harsh sunlight and bathe the interior in a mysterious, milky glow. There is a huge—it must be ten times life-size—head of the conquistador of the Amazon, Francisco de Orellana, carved in granite, with his jutting jaw, hawklike profile, and unseeing eyes, which stands guard in a back street in Trujillo while his better-known compatriot and fellow Extremeño, Francisco Pizarro, gallops across the Plaza Mayor in the same town, his sword unsheathed for all time (the sculptor did not even bother to provide the statue with a scabbard), and the plumes on his helmet flying behind him like angry bronze serpents.

The conquistadors are synonymous with Extremadura, where Cortés, Pizarro, and many hundreds of other less famous conquerors of the Americas were born. Spain is a country that was forged in battle, and the war against the Moors, the Reconquista, can be seen as a lengthy dress rehearsal for the main event, the *conquista* (Pizarro's heirs were awarded the splendid title of Marqués de la Conquista) of an entire continent that followed after 1492. Those conquistadors who managed to survive and profit from the war returned rich and built palaces in towns such as Cáceres and Trujillo that still stand, perfectly preserved, as stone monuments to the triumph of their will. The strength and beauty of these buildings, constructed of huge slabs of sandstone, with massive doorways, lie in their perfect proportions and in the complete absence of any extraneous decoration.

Go into a bar in Extremadura and order a glass of *tinto*, and you will be offered a dish of *picadillo* made of freshly slaughtered pork, garlic, and paprika. Sit down in a restaurant and you will be brought a jug of *pitarra*, wine so effervescent and young that they do not even bother to bottle it or keep it for the following year, and a heavy wooden platter of *jamón serrano*, chorizo, and a bewildering variety of other kinds of cured ham and sausage—just to keep a man going until the main course of stewed partridge, braised pheasant, or roast kid arrives.

If you decide to spend a day or two in Mérida—and you would be crazy not to—you will be confronted with those other great conquistadors and builders: the Romans. Here there are aqueducts, bridges, a theater, the ruins of a massive circus, and a statue of the emperor in battle dress, whose every marble muscle has been sculpted with the same sweat and dedication as any bodybuilder's abdomen. There is a coliseum where you can still see the pit that was flooded for aquatic gladiatorial combat and a villa whose mosaic floor proudly depicts the owner in mortal combat with a wild boar that is the size of a young bull—and quite evidently just as male.

"The most powerful man in Europe, in the world, and he just threw it all away!" I was sitting in the bar of the Palace Hotel in Madrid, which happens to be directly across the street from the Cortes, talking to a friend of a friend, Alfonso, who had spent the better part of twenty years climbing one greasy political pole or another. Recently elected a member of the Cortes, he could not contain his incredulity and exasperation at this voluntary relinquishment of power that had taken place four hundred years before. His eyes bulged as he crammed another handful of peanuts into his mouth, and he spluttered, *"Absolutamente tonto! Tonto!* And even worse, he retired to a monastery. After a lifetime spent fighting, he went to live with some monks!" The final proof that the Holy Roman emperor Charles V must have been completely off his trolley. No power. No women. What could he have been thinking? My friend refused to waste any more of his precious time speculating, but added, as he got up to leave, "I have never been to the monastery at

Yuste, but it's on your way to Cáceres, so please go and then tell me he wasn't crazy."

If you approach Extremadura from Madrid, as I did, chances are you will follow a road that takes you through La Vera, a valley so green and lush and overflowing with obvious fertility that it seems to disprove everything you have heard about the harsh character and contours of this part of Spain. But don't be deceived. The fruit trees, festooned with cherries and plums, the tender green asparagus and intensely flavored strawberries that all grow so effortlessly here, are an anomaly, particular to this tiny stretch of the region. In the valley the climate is gentler, streams of clear mountain water rush down the hillsides, irrigating the land and soothing the ear, and even the names of the villages—Jarandilla de la Vera, Villanueva de la Vera—seem to possess a lighthearted musicality. It is the kind of place a man might dream of retiring to—Iberia's answer to Florida. Which is why Charles V ended up there in 1557.

I'm not sure whether the emperor was sane or not, but his retirement home turned out to be unpretentious in the extreme. (Alfonso would have been horrified.) A steep cobbled path led up through some woods, and when I finally reached the top, the monastery's entrance was at the end of a gently sloping ramp. A eucalyptus tree stood guard outside, and after I rang the bell a couple of times, a gentleman, almost as gnarled as the roots of the tree, appeared and began to shuffle me around. Charles V's apartment was built onto the side of the existing monastery; it had been his idea to construct his bedroom so that it overlooked the altar, an architectural feature that his son, Philip II, copied at El Escorial. My guide confided that Charles V loved to fish (don't all retired men?), and then he showed me the very chair (strangely unscathed by the wear and tear of the passing centuries) by the window where he used to sit and cast his line down to the rectangular pool beneath that was specially stocked with fish eager to take the royal bait.

There was an air of melancholy about the whole place—the coffinlike litter that the bedridden emperor traveled about in was propped up in the corner of the dining room, and his study was draped entirely in black velvet—so it was a relief to finally escape into the garden, where I walked down the path behind a baby emperor, who dozed, eyelids twitching, in his stroller as his mother gently fanned him with a huge fig leaf.

The village of Jarandilla de la Vera is only a few miles from the monastery, and it was here that Charles V lived in the Counts of Oropesa's palace while his gloomy apartment at Yuste was being built. And it was here that I spent my first night in Extremadura. We were sitting in the big salon of the palace, which is now a parador, and the manager was pointing to the stone fireplace that dominated the wall behind us.

"When the emperor arrived," she said, "it was already the beginning of winter, and since this was a summer palace, it had no fireplace. So this one was built in two days. Or so they say. Maybe people worked quicker in those days. . . ." With her experience of running a hotel, and construction workers, she was obviously a little skeptical. The salon had a wide balcony, hung with white linen curtains, that overlooked the courtyard, where, as it grew darker, the only sound was the trickle of water into the square stone basin in the center and the soft hooting of owls from the surrounding trees. Later that night, as I walked back to my room, a thick mist had drifted down from the hills, blocking out the moon and the stars and diffusing the light from the metal lanterns that stood at the four corners of the patio.

The next morning, I got up early—the mist was still there, but the owls must have gone to bed—and started to drive south toward Trujillo and Cáceres. People in Spain who know the region will tell you that Cáceres is the (relatively) undiscovered jewel in its crown, that the interior decorators and Americans (a frightening combination) have already arrived in Trujillo, that the only thing in Mérida worth bothering with are its Roman ruins (the place has gone downhill ever since they left), and that at the Monastery of Guadalupe there are only eleven monks left (a shameful reflection on the state of the Catholic Church in Spain). What they didn't tell me was that I would not meet another foreigner the entire time I was there (not a single American nor a solitary interior decorator), that in Guadalupe I would discover Zurbaráns I never knew existed, that the Museum of Roman Antiquities in Mérida happens to be one of the most extraordinary examples of modern architecture in the world, and that in a back street in that same town I would have lunch in a restaurant where the chef is an unsung genius. But then, what is the point of travel if there are no surprises?

Trujillo is dominated by the spirit of Francisco Pizarro. There is the famous bronze statue in the Plaza Mayor, and if you climb up the winding alleyways toward the ruined castle that overlooks the town, you will arrive at his museum. The man who was born poor and illegitimate and who conquered the Inca empire with only 180 soldiers, before being murdered by one of them (his dying gesture was to trace the sign of the cross in the dirt with his own blood), is something of a demigod in his hometown. In 1992, the local grandees put together the museum, and when a few years later Pizarro's body was exhumed in Lima, they agreed that nothing would be more appropriate than to have his head "reconstructed" and a bust made from this true-to-life/death portrait of their local hero.

"And so an American forensic scientist was found, whose job it was first to positively identify the bones and then to create the head," explained Gregorio, who happens to be the cousin of one of the gentlemen who sponsored the project and who had invited me to have lunch when I arrived in Trujillo. We were sitting at Doña Concha's, where menus don't exist, the slightly bubbly house red wine is served in green pottery jugs, and the roast suckling pig comes to the table when it's ready. Post-*jamón* and -chorizo, but prepork, Gregorio lit another cigarette and continued with his story:

"There was a fancy reception for the unveiling of the bust, but the only problem was that the demigod turned out to look more like Quasimodo. The Marqués de la Conquista, who is Pizarro's descendant in a rather circuitous way—but we won't delve too deeply into that—was appalled, and the bust has never been seen since. But what did they expect? The conquistadors were Machiavellian soldiers of fortune, not movie stars. And you don't win wars by looking like some homosexual male model: You win them by eating food like this." He grinned and helped himself to another crisp, testosterone-packed layer of crackling.

In the afternoon, I climbed up to explore the castle. Huge and square and built with the local stone shot through with sparkling bauxite sequins, the deserted central courtyard contained a single orange tree and a mission bell, which seemed like a double echo of Mexico's open-air churches, where the Indians were baptized, and of the early California missions surrounded by orange groves. I walked through three Moorish horseshoe arches, which framed the view of the surrounding plain like a series of keyholes, and then went up some stone steps to a parapet where I could look out at the swallows and still hear, but not see, the water splashing far below in the fountain of the Plaza Mayor.

Outside, I paused in front of a sculpture far more abstract but just as hideous as the demigod's head: It consisted of two or three jagged rocks and was, Gregorio assured me, a monument to the *mestizaje*—the mingling of the blood of the Old and New Worlds. This concept is an article of faith in Mexico, and although it has less immediate meaning in Spain, in Extremadura you are constantly aware of the connections between what was once the Spanish empire and the mother country. Most obviously in the names—Alburquerque, Los Alamos, Medellin, Cartagena—but also in the similarity between the landscape and that of Mexico and the American Southwest. And then there are the treasures that flowed back to Spain: the gold and silver; the more humble, edible booty, such as chocolate, corn, potatoes, turkeys, tomatoes; and the extraordinary works of art. In El Escorial there is a bishop's miter decorated with Aztec feathers, and when a shipment of Aztec artifacts was sent by Cortés in 1520 to the emperor Charles V at his Flemish court, they went by way of Brussels, where Albrecht Dürer was the first European artist allowed to gaze upon these strange and beautiful objects. Obviously impressed, he wrote, "I saw the things that were sent to the King from the golden lands . . . it is a marvel to behold. Never in my life have I seen anything that made my heart happier."

Dusk is the best time to arrive in Cáceres. It is then that you truly feel you have fallen, like Alice in Wonderland, into a time tunnel and have left the twentieth century far behind. In keeping with the spirit of the town, I abandoned my car and started to walk up a dimly lit cobbled alley—past a sandstone doorway where the family's coat of arms displayed over the doorway was, appropriately enough, two pigs standing on their substantial hind legs, the better to feast on an oak tree laden with acorns—and finally arrived at a palace painted the color of dried bull's blood: El Parador de Cáceres. After a twenty-first-century shower and a nineteenth-century glass of Manzanilla, I decided to wander through the Old Town before dinner.

As in Trujillo, the conquistador palaces, the churches and convents, have all been meticulously restored and probably look even better now than they did in the sixteenth century. V. S. Pritchett, the English writer who first came to this part of Spain in the 1920s, described the churches of Cáceres as "places of large and simple yellow stone, blunt soldiers all of them, with earthy Baroque ornament standing out like veins on an old, wine-drinking body." They have not changed, but there was something missing. No noise, no people, no mess, no smells; none of the incidental sounds of everyday life being lived. I walked down deserted streets, looked up at the beautiful facades, and never have I yearned more to hear children squabbling or the inane buzz of a TV set, or to smell garlic frying in cheap olive oil, or to see some tattered washing hanging from a crooked line. The only sign of life I came across was outside a church, where four elderly men were sitting on a stone bench, mesmerized by the antics of a fifth, who was quite obviously the Chaplin of Cáceres. First he did a little soft-shoe shuffle, then he twirled around and took his hat off, and by the time he started on his monologue, his friends were utterly transfixed. *"Qué hombre,"* I heard one of them mutter admiringly under his breath, his eyes half-closed and a beatific smile lighting up the Audenesque wrinkles on his face.

The reason for Cáceres's mummified beauty turned out to be quite simple. The Old Town was built high up on the hill, for defense, so that when it grew, the newer part spread out in the valley below, and the two halves never melded together. The result was a kind of social apartheid, with the palaces and churches up above and the shops, banks, offices, restaurants, and bars down below. I walked down some steps, imagining that I could hear the cozy hum of traffic in the distance, turned a corner, and saw the comforting, cheesy glow of neon lights. A few more steps, and there were real live people sitting at café tables, shouting at their kids, flirting, gossiping, and watching the evening *paseo*. I ordered an espresso, and the waiter who brought it, a man whose cheek bones hinted at Gypsy blood and whose eyes suggested a life of quiet defeat, offered me another explanation for the ghost town I had just walked through.

"Those buildings you saw still belong to the same families who built them, but they are so rich that they have lots of other palaces in other parts of the country, so they hardly ever bother to come here." He did not sound bitter; that was just the way the world was—some people work in bars, and others spend their lives driving fast cars from one house to another. . . . What can a man do?

Extremadura has always been poor. Why else would so many of its men have been so eager to risk their lives across the ocean in an unknown and hostile world? The land is unforgiving, the climate harsh, and that spare beauty which takes your breath away today took plenty of Extremeños' breath away—permanently—in the past. The population has always drifted toward the big cities in search of a living, and it was surely not by accident that Buñuel chose Las Hurdes, a remote, poverty-stricken area near the Portuguese border, as the setting for his savage documentary film *Land Without Bread*, made in 1932. Although things have obviously improved immeasurably since then, the unemployment rate is still the highest in the country (thirty percent), and the region depends heavily on subsidies from Madrid and the European Union.

I arrived in Mérida late in the evening, and in a bar where the walls were papered with photographs of long-dead bullfighters and the TV showed nothing but an endless loop of Mighty Morphin Power Rangers cartoons, I listened as a group of men discussed—what else?—politics.

"It's like living on an Indian reservation. The people collect the handouts from Madrid, but then there is no work for them," a local journalist exploded to a colleague from Madrid as they both tore apart the policies of the chief executive of Extremadura, Juan Carlos Ibarra. The argument was complicated: complicated by brandy and then further complicated, for me, by my imperfect grasp of the Spanish language. A traveling salesman from Valencia, a handsome devil with a neatly trimmed mustache and sporting a navy blazer with gold buttons, joined them, ordered another round of drinks, and produced some Cuban cigars—*"Qué hombre!"*—and the discussion became even more agitated. Ibarra was "power crazed," a caudillo who had told the Madrid journalist that very afternoon, "Electricity generated in Extremadura belongs to Extremadura, not to Spain." And now—this was the final straw—he was proposing to hold a referendum in defiance of the government in Madrid! More shouting, lots more phrases bracketed with upside-down exclamation points, more *copas* of Fundador, more cigars, more espressos. I looked at my watch, saw that it was after 3 A.M., and made my excuses, and my escape, and went back to the parador and to bed.

If you walk to the central market in Mérida, keep on going straight, make a right on a narrow street that is bordered with orange trees, and follow that road uphill, after about ten minutes you will find yourself in ancient Rome. The Romans were the conquistadors of their time. They came, they saw, they conquered—but most important, they built. Theaters, bridges, aqueducts, coliseums, villas, and a still-functioning sewer system. Climb up to the highest seats in the house and look down at the stage of the theater, where concerts, ballets, and operas are still performed, and you will have some inkling of the grandeur that was Rome. Climb down and walk onto the stage and study the statues that stand between the pink, blue, and green marble columns, and you will understand that humanity has not changed at all in two thousand years. The goddess Ceres is as solid as Picasso's portrait of Gertrude Stein, a study in female serenity, her rotund body representing the bounty of the earth, her bovine face expressing the quiet, contained complacency of woman as the creator of life. To her right is Venus, the other side of the female mirror. Although her head and right arm are missing, she is still ravishing. Her waist demands to be caressed, her divinely proportioned breasts are impervious to the laws of gravity, and her rounded thighs are bare, except for a piece of fabric, so delicate it could be chiffon, that she modestly drapes across them with her left hand.

And then there was the man I could not take my eyes off. He was much bigger than me and stood, almost naked, at the edge of the stage. Like Venus, he was missing his head and both arms, but, as with her, this did nothing to diminish his allure. (Could it be that we are so used to seeing Greek and Roman statues minus limbs and heads that our eyes and brains have made a subtle adjustment and are willing to include amputees in this particular beauty pageant?) His marble body was irresistible, perfect in every detail—the shoulders, the muscular legs, and even his belly button. . . . It was then that I realized I had crossed some pornographic Rubicon and that an appreciation of Roman art had been displaced by carnal desire. It was that simple. I had actually allowed myself to wonder what it might be like to sleep with this man. Clearly I was in need of some refreshment, distraction, the company of real people, instead of unattainable marble gods.

The excitable local newspaperman of the previous evening had told me that there was only one good restaurant in the whole of Mérida, called Casa Nano, and that the owner was a friend of his. He had picked up a paper napkin and scrawled the address on it and suggested that we have lunch there the next day. Hidden away in a back street, Casa Nano was easy to miss. Heavy lace curtains excluded all daylight, and even though the sun at the Roman theater had been almost unbearable, here it was as cool and murky as the huge aquarium that dominated the front room. Fish. Eels. Lobsters. Crabs. Not a pig or a goat in sight. We sat down, and the long discussion began: What was the chef cooking that day? Where did he get his langoustines? And his Torta del Casar, was it fresh? And then there was the wine to consider. A Ribera del Duero was finally chosen, because the bodega was so small that it produced only a couple of hundred cases a year of this particular vintage. I begged for fish, any fish, and was rewarded with a grilled *rodaballo*, which was like Dover sole, only better, and came with a gently stewed confit of red and yellow peppers. The creamy sheep's milk Torta del Casar followed a salad of ripe tomatoes and translucent slices of red onion. Simple. Perfectly proportioned. And, yes, it was the best meal I had in Extremadura.

The road from Mérida to Guadalupe crosses the wide-open plain and then slowly climbs up into the steep, wooded hills that surround the monastery and shrine to the Virgin of Guadalupe. If you are not a Catholic, it is hard to grasp her supreme importance in the Hispanic world: She is the mother of all Virgins and was officially declared Virgin Queen of the Hispanic World by King Alfonso XIII in 1928. (To my English-educated ears, this sounded a bit like being Head Girl at school, but I'm sure it isn't at all.) I remember once, a few years ago outside Mexico City, watching with increasing alarm as an elderly woman crossed, on her bleeding knees, the vast plaza that surrounds the Basilica at Guadalupe. Christopher Columbus, when he was delivered safely from a storm in the Azores in 1493, swore that he would name the first land in the New World Guadalupe and that he would make a pilgrimage to the Virgin upon his safe return to Spain. Both of which he duly did. The first Indians to be brought back to Spain were baptized here, a portion of all the wealth that came from the New World made its way to the Virgin, and Don John of Austria presented her with Ali Pasha's stern lantern after the Battle of Lepanto. Even today there is a steady stream of pilgrims who come to gaze upon the nut-brown doll in her elaborate dresses (changed regularly by the monks), who presides over the church from her special glass-fronted case high above the altar.

As in Washington and Hollywood, this is a one-industry town, and that industry is the Virgin. Guadalupe itself has great charm, with its winding streets, a spectacular parador that used to be a hospital (the first autopsy in Spain was performed here in the fifteenth century), and its old shops, where the Ajax sits side by side on the shelf with bottles of homemade chestnut liquor and the plastic watering cans are festooned with garlands of dried red chile peppers. There are a few good restaurants, where the tender roast kid comes from the surrounding hills. But your reason for making the journey here is to enter the Virgin's labyrinth and to feast your eyes upon her treasures.

The contents of the monastery are as jumbled up as the stuff in one of the village stores. I came across crudely painted ex-votos (children falling out of windows and being saved by the Virgin, terrible fires whose flames have been quenched by her intervention) next to exquisite stone carvings. Down the hallway from the sacristy, which is crammed full of spare and elegant Zurbaráns, there are hideous nineteenth-century saints with rolling eyes and too much blush on their cheeks. There are scraps of cloth from the Virgin's robe, a stone from the family home in Nazareth, and a *capa rica* (ecclesiastical vestment) that looks like Christian Lacroix's idea of a Halloween costume. The cape, worn for funeral masses, is black velvet and covered with skeletons, skulls, bones, and coffins, all painstakingly embroidered, by long-dead monks, in heavy gold thread.

It was a bewilderingly eclectic collection, where the quality seemed secondary to the purpose—which is, of course, the greater glorification of God. In this vast and sprawling place, where once thousands of monks lived and served God, there are now only eleven left. I saw one of them sitting on a choir stall seat, swinging his short, chubby legs just like a bored child, and I overheard him saying plaintively to a middle-aged Japanese lady, *"Solamente once, solamente once,"* and I felt that all he really wanted was for us to go so that he could stop being one of the jumble of objects on display.

When I left Extremadura and returned to the softer, sweeter worlds of Madrid and Manhattan, I discovered that the images of the journey I had just taken meant nothing to anyone else. This is not one of those places, like Tuscany, Hong Kong, Venice, or Paris, that everyone has an opinion about or, even worse, a story that has no point or punch line and is told only to prove that they too are travelers across the world's stage. In Madrid, people politely wondered why I had chosen to visit this particular region of Spain, and in New York the response was a blunt "Extrawhere? Never heard of it." Which is always proof that you went to the right place. Nobody seemed to know about the granite head of the man who had conquered the Amazon and died there before he was fifty-six, or about the green-tinged gorges where vultures built their nests, or about the Roman coliseum where the Moors staged the first bullfights in Spain. Nobody had seen the creamy alabaster windows in the cathedral in Plasencia, or the white-robed Hieronoymite monks in the sacristy at Guadalupe, or the headless torso of the Roman god who stood guard over the theater in Mérida for two thousand years. Nobody had heard of the caudillo who was intent upon carving out his own fiefdom in this unforgiving land on the very edge of Spain. Nobody had listened to the owls in the trees of the Counts of Oropesa's palace in Jarandilla de la Vera, or seen the swallows swooping around the ruined castle in Trujillo. None of which bothered me at all, because it meant that my memories were mine and mine alone. Which, incidentally, is one of the more secret—and selfish— pleasures of travel.

1998

Dreams of the Orient

by

DAN HOFSTADTER

With his inimitable flair, the elderly Turkish writer Celik Gulersoy has described the Istanbul of his parents' day. It was a city, he tells us, of "isolated, lonely, sparsely populated districts. . . . While Kabakci Mustafa led his mercenaries from the forts at the entrance of the Bosphorus to storm various points in the city, a lady was enjoying a pleasant afternoon nap in her waterside residence, with the reflection of the waves rippling on the ceiling, and a civil servant was smelling the hyacinths in his garden by the Golden Horn, completely oblivious of what was happening elsewhere. . . . At night the houses and gardens would be bathed in moonlight, and on summer evenings the only sound would be the croaking of frogs." Like everything else in the Balkans, the Istanbul of today is a shadow of its former self. But some perfume of that bygone era, purified of the stench of gunpowder and blood, can still be found in the gardens, lanes, and fountain courts of Yildiz Park, on the hillside above Ciragan Palace.

Yildiz was the mistress of a sultan. She is believed to have lived in seclusion on this wooded slope and to have bequeathed her name to it. But in Turkish, *yildiz* also means "star" and "dahlia," and today the park is admired for its vast beds of dahlias, which stretch away toward the knolls on the far side of the Bosphorus. There are still quiet glades here, and ponds, and playing fountains. All but unknown to foreign visitors, Yildiz Park is a place where newlyweds come to have their pictures taken, and in the corner of these pictures you can sometimes make out a sliver of shimmering sea.

It is often said that the first years of a monarch's reign resemble a honeymoon, and something of this nuptial aura surrounded the Padishah Abdulhamid II's encampment here in 1877. Like the great sultans of the past, Abdulhamid wished to contribute something fine to the architecture of the capital. He decided to put a new palace complex in this park, and he commissioned a number of architects, both local and foreign, to erect an array of buildings on its grounds. These creations— the airy mansion known as the Malta Kiosk, the vaguely alpine Sale Kiosk, the Italianate armory, and various secretariats, guard lodges, and kiosks—illustrate a fanciful chapter in the story of Ottoman design. We call it (with a wink) "Occidentalism," since we sense an intention to capture the drama of the exotic West. But regardless of the form such borrowings took, the site itself was drama enough: With those sweeping views across to the headlands of Asia, no builder could go completely wrong. For a while, apace with the new construction, a spirit of optimism, of excitement, prevailed at court. And even after the honeymoon aura had begun to dissipate—even after it had completely died away—strollers could still enjoy the shade trees and the flowers and the sultan's aviaries and his zoo with its scores of gazelles and mouflons, its giraffes and chamois and monkeys, its pair of zebras. If you were lucky, you might catch sight of the Padishah himself, bending to feed a tidbit to one of his prized highland goats.

Some years ago, on a day of torrential rain, I was sitting in the Istanbul Library, immersed in Georges Dorys's *The Private Life of Abdulhamid*, when I felt a tap on my shoulder. A man with the face of an old pasha, indulged and indulgent, with tiny gleams of obstinacy in the corners of his eyes, peered down at me. Celik Gulersoy—or Celik Bey, as he is honorifically and universally known—was an assiduous presence in those precincts, since he was the library's founder. Aware of my interests, he suggested a few titles that he felt might prove amusing. He also offered to take me to see the Malta Kiosk, one of the pavilions at Yildiz that he was in the midst of restoring.

I suppose that Celik Bey was then in his mid-sixties, but he still presided over the Touring and Automobile Club of Turkey as if it were his private pashalic. Followed by a corps of rigidly correct male secretaries, we were driven up the weaving road to Abdulhamid's old estate, past scenes of heartrending dereliction—half-gutted rows of Ottoman houses, pitilessly gashed hillsides, new tower blocks that loomed like the ruins of ancient penitentiaries. Then, as we passed through the park gate, the scenery changed abruptly, as if carried into view by a rotating stage. Leafy alleys winding toward impassive facades gave intimations that a high old civilization, or at least the husk of one, lingered on in this vicinity. "I have saved what I could," said Celik Bey grimly. His eyes were the color of the storm clouds overhead.

Celik Bey is not only a writer, he is also the most eminent architectural preservationist in Turkey. Trained as a lawyer, he had the sensible idea of salvaging decaying Ottoman buildings by finding a commercial use for them. I knew of his struggle against Adnan Menderes, the brutally modernizing premier; I had heard, too, about his long duel with Bedrettin Dalan, the masterful former mayor of Istanbul who did so much to tie the city's traffic into the fantastic cat's cradle in which it now finds itself. But the Celik Bey I was meeting was different: He had acquired a sort of iron wistfulness and seemed disposed to admit that his life's battle had ended in an honorable draw.

Yildiz resembled an English park—a place to get agreeably lost in. Grottoes and folly-like structures lurked in the middle distance, half-screened by tousled trees. Apparently the buildings of the inner court had been converted into the headquarters of an Islamic research center.

From beside a cypress copse rose the Malta Kiosk, whose name was an enigma to Celik Bey ("The island was never a possession of ours") and whose elongated neoclassical order—white arcades and pilasters picked out in white against a muted green—might be described as late Victorian. Crossing a wide marble dais strewn with tea tables and chairs, we went inside. Celik Bey's conservation trust had by now completely restored the lofty reception halls, and he gestured with satisfaction at the mirror-bright floors and overhanging loggias.

We sat and talked for an hour in the mansion's sumptuous upper floor, where he kept an office, and had tea with sweet cakes. Once, when the mists lifted, we glimpsed, through the rain-washed blossoms of a fruit tree, a tramp steamer plying its way along the distant Bosphorus.

As I made my way back down to the city from Yildiz that afternoon, my thoughts returned to George Dorys. Precisely how, I wondered, had that seductive writer gained entry to the harem of Abdulhamid? I confess that from that moment to this, the question hasn't stopped puzzling me: It's like an old tune whose first bars run in my head but whose ending I can never work out.

Consider that the only men allowed into the harem, excepting the sultan himself, were the palace eunuchs. Visitors were advised to rid their thoughts of any wish to see the women's apartments, and imperial couriers were halted at the gates. It is always possible that M. Dorys disguised himself as a woman. It is also possible that he was a hermaphrodite, for he lived in an age, the fin de siècle, when hermaphrodites were privileged beings. But these explanations do not convince; no explanation convinces.

Yet I have just now been rereading M. Dorys's description of the harem at Yildiz, and it has the ring of truth. I persist in believing that he was an eyewitness, and a faithful one. By 1900, Yildiz was a domain quite literally in extremis. It was not only that the palace stood at the remotest confines of Europe, so that if you'd walked much farther to the east you'd have fallen off the continent and into the sea. It was also that Abdulhamid, who was deposed by the Young Turks in 1909, was the last sultan to rule despotically over the Ottoman Empire, the last Muslim to maintain a grand harem on European soil. An aroma of spoilage, luxurious and putrid, hung over his feminine establishment of three hundred souls. Naturally, M. Dorys tells us much that we expect to hear: that the harem women liked to dance; that they played with dolls, including dolls that swam; that they intrigued among themselves; that they reclined on sofas and followed with their eyes the plumes of blue smoke from their cigarettes; that they toyed with their prayer beads, doted upon sweetmeats and flowers, and favored a scent compounded of musk and violet. But we do not expect to hear that they used no eyeliner, "on the plea of precaution against poison"; nor that they followed "the tyrannical fashions of Paris" and wore silk or cotton dresses with bustles and hip pads. And M. Dorys sounds a queerly authentic note when he says that their favorite amusements were bicycling and photography. We can only regret that no pictures have survived from what must have been a sanctum within sanctum: the harem darkroom.

I have said that Abdulhamid's honeymoon with his realm went sour, but I haven't said how sour. It's perhaps enough to observe that though he knew by heart the protocol of the Divan, as the state chamber was called, he ignored the etiquette of happiness and made many of his people unhappy with him—those who survived his sulks and tantrums. M. Dorys notes that although Abdulhamid had in his park hundreds of pairs of parrots and doves, he had no carrier pigeons, fearing that conspirators might make use of them. The tyrant was beset by a persecution mania, which got the best of his manners and, eventually, his mind. Seeing all his subjects as potential regicides, he built two walls around his palace, filled it with telescopes to scan the horizon, compiled a photographic archive of thirty thousand suspect faces, and encouraged his officials to spy on one another. By degrees, the interior of Yildiz became a faithful simulacrum of his crazed, suspicious brain. "It is not a palace, it's a labyrinth," said one of the Young

Turks who inspected Yildiz after the sultan's fall. Yet none of Abdulhamid's precautions could long forestall that deafening hour of April 24, 1909, when the ladies of the harem, learning that their residence was surrounded by ten thousand mutinous Macedonians, screamed together in unison.

In these pages we have decided to speak only of romance, however, and there was nothing romantic about the doom of Abdulhamid. We have no desire to go into the matter: It's a tale for another day.

1997

Heart of Wildness

by

RIAN MALAN

Bill won't like my saying this, but he was beset by the jitters as we flew into Uganda. Our photographer, and a nice suburban guy with three kids and a propensity to vacation in France or the Bahamas, he'd been trawling the Net for background and hadn't liked what he found. The U.S. State Department had issued a travel warning that spoke of troop movements in national parks and banditry in the Mountains of the Moon. Hospitals were primitive, roads dangerous, and the germ threat so intense that members of President Clinton's party, which had passed through five days ahead of us, were advised to not kiss anyone and to keep their lips pursed in the shower. On top of this, Bill was reeling from the side effects of tropical disease inoculations and the psychic reverberations of a *New Yorker* article about some crazed rebels on the north bank of the Nile who believed that magic could protect them from bullets and could turn rocks into hand grenades. As we came in to land at Entebbe, his refrain was, "What the hell are we letting ourselves in for?"

What indeed? Viewed from the sensible perspective of, say, the average European or American, Uganda is one of the last places one would wish to visit, which is probably why so few do. Five years ago, there were hardly any tourists at all. Last year, a mere four thousand chanced it, and most just climbed a volcano, saw some gorillas, and got the hell out again. I mean, we're talking about a country where the power fails every second day, where AIDS is rampant and bugs are known to lay eggs under your skin or crawl up your nose and eat your brain; a country that was once a charnel house in its own right, with the killing fields of Rwanda on one side, the famine grounds of Sudan on the other, and armies of wild Karimojong tribesmen crossing the frontier on massed cattle raids, according to a newspaper we bought at the airport. It was more than enough to invoke in any white man "a sense of undefinable oppression."

Those are the words of Winston Churchill, who arrived in Entebbe in 1907 in a frame of mind not entirely dissimilar to Bill's and, to some extent, my own. He'd had a splendid time on the trans-Kenya railroad, but something about Uganda unsettled him, something he couldn't quite put a finger on. It could be the altitude, he said, or the insects, or maybe even the unbearable beauty of his first sight of Entebbe, a cluster of red-roofed bungalows on Lake Victoria. "It was too good to be true," he wrote in *My African Journey*. "It is too good to be true. Behind its glittering mask, Entebbe wears a sinister aspect."

The young British MP had come at a bad moment, it turned out. There were rebels on the north bank of the Nile, and the countryside was devastated by pestilence. Man-eating leopards prowled the jungle fringes, and the very air seemed full of malignancy. "A cut will not heal," he wrote. "A scratch festers. Even a small wound becomes a running sore." Pioneer colonists were so depressed that two had committed suicide, and even Winnie was reduced to morbid pronouncements about the curse that seemed to lie over this "curious garden of sunshine and deadly nightshade."

That said, Churchill donned his pith helmet, whistled up the porters, and set forth on safari. He and his party traveled five hundred miles in the next thirty days, trudging across savanna, bicycling down forest paths, steaming across pristine lakes under cool blue skies that were full of waterfowl and fish eagles. He began to notice things that had eluded his first glance—"birds as bright as butterflies, butterflies as big as birds," a mad profusion of flowers, forests to rival those that once covered England. He saw great herds of elephant, plains covered with game, thunderstorms "wheeling in vivid splendor across the night horizon." The natives were friendly and intelligent, the hunting superlative. By the time he reached Nimule, on the far side of the country, Churchill was enchanted. The rest of East Africa was interesting, he wrote, "but the Kingdom of Uganda is a fairy tale. You climb up a railway instead of a beanstalk, and at the end of it there is a wonderful new world."

Ninety years later, we came down from the sky, loaded our misgivings into a Land Cruiser, and took off on a journey that carried us to a similar conclusion. Uganda is a happy-go-lucky calypso song of a country, where people's pain is enormously sweetened by the bounty of nature. The soils are rich, the lakes teem with fish, and the climate is an endless summer. Ugandan peasants harvest three crops a year, where most Africans can't count on any; you can feed an entire family on an acre or so, just sitting in the shade and watching the bananas grow. This eases the desperation that might otherwise obtain in a country so poor and so recently devastated and makes it possible for people to be nice to each other, and, yes, to visitors. We were plied with beer in Kampala bars, given small gifts of fruit by peasants whose clothes were in tatters. We sang in the shower, and never got sick. We ate *boo* and *dudu* at roadside stands, and lived to tell the tale. We traveled the country from end to end, and everything we saw was beautiful. In Uganda, even the cows are breathtaking.

We began to see them about five hours out of Entebbe, lovely Ankole cattle with horns like lyres, each with its own name, apparently, and a personality much analyzed by its doting owner. This I gathered from *Sowing the Mustard Seed*, the autobiography of Yoweri Museveni, cattle farmer, soldier, and Uganda's state president. I'd bought a copy in the town of Mbarara, and it was fascinating: An earnest young revolutionary takes to the bush in 1980 with a handful of guns and twenty-nine men, hell-bent on perpetrating yet another Socialist catastrophe. But something happens to him during his long fight for power. He abandons the idea that all Africa's miseries are the white man's fault. He becomes an apostle of free markets. He starts talking about discipline, law and order, and the need for institutions based on the history, culture, and psyche of African people.

After toppling Milton Obote in 1986, Museveni starts dismantling the Ugandan state, or at least whittling away at it. He takes power from the center, gives it to "revolutionary councils" at village level. He slashes the bureaucracy, privatizes state assets, deregulates everything he can. The results are miraculous in African terms: Peace returns, inflation vanishes, and the economy starts galloping ahead at ten percent per annum. Museveni is hailed as Africa's savior, a Moses come to lead the Dark Continent out of its nightmare of violence, starvation, and economic decay. He's a dictator, to be sure, but Ugandans like Tony Sukuma, our ebullient driver, couldn't give a damn.

"People look around," he said, "and they see it's working. They say, this is the right path for the moment. Wherever you go, people are happy." It turns out that Tony spent a decade in Museveni's army fighting for a cause that came down to common decency: Down with the bloody tyrants who stole everything they could lay their hands on, and away with the soldiers who looted your village, raped your sisters, and smashed your head in if you stood in their way. He was wounded twice, but remains enormously pleased with the result of his sacrifice. "I don't want any stupid changes that will take away the peace and stability," he said. "If anybody threatens to do this, I will fight again. After all, if it wasn't for this peace, you guys would not be here, would you?"

And what a pity that would have been, because we would never have seen the sight that awaited us at the end of the road, which terminated on the summit of a sharp promontory in Queen Elizabeth National Park. Here stood the Mweya Safari Lodge, suspended in the sky between two bodies of water. Porters ushered us through the lobby, past a giant pair of elephant tusks and onto a veranda that commanded one of the most spectacular views in Africa—Lake Edward on one side, the Kazinga Channel on the other, and before us, the Mountains of the Moon, their flanks clad with mysterious forests, their snowcapped peaks lost today in cloud. We collapsed into wicker chairs, struck dumb by the sight of an alpine landscape on the equator. Waiters brought tall glasses of passion fruit juice. A lanky, bearded fanatic sat down beside us and started jabbering about birds.

Malcolm Wilson spent his asthmatic boyhood staring out of fogged-up windows at shivering sparrows in rainy English gardens. From such beginnings grew a lifelong obsession that eventually landed him here, where he was trying to establish a bird-watching center. "It's a gold mine, if you understand birding," he said. "We hold the world record for a one-day species count—397 species in a single day. There are 558 species in this park alone." He began to enumerate them: fish eagles, Palearctic ospreys, Goliath herons, the papyrus gonolek, the bare-faced go-away bird, and the legendary shoebill, a huge pterodactyl-like creature with yellow eyes and an imbecilic expression, almost impossible to see on account of its preference for impenetrable swamps. "I've spent fifteen thousand pounds of my own money trying to set this thing up," cried the birdman, "and I can't go on alone. I need help and nobody gives a damn."

Neither did I, quite frankly; birding has always struck me as boring. On the other hand, I'd never met a birder quite like Malcolm Wilson. His description of flies hatching on the lake below was inspirational. It happened often, he said, usually in the morning. Flies began to hatch and rise into the air in clouds so dense that the water appeared to be smoking. Soon an apocalyptic feeding frenzy would be under way in the sky above, with millions of swallows snatching insects out of the air and in turn falling prey to raptors that came diving out of the sun like F-16s and—*thwack*—annihilated a lesser bird in an explosion of feathers. "It's fantastic," cried the birdman, who was acting all this out with windmilling arms and a grin that was slightly lopsided as the result of an encounter with a buffalo on a footpath a hundred yards away. Irritated, it had tossed him a few times, butted him black and blue, and knelt on his face, knocking his teeth askew.

We glanced around apprehensively, and sure enough, beasts were converging from all directions. There were warthogs in the flower beds. Marabou storks sauntered across the lawns like old, stooped men in evening dress, crops dangling down their chests like scarlet cravats. A great rump of reddish brown flesh broke the horizon, and a hippo rose into view, strolling up from the lake to feed on the daisies. We changed tables, ordered beers, and watched the sun set. The birdman observed, apropos of nothing in particular, that one of the best things about this place was that you could sometimes sit here at night and watch tracer bullets arcing across the distant mountainside, where government soldiers were hunting rebels and bandits.

But we don't really want to talk about that, do we? Nah, we're on holiday. We want to repair to the dining room, where waiters are serving dinner in uniforms that seem to have been in mothballs since Uganda's fifties tourist heyday: white shirts, narrow black ties, FBI slacks, and black-rimmed spectacles, like a conclave of black Clark Kents. On the menu tonight, as always, there is fish—fillets of tilapia, hauled out of the lake this morning, deep-fried and garnished with lemon. It is an excellent fish, at least the equal of trout or salmon, especially if taken at high African altitude and washed down with cold Ugandan beer. I was groping for a light for my postprandial smoke when a waiter presented me with a good omen: a box of Double Happiness safety matches. I lit up and sat back to savor my coffee, feeling like Winston Churchill at the end of his stay.

Father of several and husband to two, Wilfred Megenyi hadn't been paid in ninety days, and worse yet, a snake had just been extracted from the hideously bloated leg of his brother, who had stepped into a black magic trap on a footpath. None of this could be vouched for, exactly, but it was the talk of Mantana Camp, a day's trek north of Lake Edward. We arrived at sunset, slept under canvas, and set forth before dawn into the Kibale Forest National Park, where Wilfred worked as a ranger. A luminously nice guy, he managed a smile at the sight of us, pulled up his Wellies, and led the way into the dim jungle, which was full of vines and spiderwebs and trees that soared to three hundred feet, stabilized by side roots resembling the fins of Apollo rockets.

Churchill loved the forests of Uganda, filling pages of his diary with descriptions of their "awful fecundity" and the "intense convulsions of life and death" under way in the rich humus underfoot. We were looking for creatures more elevated—our first cousins, the chimpanzees, which abound in Kibale Forest. We trudged through a fairyland of green glens and dells, but alas, the chimpanzees were elsewhere, and Wilfred was reduced to giving us a compensatory lecture on bush medicine: this plant to cool fever, that one to bind the gut; *katimboro* bark to engender a monstrous erection, and the flowers of the *omunyara* tree to lubricate the vagina on the receiving end of it. He cupped a hand over his nose and emitted a bizarre nasal whine, imitating a duiker ewe in her birth throes. Moments later, a troop of blue monkeys came crashing through the treetops, hoping to feast on the placenta. "Where did you learn that?" I asked. "Oh," he replied, "I used to be a poacher."

Wilfred seemed to take the chimp no-show as a personal failure, which is perhaps why he invited us back to his shamba, which lay out on the sun-drenched savanna. He showed us his mud hut, his wives, and his many sweet little offspring. We met the neighbors and inspected his plantation of coffee and *matoke* bananas, which are picked green and require cooking. In a swamp at the bottom of his garden, he'd built a fishpond that was stocked with tilapia. He lopped some leaves off a cassava plant and chucked them in. The water began to boil.

It was a great little fish farm, as fish farms go, but Wilfred had no sure way of getting the fish out of it, save for a hook fashioned from rusting wire. I delved into my luggage and found some tackle for him. He gave me a pineapple, profusely apologizing that it was the only one he had. I promised to send him some pumpkin seeds. He pressed his precious fish-farming manual into my reluctant hands. Not to be outdone, I tried to give him a few banknotes, but he refused them, so I had to slip them to a wife on the sly. It seemed the least I could do for a family that hadn't seen cash since Christmas.

Why not? Wilfred wasn't quite sure, but most national park staff seemed to be in similar straits. I made inquiries when we reached Kampala a few days later, but it was very confusing. Some said the rangers' pay had been diverted into the patriotic frenzy of street-cleaning and weed-slashing that preceded the recent visit of President Clinton. Others claimed it was lost. A few maintained that it had been stolen. Nobody seemed very worried. It was just one of those Ugandan things, apparently, like unreliable phones, bad roads, and perpetual rebellions on the periphery.

I must confess to being a bit nonplussed by these manifestations of the African ordinary. Uganda was supposed to be the New Jerusalem, the epicenter of the much-touted African Renaissance. In my imagination, it was a country of straight backs and rolled-up sleeves, with humming assembly lines, spartan leaders, and children schooled to pick up litter while singing cheerful songs about honesty and self-reliance. I was a bit dismayed to find Kampala somewhat run-down and beset by turmoil. Slack maintenance had claimed the lives of six doctors, drowned when a bridge collapsed. The sewers in some suburbs were not working. "Godfathers" of the ruling party were allegedly engaged in various swindles, and someone had just hurled a hand grenade into a crowded Kampala restaurant, killing three Burundese businessmen.

I hastened to the scene the next morning, but most passersby had no idea who had done it, or why, and the rest shrugged as if to say, relax man. I walked over to State House, hoping for an interview with President Museveni, but he was in London, so I just wandered around, taking in the sights. Downtown was the standard African jungle of office blocks and traffic chaos, but the markets were full of food, the police were friendly, and there was no discernible undercurrent of tension.

On the contrary—the mood of the city seemed astonishingly open and cheerful, considering that Uganda is a one-party state. The newspapers were full of gleeful accounts of the latest government debacles. Lampposts were festooned with pictures of candidates in a bitterly contested mayoral race. There were five of them, just about equally divided between "Movementists," who supported the government, and "multi-partyists," who didn't. The only rule seemed to be that none of them were allowed to run under their true political colors, even though everyone knew exactly where they stood. Beyond that, the campaign was a glorious free-for-all, with fistfights, near riots, and smear campaigns.

The muckraking *Uganda Confidential* assailed Mr. Birriggwa's character, claiming he'd left a wife and children destitute in America. Mr. Birriggwa stormed into the editor's office and manhandled him. The editor, Mr. Cheeye, challenged Mr. Birriggwa to a duel. Hecklers taunted Mr. Sebeggala for his lack of education, causing an inexplicable upsurge in support of his candidacy. Some said the cruel mockery had offended the electorate. Others maintained that it had actually offended the Baganda, the populous tribe from which the candidate hailed.

Around lunchtime, I sought refuge from these contradictions on the shady veranda of a restaurant called The Lion, where I met A. Kadumukasa Kironde II, aged fifty-three, a Ugandan aristocrat whose posh British accent was redolent of Eton, Bentleys, and cricket. A celebrated gourmet cook and bon vivant, he was puttering around in a chef's hat when I arrived, experimenting with exotic recipes in the kitchen. He told me to call him K.K., uncorked a bottle of "rather agreeable" South African red, and began to explain Uganda to me.

The key, he said, was to understand that the nation was led by "a master of the art of the impossible." Uganda was devastated beyond description when Yoweri Museveni came to power, riven by canyons of ethnic mistrust, haunted by the ghosts of a million civil war victims, and generally considered ungovernable by anyone. Museveni should, by rights, have failed utterly. The fact that he hadn't bore testimony, in K.K.'s opinion, to a close reading of Machiavelli, the grand master of shrewd political manipulation.

"This," K.K. continued, "is clearly evident in his style of governance." Nobody gets everything he wants, but almost everyone gets enough to keep them quiet. Politicians are free to pursue their ambitions, provided they stay within the framework of broad Musevenism. Corruption is vigorously suppressed, but you might get away with it if you're the favorite son of a powerful faction that the Big Man can't afford to alienate. Tribalism is officially a no-no, but some tribes are a bit more equal than others—a factor, per K.K., that was not entirely unrelated to minor rebellions in the backwoods and explosions in restaurants over the road. Ah, well. At least Uganda was stumbling toward the light these days, rather than sliding backward. K.K. summoned a waiter and treated me to a meal.

"My entire life has been one of paradox," he confided as we tucked into our Goanese chicken, smothered, in my case, with the delectable peanut sauce called *boo* and surrounded by the ubiquitous greens known as *dudu*. An African prince, he was hauled off to London at the age of six, when his father was called to the British bar—"Middle Temple, actually." A year or two later, he was back in Kampala, where white schools refused to admit him. After independence, he wound up in Manhattan, where his father was Uganda's ambassador to the United Nations. He returned to Kampala after the downfall of the tyrant Idi Amin, only to see his restaurant razed in the next round of street fighting. Now his cousin Ronnie was king of Buganda, but K.K.'s joint was struggling to attract tourists. "You whites are tribalistic," he observed.

I had to agree. K.K.'s cooking was excellent, and the banana gin with which he subsequently plied me was lethally effective. "Come back tomorrow," he cried, as I staggered toward a taxi. "I'll introduce you to the king." What a country. What a capital chap. What a day.

Okay, so where are we now? We're up in the wild blue yonder, in a single-engine Cessna passing over Lake Albert, a vast expanse of greasy green water dotted with fishing canoes and ominous bits of flotsam that look like crocodiles to me. To the west, the mysterious Blue Mountains rear almost vertically out of the lake, and to the north, lost in a heat haze, lies the Sudanese border— "a realm of sinister and forbidding aspect," said Winston Churchill, "where man is fanatical and often rifle-armed." It was so in 1907, and it remains thus today. Somewhere in the trackless wastes below, government power peters out, and you enter the fief of the Lord's Resistance Army (LRA), a berserk band of dreadlocked mystics who seem to specialize in slicing off their enemies' lips and seizing convent girls as concubines. Our destination— the Pakuba airstrip, on the north bank of the Nile—is considered unsafe by the U.S. State Department, but the only sign of danger as we come in to land is a herd of oribi that refuse to move out of our way until we scream over their heads at full throttle.

A Land Cruiser is waiting. We throw our gear in the back and bounce off across the savanna. Ten clicks down the road, we come upon a patch of charred, blackened sand that marks the spot where a convoy was ambushed fifteen months back by the LRA. They executed the drivers, looted their trucks, and withdrew into the reserve's northern reaches. They're still out there somewhere, so we take the south fork, which leads through a forest of singing thorn trees to the banks of the Nile, six hundred yards wide at this point, its dark waters flecked with yellow foam, rolling toward Egypt at seven miles an hour.

On a ridge above the banks looms a giant wooden stockade of the sort erected by eighteenth-century fur trappers in the wild forests of North America. This is the Paraa Lodge, a relic of Uganda's mid-century tourist heyday, recently refurbished at enormous cost in anticipation of a tourist boom that has yet to materialize. A squad of porters pounce on my luggage and lead me up a grand mahogany staircase. The lime-green walls are covered with etchings—reprints from the *Illustrated London News*, for the most part, showing Victorian explorers shooting elephants, meeting one another in jungle clearings, and fending off attacks by "forest dwarves with poison arrows." My suite is wood-paneled, with a fan in the ceiling and a mosquito net draped gracefully over the bed. Down in the kitchen, the freezers are crammed with imported delicacies that will shortly be served in a dining room the size of a ballroom. It's amazing—a grand hotel in bush so remote that the only communication with the outside world is by radio.

Outside, the vast tiled terrace is deserted, the swimming pool empty. I drink a cold beer on a cool veranda that commands a broad sweep of the river and, beyond it, the bush stretching low and level to the blue wall of the Rift Valley. This is a richly mythic landscape. Every major Victorian explorer buckled his swash out there among the thorn trees: Theodore Roosevelt hunted rhino in 1909, two years after Churchill passed through. Bogart, Bacall, Hepburn, and Huston came in 1950 to make *The African Queen*. Two years later, Hemingway almost died in a plane crash on yonder hillock, an episode that inspired *The Snows of Kilimanjaro*.

More recently, a small-town fishmonger named Alice Auma was summoned to a spot just upstream by an ancestral spirit who revealed her new destiny: She was to take up the sword in the name of Jehovah and cleanse the land of evil, beginning with administrators loyal to Museveni. This was the genesis of the Lord's Resistance Army, but we don't really want to dwell on that, do we? Nah, we're beginning to like it here on the wild frontier, poised on a knife-edge between ecstasy and terror. We want to drink gin and tonics and eat pan-seared steaks in a cabernet jus while the sun sets in barbaric splendor over the Nile. After dark, the swimming pool is like a blue jewel in the black African night, and you hear hippos crashing around in the undergrowth below. Lightning begins to play on the northern horizon, a sure sign that the rains are coming.

Next morning, we rise before dawn and go out on a game drive. It's a lovely day, cool and gray. A large herd of kob stampede across the horizon at our approach. A smudge of black on a distant hillside turns out to be a throng of ruminating buffalo. After a while, we turn back and see the same kob again, plus five giraffes and a column of ferocious driver ants heading across the savanna on some inscrutable mission. That's about it as far as wildlife is concerned. We drive home somewhat saddened.

Photographs taken here in the early sixties show a landscape as flat and open as a billiard table, all the trees having been torn down by rampaging elephants. The riverbanks heaved with hippopotamuses; there were lions and rhinos in every second donga; the antelope were too numerous to be tallied. But then the wars began, and rabble armies began to crisscross the country, living off the land. The antelope were machine-gunned and eaten, the elephants poached for their ivory. Murchison's elephant population had fallen by ninety percent. Its rhinos had been exterminated entirely.

To be fair, it should be noted that what game is left had dispersed after the rain, so there is far more of it than first meets the eye. It is also true that Museveni's government has restored control over Uganda's reserves, and that recovery is taking place at a heartening rate, with elephants giving birth to twins galore as they expand into empty ecological niches. Still, if you want to see wildlife in splendid variety and large numbers, go to a country where jumbo jets disgorge hordes of tourists who throng to zoo-like parks where they choke on each other's exhaust fumes in traffic snarl-ups around lion kills and water holes. You'll probably see the Big Five—elephant, lion, rhinoceros, leopard, and buffalo—but you'll never experience anything like the loneliness of the Ugandan wild.

About twenty miles upstream from Paraa, the Nile flows into a funnel of hard rock that narrows and narrows until all its pent-up might is constricted into a channel barely eighteen feet wide that blasts over a clifftop and into midair, only to thunder down into the abyss below with a din and violence that is almost incomprehensible. The roar of Murchison Falls is audible from ten miles away. Churchill was mesmerized by the sight of them. They were, he said, the highlight of his safari; just seeing them made the long trek worthwhile. Anywhere else, the riverbanks would be covered with resorts and casinos, and hippies would be leaping into the chasm with bungees attached, but in Uganda, time has stood still. The road that leads to the falls is a potholed abomination seldom traveled by anyone. The dusty parking lot at the end of it is absolutely empty. We had the entire magnificent spectacle to ourselves.

By my calculation, I was standing on the exact spot where Churchill stood nine decades earlier, and seeing exactly what he saw, save that the rock on which he spotted a crocodile was underwater in this season. Churchill hated crocodiles, so he raised his rifle and shot. At the sound, "the entire far bank of the river, to the extent of at least a quarter mile, erupted into hideous life." What he had presumed to be a mudbank was actually an unbroken line of basking saurians that rushed madly into the river, where their descendants were presumably still lurking— a probability that began to exercise my mind as I edged toward the foaming water, fishing rod in hand.

And now we come to a confession. Beyond all longing to see new places, this is what I had come for: to stand on this rock and do battle with the giant fish said to inhabit the pool below. They are called Nile perch, and they are the largest freshwater game fish on the planet (400 pounds reputed, 305 verified); fish like whales, and given more than anywhere in the world to lurking right here, in the swirling water at the foot of the falls, waiting to pounce on dazed and stunned prey spat out of the churning cauldron behind me.

My rod was a stout one, suitable for tuna, and the gut on it was thick and strong, terminating in a long wire trace, at the end of which a crucified baitfish wriggled. I lowered it into the raging stream and watched in dismay as it snarled on a raft of papyrus that dragged it away to the left, where it snagged in the submerged roots of an over-hanging tree. The same thing happened on the next cast, and the next. The river was swollen and full of debris, and I would have been undone had I not happened to pocket the cork from the wine drunk at last night's dinner.

Improvising ingeniously, I like to think, I used the cork as a float on my next cast, and lo, it kept my line aloof from the floating detritus. The cork bobbed around a bit, got caught in an eddy, and circled back almost to my feet, where it suddenly vanished, sucked under by a monster. I let the line run, counted to five, and then struck into something heavy. Moments later, the fish came to the surface—a great, thrashing, silver thing, mouth agape like a largemouth bass, and dancing on its tail like a sailfish. Then it took off across the pool and found the main current, and my line began to sweep downstream like the string of a kite in a gale.

It took ten minutes to win back the lost nylon, and by then the fish was exhausted. It gave up the struggle and rolled over at my feet, a thirty-pounder, to my proud eye. But I was perched atop a rock on account of the saurian menace, and it was in the water, ten feet below. The wire trace snapped as we were hauling it up, and I was left with nothing but a fishing story.

But it was enough, and I went home with a full heart. Back in Entebbe, a cool breeze was blowing off the mile-high lake, and the town that at first seemed so foreboding now looked like a South Sea island, its ramshackle houses tucked away under banana and mango trees and overrun by rioting frangipani. As we rose into the sky, the colors were like a Gauguin painting, the red billboards for Sportsman cigarettes playing off against black Guinness signs, bright yellow phone booths, and schoolchildren in uniforms of pastel pink and blue. Uganda has terrible problems, to be sure, but it's a special place, the land of Double Happiness safety matches. Like Churchill before us, we were beset by the thought that the best was behind us, and that what lay ahead would never quite measure up. "Beauty dies out of the landscape," he wrote as he steamed away, "and richness from the land." He was brokenhearted. So were we.

1999

ABOUT THE AUTHORS

André Aciman (b. 1951), an American writer and scholar of seventeenth-century literature, was born in Alexandria, Egypt. A professor of comparative literature at the Graduate Center of the City University of New York, he is the author of several books, including his Whiting Award–winning memoir *Out of Egypt* (1995), an account of his Jewish childhood in postcolonial Egypt, and two novels, *Call Me By Your Name* (2007), a *New York Times* Notable Book of the Year, and *Eight White Nights* (2010). His latest collection of essays is *Alibis: Essays on Elsewhere* (2011). Aciman's work has appeared in *The New Yorker*, the *New York Review of Books*, the *New Republic*, and other publications in addition to *Condé Nast Traveler*. Of his Monet-inspired trip to Bordighera, Italy, he said, "The whole piece is about accidents and method all working together. I get there and am totally lost, and then trust in some sort of entity or organizing principle. Ultimately I think art is about how we go after things that seem totally whimsical, then discover what we trusted we would find."

Russell Banks (b. 1940) is a member of the American Academy of Arts and Letters. He is the author of five story collections and twelve novels, most recently *Lost Memory of Skin* (2011), set in South Florida. Two of his novels, *Affliction* (1989) and *The Sweet Hereafter* (1991), were made into critically acclaimed films. Banks's work has been translated into twenty languages and he has received numerous international prizes and awards. He lives in upstate New York and Miami.

Joan Juliet Buck (b. 1948) is a frequent contributor to *Condé Nast Traveler* as well as to *W*, the *New York Times Magazine*, and *Newsweek*, among others. Editor in chief of French *Vogue* from 1994 to 2001 and the author of two novels, Buck is also an actress. In 2009, she portrayed Madame Elisabeth Brassart, proprietress of Le Cordon Bleu cooking school, in the film *Julie & Julia*; in 2010, she played Marguerite Duras at La MaMa in New York. In 2012, Buck will be working in residency at Tucson's Museum of Contemporary Art and storytelling on the road with George Dawes Green's "Unchained Tour." After her trip alone to Rome for *Condé Nast Traveler* in 2007, she returned in 2011, "to show the city to someone I love."

William Dalrymple (b. 1965) began life in Scotland but has lived in New Delhi on and off for the last twenty-five years. He is the author of seven prize-winning books about India and the Islamic world, including *City of Djinns* (1993), *White Mughals* (2003), *The Last Mughal* (2006), and *Nine Lives: In Search of the Sacred in Modern India* (2009), as well as radio and TV documentaries, among them *The Long Search* for BBC Radio 4 (2002) and *Indian Journeys* for the BBC (2002). The recipient of honorary doctorates from the Universities of St Andrews, Aberdeen, and Lucknow, he will be a visiting fellow at Princeton in September 2012. He is currently at work on a history of the First Anglo-Afghan War and on a show of Mughal art for the Asia Society in New York City.

An ethnographer, writer, photographer, and filmmaker, **Wade Davis** (b. 1953) is an Explorer-in-Residence at the National Geographic Society. His work investigating folk medicines implicated in the creation of zombies in Haiti became the 1986 international best seller *The Serpent and the Rainbow* and was turned into a motion picture. In 2011, he published two books: *Into the Silence: The Great War, Mallory, and the Conquest of Everest* and *The Sacred Headwaters*, about impending development on British Columbian land sacred to the First Nations. In 2012, Davis will publish three books: a collection of photographs taken from 2000 to 2010, the edited journals of Alpine Club of Canada founder Arthur Oliver Wheeler, and a work of literary nonfiction on the Grand Canyon of the Colorado.

E. L. Doctorow (b. 1931) is the author, most recently, of *All the Time in the World: New and Selected Stories* (2011). His eleven novels include *Homer & Langley* (2009), *The March* (2005), *Billy Bathgate* (1989), *Ragtime* (1974), and *The Book of Daniel* (1971). His work has been published in thirty-two languages, and several of his short stories and novels have been adapted for television and film. Among his honors are the National Book Award, three National Book Critics Circle Awards, two PEN/Faulkner awards, the Edith Wharton Citation of Merit for Fiction, the William Dean Howells Medal of the American Academy of Arts and Letters, and the presidentially conferred National Humanities Medal. He lives in New York.

Martha Gellhorn (1908–1998) was a noted war correspondent and travel journalist. Her fifty years of reporting on armed conflict began with the Spanish Civil War (where she traveled with her future husband, Ernest Hemingway), extended through World War II (where she was one of the first reporters to reach Dachau after the camp was liberated), and ended with her covering at the age of eighty-one the U.S. invasion of Panama. Among her dozens of books are collections of journalism—*Travels with Myself and Another* (1978), *The View from the Ground* (1959), and *The Face of War* (1959)—and novels, including *A Stricken Field* (1940), set in wartime Czechoslovakia, and *The Lowest Trees Have Tops* (1967), about McCarthyism.

Dan Hofstadter (b. 1943) is the author of *The Earth Moves: Galileo and the Roman Inquisition* (2009); *Falling Palace: A Romance of Naples* (2005), a finalist for the PEN/Martha Albrand Award for the Art of the Memoir; *The Love Affair as a Work of Art* (1996), nominated for the National Book Critics Circle Award; *Goldberg's Angel* (1994); and *Temperaments* (1992). A regular contributor to *The New Yorker* for eight years, he has also written for the *New York Times* and several national magazines. He teaches at Bennington College and lives in upstate New York.

The art critic for *Time* magazine for more than thirty years, renowned cultural critic **Robert Hughes** (b. 1938) is the author of eleven books of nonfiction, most recently *Rome: A Cultural, Visual, and Personal History* (2011), which spans more than two thousand years of the Italian capital's fortunes. Previous books include the highly influential *The Shock of the New* (1981); *The Fatal Shore* (1987), a history of his native Australia; *Heaven and Hell in Western Art* (1968); *Goya* (2003), a biography of the artist; and *Things I Didn't Know* (2006), a memoir. Hughes, who now lives in New York City, has been awarded countless literary prizes and distinctions, most recently an Arts and Letters Award in Literature from the American Academy of Arts and Letters.

Pico Iyer (b. 1957) was born in Oxford, England, to Indian parents. When he was seven, the family moved to California. At nine he started commuting six times a year between his parents' home in Santa Barbara and boarding schools in Oxford. During his twenty-five years as a contributing editor for *Condé Nast Traveler*, he has reported from many countries, including Argentina, Vietnam, Cambodia, Ethiopia, and Bolivia. Over two successive New Years beginning in 2008, he traveled to holy cities Varanasi and Jerusalem for the magazine. "In both cities, what fascinated me was the interplay of holiness and humanness," he says. "These places speak at once for our highest longings and our best selves, and also become a home to our most contentious and territorial impulses." He is the author of eight works of nonfiction, as well as novels set in Iran and revolutionary Cuba. His books of travel writing include *Video Night in Kathmandu* (1988), *The Lady and the Monk* (1991), *Falling Off the Map* (1993), *The Global Soul* (2000), and *Sun After Dark* (2004). His latest book, *The Man Within My Head* (2012), sees the world through the lens of his longtime fascination with Graham Greene, and unfolds in many settings, from Bhutan to Bogota, from Saigon to Ethiopia. He divides his time between California and Japan.

London-born **Norman Lewis** (1908–2003) is widely regarded as one of the twentieth century's finest travel writers. He once summed up his style as "revealing little descriptions; I think of myself as the semi-invisible man." Though his work exposed man's follies, whether those of dictators in Burma (*Golden Earth,* 1952) or missionaries in Latin America (*The Missionaries,* 1988), his writing is unremittingly enjoyable for what *The Guardian* called "his subtle, refulgent musical magic." A stint in the British intelligence corps during World War II as well as the acquisition of Sicilian in-laws inspired Lewis to write his unparalleled study of the Mafia, *The Honoured Society* (1964). The work so impressed then–*New Yorker* editor William Shawn that he serialized it in its entirety. Lewis also authored more than a dozen novels, including *The Sicilian Specialist* (1975), a best seller in both the United States and the then–Soviet Union, as well as a two-volume autobiography, *Jackdaw Cake* (1985) and *The World, The World* (1996).

Rian Malan (b. 1954), an eighth-generation Afrikaner, is best known as the author of *My Traitor's Heart: A South African Exile Returns to Face His Country, His Tribe, and His Conscience* (1990). This best-selling account details South Africa's racial discord during the 1980s as well as the writer's conflicted feelings as a descendant of one of the principal architects of apartheid policy. He is also a widely published journalist and a documentary television producer and presenter, as well as a musician and songwriter who has released a CD of his own songs, *Alien Inboorling* (2005).

A *Condé Nast Traveler* senior correspondent based in New York and Berlin, **Guy Martin** writes about Eastern Europe, his native South, and post-9/11 security issues. He has also written for other magazines, including *Wired* (UK), *The Observer* (London), *Garden & Gun,* and *The New Yorker.* He found the film studio Babelsberg in Berlin illustrative of the city's changing fortunes: "When I got there, history had come full circle. Babelsberg's then-boss, West German director Volker Schlöndorff, was having a fine time running around renaming the streets in between the sound stages for all the German film stars that Hitler had kicked out—namely, Fritz Lang, Billy Wilder, and Marlene Dietrich," he recalled. "In a nutshell, that's Berlin."

The author of seven novels and three collections of essays on wine, **Jay McInerney** (b. 1955) is a regular contributor to *New York Magazine*, the *New York Times Book Review*, the *Independent*, and *Corriere della Sera*. His short fiction has appeared in *The New Yorker*, *Esquire*, *Playboy*, and *Granta*. In 2006, *Time* magazine cited his 1984 debut, *Bright Lights, Big City*, as one of nine generation-defining novels of the twentieth century; the James Beard Foundation gave him its M.F.K. Fisher Distinguished Writing Award, and his novel *The Good Life* (2006) received the Grand Prix Littéraire de Deauville. He lives in Manhattan and in Bridge-hampton, New York.

Cristina Nehring (b. 1973) is the author of *A Vindication of Love: Reclaiming Romance for the Twenty-First Century* (2009), a scholarly history of eros from ancient times to the present. A highly acclaimed and consistently provocative critic and essayist, Nehring has written for *The Atlantic*, *Harper's Magazine*, the *New York Times Book Review*, *New York Magazine*, the *American Scholar*, the *Los Angeles Times*, and the *London Review of Books*, among others. Most recently, she has published a memoir, *Journey to the End of Light: A Story of Love, Leukemia and Transformation* (Kindle Singles, 2011).

The author of twenty-nine books, **Edna O'Brien** (b. 1930) made her literary debut with the Country Girls Trilogy (1960–1964), which was widely acclaimed despite being banned in her native Ireland. Her novel *Lantern Slides* was awarded the *Los Angeles Times* book prize in 1990. O'Brien, who has also written numerous plays, children's books, and essays, won the 2011 Frank O'Connor International Short Story Award for her collection *Saints and Sinners*. She lives in London and is writing a memoir.

Jonathan Raban (b. 1942) is a British travel writer, essayist, and novelist. He is author of, among others, *Soft City* (1974), *Arabia Through the Looking Glass* (1979), *Old Glory* (1981), *Foreign Land* (1985), *Hunting Mister Heartbreak* (1991), *Bad Land* (1996), *Passage to Juneau* (1999), *Waxwings* (2003), *Surveillance* (2006), and, most recently, *Driving Home: An American Journey* (2011). His awards include the National Book Critics Circle Award, the Thomas Cook Travel Book Award, the Royal Society of Literature's Heinemann Award, the PEN USA Creative Nonfiction Award, the Governor's Award of the state of Washington, and an honorary doctorate from the University of Hull. He lives in Seattle.

Julia Reed (b. 1960) grew up in Greenville, Mississippi. As a college student at Georgetown and American University, she interned at *Newsweek*, where she is now a contributing editor and the author of the magazine's monthly "Food and Drink" column. A senior writer and contributing editor at *Vogue* for twenty years, she is also the author of *Queen of the Turtle Derby and Other Southern Phenomena* (2004), a collection of essays about the South, as well as *The House on First Street: My New Orleans Story* (2008) and *Ham Biscuits, Hostess Gowns, and Other Southern Specialties: An Entertaining Life (with Recipes)* (2008). Reed contributes regularly to the *New York Times*, the *Spectator*, and *Southern Accents*. She lives in New Orleans with her husband.

Belgian-born **Luc Sante** (b. 1954) returned home for the first time in nearly twenty years to write about the place for *Condé Nast Traveler*, and the experience led to the writing of his third book, *The Factory of Facts* (1998). His other books include *Low Life* (1991) and *Kill All Your Darlings* (2007). The recipient of numerous prizes, including a Whiting Writers' Award, a Grammy Award for Best Album Notes, and an Infinity Award from the International Center of Photography, he teaches creative writing and the history of photography at Bard College. He lives in upstate New York.

Stephen Schiff is a screenwriter whose work includes *Lolita* (1997), *The Deep End of the Ocean* (1999), *True Crime* (1999), and *Wall Street: Money Never Sleeps* (2010). Of his trip to Vienna for *Condé Nast Traveler*, he recalls: "The late, very great photographer Helmut Newton and I would meet by night and recount our exploits—and sometimes embark on a few more." A finalist for the Pulitzer Prize in Criticism, Schiff worked as a staff writer at *The New Yorker* for nine years and as a critic for *Vanity Fair*. Projects in the works include the television series *Ultimate Rush*, for which he is writer-producer, and a biography of Norman Mailer, to be published by Henry Holt and Company.

Henry Shukman (b. 1962) has worked as a trombonist, a trawlerman, and a travel writer. His first poetry collection, *In Doctor No's Garden* (2002), won the Aldeburgh First Collection Prize and was a Book of the Year in *The Times* (London) and *The Guardian*. His novels include *Sandstorm* (2005) and *The Lost City* (2008). His fiction has won an Arts Council England Writers' Award and has been a finalist for the O. Henry Award. He lives in New Mexico, where he teaches at the Institute of American Indian Arts.

Journalist **Patrick Symmes** (b. 1964) specializes in reporting on insurgencies and global environmental problems. In addition to *Condé Nast Traveler*, he contributes to *Harper's Magazine*, *Outside*, and *Newsweek*, and is the author of books *Chasing Che: A Motorcycle Journey in Search of the Guevara Legend* (2000) and *The Boys from Dolores: Fidel Castro's Classmates from Revolution to Exile* (2007). His trip to Italy's Emilia-Romagna region was the first time he took a cooking class while covering a story, "but now I bring back a dish from every international assignment—there is nothing more relaxing than getting away from tough spots and cooking." His second story in this volume, which traces the route of the Hudson River north from lower Manhattan to Lake Tear in the Clouds, "was bittersweet for me—it hit newsstands in September 2001, with a large picture of kayakers in front of the Twin Towers."

Calvin Trillin (b. 1935) is an American reporter, humorist, and memoirist. As accomplished at writing serious reportage as light humor, he has worked as a staff writer for *The New Yorker*, *The Nation*, and *Time* magazine. Every week since 1990, he has contributed topical comic verse to *The Nation*. Among his more than two dozen books are three memoirs—*Remembering Denny* (1993), *Messages from My Father* (1996), and *About Alice* (2006), a best seller about his late wife and muse. A self-described "happy eater," Trillin has compiled his three books on the pastime—*American Fried* (1974), *Alice, Let's Eat* (1978), and *Third Helpings* (1983)—into a single volume entitled *The Tummy Trilogy* (1994). His most recent book is *Quite Enough of Calvin Trillin: Forty Years of Funny Stuff* (2011). Of his trip to Cuenca, Ecuador, in 2010, the septuagenarian recalls tirelessly walking through the town yet suffering no ill effects from the thin air at eight-thousand-plus feet. "I took it easy the first day, and Cuenca itself is pretty flat," he says. "I don't think I'd want to try any San Francisco–like hills there, though." He lives in Greenwich Village, in New York City.

After writing about music and popular culture in London, **James Truman** (b. 1958) moved to New York in 1981 and switched to being an editor. After four years as editor in chief of *Details*, he became the editorial director of Condé Nast Publications in 1994, a position he held until 2005. He currently lives between Manhattan, upstate New York, and Northern California, and is working on projects involving organic farming, music, wine, and the hospitality business. His desire to visit Bhutan rose from his interest in Buddhism but deepened after meeting travelers who had recently returned. "I became fascinated by how this remote, inaccessible little country in the Himalayas seemed to have captured the hearts of everyone who visited." The spell, he learned, was cast by a combination of its magical topography and a system of government that promotes national happiness. "I interviewed politicians, lamas, and ordinary citizens and was always impressed by their engagement in their country's future," he said. "It's certainly possible to hold a romantic vision of Bhutan as a Buddhist Shangri-la, and it might even be true, but the real miracle is that this tiny kingdom has organized a better-functioning democracy than many advanced nations."

Gully Wells (b. 1950) has been an editor and writer at *Condé Nast Traveler* for more than twenty years. Of the countless destinations she has written about—everywhere from Russia, Mexico, France, and Jamaica to Italy and Estonia—Spain is a favorite, and has been since her first trip there while in college. "I began a love affair with a Spanish man at Oxford," she said. "In 1972 he took me to Spain; it was before Franco died and the country had been cut off from the rest of Europe for thirty years. It felt more foreign than any place I'd ever been and I was totally fascinated, and have been going back ever since." Of Extremadura, the rugged western region she wrote about in 1998, she said, "Since it is quite remote and doesn't appeal to many tourists, it is wonderfully empty. For me, it is the essence of Spain: tough, harsh, and beautiful." Wells is the author of *The House in France* (2011), a memoir set in France, London, and New York. She lives in Brooklyn with her family.

Amy Wilentz (b. 1954) fell in love with Haiti while researching her first book, *The Rainy Season: Haiti Since Duvalier* (1989), which was nominated for the National Book Critics Circle Award. Her story about the country for *Condé Nast Traveler* ran just months before the devastating January 12, 2010, earthquake. She has returned several times since then and is working on a new book about Haiti. "Haiti has had a lot of troubles in its history—it is the first black republic, and so it had a complicated history including centuries of pariah status," Wilentz said. "But things were looking up before the earthquake and I don't see why, within the decade, things can't be looking up again." Her article about Senegal, published in 2007, was in part inspired by the Haitian people: "I thought I should go to West Africa to know where these people came from. I found Dakar pulsing with life, a great mixture of French and black African cultures, along with a Muslim influence that adds to the fascinating stew." Wilentz's other books are *Martyrs' Crossing* (2000) and *I Feel Earthquakes More Often Than They Happen: Coming to California in the Age of Schwarzenegger* (2006). She is a winner of the Whiting Writers' Award, the PEN/Martha Albrand Award for the Art of Nonfiction, and the American Academy of Arts and Letters Rosenthal Award. A former Jerusalem correspondent for *The New Yorker*, Wilentz has also been a longtime contributing editor at *The Nation*. She's a professor of literary journalism at the University of California at Irvine, and lives in Los Angeles with her husband and three sons.

ABOUT *CONDÉ NAST TRAVELER*

Since its launch in 1987, *Condé Nast Traveler* has remained committed to its philosophy of "Truth in Travel." The magazine is independent of the travel industry; this means that its editors and reporters never accept free or discounted trips and accommodations and, as far as possible, travel anonymously. They experience travel the way you do—the good and the bad—and are free to report their findings honestly, with no obligations, conflicts of interest, or ulterior motives. Their reports are therefore impartial and authoritative.

For more information about the magazine, visit condenasttraveler .com.

Acknowledgments

First and foremost I would like to thank all the writers who have contributed to *Condé Nast Traveler* over the past twenty-five years. Their roamings and wanderings, their curiosity and observations, and the varied but invariably inspired ways in which they committed them to paper and computer screens have given this magazine its soul, substance, and style. When we published the first volume of *The Condé Nast Traveler Book of Unforgettable Journeys* in 2007, on the occasion of the magazine's twentieth anniversary, the choice of which writers and pieces to include seemed daunting—for every one selected, so many others worthy of inclusion could not be. The balance has been partially righted now, with the publication of this second, twenty-fifth anniversary edition—but only partially so. There are many stories left to gather and showcase, and each monthly edition of the magazine offers up fresh candidates.

My gratitude goes to my predecessors as editor in chief of *Condé Nast Traveler*—Sir Harold Evans, the magazine's founding editor, and Thomas J. Wallace, under whose inspired and vigilant stewardship many of these stories were originally commissioned—as well as to senior consulting editor Clive Irving, our presiding sage since the magazine's inception. On behalf of all of us at *Condé Nast Traveler*, I would like to thank S. I. Newhouse, Jr., chairman of Condé Nast, for so steadfastly supporting the magazine and continuing to recognize the value and imperative of our Truth in Travel philosophy.

I am immensely grateful to Stephen Morrison, former editor in chief of Penguin Books, for suggesting that we collect our stories and

Acknowledgments

to the entire terrific Penguin team: Rebecca Hunt, Norina Frabotta, Sharon Gonzalez, Paul Buckley, and Jaya Miceli. And thanks as well to the *Condé Nast Traveler* team—Gully Wells, Dee L. Aldrich, Dana Dickey, Marita Begley, Priscilla Eakeley, Gail M. Scott, Sylvia Espinoza, and Jessica Tauber—who helped make this volume a reality. Last but not least, my gratitude goes to editor at large Hanya Yanagihara, who back in 2006 pointed out the obvious—that our stories should be books.

—*K.G.*